Mental Health in Social Work: A Casebook on Diagnosis and Strengths-Based Assessment

JACQUELINE CORCORAN

Virginia Commonwealth University

JOSEPH WALSH

Virginia Commonwealth University

PEARSON

Boston   New York   San Francisco
Mexico City   Montreal   Toronto   London   Madrid   Munich   Paris
Hong Kong   Singapore   Tokyo   Cape Town   Sydney

Dedication

With love to my sisters Sue, Kathy, and Marianne
—Joe

In memory of Doreen Corcoran
—Jacqueline

Senior Acquisitions Editor: Patricia Quinlin
Editorial Assistant: Carly Czech
Senior Marketing Manager: Wendy Albert
Production Supervisor: Roberta Sherman
Editorial-Production and Electronic
  Composition Services: Nesbitt Graphics, Inc.

Composition Buyer: Linda Cox
Manufacturing Buyer: Debbie Rossi
Interior Design: Nesbitt Graphics, Inc.
Cover Administrator: Joel Gendron

For related titles and support materials, visit our online catalog at www.ablongman.com.

Between the time website information is gathered and then published, it is not unusual for some sites to have closed. Also, the transcription of URLs can result in unintended typographical errors. The publisher would appreciate notification where these errors occur so that they may be corrected in subsequent editions.

ISBN-13: 978-0-205-48299-3   ISBN-10: 0-205-48299-6

Cataloging-in-Publication data unavailable at press time.

Printed in the United States of America

10 9 8 7 6 5 4   12 11 10

Contents

————— ▼▲▼ —————

Preface

—— ▼▲▼ ——

Mental Health in Social Work: A Casebook on Diagnosis and Strengths-Based Assessment is a graduate-level textbook that will help students and professionals learn to understand clients holistically as they proceed with the assessment and intervention process. A major purpose of *Mental Health in Social Work* is to familiarize readers with the American Psychiatric Association Diagnostic and Statistical Manual (DSM) classification of mental disorders. The primary reasons that social workers need to become conversant with the DSM are: 1) to offer clients appropriate referrals and treatment; 2) to communicate effectively with other mental health professions; and 3) to be eligible for third-party reimbursement.

Chapter One will present an **overview of the DSM and the multi-axial diagnostic system.** Subsequent chapters follow the order of the DSM; that is, disorders of infancy, childhood, and adolescence are presented first, followed by dementia, substance-related disorders, schizophrenia, mood disorders, anxiety disorders, eating disorders, and personality disorders. Disorders chosen for this book are those that social workers commonly see in clinical and social service settings and have sufficient research information supporting them[1].

The learning in *Mental Health in Social Work* primarily occurs through a **case study method;** students are asked to respond to case illustrations that are presented in each chapter. Cases (two to three in each chapter) have been selected to represent the diversity of people with whom social workers intervene. Answers to the questions posed about each case are provided in an Instructor's Manual, and should be discussed in class and/or through feedback on case study assignments.

While gaining competence in DSM diagnosis, the reader is also taught to maintain a critical perspective on the various DSM diagnoses and the medical model as promulgated through the DSM. The field of social work has a focus not just on the individual, but on the person within an environmental context, and concerns itself with strengths as well as problems. Additionally, social work has a traditional commitment to oppressed and vulnerable populations. Since the DSM is limited in these areas, *Mental Health in Social Work* **will include the biopsychosocial risk and resilience perspective, which takes into account both risks and strengths at the individual and environmental levels.** In Chapter 2, the biopsychosocial risk and resilience perspective is described in depth. Each chapter then explores the relevant risk and protective influences for each disorder, highlighting some of the particular risks for special populations, including children,

---

[1] For instance, reactive attachment disorder is not included, even though child clients may carry this diagnosis because there has been little research on the disorder itself, despite the fact that there has been a lot gathered throughout the years on attachment theory and attachment styles.

iv

women, the elderly, minorities, people with disabilities, gay and lesbian individuals, and those from low socioeconomic strata. **Students are asked to complete risk and resilience assessments for the case studies presented.** Moreover, we provide guidelines on how to conduct a clinical interview that is consistent with a strengths-based perspective, drawing mainly on solution-focused and motivational interviewing techniques (Chapter 3). This emphasis on strengths ensures that students will keep a balanced appraisal of both client strengths and limitations to counteract the pathology focus of the DSM.

Another emphasis in *Mental Health in Social Work* is **evidence-based treatment,** a recent movement in social work and various other health and mental health disciplines. The Council on Social Work Education states that direct practice content should include "…identifying, analyzing, and implementing empirically based interventions designed to achieve client goals" (CSWE, 2004, p. 10). The meaning of evidence-based practice can be debated (Norcross, Beutler, & Levant, 2006), but has been generally defined as the prioritization of research evidence when social workers consider how to best help clients. However, client preferences and available resources must also be part of the process of clinical judgment in addition to research studies (Sackett, Straus, Richardson, Rosenberg & Haynes 2000). In considering the hierarchy of evidence, whenever possible we rely on systematic reviews and meta-analyses, which are considered "first-line evidence" (Petticrew & Roberts, 2006). These systematic reviews aim to comprehensively locate and synthesize the treatment outcome literature in a particular area. If the review lends itself to combining the results of primary studies in a quantitative way, then it is referred to as meta-analysis (Petticrew & Roberts, 2006).

From these reviews of the literature, *Mental Health in Social Work* **presents treatment guidelines for each disorder covered in the book, and through the case studies, students will learn how to form evidence-based treatment plans.** At the same time, in keeping with the importance of the environmental context, interventions address the broad nature of the concerns that people bring to social work professionals. For instance, if socioeconomic problems, such as lack of health insurance and unemployment, are part of the client's presenting problems, then intervention will appropriately address these concerns, as they are critical to a person's well-being and healthy functioning.

In summary, we believe that clients are best served by the holistic approach to direct practice emphasized in this book. In this way the humanistic values of the social work perspective are preserved, and students who use this book will be well prepared to function as effective and empathic practitioners.

Acknowledgments

The case studies that make up this book are based on our clinical practice and the contributions of our students and other professionals. As the application of assessment competencies is a core element of this book, we are truly grateful to the following students who offered case contributions:

Susan Bienvenu, Treva Bower, Lindsay Doles, Martha Dunn, Gidget Fields, Lisa Genser, Carolynn Ghiloni, Christine Gigena, Dana Gilmore, Kristine Kluck, Elizabeth

Lincoln, Pamela McDonald, Jodee Mellerio, Cynthia Ormes, Kristi Payne, Constance Ritter, Zoe Rizzuto, Heather Roberts, Anne Ross, Amelia Schor, Tina Shafer, Rebecca Sorensen, Megan Vogel, and Raquelle Ward. We are also indebted to the following social work professionals: Kim Giancaspro, Kris McAkeavey, and Adina Shapiro. Most of all, we want to thank Shane Fagan for tirelessly reading over case studies and offering her valued clinical opinions.

Moreover, we thank the reviewers for their suggestions: Chrystal Baranti, California State University; Laura Boisen, Augsberg College; Daphne S. Cain, Louisiana State University; Rebecca T. Davis, Rutgers University; and Judith H. Rosenberg, Central Connecticut State University.

As always, thanks to Patrick Corcoran for his diligent and conscientious proofreading, helping us to prepare the best book we can put forward.

1

— ▼▲▼ —

Diagnosis and the Social Work Profession

Henry Williams, a 59-year-old African-American man, was in the hospital after undergoing surgery for removal of a brain tumor. His past medical history included seizures, insulin-dependent diabetes mellitus, and pancreatitis (an inflammation of the pancreas that causes intense pain in the upper abdomen). Currently, Mr. Williams was taking several medications, including Dilantin (used to treat epilepsy), insulin, and steroids (to decrease swelling around his tumor).

About six days after the surgery Mr. Williams woke up in the middle of the night and was very loud in "casting the demons out," as he called it. The nurse tried to calm him, but Mr. Williams was so incensed that he picked up a small monitoring machine next to his bed and threw it at her. Security officers and the on-duty physician assistant were called to calm the patient.

The next morning the neurosurgery team requested a psychiatric exam, but since it was a Friday Mr. Williams was not examined until the following Monday. His family visited over the weekend, and he repeatedly became agitated, even accusing his wife of cheating on him. He was upset and emotional during those visits, and it took him a while to calm down after his family left.

On Sunday night, Mr. Williams got up at midnight and threatened his roommate. Mr. Williams yelled that his roommate was cheating on him with his wife and they were plotting to kill him. Because his roommate feared for his safety, he was moved to another room, while the nurse tried to calm Mr. Williams.

When the psychiatric team, accompanied by the social work intern, finally examined Mr. Williams, he said he felt great but was hearing voices, most prominently that of his pastor. He reported that he saw demons at night and was attempting to fight them off. He also stated that he thought someone wanted to kill him to benefit from his life insurance policy. In addition, Mr. Williams told the psychiatrist that his wife had not come to visit him for some days (this was not true; she had been there twice over the weekend) but that his son had been at his bedside in the morning and that he had enjoyed the visit.

His wife heard about the incident with the roommate and said she would not take Mr. Williams home because she was afraid of him. She told the social work intern that Mr. Williams had behaved similarly in the past. She would sometimes wake up in the middle of the night and find him standing next to the bed or leaning over her body, staring at her. When she confronted her husband, he would pass it off as a joke, saying he was making sure she was really in bed and had not gone out. (They had separate bedrooms.) She also told the intern that although she had never cheated on her husband, he had had an affair several years ago. After she found out, they went to marriage counseling together, but the marriage had been "rocky" ever since.

The case described above is one in which the client, Mr. Williams, appears to have a mental disorder. Almost half of all Americans (46.4 percent) will meet the criteria for a mental, emotional, or behavioral disorder sometime during their lives (Kessler, Berglund, Demler, Jin, & Walters, 2005). The various disorders are catalogued and described in the *Diagnostic and Statistical Manual of Mental Disorders* (DSM), published by the American Psychiatric Association (APA). The DSM is the standard resource for clinical diagnosis in this country. The first edition of the DSM came out in 1952, and the manual has undergone many revisions during the last 50 years. The latest version is DSM-IV-TR (Text Revision) (APA, 2000), and another revision is planned for 2010.

The definition of *mental disorder* in the DSM is a "significant behavioral or psychological syndrome or pattern that occurs in an individual and that is associated with present distress (e.g., a painful symptom) or disability (i.e., impairment in one or more important areas of functioning) or with significantly increased risk of suffering death, pain, disability, or an important loss of freedom" (p. xxxi). A disorder ". . . must currently be considered a manifestation of behavioral, psychological, or biological dysfunction in the individual" (p. xxxi). The DSM represents a medical perspective, only one of many possible perspectives on human behavior. The medical definition focuses on underlying disturbances *within* the person and is sometimes referred to as the *disease model* of abnormality. This model implies that the abnormal person must experience changes within the self (rather than create environmental change) in order to be considered "normal" again.

In its desire to promote the "objectivity" of its manual, the APA does not recognize the notion of mental illness as a *social construction*. A social construction is any belief system in a culture that is accepted as "factual" or "objective" by many of its members, when in fact the belief system is constructed by influential members of that society (Berger & Luckmann, 1966; Searle, 1995). The medical profession now holds great influence in Western society, so when mental health diagnoses are presented as scientifically based "disorders," many people will accept them as such. Social constructionism asserts that many "accepted" facts in a society are in fact ideas that reflect the values of the times in which they emerge.

The foregoing information may explain why the DSM classification system does not fully represent the knowledge base or values of the social work profession, which emphasizes a transactional, person-in-situation perspective on human functioning. Still, it is extensively used by social workers, for many positive reasons. Worldwide, the medical profession is preeminent in setting standards for mental health practice, and social workers are extensively employed in mental health settings, where clinical diagnosis is considered necessary for selecting appropriate interventions. In fact, social workers account for more than half of the mental health workforce in the United States (Gambrill, 2002). Competent use of the DSM is beneficial to social workers (and clients) for the following reasons:

• Social workers are employed in a variety of settings, not just mental health agencies and facilities, where they meet people who are vulnerable to mental health disorders because of poverty, minority status, and other social factors. No matter what their setting, social workers should be able to recognize the symptoms of possible disorders in their clients and appropriately refer them for treatment services.

• The five-axis diagnostic system (which considers mental disorders, developmental disorders, medical problems, environmental stressors, and a global assessment of client functioning) provides the basis of a comprehensive bio- (Axis III), psycho- (Axes I, II, and V), and social (Axis IV) assessment.

• An accurate diagnosis propels the development of a suitable intervention plan.

• The diagnostic categories enable social workers to help clients, and possibly also their families, learn about the nature of the person's problems. Although some stigma is often attached to the assignment of a diagnostic label, many people take a certain comfort in learning that their painful experiences can be encapsulated in a diagnosis. It validates their experience, lets them know that other people suffer from the same disorder, and offers hope that their problems can be treated.

• Use of the DSM allows practitioners from various disciplines to converse in a common language about clients.

• The DSM perspective is incorporated into professional training programs offered by a variety of human service professions and portions of state social worker licensing examinations.

• Insurance companies usually require a formal DSM diagnosis for client reimbursement.

For these many reasons, social workers need to gain competence in DSM diagnosis, and enabling them to do so is a major purpose of this book. To that end, each chapter covers a particular mental disorder and is illustrated with two to three case studies on which readers can practice their skills and knowledge. Cases have been selected to represent the diversity of people with whom social workers intervene. The disorders chosen for this book are those that social workers may see in their employment or field settings and that have sufficient research information behind them. For instance, reactive attachment disorder is not included, even though child clients may carry this diagnosis, because there has been little research on the disorder itself, despite the fact that many data have been gathered throughout the years on attachment theory and attachment styles.

We will now turn to an overview of the DSM multi-axial classification system, using the case that opened the chapter as an illustration. We will then describe some of the tensions involved in DSM diagnosis as practiced by social workers and discuss how this book will help develop social workers' skills in ways that will overcome some of the limitations of the DSM approach for clinical practice in social work.

The DSM Classification System

Following is a description of the DSM five-axis classification of mental disorders, along with some general guidelines for its use (APA, 2000).

Axis I   Beginning with the problem that is most responsible for the current evaluation, the mental disorder or other condition that may be a focus of clinical attention (a V-code diagnosis) is recorded under Axis I. The mental disorders, including adjustment disorders, will make up the chapters of this book. Although they are typically not given on their own, since they are not reimbursed by insurance, the V-codes are given in three different situations: (1) when no mental disorder is present but a problem needs clinical attention; (2) when there is a problem unrelated to the mental disorder; or (3) when a problem related to the mental disorder is sufficiently severe to warrant clinical attention of its own (APA, 2000).

When uncertain if a diagnosis is correct, the social worker should use the "provisional" qualifier. If a person no longer meets criteria for a disorder that may be relevant to his or her current condition, the qualifier "past history" can be given. For example, if a woman seeks help for depression while she is pregnant, it may be important to note if she had an eating disorder history.

Axis II   This axis includes the disorders that are considered to have more of a constitutional basis and includes the personality disorders and mental retardation. They are considered to represent relatively chronic conditions that can put the person at risk for a variety of Axis I disorders. If a personality disorder is the most important reason for the client's request for evaluation, the social worker should add the term "principal diagnosis."

Axis III   This axis includes the person's general medical conditions, which may have a direct bearing on an Axis I diagnosis or may affect (or be affected by) management of an Axis I or II diagnosis. The source of the information should also be listed here, such as "according to the client" or "confirmed in the chart by a physician."

Axis IV   This axis is used to record psychosocial and environmental problems that have occurred in the last year and are a focus of clinical attention. These involve problems with the following: primary support group, economic or social

environment, access to health care services, educational system, interaction with the legal or criminal systems, occupational setting, housing problems, as well as any other psychosocial stressors, such as phase-of-life and accultura-tion problems. The social worker should record the formal term and also add descriptive information about the stressor, such as "educational problem— failed past year of school."

Although Axis IV does not relate to problems within the individual, only environmental conditions, no differentiation is made between environ-mental problems that are contributing to a person's disorder (risk influences) and those that are consequences of the disorder. For example, educational problems in a child with oppositional defiant disorder (ODD) often arise because of disruptive behaviors displayed at school; it is not that the educational problems result in ODD.

Axis V   Global assessment of functioning (GAF) indicates the level of a client's social, occupational, and psychological functioning on a 100-point scale reflecting a continuum of mental health and illness. It comprises two scores: one reflecting the client's current GAF (the past week), and another reflect-ing the client's highest level during the past year. The DSM includes anchor descriptions for each ten points on the scale. The reader should note that GAF scores, like many aspects of the DSM, are subject to interpretation. GAF scores tend to have low reliability, as individual clinicians vary widely in their assignment of scores.

Following is a list of "hierarchical principles" that can help the practitioner decide which diagnoses to use in situations where several might be feasible:

- "Disorders due to a general medical condition" and "substance-induced disorders," which include not only substances people consume but also medications they are pre-scribed, preempt a diagnosis of any other disorder that could produce the same symptoms.
- The fewer diagnoses that account for the symptoms, the better. This is the rule of "parsimony." Practitioners need to understand the "power of the diagnostic label," in its negative as well as positive aspects, and use diagnostic labels judiciously. For example, post-traumatic stress disorder (PTSD) and reactive attachment disorder are sometimes diagnosed simultaneously in children. Although they share some presentation, when they are used together the diagnostic picture becomes imprecise and does not lead to a coherent treatment plan.
- When a more pervasive disorder has essential or associated symptoms that are the defining symptoms of a less pervasive disorder, the more pervasive disorder is diag-nosed if its diagnostic criteria are met. For example, if "oppositional defiant disorder" and "conduct disorder" are both present, the social worker should use the "conduct dis-order" diagnosis, since its range of criteria overlaps with the former diagnosis (see Chapter 6 for case examples).

• When the client's presentation seems to match several diagnostic categories, the social worker should use the least severe diagnosis possible, to treat the client with respect and to avoid stigma and the negative social effects of labeling. While there is no "official" ranking of diagnoses by severity, some categories do seem to be less stigmatizing than others, in that they are more common and shorter term in nature (such as an adjustment disorder versus depression, or depression versus a psychotic disorder or a personality disorder). Thus the social worker may assign a client an adjustment disorder diagnosis or a V-code (although the latter is not usually reimbursable by insurance companies).

The principles outlined above are of course applied only after a comprehensive client assessment is carried out. Each chapter in this book includes assessment principles relevant to specific disorders, but here we present some general guidelines for the assessment of a client's mental, emotional, and behavioral functioning.

Mental Status Examination (MSE)

An MSE is a process by which a social worker or other human services professional systematically examines the quality of a client's mental functioning. Ten areas of functioning are considered individually. The results of the examination are combined with information derived from a client's social history to produce clinical impressions of the client, including a DSM diagnosis. An MSE can typically be completed in 15 minutes or less. One commonly used format for an MSE evaluates the following areas of client functioning (Folstein, Folstein, & McHugh, 1975):

- *Appearance*. The person's overall appearance in the context of his or her cultural group. These features are significant because poor personal hygiene or grooming may reflect a physical inability to care for one's physical self or a loss of interest in doing so.
- *Movement and behavior*. The person's manner of walking, posture, coordination, eye contact, and facial expressions. Problems with walking or coordination may reflect a disorder of the central nervous system.
- *Affect*. This refers to a person's outwardly observable emotional reactions and may include either a lack of emotional response or an overreaction to an event.
- *Mood*. The underlying emotional tone of the person's answers.
- *Speech*. The volume of the person's voice, the rate or speed of speech, the length of answers to questions, and the appropriateness and clarity of the answers.
- *Thought content*. Any indications in the client's words or behaviors of hallucinations, delusions, obsessions, symptoms of dissociation, or thoughts of suicide.
- *Thought process*. The logical connections between thoughts and their relevance to the conversation. Irrelevant detail, repeated words and phrases, interrupted thinking, and illogical connections between thoughts may be signs of a thought disorder.

- *Cognition.* The act or condition of knowing. The social worker assesses the person's orientation with regard to time, place, and personal identity; long- and short-term memory; ability to perform simple arithmetic (counting backward by threes or sevens); general intellectual level or fund of knowledge (identifying the last five presidents, or similar questions); ability to think abstractly (explaining a proverb); ability to name specified objects and read or write complete sentences; ability to understand and perform a task (showing the examiner how to comb one's hair or throw a ball); ability to draw a simple map or copy a design or geometrical figure; ability to distinguish between right and left.
- *Judgment.* The social worker asks the person what he or she would do about a commonsense problem, such as running out of a prescription medication.
- *Insight.* A person's ability to recognize a problem and understand its nature and severity.

Abnormal results for an MSE include any evidence of brain damage or thought disorders, a mood or affect that is clearly inappropriate to its context, thoughts of suicide, disturbed speech patterns, dissociative symptoms, and delusions or hallucinations.

> **Question:** Now that you have read a description of the multi-axial system, hierarchical principles, and an MSE, can you work out a multi-axial diagnosis for Henry Williams before reading ahead?

Multi-Axial Diagnosis

Axis I:

Axis II:

Axis III:

Axis IV:

Axis V:

Multi-Axial Diagnosis of Mr. Williams

Axis I: 292.12 Psychotic disorder with hallucinations induced by steroids
          V61.10 Partner relational problem

Axis II: V71.09 (no diagnosis on Axis II)

Axis III: 250.01 Insulin-dependent diabetes mellitus
          225.2 Meningioma (cerebral)
          345.10 Seizure disorder
          577.1 Pancreatitis

Axis IV: Problems with primary support group (marital problems)

Axis V: GAF score: 35

Rationale for the Diagnosis

Psychotic disorder with hallucinations induced by steroids was diagnosed because the symptoms started a few days after the patient started to take the medication. Steroids can affect the limbic system, causing aggression and emotional outbursts. Although this diagnosis would have to be made by medical personnel, the social worker should be aware that the symptoms of apparent mental disorders may result from a medical condition or from medication used to treat the condition.

The specifier "with hallucinations" was used because the patient's hallucinations (casting out the demons) seemed to predominate over his delusions (thinking that his wife was cheating on him). The latter appeared to have a basis in reality, even though he was the one who had had an affair. Projection of his own behavior onto his wife may have caused the delusion. It should also be noted that Mr. Williams had just had a brain tumor removed; changes in mood and affect are fairly common in these patients. A diagnosis of psychotic disorder due to a medical condition can be excluded, however, because Mr. Williams did not show symptoms before or right after the craniotomy was performed. Instead they developed six days after the surgery. The V-code, partner relational problem, was also diagnosed due to the long-standing marital problems that have recently resurfaced due to Mr. Williams's accusations.

The GAF score of 35 was given because Mr. Williams is experiencing major symptoms, including impaired reality testing, hallucinations, and delusions, which cause him to behave aggressively and seriously impair his relationships with others. Although Mr. Williams's current GAF score is very low, there is considerable hope that he will be able to return to his previous level of functioning, because his symptoms appear to be the temporary side effects of the steroids he was given in the hospital.

Limitations of the DSM

Any classification of mental, emotional, and behavioral disorders is likely to be flawed, as it is difficult for any system to capture to complexity of human life. As noted earlier, the DSM classification system is based on the medical model of diagnosis, while the profession of social work is characterized by the consideration of systems and the reciprocal impact of persons and their environments on human behavior (Andreae, 1996). That is, for social workers the quality of a person's social functioning should be assessed with regard to the interplay of biological, psychological, and social factors in his or her life. Three types of person-in-environment situations likely to produce problems in social functioning include life transitions, relationship difficulties, and environmental unresponsiveness (Carter & McGoldrick, 2005). Social work interventions, therefore, may focus on the person; the environment; or, more commonly, both. Some other limitations of the DSM from the perspective of the social work profession are described below. Additionally, each chapter will offer critiques of the particular DSM diagnosis and/or the medical perspective underlying it. The reader will also be asked to offer a critical perspective when presented with each of the case illustrations.

One of the criticisms of the DSM is that the reliability of diagnosis (agreement among practitioners about the same clients) is not high for some disorders, and generally has not risen since DSM-II (Duffy, Gillig, & Tureen, 2002). Second, psychiatric diagnoses are often based on cultural notions of normality versus abnormality and mental health versus illness (Maracek, 2006). For example, homosexuality was considered a mental disorder until 1974, when political pressure on the creators of the DSM was successfully applied (Kutchins & Kirk, 1997). Today, some question the validity of the diagnosis of gender identity disorder, claiming that it represents an unusual but valid gender orientation (Hill, Rozanski, Carfagnini, & Willoughby, 2005).

Third, arising as it does from the psychiatric profession, the DSM may overstate the case for biological influences on some mental disorders (Cooper, 2004; Healy, 2002; Johnston, 2000). For instance, heritability for both major depression and anxiety is about 30 to 40 percent (Hettema, Neale, & Kendler, 2001; Sullivan et al., 2000); for substance use disorders heritability is about 30 percent (Walters, 2002). While other biological factors may play a role in the development of mental disorders aside from genetics (for example, complications at birth, exposure to lead), social factors (family environment, community, social support, income levels) certainly play a large role as well.

In a related vein, the DSM tends to view clients in isolation and decontextualizes the disorder from the person and the life circumstances that have given rise to it (Westen, 2005). Generally speaking, the DSM does not highlight the roles played by systems in the emergence of problems. Some parts of the DSM do so, however, primarily with the "adjustment disorders," in which people are seen as having difficulty adjusting to environmental stressors. Further, the V-codes allow practitioners to articulate relational issues, and Axis IV is also helpful in balancing the personal and the social aspects of life.

Fifth, some feminists argue that the DSM is gender-biased, according a higher prevalence of many disorders to women (notably depression, anxiety, and many of the personality disorders) (Wiley, 2004). The DSM has been criticized for blaming women for their responses to oppressive social conditions (Blehar, 2006).

Sixth, because not all symptoms need to be met for any diagnosis to be made, two people with the same diagnosis can have very different symptom profiles. There is also an acknowledged abundance of "subthreshold cases" (those that do not quite meet the minimum number of symptom criteria), even though these may produce as much impairment as those that meet full diagnostic criteria (Gonzalez-Tejara, Canino, Ramirez, et al., 2005). This problem of a lack of specificity has been dealt with in part by the addition over time of new subtypes of disorders, and also by the introduction of "severity" qualifiers (mild, medium, severe).

Due to this limitation of the DSM, many people have argued that mental disorders should be assessed through a dimensional approach on a continuum of health and disorder. Measurement instruments assess symptoms in a dimensional context rather than through a categorical system like the DSM, in which a person either meets certain criteria or does not. In this book we may occasionally mention some measures that might be useful for assessment, but the focus is on DSM diagnosis. The interested reader is referred to other books that focus on measurement instruments (e.g., Fischer & Corcoran, 2007; Corcoran & Walsh, 2006; Hersen, 2006).

Seventh, the problem of comorbidity, in which a person may qualify for more than one diagnosis on an axis, is a point of significant confusion among practitioners. The reader will note that throughout this book, comorbidity rates for disorders are often substantial. The APA encourages the recording of more than one diagnosis on an axis when the assessment justifies doing so. But many disorders (for example, anxiety disorders and depression) correlate strongly with one another (Kessler, Chiu, Demler, & Walters, 2005). It may be that an anxious depression differs from either a "pure" major depressive disorder or anxiety disorder in critical ways. In addition, research on treatment generally confines itself to people without comorbid disorders, so that results are often not generalizable to the treatment population at large.

Finally, the DSM makes no provisions for recording client strengths. Strengths-oriented practice implies that practitioners should assess all clients in light of their capacities, talents, competencies, possibilities, visions, values, and hopes (Saleeby, 2001). This perspective emphasizes human *resilience*—the skills, abilities, knowledge, and insight that people accumulate over time as they struggle to surmount adversity and meet life challenges. In the next two chapters, we will discuss the appraisal of strengths—both at the individual and environmental levels.

2

— ▼▲▼ —

Biopsychosocial Risk and Resilience Framework

This book uses the biopsychosocial risk and resilience framework to organize information on how mental disorders develop and how internal and external influences affect individual adjustment after a diagnosis is made. Adjustment involves the extent to which a person recovers from the condition and/or the response to intervention (Gowers & Bryant-Waugh, 2004). Although the biological and psychological levels relate to the individual, the social aspect of the framework captures the effects of the family, the community, and the wider social culture. The processes within each level interact, prompting the occurrence of emotional or mental disorders (Shirk, Talmi, & Olds, 2000) and the propensity toward resilience, or the ability to function adaptively despite stressful life circumstances.

We emphasize risk and protective mechanisms or processes rather than "factors," which imply a static quality (Deater-Deckard et al., 2005). Risks can be understood as hazards occurring at the individual or environmental levels that increase the likelihood of impairment developing (Bogenschneider, 1996). Protective mechanisms involve the . . . personal, familial, community, and institutional resources that cultivate individuals' aptitudes and abilities while diminishing the possibility of problem behaviors (Dekovic, 1999). These protective influences may counterbalance or buffer against risk (Pollard, Hawkins, & Arthur, 1999; Werner, 2000) and are sometimes the converse of risk (Jessor, Van Den Bos, Vanderryn, Costa, & Turbin, 1997). For instance, at the individual level, poor health presents risks while good health is protective. It must be noted that research on protective influences is limited compared with information on risks for various disorders (Donovan & Spence, 2000).

The biopsychosocial emphasis expands the focus beyond the individual to a recognition of systemic factors that can both create and ameliorate problems. The nature of systems is such that the factors within and between them have transactional and reciprocal influence on one another, with early risk mechanisms setting the stage for greater vulnerability to subsequent risks. The development of oppositional defiant disorder and

conduct disorder is a case in point that shows how the presence of certain risk or protective mechanisms may increase the likelihood of other risk and protective influences.

Moffitt (2003) hypothesizes that a neurologically vulnerable and difficult child develops disruptive behavior in the context of interactions with parents. Deficits in cognition and verbal skills (Loeber & Coie, 2001) and early difficult temperament, which is defined as negative emotionality, intense and reactive responses to stress and frustration, and inflexibility (Nigg & Huang-Pollock, 2003) may be biological or hereditary. These factors in turn evoke negative reactions from parents. These responses then heighten the child's tendency toward difficult behavior. At the same time, parents who abuse substances or who are themselves diagnosed with antisocial personality disorder tend to have children at an earlier age than other parents do and demonstrate less effective parenting practices (Loeber et al., 2002). Assortive mating is an additional factor, in that people with antisocial tendencies couple and produce children who are not only at genetic risk but may also be raised in detrimental environments. Family poverty, neighborhood crime, inadequate social support, and limited community resources may further inhibit parenting effectiveness (Loeber & Coie, 2001). Parents may eventually attempt to avoid the negative interchanges and the strain involved in taking care of a child with conduct problems (Bussing, Gary, Mason, Leon, Sinha, & Garvan, 2003). Rejection and avoidance of the child further erode discipline and supervision (Capaldi & Patterson, 1994).

Negative interactions in the home environment eventually extend into the realm of school and peer groups (Moffitt, 2003). Difficulties with teachers may contribute to poor school performance. Alienation from the norms of the school system may develop, and by the time such children are about 10 or 11 years of age they bond together in deviant peer groups (McMahon, 1994). If such individuals live in poverty, they have restricted opportunities and are therefore more likely to seek out deviant means to obtain fulfillment and a sense of identity (Prinz & Miller, 1991).

Although precise mechanisms of action are not specified, data have begun to accumulate that four or more risk influences may overwhelm an individual and represent a threat to adaptation (Epps & Jackson, 2000; Garmezy, 1993; Kalil & Kunz, 1999; Runyan et al., 1998). Risk seems to have a stronger relationship to problem behavior than does protection (Devocik, 1999). While some have found that the more risks, the worse the outcome (Appleyard, Egeland, van Dulmen, & Sroufe, 2005), others have argued that risk does not proceed in a linear, additive fashion (Greenberg, Speltz, Deklyen, & Jones, 2001). Neither are all risk factors weighted equally. The associations between risk and protection and outcomes are complex and may involve changing conditions across development.

The chapters in this book delineate the risk and protective influences for both the onset of particular disorders and an individual's adjustment or recovery. Some of the influences discussed in each chapter are nonspecific to that particular disorder; in other words, certain risks and protective mechanisms play a role in multiple disorders. These common mechanisms, discussed at the individual and social levels, are good targets for intervention and prevention and are given an overview here.

Individual Factors

Individual factors include the biological and psychological realms. Within biology we will discuss genes, neurotransmitters, temperament, health, developmental stage, and intelligence. At the psychological level we will explore individual patterns of behavior.

Biological Mechanisms

GENES AND HERITABILITY

Genes determine the extent of liability for the development of disorders (Bulik, 2004). Although information on the genetic influences of all mental disorders is not available, the disorders differ in the extent to which they are attributed to genetic causes. For instance, heritability for major depression ranges from 31 to 42 percent (Sullivan et al., 2000); similarly, anxiety disorders seem to be moderately heritable. The hypothesis is that emotional disorders such as depression or anxiety may stem from a general genetic vulnerability, with environmental mechanisms determining the specific disorder (Williams, Reardon, Murray, & Cole, 2005). Certain other disorders, such as bipolar disorder and schizophrenia, are more heritable than the emotional disorders (U.S. Department of Health & Human Services [DHHS], 1999).

Specific genetic markers have been linked to some mental disorders. For instance, mutations in any of four genes (located on chromosomes 1, 14, 19, and 21) are implicated in the development of autistic disorder (Polleux & Lauder, 2004). Indeed, genetic models for many disorders increasingly involve a number of genes rather than a single-gene theory (Williams et al., 2005). Even for disorders assumed to have genetic causes, those conditions result not only from abnormalities in inherited genes but also from certain gene combinations or other errors in genes caused during pregnancy by such events as infections and exposure to x-rays (Arc, 2007).

NEUROTRANSMITTERS

Many people describe mental disorders as caused by "chemical imbalances in the brain." Neurotransmitters are the chemicals that convey communication between neurons. These substances are naturally regulated by breaking down in the spaces between cells or through reuptake into transmitting cells. Problems with neurotransmitter action have been associated with various mental disorders. For example, a lack of serotonin has been associated with depression, anxiety (Ebmeier, Donaghey, & Steele, 2006), and borderline personality disorder (Ni, Chan, & Bulgin, 2006), while high levels of serotonin have been linked to autism (Waldman & Gizer, 2006). Inflated levels of norepinephrine have been associated with borderline personality disorder (Gurvits, Koenigsberg, & Siever, 2000), and problems with dopamine have been correlated with schizophrenia (Finlay, 2001) and attention-deficit hyperactivity disorder (ADHD) (Levy, Hay, & Bennett, 2006).

The notion of a "chemical balance" as the cause of a mental disorder is a reductionistic way to view disorders, as most arise from a complex interplay of biological, psychological, and social processes. In addition, correlation should not be confused with causality. That is, psychosocial events can affect brain functioning and the action of neurotransmitters (Andreasen, 2001; Cozolino, 2002).

Much of what is known about neurotransmitters and their role in causing mental disorders has been hypothesized from the effects of medication. Valenstein (1998) discusses the limitations of these theories with respect to depression. First, it is not possible actually to measure the levels of neurotransmitters in the human brain. Only indirect measures can be relied upon, and when these are used, low levels of critical neurotransmitters are not reliable indicators of mental disorders.

Early antidepressants were thought to work by increasing norepinephrine in the nervous system. Newer antidepressants inhibit the reuptake of serotonin and norepinephrine, and it is suspected that all antidepressants have effects on other neurotransmitters such as gamma-aminobutyric acid (GABA), dopamine, and the opioids. However, some medications alleviate depression, even though they affect other transmitters. For instance, tricyclics tend to work on acetylcholine. The complexity of neurotransmitter action is generally unknown and theories tend to be reductionistic when pinpointing one or two neurotransmitters as culpable in the development of a particular mental disorder (Valenstein, 1998).

Another problem with theories based on brain chemistry is that medications need to be taken for a few weeks in order to demonstrate their impact on mood. However, they produce maximum elevation of neurotransmitter activity in only a couple of days. Since each neuron both receives and transmits from tens of thousands of other neurons, a medication that focuses on one type of neurotransmitter will actually have an exponential effect throughout other chemical systems. Hence, it is difficult to account for the changes that might be responsible for improved mood. In other words, biological theories have not considered the potential complexity involved in brain functioning (Valenstein, 1998).

TEMPERAMENT

Temperament provides the foundation for personality. It includes qualities that are biologically driven, are observed from infancy, and are moderately stable across the life span and in different contexts (Deater-Deckard, Ivy, & Smith, 2005). Temperament involves activity level, intensity, attention span, quality of mood (irritability or explosiveness), adaptability, flexibility, and rhythmicity (the regularity of sleep-wake cycles, eating, and elimination) (Barkley, 2000). To a certain degree, a child's temperament will elicit behaviors from caregivers that will crystallize these traits, which will increase the likelihood that these behavior patterns will endure over time (Johnson et al., 2005). "Children who are irritable, easily distressed by changes in the environment, and more distractible may be less able to cope with adversity and more likely to attract or elicit harsh and rejecting parenting" (Deater-Deckard et al., 2005, p. 52). On the other hand, positive temperamental traits, such as good-naturedness, precociousness, maturity, inquisitiveness, willingness to take risks, optimism, hopefulness, altruism, and personableness help people cope with life stress and attract others to them (Henggeler et al., 1998).

Another temperamental style associated with mental disorders is temperamental sensitivity, which is characterized by a range of emotional reactions toward negativity, including fear, worry, sadness, self-dissatisfaction, and hostility (Donovan & Spence, 2000). This tendency predisposes people to both anxiety and depression, which often occur together. Certain temperaments may present risk or protection. For example, behavioral inhibition, which involves timidity, shyness, emotional restraint, and withdrawal when introduced into unfamiliar situations (Kagan et al., 1988, as cited in Donovan & Spence, 2000) puts a person at risk for anxiety disorders but protects against the development of oppositional defiant and conduct disorders (Burke, Loeber, & Birmaher, 2002).

PHYSICAL HEALTH

Good physical health is a protective mechanism for many disorders; this includes perinatal health, defined as the absence of pregnancy and birth complications (Werner, 2000). Complications during pregnancy and delivery may place individuals at risk for mental disorders, including ADHD (Bhutta, Cleves, Casey, Cradock, & Anand, 2002; Root & Resnick, 2003; Samudra & Cantwell, 1999), eating disorders (Favaro, Tenconi, & Santonastaso, 2006), bipolar disorder (Kinney, Yurgelum-Todd, Tohen, & Tramer, 1998), and schizophrenia (Verdoux, Geddes, Takei, Lawrie, Bovet, et al., 1997). Further, certain maternal behaviors during pregnancy may increase the child's risk for some disorders. A pregnant mother's prenatal drug use, excessive alcohol intake, and malnutrition during pregnancy are risk influences for the onset of mental retardation (Arc, 2007). Cigarette smoking during pregnancy has been associated not only with the child's development of mental retardation (Arc, 2006) but also with conduct disorder (Loeber et al., 2002) and ADHD (Linnett, Dalsgaard, Obel, et al., 2003). Medical conditions, such as heart attack, cancer, stroke, diabetes, and HIV increase the risk of depression (Ciesla & Roberts, 2001; Karasu et al., 2002). Untreated depression can also inhibit recovery from disease. It can increase the level of impairment, interfere with healing, and impede an individual's motivation and ability to follow through with prescribed treatment.

DEVELOPMENTAL STAGE

Mental disorders usually emerge early in life. About 50 percent of cases have their onset by the age of 14, and 75 percent begin by age 24 (Kessler, Berglund, Demler, et al., 2005). The risk of mental disorders continues to be high until after the age category 30 to 44; prevalence then declines for people who have matured out of this high-risk age range. For example, borderline personality disorder (Paris, 2003) and antisocial disorder may remit as afflicted individuals mature into their 40s.

In Werner and Smith's (2001) longitudinal study on resilience, many people whose lives had been characterized by adversity and mental health or learning disabilities in their teens were able to make a positive adjustment by age 40. Protective influences for positive adaptation involved education at community colleges, educational and vocational skills garnered during military service, a stable marriage, active participation in a religious faith, and experience of life-threatening accident or illness.

INTELLIGENCE

Intelligence quotient (IQ) is a protective factor, producing higher school performance despite life stress and more effective problem solving in peer social situations (Wachs, 2000). Conversely, low IQ is a central risk factor for antisocial behavior, over and above socioeconomic status and race. More specifically, reading and reasoning skills have been identified as critical to a child's long-term development (Werner & Smith, 2001). Parental education is also key, extending from adjustment in childhood, all the way into middle age (Werner & Smith, 2001).

Psychological Mechanisms

SELF-EFFICACY AND SELF-ESTEEM

Children with positive self-concepts and a self-perception characterized by an internal sense of control, a belief that they can influence their environment and show effective coping strategies, are better equipped to face life stressors (Wachs, 2000; Werner & Smith, 2001).

COPING STRATEGIES

A tendency toward rigid belief systems and certain cognitive distortions puts people at risk for mental disorders. For example, depression is related to significant cognitive distortions, such as Beck's conceptualization involving the "cognitive triad" of depression: thoughts about the self as worthless, the world as unfair, and the future as hopeless (Beck, Rush, Shaw, & Emery, 1979). In addition, youth with conduct problems display distortions in how they perceive and code their social experiences (called cognitive processing) (Kazdin, 2001). These include the inability to produce a variety of strategies to manage interpersonal problems; difficulty figuring out ways to achieve a particular desired outcome; difficulty identifying the consequences of a particular action and its effects on others; a tendency to attribute hostile motivations to the actions of others; and misunderstanding of how others feel. The combination of perceived threat and limited options for managing social situations makes antisocial youth more likely to respond with aggression rather than with more productive problem-solving strategies.

The nature of one's coping strategies is also a general risk or protective resilience mechanism. For example, certain coping strategies are problematic for the development of anxiety and depressive disorders. One type of problematic coping pattern involves avoidance coping. For instance, anxiety disorders develop partly because individuals avoid situations that trigger anxiety. They do not allow themselves to tolerate a situation until the anxiety begins to dissipate. Unfortunately, a style of avoidance for dealing with depression might lead an individual to experience more life stress and depressive symptoms as a result (Holahan, Moos, Holahan, Brennan, & Schutte, 2005).

Rumination is another detrimental coping pattern. Rumination is the proclivity to focus on the symptoms of a distressed mood, or to mull over the reasons for its occurrence in an incessant and passive way (Nolen-Hoeksema, 2002), rather than using problem-solving strategies (Hino, Takeuchi, & Yamanouchi, 2002). It is not only the internalizing disorders that are linked with problematic coping; conduct problems in girls have also been associated with poor coping skills (Burke, Loeber, & Birmaher, 2002).

Interpersonal skills can also be subsumed under the category of coping strategies. These skills involve the ability to create and maintain relationships and to communicate effectively and assertively (Henggeler, Schoenwald, Borduin, Rowland, & Cunningham, 1998).

Social Mechanisms

Family factors have a major influence on whether an individual with a biological vulnerability develops a mental disorder. For instance, family characteristics explain more of the variance in conduct disorder (Dekovic, 1999) and adolescent substance use than do any other factors (Hopfer, Stallings, Hewitt, & Crowley, 2003). Families transmit both genetic material and an environmental context for children (Wachs, 2000), although the extent to which heredity or the family environment explains the influence of the family is not always well understood. Other important influences in the social environment include neighborhood context, church, school, and other community resources available to families. The influence of each of these mechanisms will be discussed, although it is important to point out that these aspects of the community context interact with one another (e.g., schools are part of the neighborhood) and with other levels (e.g., individuals and families make up neighborhoods).

Family

FAMILY FUNCTIONING

Several patterns are indicative of families in which mental disorders develop, among them hostility, conflict, isolation, low cohesion, enmeshment, and an absence of nurturing. Certain family variables center on the parent-child relationship. Parental rejection of the child, inconsistent and ineffective discipline, lack of supervision, and lack of involvement in the child's activities are also mechanisms of risk.

Parent-infant attachment is especially central. The developing child requires a sense of security that caregivers will respond in warm, consistent, and sensitive ways to his or her needs (Bowlby, 1969, 1973, 1980). Early attachment is hypothesized to result "in the development of 'working models,' schemata about the self, others, and relationships that will guide functioning across the life span" (Davila, Ramsay, Stroud, & Steinberg, 2005, p. 216). Indeed, attachment style has been shown to afford stability into adulthood (Hazan, Campa, & Gur-Yaish, 2006). "Although insecure attachment itself may in some cases be severe enough to qualify as a disorder (e.g., reactive attachment disorder)" (Davila et al., 2005, p. 217), most of the time, it will only be one mechanism contributing to the development of a disorder.

A critical function of secure caregiving is that it provides "children with a context in which they learn about and develop the ability to identify, tolerate, and express a range of emotions . . . (defined as emotion-regulation skills). However, when caregivers are unable to reflect upon and regulate their child's and their own emotional states, children do not have the opportunity to develop effective strategies to respond to their own emotions or the emotions of close others" (Davila et al., 2005, p. 229).

Further risks in the context of the family involve instability and parental conflict, such as discord, separation and family violence, and high parental stress (Loeber et al., 1998). Chronic marital discord and family violence are associated with risk of maternal mental health, for example, increased incidence of depression and post-traumatic stress disorder (Golding, 1999), and aversive parenting practices (Krishnakumar & Buehler, 2000). Any psychopathology afflicting parents that compromises their abilities also constitutes a risk (Steinberg, 2000). Such factors include parental depression, substance use problems, antisocial personality disorder and criminal offending, or the presence of any other psychiatric disorders.

Conversely, family stability, a stable parental relationship (including parental agreement on values and discipline), and social support for parents are seen as protective. Families that have effective discipline skills, healthy cohesion, and positive communication help buffer their children against mental disorders. For example, adolescents whose parents provide emotional support and structure the environment with consistent rules and monitoring tend to group with peers who share similar family backgrounds (Steinberg, 2000). Supportive parenting in turn affects the characteristics of the child, in that he or she learns to regulate emotional processes and develop cognitive and social competence (Wachs, 2000). Individual characteristics of parents are also key; parents who have problem-solving ability and resourcefulness, experience low stress, and demonstrate frustration tolerance and patience are more effective in their role as parents (Henggeler et al., 1998).

HOUSEHOLD COMPOSITION

Household composition refers to familial structure and includes size of the family, the number of parents in the home, and the spacing of children's births. Larger family size (more than three children) is a risk factor, as precious family resources are then spread among many children (Werner, 2000). Living in a single-parent family has also been identified as a risk factor. Whereas in two-parent families two adults can provide financial security, guidance, and emotional support (Young, Jensen, Olsen, & Cundick, 1991), single parents are more likely to work full-time and therefore not be as available for supervision, monitoring, or time spent with the child (Newcomer & Udry, 1985). Rapid childbearing (defined as less than a two-year spacing between children) further presents risk, as it limits the amount of time devoted to the first child (Klerman, 2004).

Another risk for some mental disorders is the structure of Western society, in which the upbringing of most children is limited to one or two primary caregivers, without additional consistent parent figures available to "fill in" when these caregivers prove to be inadequate (Alarcon, 2005). In contrast, in some cultural groups, such as Latinos and

African-Americans, extended family may routinely provide major parenting roles. Western society's reliance on the nuclear family fails to provide opportunities for children to have "second chances" to develop healthy attachments when these might be developmentally beneficial. Characteristics of the extended family that offer protection include the provision of material resources, child care, supervision, parenting, and emotional support to the child (Henggeler et al., 1998).

TRAUMATIC EVENTS AND LOSS

These have been organized under family factors because events such as sexual abuse and physical abuse often occur in the context of the family. Sexual and physical abuse are broad risk mechanisms and have been associated with the development of conduct disorder, oppositional defiant disorder (McGee & Williams, 1999), depression (Fergusson, Horwood, & Lynskey, 1996), anxiety (Phillips, Hammen, Brennan, et al., 2005), and borderline personality disorder (Zanarini, Yong, Frankenburg, Hennen, Reich, et al., 2002). When abuse and neglect are severe, children may be removed from their own homes and placed into foster care, and these situations put them at high risk for mental health problems (DHHS, 2001).

Neighborhood

Although individual and family characteristics are major contributors to child and young adult outcomes, neighborhood factors are also key (Ellen, 2000; Leventhal & Brooks-Gunn, 2003). Living in poor and disadvantaged communities creates substantial risks of antisocial behavior in children. Such risks include poverty, unemployment, community disorganization, availability of drugs, the presence of adults involved in crime, overcrowding, community violence, and racial prejudice (Hill, 2002; Loeber et al., 2000; McGee & Williams, 1999). Parenting abilities are often challenged by the many stressors that attend living in a low socioeconomic stratum, among them unemployment, underemployment, the lack of safe child care, the lack of transportation, inadequate housing, and exposure to crime. These stressors may not only negatively affect parenting but may also inhibit access to general health and mental health care services.

An extensive review of the literature on neighborhood effects (Leventhal & Brooks-Gunn, 2003) found evidence that living in a disadvantaged neighborhood had negative consequences for young children's mental health functioning. Moreover, a recent study of 2,805 children found that those living in poor neighborhoods were more likely to have mental health problems, particularly internalizing disorders (Xue, Leventhal, Brooks-Gunn, & Earls, 2005). Over time, as children mature, effects become more deleterious. For adolescents, not only impaired mental health, but also criminal behavior, early sexual activity, and teenage pregnancy are associated with living in poor neighborhoods (Levanthal & Brooks-Gunn, 2003).

Neighborhoods can, however, represent a source of protection. While neighborhood peers may exert negative influences on such behaviors as drug and alcohol use and criminal activity, some studies have found that adult neighbors who offer structure and monitoring can be an important source of support for children experiencing risks in their own families (Werner & Smith, 2001). As well as providing informal social control and social cohesion, neighbors involved in local organizations help to sustain the mental health of children who live in neighborhoods marked by disadvantages (Xue et al., 2005). Studies have also shown that middle-class and affluent neighborhoods have generally positive effects on educational attainment and achievement for adolescents, and neighbors of high socioeconomic status (SES) contribute to younger children's verbal ability, IQ, and academic achievement.

Social Support Networks

"Social support is widely viewed as a multidimensional concept and is commonly defined as the availability of a network of people on whom a person can rely in times of need. There are different types of social support (e.g., emotional, financial, informational, or enacted support)" (Hankin & Abela, 2005, p. 265). Social support networks can provide risk or protective influences. Social isolation and the lack of connection and social skills put people at risk for internalizing and eating disorders (Striegel-Moore & Cachelin, 1999). Deviant and substance-using peers present risks for the development of conduct problems (Hill, 2002) and substance use disorders. Lack of social support for abstinence hinders the chances of a person's recovery from substance use disorders (Bond, Kaskutas, & Weisner, 2003).

While positive social support acts as a buffer against the development of many mental disorders, it also plays a strong role in adjustment for all the disorders discussed in this book. The number and variety of social supports (extended family, friends, neighbors, coworkers, and church members) appear to be important (Henggeler et al., 1998). For youth, such supports encourage involvement in a peer group that is engaged in prosocial activities, hobbies, and interests.

A particular type of social network involving church or religious participation has been associated with positive physical and mental health, as well as with buffering the effects of neighborhood risks (Taylor, Ellison, Chatters, Levin, & Lincoln, 2000; Werner & Smith, 2001). Religious attendance and religiosity have also been significantly associated with a decreased likelihood of drug use among adolescents (Albrecht, Amey, & Miller, 1996; Miller, Davies, & Greenwald, 2000). In addition, for African-American youth, religious involvement may buffer the impact of neighborhood risk on criminal offending (Johnson, Jang, Li, & Larson, 2000). Research further indicates a positive relationship between religious involvement and adult health outcomes and coping with stress (McCullough, Larson, Hoyt, & Koenig, 2000).

More formal support systems may also enhance protection. Research has shown that participation in out-of-school activities and availability of community supports have positive outcomes for children in terms of educational attainment and health status. Empirically validated programs such as Big Brothers and Big Sisters (e.g., Thompson & Kelly-Vance, 2001), Head Start (e.g., Currie & Thomas, 1995), and other youth organizations present substantial protective factors (Werner, 2000).

Physical Health and Mental Health Care Access

The lack of necessary formal supports, especially health care services, can be a risk factor for families. For example, regular prenatal care, childhood immunizations, and routine developmental screenings protect against the development of mental retardation (Arc, 2007). Health professionals are responsible for screening for some childhood disorders, such as autism, and early detection is critical for good outcomes (Volkmar, Charwanda, & Klin, 2004).

In the United States, the system of mental health treatment consists of a patch-work of ad hoc services (DHHS, 2001, p. 33). There are four chief sectors for mental health care:

1. The specialty mental health sector, including mental hospitals, residential treatment facilities, psychiatric units of general hospitals, and specialized community agencies and programs (such as community mental health centers, day treatment programs, and rehabilitation programs).
2. The general medical and primary care sector.
3. The human services sector, which comprises social welfare (housing, transportation, and employment), criminal justice, educational, religious, and charitable services.
4. The voluntary support network, including self-help groups and organizations devoted to education, communication, and support.

Unfortunately, there is no systematic way for people to obtain needed mental health services; often those with the greatest and most complex needs, and the fewest resources, are underserved. "Lack of access to health care, and lack of health insurance in particular, is a principal factor in limiting adequate treatment for serious and chronic conditions, including major depression and other prevalent mental illnesses" (Tondo, Albert, & Baldessarini, 2006, p. 518). For example, among people who made an effort to get treatment for substance use disorders, 42.5 percent reported cost or insurance barriers (SAMHSA, 2006).

Typically, people do not receive timely treatment for mental disorders. The median delay across disorders for receiving treatment is nearly a decade (Wang, Berglund, Olfson, et al., 2005). If people are left untreated, they may be more vulnerable to future episodes that may be even more severe in nature. Further, as disorders become entrenched, they may become more resistant to treatment.

Several factors have been associated with treatment delay (Wang et al., 2005). Early onset of a disorder, defined as child or adolescent onset, is of particular concern, since untreated early-onset disorders can result in school and subsequent occupational failure, early childbearing and marriage, and marital problems. Other factors associated with treatment delay include male gender, minority status, lower education (except for substance use disorders), and being married and having social support (presumably because of lesser need for support from formal sources).

School

The importance of children's perception of school as safe and teachers as supportive adults who convey caring and regard for their students and have high expectations for children's scholastic ability is confirmed in most studies of at-risk children (Baker, 1999; Bowen et al., 1998; Garmezy, 1993). Other key protective characteristics of schools include appropriate and effective classroom management practices; concerned school personnel; the availability of prosocial after-school activities such as art, drama, athletics, and special-interest clubs; and efforts to engage families in their children's education (Henggeler et al., 1998).

The protective effect of school relationships may persist well beyond elementary school, with early child-teacher relationships predicting long-term positive school outcomes (Hamre & Pianta, 2001). A national longitudinal study further found that perceived school connectedness is important to adolescents, providing a protective factor against numerous health risk behaviors (Resnick et al., 1997).

Schools can also present risk for children. Durlak's (1998) review of 1,200 outcome studies found that in poor-quality schools, characterized by such attributes as a nondemanding curriculum, ineffective leadership, and generally poor relationships among school personnel and with parents, students are more likely to drop out, have higher rates of teen pregnancy, and have higher rates of behavior problems.

Societal Conditions

The United States has "overarching social, political, legal, economic, and value patterns" (Greene & Livingston, 2002, p. 79) that can both contribute to individual problem situations and provide protection against risk. These macro-level influences, however, do not occur in isolation from risk and protective mechanisms at the other levels. For example, employment may open opportunities for interactions with others and expansion of social support networks, which in turn may help the family provide a safe and secure home. As noted earlier, the nature of systems is that the processes within each system influence one another.

On the protective side, social policies can have positive effects on the income and employment of individuals. For example, Social Security payments to the elderly have a significant effect on reducing the percentage of those who are poor, while Medicare covers many of their major health care costs. For the working poor, economic supports include such programs as the earned income tax credit and food stamps, which help them meet household expenses (for a review of income support policies see Scholz & Levine, 2000). Strong child-support policies have also been shown to improve the income of single-mother families (Garfinkel, Heintze, & Huang, 2001).

Poverty, discrimination, and segregation are risks that affect individual-level functioning, whereas social and income supports, tax policies, and legal sanctions provide protection against these risks. We will now explore further some of the risks associated with being poor, being a member of an ethnic minority, and being female in U.S. culture.

Poverty

Low SES is associated with the development of a number of mental disorders, such as oppositional defiant disorder and conduct disorder (Hill, 2002; Loeber et al., 2000; McGee & Williams, 1999), anxiety disorders, and schizophrenia (Wadsworth & Achenbach, 2005; Mulvany, O'Callaghan, Takei, Byrne, & Fearon, 2001). People of the lowest SES have a two- to threefold likelihood of having a mental disorder compared with the general population (DHHS, 2001). Those living in poverty are more exposed to stressful circumstances such as crime; violence; availability of drugs; and lack of safe child care, convenient transportation, quality health care, and adequate housing. For example, poverty is a risk factor for mental retardation (MR) because of its association with malnutrition, disease, inadequate prenatal and general medical care, and environmental health hazards (Arc, 2007). The poor are also less likely to be protected against these stressors by social or material resources. Finally, since the presence of a mental disorder, such as schizophrenia, usually results in academic and occupational impairment, those with mental disorders may end up living in poverty due to these impairments.

Ethnicity

Overall, ethnic minorities have rates of mental disorder similar to those among the white mainstream population. Some minorities, however, especially African-Americans, are overrepresented among certain subgroups that are vulnerable to mental disorders, including people who are homeless, incarcerated, or in the foster care system (DHHS, 2001). Many people in these subpopulations are not counted in national surveys of mental disorders. In addition, ethnic minorities are also disproportionately poor and are therefore subject to the attendant risks that have been detailed above. Further, "minorities' historical and present day struggles with racism and discrimination . . . affect their mental health and contribute to their lower economic, social, and political status" (DHHS, 2001, p. 4). Perceived discrimination has a strong association with measures of stress and mental health (Kessler, Mickelson, & Williams, 1999). Moreover, "(r)acial stereotypes and negative images can be internalized, denigrating individuals' self-worth and adversely affecting their social and psychological functioning" (DHHS, 2001, p. 39).

Even though the prevalence of mental disorders among most minority groups is similar to the white mainstream, minorities are underserved when it comes to treatment settings. As well as a lack of access to health care, minorities may hold even more stigmatizing attitudes toward mental illness than does the general population, making them less likely to seek treatment (DHHS, 2001). Moreover, minorities are more likely to turn to the general health care system for problems they experience. The problem is that primary care providers typically do not have the time or the expertise to diagnose and treat mental disorders, especially when their patients already have physical disorders that they can recognize and treat (DHHS, 2001). Minorities may also seek help from informal sources such as family, friends, religious leaders, and indigenous healers.

Other barriers to treatment of mental illness include the fragmented organization of mental health services in the United States, providers' "lack of awareness of cultural issues, bias, or inability to speak the client's language, and the client's fear and mistrust of treatment" (DHHS, 2001). In addition, although the helping professions have recently begun to move toward evidence-based practice, there is a shortage of research on treatment outcomes for the major mental disorders among people from different ethnic groups (DHHS, 2001). In addition, there has been a call for "cultural competence," which involves sensitivity to culture and the development of "skills, knowledge, and policies to deliver effective treatments" (p. 36). Few models of culturally sensitive services have been tested, so we know little about either the key ingredients needed or their effect on treatment outcomes for ethnic minorities.

Conclusion

At this stage the biopsychosocial risk and resilience framework has several limitations. For example, some of the risk mechanisms named may not be in place prior to the development of a disorder, that is, they may be concurrent to or a consequence of the disorder. For instance, poor school performance has been named as a risk influence in oppositional defiant disorder and conduct disorder, but is that a part of the disorder, a consequence of having the disorder, or a true risk for the disorder? For most mental disorders the research on protective factors has lagged behind the study of risk, and the relative contributions of risk factors at different stages of development have not typically been identified (Striegel-Moore & Cachelin, 1999; White, 2000).

Despite these limitations, the biopsychosocial risk and resilience framework holds a number of advantages for the assessment of mental disorders. It can provide a theoretical basis for social workers to conceptualize at several levels and can assist them in identifying and bolstering strengths as well as reducing risks. The framework offers a balanced view of systems in that it looks at both risks and strengths, as well as recognizing the complexity of individuals and the systems in which they are nested.

3

— ▼▲▼ —

Strengths Assessment

Marlatta is a 43-year-old African-American woman who presents to a private, nonprofit community mental health center for services. She is on parole for three to nine years for being an accomplice to an armed robbery. Her most recent incarceration was one of four she has served.

Marlatta reports starting to drink alcohol at age 12, smoking marijuana and phencyclidine (PCP) at age 13, using acid at 20, and smoking crack when she was 24 years old. Since that time her substance use has centered on crack cocaine and alcohol. She was clean for the four and a half years of her incarceration and the first year of her parole, but she started using drugs again within the last two months because of experiencing severe depression.

Marlatta reports first feeling depressed after her mother died six years ago, and she was hospitalized for symptoms of depression about five years ago. She reports that for the past two and a half months she has been having "bad thoughts" about herself (hating herself, wondering why she's alive), having problems sleeping, not feeling like doing anything, feeling "a lot of pain in my nerves," and thinking about throwing herself in front of a car.

Marlatta has been using crack cocaine an average of once a week (with a binge lasting on average for three to four days) during the past two months, and she has been drinking alcohol almost every day. She admits to engaging in sex for drugs and not always having her partner use a condom. Marlatta reports to a parole officer but has not checked in for the last few weeks during the height of her substance use.

Marlatta was raised by her mother along with two other sisters and a brother. She and her siblings all had different fathers, none of whom remained involved with the family. She says that many of her family members abused drugs and alcohol and never received help. Marlatta's mother, father, brother, and one of her sisters are deceased. Her other sister lives in the area but has no contact with Marlatta. The sister has a mental illness, but Marlatta is not sure of the diagnosis. Marlatta's strongest relationship now is with her niece, with whom she currently resides.

Marlatta was sexually abused by her maternal uncle at age nine and dropped out of school in seventh grade. She has limited literacy. She had her spleen removed five years ago after an assault by her boyfriend with a baseball bat.

While incarcerated, Marlatta received psychotropic medication and psychotherapy. When she was released, Marlatta went into a halfway house and then a treatment center, and she was eventually referred to another community dual-diagnosis treatment center. While in the halfway house, she was enrolled in adult education classes. Marlatta held brief jobs in housekeeping and maintenance with a supported employment agency or a temp agency. However, she lost each job as a result of her drug use. Marlatta is currently supported by welfare benefits (Medicaid and Supplemental Social Security Income).

Strengths-Based Assessment

In Chapter 2 we covered the risk and resilience framework, which was presented as a systematic way to assess for a client's strengths (protective influences) at the biological, psychological, and social system levels. In this chapter we will continue to focus on strengths-based assessment, drawing on solution-focused therapy (Bertolino & O'Hanlon, 2002; deJong & Berg, 2002) and motivational interviewing (Miller & Rollnick, 2002). The practices detailed below lend themselves to an assessment process that works to elicit and enhance client strengths. Table 3.1 encapsulates the balance in the assessment process between risks and strengths.

A case has also been presented for consideration. The above version is a typical DSM assessment, whereas the version at the end of this chapter will show an assessment that maintains a balance between the problems and strengths that individuals invariably display. Before reading further, take some time to reflect on the case scenario above and respond to the following questions:

1. What is your reaction toward this client?

TABLE 3.1 Balanced Assessment of Strengths and Risks

Presenting problem	List of symptoms Onset and duration	Emphasis on client's language Coping strategies Exceptions to the problem
Treatment history	Previous treatment history	What was helpful/not helpful?
Personal history	Developmental milestones Medical history Diet, exercise Physical, emotional, sexual abuse	Physical, psychological, social, spiritual, environmental assets How did you cope? How were you able to survive that time? What needs to happen so that you are safe?
Substance abuse history	Patterns of use: onset, frequency, quantity Drugs/habits of choice: Consequences: physical, social, psychological	Periods of using less and periods of abstinence What are the advantages/disadvantages of use?
Suicide risk	Previous suicide attempts Current suicidality	If you've had thoughts of hurting yourself, what did you do to get past that point? Things sounded really hard then. How did you manage? How did you stop things from getting even worse? What needs to happen now so that you feel a bit better?
Family history	Description of relationships History of illness, mental illness	Supportive relationships
Community involvement	Legal history Neighborhood risk Problematic relationships	Cultural and ethnic influences Community participation Spiritual and church involvement Other social support Neighborhood assets
Employment and education	Educational history Employment history	Achievements, skills, and interests
Goals	Goals	Future without the problem What do you want to get out of treatment? What will your life look like when treatment is successful?

Sources: Bertolino & O'Hanlon, 2002; Graybeal, 2001.

2. What strengths does this client have?

3. What questions would you ask to gain a more comprehensive understanding of the client's strengths?

Guidelines for Eliciting and Enhancing Client Strengths

The first guideline for the social worker is to develop an awareness of strengths and identify them to clients. Many possible strengths and protective influences were named in Chapter 2, and each subsequent chapter lists protective mechanisms pertinent to particular disorders. These strengths should be openly conveyed to clients. Often, by the time people seek help from a social worker, the problem may have enveloped them to such an extent that they may have lost sight of their resources. For example, if a person seems to have a solid social support system, he or she needs to be told that this is a strength critical to adjustment. One could take this intervention a step further and ask about the resources people have used to develop these strengths. Such a client could be asked, "What would your husband say makes you a good partner?" or "Why do your friends like to be around you?"

The social worker must further be alert to the strengths individuals bring to other contexts, such as work settings (e.g., organizational skills, assertiveness, problem-solving abilities), hobbies (e.g., gardening, crafts, handiwork, sports), and pastimes (churchgoing, socializing with friends). The social worker can also ask directly about strengths: "What do you do well?" "What are your best qualities?" "What would other people say you do well/is good in you?"

It must be emphasized that when people talk about the suffering and pain they've been through, they need to be validated. They can then be asked about the resilient qualities they have shown to "make it this far, despite the pain in their life." The social worker can inquire about the aspects of the client's life that are still intact despite the problem, such as relationships, hobbies, interests, employment, academics. The social worker can plumb for the resources that were drawn upon in these areas. Inquiry can further center on personal or family qualities or strengths that have developed as a result of dealing with the illness. A recent quantitative review found that when people are able to find benefits after a major stressor, they experience less depression and greater well-being (Helgeson, Reynolds, & Tomich, 2006). These lines of inquiry show that many facets of difficult circumstances can be explored to find the strengths.

Another way of validating the extent to which people have struggled is through the use of the solution-focused intervention of coping questions. Questions such as the following ask clients to reflect upon the resources they have used to manage their struggles:

- "How have you coped with the problem?"
- "How do you manage? How do you have the strength to go on?"
- "This has been a very difficult problem for you. How have you managed to keep things from getting even worse?"

A major intervention using solution-focused therapy is exception finding (deJong & Berg, 2002), which involves inquiry about symptom-free periods or times that were "a little bit better." Even the most severe mental illnesses include periods of remission or at least reduction in symptoms. On a daily basis, there may be at least brief periods when the problem is not as bad.

When people are seeing a social worker for a possible mental disorder, they tend to experience their symptoms as all-encompassing and all-consuming. For example, a depressed person typically sees the past as depressing and the future as hopeless. These are biased perceptions based on present mood.

By asking questions about what the person did during these times that made a difference and the supports that were used, people get in touch with the strengths and resources on which they have drawn to deal with difficult circumstances.

Sometimes people will respond by crediting situations, events, and people outside themselves for any differences they have experienced. But the social worker should find a way to give people responsibility for any changes made. For instance, if a client says she remained sober only while incarcerated, the social worker can respond that people who are interested in abusing substances seem to be able to still find a way to do so, even when they are "inside." So what caused them to commit to sobriety this time?

Another way to identify problem-free times is through a technique called externalizing the problem (Bertolino & O'Hanlon, 2002; White & Epston, 1990), in which a linguistic distinction is made between the presenting problem and the person. Through language, the problem behavior is personified as an external entity (*the* depression, *the* mood swings, *the* voices), rather than being seen as a dysfunction integral to the individual. The purpose is to free the person from the belief that the problem is a fixed and inherent quality. It introduces fluidity into a problem that may have become rigid and seemingly fixed, so that the oppressive nature of the problem is lifted, and more options for behavior may be revealed.

After identifying the externalized entity, the next step is to empower people to fight against it by asking what are referred to as "relative influence" questions (when do they have influence over their problems and when do their problems have influence over them?). Individuals can be invited to extend their awareness of how they combat their problems through the following questions:

- What's different about the times you're able to control the [the mental health symptoms, the diagnostic label]
- When are you able to overcome the temptation to . . . ?
- What percentage of the time do you have control over . . . ? What are you doing during these times?

An additional technique of solution-focused therapy is to inquire about past help seeking. People with mental health problems are often demoralized by extensive treatment histories. A line of questioning such as the one detailed below offers several benefits. First, it validates people's efforts to help themselves. It acknowledges that they have been trying to overcome their problems. Second, it informs the social worker about what the client has already tried. If one already knows what is not helpful for a client, that particular intervention should not be repeated. Third, it conveys that the client is the expert on himself or herself. The following questions convey the resources people bring to past help-seeking efforts:

- What did you find helpful about previous therapy (individual, couples, family, group, etc.)?
- What did the therapist do that was helpful?
- How did that make a difference for you?
- What wasn't so helpful?

Although medication is a critical element of the treatment protocol for many mental disorders, the case for medication has sometimes been overstated. For example, not even half of people experience a 50 percent reduction of depressive symptoms as a result of being on antidepressants (Trivedi, Rush, Wisniewski, et al., 2006), and most (74 percent) discontinue antipsychotic medications because of the side effects they experience (Lieberman, Stroup, McEvoy, et al., 2005).

Many consumers have an external locus of control toward medication; that is, they attribute changes in their behavior to the effects of medication rather than being empowered to see the changes as a result of their own efforts and qualities. The social worker can ask questions such as these if the client is currently or has previously been on psychotropic medication:

- How was the medication helpful to you? How was it not helpful?
- What, if anything, did the medication allow you to do that you wouldn't have been able to do otherwise?

- What percentage of the change you've experienced is a result of the medication, and what percentage do you think is your own doing?
- What qualities do you possess that enabled you to work with the medication to improve things for yourself?

The social worker should further be alert for opportunities to build client motivation. Motivational interviewing, a brief treatment model (one to four sessions), was formulated to produce rapid change by mobilizing the client's motivation. It was designed for substance use disorders but adapted to other problems in which there is ambivalence about change (Miller & Rollnick, 2002).

Empathic listening and affirming statements are used in a systematic way to direct the process toward building client motivation. The social worker selectively reflects and affirms change talk and asks the client to elaborate on statements about change. Additionally, to bolster motivation for change (Miller & Rollnick, 2002), the social worker works to create a discrepancy between the client's values and goals, such as long-term mental health, and the problem (failing to do things that one knows will help one's disorder) that stands in the way of these goals.

The interested reader is encouraged to pursue other sources for more information about motivational interviewing (see Miller & Rollnick, 2002); here we will mention one technique, called the decisional balance, aimed at getting the client to weigh the advantages and disadvantages of the problem behavior. In this technique, the social worker asks the client to recount some of the pros of the problem behavior: "What do you get out of drinking?" "How is the eating disorder working for you?" When people feel someone else understands the reasons they seek out problematic behaviors, they are less likely to show defensiveness against change. Then the practitioner can switch to asking about "the not so good things" about drinking/purging/isolating from social contact/not taking medication. The client then details the advantages and disadvantages of changing. The process of gathering this information provides a great deal of information about the problem behavior necessary for diagnosis. It also makes it easier for clients to argue for their own change as they weigh the pros and cons of their current behaviors and their perceptions about change.

As the final part of the assessment, the social worker can help clients to orient toward the future and build a vision of a problem-free future. Sometimes when people are mired in their symptoms, they have difficulty seeing beyond their current unhappy circumstances. Asking people what their lives will look like after their problems are solved frees them from these circumstances to consider a different future. This process may fuel a sense of hope and may also help individuals develop a blueprint for what changes need to be made. Future-oriented questions include the following:

- Imagine yourself in the future when the problem is no longer a problem. Tell me where you are, what you are doing and saying, and what others around you are doing and saying.
- When you do succeed in getting past this and are looking back on it now, what most likely is it that worked? How did it happen?

These techniques show how the social worker, while collecting relevant information for the formulation of a diagnosis, can also keep focused on the strengths and resources of the individual. People who are empowered with regard to their strengths are more likely to feel a sense of hope about themselves and their future. If strengths and resources are galvanized during the assessment process, the client can begin a process in which a different perspective (about the self, about the problem) can inspire changes in behavior. People who feel empowered and hopeful are also more motivated to engage in intervention.

We now turn our attention back to Marlatta, the client who was presented at the beginning of this chapter.[1] This time, the assessment will be strengths-based.

Strengths-Based Assessment

Marlatta is a 43-year-old, African-American woman who presents to a private nonprofit community mental health center for services. She has an engaging personality and good social skills. She is attractive and well dressed.

Marlatta complains of feeling depressed and using crack cocaine and alcohol to help herself feel better. While under the influence of drugs or alcohol, she recently felt like committing suicide. She says she fleetingly thought of throwing herself in front of a car but did not consider doing so for any length of time. She was able to get past that point by thinking of her niece's family with whom she lives.

Marlatta says that she feels better when she is with people who care about her. She sees that when her depression is no longer a problem, she will be able to spend more time with her niece and her niece's children as well as develop friendships with "people who don't use drugs." Her niece's children love Marlatta and enjoy being with her. Marlatta has been helping her niece shop for groceries for the children, and she provided support when her niece's baby went to the hospital for treatment for a seizure. During that time Marlatta was reliable and was able to provide effective child care.

Marlatta is currently on parole for being an accomplice to an armed robbery. She is concerned about her crack use because she does not want to return to prison and is motivated to do "whatever it takes" to avoid another incarceration. While in prison and in treatment facilities after she was released, Marlatta received medication and therapy. She says she liked the fact that the therapists "really listened" to her, and they helped clarify her feelings. She also learned techniques for "staying clean." Residential treatment was helpful because "it kept me off of the streets." She did not find it helpful when one of the therapists probed Marlatta about the sexual abuse by a maternal uncle that she experienced at the age of nine. Marlatta said she had blocked it out, and the therapist "kept trying to get at it." Marlatta says that she would like more therapy, however, because it was so helpful for her overall. She also says that the medication was beneficial in that it kept her from thinking so many bad things about herself.

---

[1]We acknowledge Graybeal's (2001) work as an inspiration for setting up these contrasting views of assessment.

Marlatta was able to maintain her sobriety for 11 months beyond her 4.5-year incarceration. One strategy she used was "staying away from my old neighborhood and people on the street," until one day she found herself taking the familiar bus route to the old neighborhood. In discussing it further, Marlatta said she had been thinking about her mother, which caused her to feel sad and lonely.

She states that when she was not using drugs, she had things to do to occupy her time. For instance, when she was involved with her niece's children and had a janitorial job at the convention center, she was clean. She also says that when she does not feel depressed, she uses drugs less. Using helps her to "feel better" and to keep from thinking about her mother. When she feels depressed, she copes by seeking affection and support. Currently, her support comes primarily from men, but she says she is not sleeping with them. "They just take care of me and we drink together." Marlatta says she seeks support from her niece, but recently her niece has been facing difficulties of her own and is unable to be supportive right now.

When asked how she is able to stop things from getting even worse, she says that she knows she has to stop smoking crack "when it's time to get back to reality." Usually, that means when the weekend is over or when she needs to see her parole officer. Marlatta admits that when she has to see her parole officer twice a week versus once a month, she is better able to restrict her drug use. She also stayed clean when she lived in a transitional home or when she was taking GED classes. In sum, Marlatta recognizes many strategies that she employs to prevent herself from using substances.

Marlatta is closest to her niece and niece's children. She appreciates her niece's willingness to give Marlatta a place to stay as well as provide support in her recovery from substance use and mental illness. Marlatta says that the kids appreciate her because she is providing financial help to their mom to have "good food in the house . . . actual meals." She says that her niece would say that Marlatta's best qualities revolve around her personality and her sweet spirit. Marlatta knows that she can go to her niece for help.

Marlatta said that she had a "tough" upbringing. Her mother raised her and her siblings (two sisters and one brother) alone. Marlatta is currently not close to anyone in her family except for her niece. Her father, mother, and two siblings have already died. Many of her family members had substance use problems for which no one received treatment. Marlatta didn't know of any other mental illness in her family of origin, except for her surviving sister, although Marlatta isn't sure of the diagnosis.

Marlatta still misses her mother, who died six years ago. She said her mother was her "heart," and "she did a good job with what she had, which wasn't much." She said her mother never gave up on her.

At age nine Marlatta was sexually abused by her maternal uncle for a year when he lived with the family. When she told her mother about the abuse, her mother made Marlatta's uncle leave the house, and it didn't happen again. Marlatta said that the way she coped with the abuse was to "forget about it" and "put it away." As for other abuse, she had her spleen removed after an assault with a baseball bat by her boyfriend at the time. After this incident, she left the boyfriend and has not been involved in another abusive relationship.

Although Marlatta has only a seventh-grade education, she enrolled in adult education courses when she was in the transitional housing program. She says she enjoyed the classes and was learning a lot. She stopped taking the classes only because her time was up at the residential program. She is interested in resuming her studies, and their completion will result in a GED.

Marlatta is currently unemployed but is motivated to work again, especially in food service or cleaning. She names her strong points as an employee as (1) her ability to converse with others, (2) her willingness to do what she is asked, and (3) her assertiveness. Marlatta has accessed government benefits, including Medicaid and Social Security Income, to meet her basic needs.

Marlatta enjoys being with people, including children. She likes listening to music, roller skating, playing cards, shopping, and watching television.

When asked to envision a future without the problem, Marlatta had a difficult time seeing her life clear of drug addiction. She feels that it is pervasive and has such a grip on her that she doesn't think it realistic to be clean for longer than 11 months. She seemed to feel more hopeful when the social worker reframed the nature of relapses as an opportunity for greater awareness of high-risk situations and the coping strategies that she needs to develop to address these challenges.

When asked motivational questions about her problem ("What is there about using crack that you or others might see as a concern?"), Marlatta said, "My niece is scared that the cops are gonna come up in her house and break down her door to try to find me and send me back to jail. She is concerned about what that will do to the kids. I don't want to go back to jail and be around a bunch of women all day long. I want to move on in my life."

A decisional balance was enacted to determine the advantages and disadvantages of Marlatta's substance use. The advantages are that it helps her cope with depression and loneliness. As for the disadvantages, using drugs places Marlatta at risk for another arrest, which will triple her time in jail. It also places her at risk for STDs, because she trades sex for drugs. The benefits are only temporary and require a lot of footwork on her part to get the money for the next use. Marlatta states that when she is using, she does not eat or sleep, nor is she concerned about other people.

The social worker then oriented Marlatta to a future without the problem by asking her to imagine that she had been clean for one whole year. She was next asked to picture herself as a fly on the wall on the first anniversary of her sobriety. Marlatta described the following scene: "I guess I'd be in my own place, listening to my music. I would have a friend over and we would be eating pigs' feet. I would be able to go shopping because I have a part-time job. I would also be enrolled in adult education classes again. I would be seeing my parole officer a whole lot less and be working toward getting off parole." When asked what she thought would work for her if she decided to make a change, Marlatta responded, "Going into a treatment program that is coed. If I were in a treatment program all day long surrounded by only women, it would remind me too much of jail and I would not stay."

Summary

Marlatta struggles with depression and substance use abuse but is motivated to seek treatment and employment. She successfully completed treatment in the past and maintained sobriety for almost a year. Marlatta has demonstrated resilience in surviving a difficult upbringing and in being able to leave a violent relationship as an adult. At this time, she seems to need increased support to maintain her sobriety. Since relationships, in particular, are important to her, increased social support might help her cope with feelings of depression and urges to use, as well as to provide her with accountability.

Questions to Consider

Now that we have covered two alternative assessments, consider the following questions:

1. What is your reaction to this case presentation, contrasting it with the one presented earlier?

2. What strengths do you now see in this client?

3. What other lines of inquiry could you pursue to elicit more strengths?

4

— ▼▲▼ —

Autistic Disorder

Emmanuel is a five-year-old Guatemalan boy who has just started kindergarten. He is an artistic and active child who enjoys playing in the playground, listening to music, and doing puzzles. On his first day of school Emmanuel had a hard time separating from his parents. He cried almost continuously through the day, tried to run away from the classroom and playground, and threw tantrums when the classroom teacher tried to redirect him. Emmanuel continually asked for his mom or dad and could not be calmed down. The teacher reported that he seems to have difficulty with transitions, such as from the classroom to the cafeteria, and he does not follow directions unless the teacher or her assistant directs him through the individual steps. The teacher also noted that Emmanuel appears to have difficulty in other areas of development. His speech is functional but not pragmatic, meaning that he is able to form the words necessary for speaking but cannot use them as a social tool to interact verbally with others. He does not approach other children and does not react to their attempts to play or talk.

The range of "autism spectrum disorders" (ASDs) includes autistic disorder itself, Asperger's disorder, Rett's disorder, and pervasive developmental disorder not otherwise specified (PDD-NOS). Autism is a neurological-developmental disorder with an onset during the first three years of life. The child with autism demonstrates severe impairments in social interaction and communication, as well as odd repetitive behaviors and restricted interests (Schreibman, Stahmer, & Akshoomoff, 2006). More than anything else, autism is characterized by impairments in social relatedness (Volkmar, Charwanda, & Klin, 2004). These include a lack of awareness of the feelings of others, an inability to express emotions, and the absence of a capacity for social and symbolic (imaginative) play. On the other hand, persons with autism often possess impressive isolated skills such as memorization, visual and spatial awareness, and attention to details.

Asperger's disorder is sometimes used to describe higher-functioning individuals with autism (Smith, Magyar, & Arnold-Saritepe, 2002). In Asperger's disorder, early cognitive and language development are apparently normal, but the child has unusual interests that he or she pursues with intensity (Holter, 2004). The child's attachment patterns to family members are well established, but he or she does not tend to attach to peers and new adults. Because the behavioral abnormalities are less pronounced, the child's referral for assessment is usually later than with suspected autism. The social difficulties of Asperger's disorder are lifelong, but such persons are more likely to secure employment, live independently, and establish a family (Volkmar et al., 2004).

PDD-NOS is diagnosed in cases where there is impairment in the three areas that are "core" to autism, but the full features of autism or another PDD are not met (Koyama, Tachimor, & Osada, 2006). The deficits in social and other skills are less severe than in classic autism. The issue of whether meaningful subtypes might be defined within the broad PDD category remains a topic of debate. The limited data available suggest that such persons have a better prognosis than persons with autism (Howlin, 2005).

Prevalence and Comorbidity

The reported incidence of autism has increased worldwide in recent years. This increase may be due to a broader application of the criteria, more frequent inclusion of other PDDs in the diagnosis, and an increased alertness to assessing children for the disorder (Chakrabarti & Fombonne, 2005). There is even some diagnostic variability across states (Mandell & Palmer, 2005), which is believed to be an indicator of differences in the training of education professionals, the availability of pediatricians, and the accessibility of health care resources.

A review of prevalence studies indicates that autism occurs at a rate of about 7.1 per 10,000; the rate for all ASDs is about 20 per 10,000 (Williams & Brayne, 2006). The Centers for Disease Control and Prevention (Rice, 2007) found that the prevalence of ASDs was 6.6 per 1,000 children in the United States. Autism occurs in all social classes and races, although Caucasian children are more likely to be diagnosed than African-American children (Rice, 2007). The reason for this difference is not understood, but may be due to a greater likelihood for Caucasians to be evaluated for an autism spectrum disorder. Studies consistently find that ASDs occurs more often in males than females, with a 4.3 to 1 ratio (Rice, 2007).

On average, the rate for ASDs in eight-year-old males is 11.5 per 1,000 and 2.7 per 1,000 for females. The available data suggest that children and adolescents with ASD experience a range of comorbid disorders. Precise data are not available on these rates, however, because there are no formal ASD assessment instruments that include attention to comorbid disorders (Matson & Minshawi, 2006). Common comorbid disorders include mental retardation (44 percent of cases), seizure disorders (25 to 30 percent), depression (4 to 57 percent), anxiety disorders (7 to 84 percent), overactivity and attention problems (21 to 72 percent), and tic disorders (7 to 29 percent) (Aman & Langworthy, 2000; Bernard et al., 2002; JAACAP, 1999; Lainhart, 1999; Matson & Minshawi, 2006; Richdale, 1999; Rice, 2007). The likelihood of comorbid disorders is largely due to the broadly debilitating features of the ASDs, their associated medical disorders, and the problematic life experiences related to having autism. Aggression and self-injury (head banging, finger or hand biting, head slapping, and hair pulling) are common behavioral symptoms for children with comorbid pathologies. These behaviors are rarely intentional, but are due to biological factors (such as seizures), cognitive and emotional impairments (leading to impulsivity and low frustration tolerance), inability to communicate anger verbally, difficulty managing change, learned behaviors to avoid certain tasks or situations, and misreading of others' intent as threatening (Lainhart, 1999).

Assessment of Autism

With autism the goals of assessment are to determine first whether or not a child has the disorder and then to offer appropriate interventions to maximize the child's potential for change (Jordan, 2001). Professionals must set the stage for a long-term collaborative relationship with parents and help them become better-informed advocates for their child.

A recent thrust in health care is the early diagnosis of autism, so that intervention can begin as soon as possible. Certain factors are associated with the early or later diagnosis of autism. Early diagnosis is associated with urban residence, middle socioeconomic status (SES), pediatric referral to a specialist, having a child with severe language deficits, and symptoms such as hand flapping and toe walking (Mandell, Novak, & Zubritsky, 2005). Later diagnosis is associated with rural residence, low SES, having a child who displays oversensitivity to pain, having a child with a hearing impairment, and having seen at least four primary care providers. Ironically, conduct of developmental tests by a pediatrician does not correlate with an earlier diagnosis, in part because two-thirds of pediatricians report that they do not feel capable of conducting such assessments (Halfon, Regaldo, McLearn, Kuo, & Wright, 2003). Parental concern is a more important factor than pediatric testing in identifying a child with autism (Mandell et al., 2005). Studies show that 90 percent of parents of autistic children recognize a significant abnormality in the child by age 24 months (Volkmar, Lord, Bailey, et al., 2004).

In the first year of life the child typically displays unusual social development, being less likely to imitate the movements and vocal sounds of others, and exhibits problems with attention and responding to external stimulation. Between one and three years of age, when parents are most likely to seek evaluation, differences from peers are readily apparent, and the child's idiosyncratic, self-absorbed behaviors and communication problems are striking. Parents report their child's regression from a higher level of functioning in 20 to 40 percent of cases (Volkmar, Lord, Bailey, et al., 2004).

Researchers at the Centers for Disease Control found that children with ASDs were initially evaluated at a mean age of 48 months but were not diagnosed until 61 months (with no differences by gender or SES) (Wiggins, Baio, & Rice, 2006). More severely impaired children were diagnosed earlier. Most practitioners (70 percent) did not use a diagnostic screening instrument in the process, and 24 percent of children were not diagnosed until after entering school.

Assessment is a challenging process, because no biochemical tests are available to assess for the disorder; nor does a single behavior or set of behaviors unequivocally denote autism (Jordan, 2001). Assessment should be multidisciplinary in nature, including evaluations by a clinical or school psychologist, medical doctor, and speech and language pathologist as well as a social worker. The core assessment comprises the following (Ozonoff, Rogers, & Hendren, 2005; Smith et al., 2002):

- Information from parents about mother's pregnancy, labor, and delivery; the child's early neonatal course; the parents' earliest concerns about their child; family history of developmental disorders; symptoms in the areas of social interaction, communication/play, and restricted or unusual interests; the presence of problem behaviors that may interfere with intervention such as aggression, self-injury, and other behavioral oddities; and the child's prior response to any educational programs or behavioral interventions.
- Direct observations in structured (school) and unstructured settings (home) and in interactions with peers, parents, and siblings.
- A medical evaluation, which includes information about possible seizures, visual and hearing examinations for possible sensory problems, and testing for lead levels if the child has had exposure.
- Cognitive assessment to establish the level of intellectual functioning.
- An assessment of adaptive functioning and social skill development.
- A speech and language assessment.

Neuropsychological testing might also be indicated for children with some verbal ability in order to gain a sense of their strengths and limitations for treatment and education planning (Ozonoff et al., 2005).

Professionals are encouraged to use formal instruments to assist in their diagnostic assessments. A variety of instruments are available that can be used in this way (Ozonoff, Rogers, & Hendren, 2005; Volkmar, Charwanda, & Klin, 2004; Volkmar, Lord, Bailey, Schultz, & Klin, 2004). Two instruments, both clinician-administered, are considered the "gold standards" for assessment of autism (Ozonoff et al., 2004): the Autism Diagnostic Interview-Revised (Lord et al., 1994); and the Autism Diagnostic Observation Schedule (Lord et al., 2000). Another recommended measure is the Social Communication Questionnaire, which is a parent report version of the Autism Diagnostic Interview-Revised (Berument, Rutter, Lord, Pickles, & Bailey, 1999; Rutter, Bailey, & Lord, 2003). An additional well-known assessment tool for general disability is the Checklist for Autism in Toddlers (Baron-Cohen et al., 2000), while the Pervasive Developmental Disorders Screening Test (Siegel & Hayer, 1999) and the Screening Tool for Autism (Stone et al., 2000) are used to assess the specific disorder of autism. Some newer instruments that assess general developmental disabilities include the Social

Responsiveness Scale (Constantino & Todd, 2003) and the Children's Communication Checklist (Bishop, 1998).

Although Emmanuel started kindergarten this year and has never been in a preschool setting, he can write all letters of the alphabet, as well as his own and his sister's name. He is also able to write numbers and recite up to three-digit numbers. His spelling is artistic and almost looks like a form of calligraphy, especially his numbers. His family states that they never taught him any of these skills.

Emmanuel uses very few of his own words and sentences but repeats what other people say and sometimes recites whole conversations from cartoons (echolalia). An example of echolalia is when he answers questions like, "Are you hungry?" with "Are you hungry?" instead of giving an affirmative or negative answer. This affects his interaction with people, as he responds the same way to questions they pose. For example, if asked, "What is your name?" his answer would be, "What is your name?" Further, Emmanuel confuses pronouns (he says, "You want to go home" instead of "I want to go home."). When upset, Emmanuel makes guttural noises or screams unintelligibly. He also seems very sensitive to certain sensory inputs, especially loud noises, such as laughter or the hubbub of many people speaking at the same time. These seem to bother him greatly, and he reacts by covering his ears and screaming as if in pain.

Generally, Emmanuel seems to have no interest in his peers. He maintains very little eye contact and does not pick up social cues. For example, he is unable to play "tag" because he does not understand what to do when he is "it"; he cannot follow his classmates' example of getting in line. He prefers to play on his own and does not engage in imaginative play. When Emmanuel gets excited, he will flap his hands rapidly, clap his thighs and crotch, and tap his face. In comparison with his peers he appears aloof or in a world of his own.

Despite his lack of social skills, Emmanuel can manage many one-on-one situations with adults. He is able to interact in a limited way with one person at a time and participates in activities suggested by that person if those activities interest him. It is in these situations that he displays what resembles a sense of humor, although he seems to be amused only by his own jokes and does not react to other people's funny remarks or faces. The social worker who assisted him during the first two days of school reports that he has very limited interests. He is content with writing numbers and letters over and over and was willing to take turns with the social worker. He appeared to enjoy naming the numbers she wrote but showed distress when she did not use the same calligraphic style of spelling that he himself used. The social worker also reported that Emmanuel frequently writes down numbers to soothe himself after getting upset.

Emmanuel's parents report that he acts rather impulsively at times. They state that he likes to "help" with chores in the house. On one occasion he attempted to do the laundry and emptied a whole bottle of bleach on a basket of colored clothes, thus ruining them. They say he is not aggressive, however.

Emmanuel's school personnel completed a thorough assessment, which included a review of his medical history. They conducted a series of tests, including a speech and language evaluation, the Wechsler Intelligence Scale, the Childhood Autism Rating Scale, the Developmental Behavior Checklist, the Vineland Adaptive Behavior Scale, educational evaluation and observation, and collection of the social history of the child. These revealed an average IQ (95) but below-average language skills. Instead of using words of his own, Emmanuel employs idiosyncratic expressions. He lacks social skills and shows some developmental delays in areas of self-help and adaptation. For example, he becomes easily frustrated when he cannot unzip his jacket and does not accept certain school rules, like putting his backpack in his locker, if they go against his usual pattern of behavior.

Emmanuel comes from a caring family. Family members have been aware of Emmanuel's atypical development but related it to his lack of schooling and interaction with peers. They also report that his language development was delayed—he didn't babble until the age of two and a half. He started imitating others and reciting sentences by age four. His parents attributed this delay to the fact that two languages (English and Spanish) are spoken in the home. They assumed that this lack of consistency led to Emmanuel's difficulties with language development. At this point, his mother speaks to him in Spanish, while all other family members go back and forth between English and Spanish. Emmanuel himself speaks English, which he started using at the age of two and a half. He understands Spanish, but speaks it only when distressed.

The parents are open to treatment and agreed to the special education eligibility process. All family members demonstrate affection toward and concern for Emmanuel. His mother and sister report some inconsistency in parenting, however, as his father seems to give in to all of Emmanuel's wishes. Emmanuel is clearly his father's favorite child. His father carries Emmanuel home from school although he is a physically strong and healthy boy, and he will always interrupt his activities if Emmanuel demands his attention. His mother tries to use a more structured approach to discipline and reports letting him cry if he does not get what he wants, such as when he demands candy in a store. According to Emmanuel's mother, these differences in parenting are also a source of marital disputes.

The family resides in a three-bedroom apartment in a working-class neighborhood. The family is living in the United States legally and receives disability benefits due to the father's medical condition (a job-related leg injury). Up to this point, Emmanuel stayed at home with his father while his mother worked as a maid. His sister (age 17) attends the local community college and his brother (age 13) is a seventh grader at a public middle school. The parents understand little English and need the assistance of their daughter or a translator to engage in meetings with school personnel. Extended family live in the area, and large family gatherings are common. The family is also involved in their Catholic church and has access to support services there.

Directions Part I, Multi-Axial Diagnosis: Given the case information, and your responses to the questions below, prepare the following: a multi-axial diagnosis, the rationale for the diagnosis and GAF score, and additional information you would have wanted to know in order to make a more accurate diagnosis.

Questions to consider when formulating a diagnosis for Emmanuel

1. What are Emmanuel's significant symptoms with regard to a possible mental disorder?

2. How long have Emmanuel's problem behaviors been evident?

3. Has any stressful event occurred in Emmanuel's life recently that might account for any of his symptoms?

4. To what extent do Emmanuel's (and his parents') cultural traditions contribute to his problem behaviors?

5. Given that Emmanuel has a developmental disorder, with what other disorders of childhood and adolescence (if any) do his symptoms overlap?

6. What are the major differences among the ASDs that might be considered in this case?

Multi-Axial Diagnosis

Axis I:

Axis II:

Axis III:

Axis IV:

Axis V:

Rationale and Differential Diagnosis

Additional Information Needed

Biopsychosocial Risk and Resilience Influences

Onset

Autism is at its core a genetic, neurobiological disorder, although its specific causes have not yet been identified (Volkmar, Charwanda, & Klin, 2004). There is no association of autism with any psychological or social influences in the absence of biological mechanisms. Still, certain populations are more at risk for the disorder because of their biological characteristics or tendency to have a later age of diagnosis (see Figure 4.1). Although autism has many potential causes, in this discussion we will explore risks due to heredity and brain abnormalities.

HEREDITY

Evidence that autism is a neurodevelopmental disorder is indicated by the high rates of heredity transmission that have been found for ASDs. The concordance rate for autism in identical twins ranges from 36 to 91 percent, depending on the diagnostic criteria used (Veenstra-Vanderweele & Cook, 2003). In other family studies, 2 to 4 percent of siblings also develop autism, which is 50 times more likely than in the general population.

FIGURE 4.1 Autism in Vulnerable and Oppressed Populations.

FEMALES
- Overall, ASDs are more prevalent in males than females (except for Rett's disorder) but females tend to be more severely affected because of a greater likelihood of mental retardation.[1]

LOW SES
- Low SES is one of the factors associated with later diagnosis of autism.[2]

---

[1]Smith et al., 2002.
[2]Mandell, Novak, & Zubritsky, 2005.

Autism probably involves 10 or more genes, with two to four genes that must interact to produce symptoms (Veenstra-Vanderweele & Cook, 2003). The strongest evidence to date points to evidence on the following chromosomes:

- #2, which includes genes that control growth and development early in life.
- #7, which includes a region that pertains to speech and language.
- #13 and #15, both of which include genes that, when damaged, can cause behavioral symptoms associated with autism.
- #16, which is associated with tuberous sclerosis, a rare genetic multisystem disorder characterized by seizures, mental retardation, and skin lesions.
- #17, deficiencies which are associated with metabolic and serotonin deficiencies.
- The X (or sex-specific) chromosome, associated with Rett's syndrome and fragile X (a syndrome of mental retardation that features a variety of physical abnormalities).

In one recent study of several hundred subjects it was found that advanced paternal age (over 40), but not maternal age, was associated with an increased risk of ASD (Reichenberg, Gross, Weiser, Bresnahan, Silverman, et al., 2006). Possible biological mechanisms include mutations associated with advancing age or alterations in genetic imprinting.

BRAIN ABNORMALITIES

Approximately 60 to 70 percent of persons with autism experience distinct neurological abnormalities and some degree of mental retardation (Peliosa & Lund, 2001). Several brain abnormalities have been identified. Brain imaging studies indicate that autism is associated with enlarged overall brain size (as much as 10 percent larger than nonautistic toddlers) and decreased size and activity in specific areas of the brain (Volkmar, Lord, Bailey, Schultz, & Klin, 2004). These areas possibly include the midsagittal area of the cerebellum, thought to be involved in the sequencing of motor activities; the lower hippocampus (in the midbrain), associated with complex learning processes; the amygdala (located in the temporal lobe), which is believed to contribute to the recognition of faces and emotional expression; and a portion of the brain stem associated with attention. Children with autism may have an overgrowth of neurons, coupled with an underdeveloped organization of neurons into specialized systems in some areas of the brain, although findings have not received consistent replication (Smith et al., 2002).

Problems in a number of neurotransmitter systems (the chemicals in neurons that send messages to each other) include serotonin, dopamine, norepinephrine, acetylcholine, oxytocin, endogenous opioids, cortisol, glutamate, and gamma-aminobutyric acid (GABA) (Lam, Aman, & Arnold, 2005). Overall, the most empirical evidence for a role in autism points to serotonin. There is less support for the notion that dysfunctions of norepinephrine or the endogenous opioids are related to autism. The role of dopamine has not been shown to be compelling thus far, though conflicting findings suggest a need for further study. Promising new areas of study may include possible dysfunction of the cholinergic system, oxytocin, and amino acid neurotransmitters. There is also a need for studies that control for subject variables such as race, gender, and pubertal status.

With regard to deficits in brain functioning, autism has been conceptualized in various ways (Volkmar, Lord, Bailey, Schultz, & Klin, 2004), among them the following:

- A disorder of *central coherence*, in which the person is unable to process information holistically and instead develops a bias toward part-oriented processing.
- A disorder of *executive function*, in which the person is unable to process bits of information or regulate behavior, and is thus inclined toward rigid, repetitive behaviors and impoverished interactions.
- A deficit in *social cognition*, in which the person fails to understand the internal mental states of other people and has difficulty making attributions of mental states to others and themselves.

COURSE OF AUTISM

Advances in nervous system assessment may eventually facilitate more effective interventions for autism's core symptoms, but for now social workers can best focus on the adjustment of persons with autism. With early detection and intervention, the prognosis for autism seems to improve.

Currently, one-third of children with autism ultimately achieve some level of independence and self-sufficiency in adulthood. Although those adults still demonstrate social deficits, they usually have high levels of cognitive and communicative skills (Billstedt, Gillberg, & Gillberg, 2005). The other two-thirds of children with autism require intensive care as adults.

Other than the timing of intervention, protective influences for the course of autism and other ASDs include later age of onset (after 24 months) as well as the child's early acquisition of nonverbal communication, functional play skills, and speech capacity (Volkmar, Lord, Bailey, et al., 2004). Unfortunately, 50 percent of the autistic population do not develop speech, and a majority fail to use speech in a functional manner (Peliosa & Lund, 2001).

Children with IQs above 60 are also more responsive to intervention, as these scores correlate with later academic and work achievement. In addition, lack of aggression and self-injurious behaviors offers protection, as these individuals are better able to manage home and community placements (Lainhart, 1999).

Another protective influence on the course of the disorder is the quality of parents' interactions with their children, which may affect the development of language skills over time. In one 16-year longitudinal study, parents' level of parallel participation during play with their children had a positive impact on the development of the child's language skills (Siller & Sigman, 2002).

Directions Part II, Biopsychosocial Risk and Protective Factors Assessment: Formulate a risk and protective factors assessment, both for the onset of the disorder and the course of the disorder, including the strengths that you see for this individual.

TABLE 4.1 Biopsychosocial Risk and Resilience Assessment for the Onset of the Disorder

RISK INFLUENCES	PROTECTIVE INFLUENCES
Biological	
Psychological	
Social	

TABLE 4.2 Biopsychosocial Risk and Resilience Assessment for the Course of the Disorder

RISK INFLUENCES	PROTECTIVE INFLUENCES
Biological	
Psychological	
Social	

What Techniques Could You Use to Elicit Additional Strengths in This Client?

Interventions for Autism

No interventions have yet been found that affect the core features of autism to an extent that the person can achieve normal functioning (Volkmar, Charwanda, & Klin, 2004). Interventions can often improve the person's functioning, with early detection and treatment as critical components. Intervention programs should be comprehensive and should include professionals from a variety of disciplines. The range of interventions should include special education; family education, support, and involvement; behavioral management; and possibly medication (American Academy of Pediatrics, 2001; Volkmar, Lord, Bailey, et al., 2004). We will also discuss social skills training and some of the intervention needs for adolescents and adults with pervasive developmental disorders.

Special Education

All children with autism are entitled to an Individualized Educational Plan (IEP). Ancillary services such as speech or language therapy, occupational therapy, and physical therapy are often required as a part of this plan (Volkmar, Lord, Bailey, et al., 2004). Continuous programming, including summer programming, is more effective than episodic intervention, because children with autism often regress in the absence of services. Professionals should be prepared to collaborate with teachers and other school personnel and to work with parents to obtain appropriate educational placements and other community resources.

Family Education, Support, and Involvement

Parental involvement should be encouraged to enhance consistency in intervention at home and at school and to facilitate the child's generalization of skills across settings. Family members can also be invited to join various parent and family groups for information and support. In addition to experiencing overwhelming caregiver burdens, many parents of children with autism feel guilt, sorrow, anger, and stress; siblings may be affected in similar ways (Magda, Schopler, Cueva, & Hallin, 1996).

Behavioral Management

Research has demonstrated the beneficial effects of behavioral interventions (known as applied behavioral analysis, or ABA) in both home and school settings (Eikeseth, Smith, Jahr, & Eldevik, 2002; Volkmar, Lord, Bailey, et al., 2004). These interventions can improve clients' skill areas, such as receptive and expressive language, social and play activities, and self-help. The results of studies of treatment programs for autism in general indicate that they are not as effective as once hoped, however (Matson & Minshawi, 2006). One limitation involves the challenge for families of maintaining the intensity recommended by some intervention programs (such as the number of hours of face-to-face involvement and regular use of specific exercises). Still, despite various methodological flaws, a sufficient number of replications exist to declare ABA methods "promising."

Medication

The core features of autism do not respond to medication. Drug intervention, however, may help control the symptoms of aggression, self-injury, inattention, and stereotyped movements (Volkmar, Lord, Bailey, Schultz, & Klin, 2004). In the past decade there has been an interest in the newer antipsychotic medications, particularly risperidone, for this purpose, although side effects (weight gain and drowsiness) are a concern.

The effectiveness of the selective serotonin reuptake inhibitor (SSRI) medications supports evidence that autism and ASDs are associated with abnormalities in serotonin function (Kolevzon, Mathewson, & Hollander, 2006). For repetitive and maladaptive behavior in adults, fluvoxamine has been found effective, and fluoxetine has been validated for children's repetitive behavior (Posey, Erickson, Stigler, & McDougle, 2006). Still, children appear to be more sensitive to the adverse effects of the SSRI medications (including agitation), and the weight of evidence to support their use is weak. Other medications, such as stimulants and anticonvulsants, have been used to regulate the behaviors of persons with autism, but there is no compelling evidence for their utility at present.

Social Skills Training

Interventions emphasizing social skills developments for persons with autism have emerged as a major theme in the treatment literature in recent years (Matson &

Minshawi, 2006). Much of this literature has focused on somewhat older children. These interventions can be carried out through integrated peer groups, classwide interventions, adult social groups, and videotapes to help the clients perceive themselves as they try to gain new interactional skills.

Interventions for Adolescents and Adults

For adolescents, intervention emphasis should be placed on adaptive and vocational skills to prepare for independent living. Sexual development in adolescence brings some additional behavioral problems, which may be addressed using education and behavioral techniques. Such techniques include teaching basic social skills through operant conditioning (introducing oneself, responding to requests, not touching other persons inappropriately) (Holter, 2004). Among adults, the identification of community resources and supports for long-term care planning is critical.

Directions Part III, Goal Setting and Treatment Planning: Given your risk and protective factors assessments of the individual, your knowledge of the disorder, and evidence-based practice guidelines, formulate goals and a possible treatment plan for this individual.

Critical Perspective

Autistic disorder may be better conceptualized as a continuum of disorders, with varying degrees of impairment that imply different interventions (Volkmar, Lord, Bailey, et al., 2004). The DSM IV does not distinguish between these levels of impairment, and it is often difficult to establish a diagnosis of autistic disorder that is clearly distinct from the other ASDs, which include Asperger's disorder, and PDD-NOS. Due to the symptom overlap between the various PDD disorders, it is debated whether autistic disorder is truly distinct from the others. Further debate ensues over the significant distinctions between high-functioning autism and Asperger's syndrome, and few studies find clear support for separate classifications (Kasari & Rotheram-Fuller, 2005).

As a result of the diagnostic difficulties described above, there is some disagreement as to whether autism should be assessed using a categorical (as in DSM-IV) or a dimensional classification system (Volkmar, Charwanda, & Klin, 2004). In DSM-IV a client either does or does not qualify for a diagnosis. A dimensional system would allow professionals to identify levels of disability more clearly in each of the core areas of autism and thus consider ASDs along a single spectrum of ability and disability.

Directions Part IV, Critical Perspective: Formulate a critique of the diagnosis as it relates to this case example. Questions to consider include: Does this diagnosis represent a valid mental disorder from the social work perspective? Is this diagnosis significantly different from other possible diagnoses? Your critique should be based on the values of the social work profession (which are incongruent in some ways with the medical model) and the validity of the specific diagnostic criteria applied to this case.

CASE 2

Hao, a five-year-old child whose parents emigrated from Vietnam many years ago, was recently expelled from his parochial school kindergarten class and advised to seek placement at the public school. The reason for the expulsion was his inability to relate to other children in class, incessant hand washing, and inability to follow instructions. Hao could not follow the classroom routine and would stay only for activities in which he was interested, such as those focusing on math or science topics. At times he would grow so frustrated with what he saw as disruption to his favored activities that he had temper tantrums at school. His parents, Lang and An, are extremely disappointed and upset over Hao's expulsion and are not sure what the future holds for him.

Lang and An had no previous thoughts of seeking out services for their son until now. It was only when Hao faced the structure of the kindergarten day that problems emerged. Lang, a 43-year-old Vietnamese woman and primary informant during this assessment, enrolled Hao in preschool at the age of four and did notice at that time that Hao was not connecting personally with other children. She said, "Hao only wanted to play alone. He ran around the yard while other children played together." But when Lang asked the teachers about this, they said that Hao was a sweet little boy who displayed no unusual behaviors and that all children mature at different rates. Lang believes that the preschool teachers' patience served to elicit positive behavior from Hao. Hao thrived in preschool and responded well to the staff's consistent positive reinforcement. Hao never had a tantrum in preschool.

Lang tried for years to conceive before having Hao. She was able to access quality prenatal care and experienced a good pregnancy and vaginal delivery with no complications. Hao was a healthy infant, who weighed 7 pounds, 4 ounces at birth. Hao walked at 11 months of age, had a vocabulary of about 20 words when he was 18 months (which is considered normal), and was toilet trained at 24 months of age. He also began to read at 24 months of age and learned how to use a computer before he was 36 months old. Hao now dedicates a significant portion of time to figuring out how to operate minute functions on the computer, fixing computer parts, and playing math and science games on the computer.

Hao is also gifted musically. He can play a song on his electric keyboard after hearing it only once. Hao was recently tested and found to have an IQ of 130. Hao was extremely interested in the testing process, asking questions about the instruments and questions. Sometimes he would ask the psychologist questions in response to her questions.

Lang appreciates the importance of Hao's gifts and nurtures his curiosity with books, musical instruments, and computer games. At the same time, she and An are both concerned about these attributes in terms of their impact on Hao's relationships with others. They believe Hao functions at such a high level that he would alienate peers by obsessing about his computer and academic pursuits and not just playing like a "normal five year old."

Lang encourages Hao to dress himself, select his own breakfast (he is able to pour his own cereal and milk), and care for his books and toys. Hao needs help buttoning his clothing and tying his shoes because of a slight delay in fine-motor skills.

Lang notices a difference between her more compliant nieces and nephews and Hao, who would prefer to follow his own set of rules rather than those set forth by his family. Lang states that mealtimes are especially difficult for their family, because Hao refuses to sit for longer than two minutes and ignores them when they speak to him. Lang and An value order, not unlike most Vietnamese parents, according to Lang; Hao's frequent disruptions during meals are difficult to bear. Hao sits for two minutes at a time and then gets up to draw or write in his notebook. When he does sit at the table, Hao takes over an hour to finish a meal that should take thirty minutes to eat.

Hao tends to ignore his parents when they try to discipline him. When Hao does not follow instructions, he is responsive to time-outs, strong verbal communication, and direct eye contact from Lang. Time-outs have proved a deterrent to disruptive behavior, as Hao hates receiving time-outs. Lang and An try to be consistent in their approach to discipline. When asked how she has managed to be patient and firm with Hao in the face of his erratic behavior, Lang stated that it is very difficult but she has to do it in order to be a good mother for Hao. She stated that Hao needs extra attention and patience and that her faith helps her through tough times.

Hao has suffered from severe allergies since he began eating solid foods. Hao is allergic to peanuts, eggs, and milk and breaks out in eczema as a result. Lang and An are closely involved with Hao's pediatrician, and Lang constantly monitors his food intake. As a result, Hao has suffered few outbreaks of eczema in recent years.

Every Saturday and Sunday An brings Hao to the park, where they enjoy playing basketball, soccer, and other sports. An becomes frustrated with Hao's excessive laughter during these activities. At times An loses his patience and threatens to leave the park. Lang indicated that Hao's loss of control is unacceptable in the Vietnamese culture; children are expected to be more in control of their emotions by the time they are Hao's age.

Lang and An are healthy and report no chronic physical or mental illness in themselves or their own families. Lang is a high school graduate who is a trained hairdresser, and An is a college graduate currently working as an information technologist. They enjoy a financially secure life and comfortable existence. Lang has been able to stay home and care for Hao because of this financial security but is excited about getting back into hairdressing. She knows that she will be much happier when she is cutting hair again in that she will have a personal and professional outlet.

As An works long hours, Lang bears the brunt of the responsibility for Hao. She complains of feeling exhausted and helpless. This difficulty has placed an occasional strain on Lang's marriage with An. Lang feels relieved when her husband is available to help. An cooks dinner on weekends and will sometimes use his flex-leave to take Friday off, which allows Lang to have time to herself.

On weekends, Lang and An spend time with An's family. Lang enjoys this time, as she has a positive relationship with them. They eat meals and enjoy birthday parties together, and sometimes Lang will go shopping with her sister-in-law.

Hao has 11 first cousins. Hao sees them almost every weekend for birthdays, at church, and during dinner get-togethers. Hao and his first cousin, six-year-old Thanh, get along well, although Hao tends to focus too much on academics with Thanh. This irritates Lang, who picks up on Thanh's lack of interest, but Hao is unable to see it. Lang will at times firmly instruct Thanh to ignore Hao's questions about math, science, and reading, suggesting other toys and games they might enjoy instead. Hao's aunts and uncles don't always understand why his parents encourage his "different" personality and express distaste over what they perceive as his unusual habits.

Lang summed up her feelings about Hao's most pressing issue. Lang emphasized that while Hao is gifted intellectually, he is not developing socially. Lang stated, "I don't care if he is smart. How is he going to have friends and someday find a wife if he is this way?"

Lang explained that both she and her husband were "boat people." She escaped from Communist Vietnam 25 years ago and spent three years in Cambodia until she was able to locate a family member in the United States who was able to sponsor her. An had arrived in the United States five years before Lang arrived. The couple met in the United States and married 15 years ago. Lang stated that her faith in God and her determination helped her to persevere through many difficult obstacles when trying to come to the United States.

For Lang, An, and Hao, English is their second language. Vietnamese is spoken in the home, and the family holds traditional Vietnamese values. For example, Lang explained that family cohesiveness, spirituality, and work are important to them.

Lang reported that in Vietnam, Hao's behavior would be considered completely unacceptable and totally outside the norm. She stated that she was able to think "less Vietnamese and more American" about Hao when she observed the patience of American teachers in managing Hao. She is hopeful about the future and recognizes that she and An would not be receiving the support for Hao in Vietnam that they receive here. In Vietnam children are warned against bad behavior by being threatened with a wooden spoon. Often, children are hit with the spoon if they continue to misbehave. Lang reports that she has threatened Hao with the spoon only occasionally. Lang stated that when Hao misbehaves she gets down on her knees, uses direct visual contact, and speaks firmly. Lang has used time-outs successfully in the past and will continue to use them.

Lang, An, and Hao are devout Catholics and rely heavily on the guidance of their faith. Lang indicates that she prays often and speaks to her priest when she feels overwhelmed. Lang indicated that her priest has helped her to understand Hao better and told her that God made Hao and he should be accepted and loved. Lang gets a great deal of support from her priest and is able to find strength and patience through prayer. Lang sometimes prays at the dinner table when Hao is not cooperating and reports that it helps her not lose her patience with him. Lang often engages Hao in prayer to remedy his inattentiveness. This approach generally works, and Lang reports that Hao will sit and pray with her for periods of up to a minute or two.

Observations of Hao in his kindergarten classroom revealed that he speaks very loudly and in close proximity to other people's faces. The teacher says that he is unable to retain her instructions about standing back or speaking more quietly. Typically, Hao flatly looks off into space while the teacher speaks. His face displays little emotion. He does not react to questions or comments made by the teacher.

Please go to the Appendix for directions to this case. The following questions will help to guide your thinking about a possible multi-axial diagnosis.

Questions to consider when formulating a diagnosis for Hao

1. What are Hao's significant symptoms with regard to a possible mental disorder?

2. How long have Hao's problem behaviors been evident?

3. Have any stressful events occurred in Hao's life recently that might account for any of his symptoms?

4. To what extent do Hao's (and his parents') cultural traditions contribute to his problem behaviors?

5. How does a social worker make the distinction between autistic disorder and Asperger's disorder in this case?

6. What disorders of childhood and adolescence do Hao's symptoms possibly represent?

CASE 3

DeShon Johnson is a five-year-old African-American male kindergarten student who has been referred to his school's Child Study Team. He is distant and aloof, does not relate to classmates and his teacher, and rarely makes eye contact. He does not play imaginatively like the other children in his class, although his mother says he entertains himself well, usually playing with small household items such as kitchen utensils, pencils, or small toys such as matchbox-style cars, for hours on end. He also likes being outside.

His mother reports that at times DeShon easily becomes frustrated, upset, and defiant—crying, screaming, and throwing himself to the floor—

especially when having to transition from one activity to another. These tantrums last from five to 30 minutes and occur once or twice per day. DeShon's mother and her boyfriend react to these tantrums by either ignoring, yelling, or spanking him. Nothing, according to his mother, changes the nature of his tantrums.

At most times, his affect is flat. He is sensitive to tactile experiences, particularly with regard to food texture. For example, DeShon refuses to eat any food items that are crunchy or hard in consistency. He likes soft foods, such as yogurt, bananas, and soggy cereal. Although DeShon does talk, he displays echolalia, often repeating what others say to him. He also rocks back and forth and waves his hands in front of his face.

According to his mother, Ms. Turner, DeShon's birth history was normal, and he was healthy upon delivery. His mother stated that she became some-what concerned about her son when he was between 18 and 24 months of age. She noted that DeShon's speech, which had apparently been developing relatively normally, stopped progressing. The little eye contact that DeShon had previously made became even less frequent. She also noted that DeShon seemed increasingly uninterested in social interaction, even with her, his older siblings, and others with whom he was quite familiar. Toilet training was reportedly an extensive, time-consuming, and difficult process for DeShon. Despite these concerns, DeShon did not receive consistent medical care and follow-up on referrals to specialists because of the family's frequent moves, lack of financial resources, and temporary homelessness. Consequently, DeShon entered kindergarten with no formal diagnosis or treatment plan.

DeShon Johnson resides with his mother, her male partner, and two older teenage siblings. Ms. Turner is 30 years old and attended school until the eighth grade, when she became pregnant with DeShon's 15-year-old brother. Each of her children has a different biological father. She is currently unemployed but has occasionally worked in the food services field. DeShon's biological father (Torrence Brown) is 39 years old and has been intermittently incarcerated since the age of 15 for drug charges. He has sporadic contact with DeShon and provides no financial support.

The family has Medicaid health coverage. However, DeShon's mother tends to let coverage lapse for a few months each year because she does not complete the required renewal paperwork in a timely manner. At the same time, DeShon's mother is fairly familiar with social services agencies and how to get assistance and financial help when she is in a tight spot.

Ms. Turner's boyfriend is 38 years old and has a tenth-grade education. At times he is employed as a painter. He has lived with the family off and on for approximately three years but has two children in other households living with their respective mothers.

DeShon's mother is able to meet the basic needs of her children: food, clothing, bathing, and shelter. While she obviously loves her children, she is inconsistent in disciplining them. She and her boyfriend often become frustrated with DeShon's challenging behaviors and communication difficulties and tend to rely on yelling and spanking for discipline.

Ms. Turner's stepmother and her aunt and uncle offer emotional support to the family; in addition, she sees other extended family members on occasion, perhaps several times per month. However, most members of her family are also struggling financially, so they are not able to offer financial aid.

The family lives in an apartment complex near the school. Although some parents in this area are reluctant to allow their children to play outside due to potential danger, DeShon's mother perceives the neighborhood as being much safer than some of her past neighborhoods.

DeShon attended no preschool or day care prior to entering public kindergarten as a five year old. During the first few days of school, DeShon's teacher recognized that not only had DeShon lacked exposure to any form of structure in his young life, but he seemed unusually detached from social interactions. This veteran teacher realized that DeShon was likely developmentally delayed, and she immediately referred him to the Child Study Team for an evaluation.

Upon learning of his behavioral characteristics and early history, the Child Study Team recommended that DeShon undergo full assessments—psychological, educational, and sociological evaluations. This school system provides comprehensive services to children with special needs, and the special education teachers are experienced and dedicated. DeShon's mother is willing to seek and accept whatever assistance the school can offer.

Testing showed that DeShon has an IQ of 60 and that his strongest learning style is through visual means. His receptive listening skills are very poor. A medical exam indicated no known physical conditions that could have caused his current symptoms.

Please go to the Appendix for directions to this case. The following questions will help to guide your thinking about a possible multi-axial diagnosis.

Questions to consider when formulating a diagnosis for DeShon

1. What are DeShon's significant symptoms with regard to a possible mental disorder?

2. How long have DeShon's problem behaviors been evident?

3. Have any stressful events occurred in DeShon's life recently that might account for any of his symptoms?

4. How does one decide if DeShon's symptoms meet the criteria for one developmental disorder over another?

5

— ▾▲▾ —

Attention-Deficit Hyperactivity Disorder

Mrs. Bronsky, a 32-year-old Caucasian woman, brought her two children—Pauline, age 10, and Billy, age 8—to the agency because her new husband's 15-year-old nephew had sexually abused them.

Mrs. Bronsky says that Billy has always been a difficult child, independent of the sexual abuse. When asked to do chores or homework or given any instruction, he argues and refuses point blank. If he is doing something annoying to his mother, such as banging a toy against the wall and creating scuff marks, he keeps doing it, almost as if he enjoys getting on everyone's nerves.

His teachers report that Billy argues about teacher commands and refuses to do schoolwork. When they correct him on misbehavior, he blames classmates. Not surprisingly, he has always received poor conduct grades in school. He has also just barely passed each grade and is currently scraping by. His math and science grades are now at the failing level. Mrs. Bronsky says that he has not undergone any testing at the school; nor does he have an Individualized Education Plan (IEP). However, his teacher has suggested that Billy take Ritalin. Mrs. Bronsky states that she doesn't want her son on medication and has heard that some herbal remedies might help him. She admits that Billy does seem to have some difficulty keeping his attention on tasks. He is easily distracted (looking out the window at school and getting involved with what is happening out there rather than what the teacher is saying), doesn't seem to be listening when someone tells him something (but Mrs. Bronsky suspects that he's purposely being difficult), and loses and forgets things (his Math book, his homework, or what the teacher has told him). Again, Mrs. Bronsky thinks these are purposeful behaviors to avoid the work rather than actual forgetfulness.

Attention-deficit hyperactivity disorder (ADHD), one of the disruptive behavior disorders, is characterized by a chronic pattern of *inattention* or *hyperactive/impulsive behavior* (or both)

that is more severe than what is typically observed in peers (APA, 2000). Persons with the "inattention" subtype of the disorder manifest a failure to attend to details and make many careless mistakes, while those with the "hyperactive" subtype are characterized by restlessness and impulsivity. The ADHD diagnosis was once largely restricted to children and adolescents, but it is know known that the condition can persist into adulthood.

Prevalence and Comorbidity

A recent study by the U.S. Centers for Disease Control (Centers for Disease Control and Prevention, 2005) reported an ADHD prevalence of 7.8 percent among children aged 4 to 17, with the prevalence increasing gradually with age. According to a review by Barkley (2004), in community samples almost 45 percent of persons with ADHD may have at least one comorbid disorder. The rates of oppositional defiant disorder (ODD) or conduct disorder (CD) vary according to studies. One review put the rate at between 25 and 75 percent (Wolraich et al., 2005), while another found a rate of between 54 and 67 percent (Barkley et al., 2004). A meta-analysis found that 36 percent of males and 57 percent of females with conduct problems also had ADHD (Waschbusch, 2002). Having both CD and ADHD is the strongest predictor of risk for substance use disorders in ADHD children when they reach adolescence and adulthood (Barkley, 2004). Substantial comorbidity also exists between ADHD and the mood disorders (15 to 75 percent), anxiety disorders (25 percent) (Pliszka, 2000), and learning disorders (20 percent) (Tannock & Brown, 2000).

Assessing ADHD

The way in which ADHD assessments are conducted depends on the age of the client. The diagnosis is particularly difficult in preschool children because of the lack of valid measurement tools and the difficulty of sorting out the possible psychological or environmental contributors to the child's symptoms (Shepard, Carter, & Cohen, 2000). Further, a national survey has indicated that the majority of primary care physicians do not use DSM criteria to diagnose ADHD (Chan, Hopkins, Perrin, Herrerias, & Homer, 2005), and one-fifth to one-third do not routinely incorporate teacher and school information into the evaluation process.

Most comprehensive assessments do not occur until elementary school. The social worker can assume primary responsibility for certain aspects of this assessment (clinical interviews with the child and parent, assessment of parent-child interactions, interviews with teachers, and implementation measures). Other aspects of the assessment require referrals for medical and psychological evaluation. In summary, assessment at the school-age stage should comprise the following (Root & Resnick, 2003):

- A physical examination and a review of health records.
- Interviews with the child, parents, teachers, and any other significant persons. It must be noted that children tend to underreport their symptoms (Pelham, Fabiano, &

Massetti, 2005). In addition, teachers are usually the first people (followed by parents) to suggest that children be evaluated for ADHD (Sax & Kautz, 2003), and their judgment of a child's symptoms tends to be valid (Mannuzza, Klein, & Moulton, 2002).

- Rating scales completed by parents and teachers can also provide useful information. The Swanson, Nolan, and Pelham-IV Questionnaire (SNAP-IV) (Swanson, 1992; Swanson, Schuck, Mann, et al., 2001) has both parent and teacher versions for children ages 5 to 11 and is available online.
- A review of school records (report cards, achievement tests, and attendance).
- Behavioral observations of the child and of parent-child interaction.

Differentiating between ODD and ADHD is also important. Children with ODD behave in a way that purposely annoys and antagonizes others, whereas ADHD symptoms are displayed without regard to others. However, it must be noted that both disorders often co-occur. It is important to explore a trauma history. Common traumas include abandonment, physical or sexual abuse, or observation of family or community violence. Some of the symptoms of post-traumatic stress disorder (PTSD) may mimic those of ADHD (Perrin et al., 2000). Chronic hyperarousal and physiological reactivity to cues from the traumatic event can appear as hyperactivity and impulsivity. Intrusive thoughts of a trauma can interfere with attention and concentration.

In addition to the above steps, a clinical interview with adults should include a discussion of ADHD symptoms present in childhood and symptoms, "such as procrastination, overreacting to frustration, poor motivation, insomnia, and difficulty with time management" (Weiss & Weiss, 2004, p. 27). Adult variants of hyperactive symptoms include workaholism, difficulty sitting through meetings at work, unwillingness to wait, and speeding. The clinician should further inquire about a history of drug and alcohol use (since ADHD can be comorbid with substance abuse). If possible, a collateral (a spouse, partner, parent) should be interviewed to provide a more objective appraisal of the client's symptoms (Murphy & Adler, 2004).

Mrs. Bronsky says she has not talked to the children about the sexual abuse, both because they have been interviewed so many times and because they do not bring it up. She would prefer that they just all forget about it, but the women at the children's advocacy center emphasized that her children will need counseling. She reports, though, that the professionals attribute all of Billy's problems, such as his lack of following through with rules and his bed-wetting, to the abuse. As long as she can remember, however, Billy has had these problems. Mrs. Bronsky denies that he has had nightmares, changes in sleep or eating patterns, or any other specific fears since the abuse occurred. She reports that both Pauline and Billy liked their cousin who abused them and now ask when they can play with him again. When asked how she responds to those requests, Mrs. Bronsky says she tells them, "Now you know after what you said that you can't play with him ever again." When you explore with her what this could mean to the children, she says that she makes it clear that the abuse was the older cousin's fault, that he has a problem and needs a lot of counseling, and that they did the right thing in telling about it.

When asked about the bed-wetting, Mrs. Bronsky said that that is another long-standing problem, that Billy wets his bed almost every night and has done so ever since he was little. She says he rarely wets himself during the daytime. When asked how she has tried to address the problem, she says that she tries to limit his liquid intake after a certain time of day and makes sure he uses the bathroom before he goes to bed. She says that for the past year, Billy has occasionally (once a month) passed feces into his clothing during the daytime. She has had him checked medically, and no problem has been found. She says that she sees neither the bowel movements nor his urination as oppositional behaviors, because he is extremely embarrassed about these "accidents." When asked, she claimed that the doctor has given her no advice on how to handle these problems, other than to have Billy be responsible for washing his own sheets and clothing. She notes that he sometimes hides the sheets and clothes because he is embarrassed.

Mrs. Bronsky reports that she was married to Pauline and Billy's father for nine years and that he was physically abusive to her, but not the children. She admits that they witnessed some of the violence and would cry, but she denies that it had any lasting impact on them in terms of nightmares, flashbacks, or other fears. She says her husband hung out with a motorcycle gang and used to have a problem with "taking speed" in their early marriage, but now merely drinks heavily. She states that he eventually left her two years ago to be with another woman.

Mrs. Bronsky reports that her children have regular visitation with her ex-husband and have consistently denied to all who have asked that he is abusive to them. The children tell the therapist that they like his girlfriend, and that he is not drunk when they are over there, although he does sometimes drink beer. They enjoy their visits to his house. When asked the reason their parents are not together anymore, they say that he went to live with his girlfriend and do not mention the family violence.

Mrs. Bronsky says she has been married to her new husband, Don, for one year, and that she is happy because he is so much better than her ex-husband. He is not violent to her and holds a regular job. When asked how her new husband reacted to the report of Pauline and Billy's sexual abuse by his sister's son, she said that he believes it happened but doesn't want any part of the whole problem. He has played as minimal a role as possible in the police and the child protective services investigations. For example, Mrs. Bronsky has gone alone to the child advocacy center with her children to be interviewed and to have their medical examinations. When asked if the sexual abuse in the family has put any stress on her relationship with her husband, Mrs. Bronsky denies it. She says her husband is very good with her children, although when the children were alone together with the therapist in the second session, they reported, "Don yells a lot" at them and at their mother.

When the therapist was alone with Billy for the first session, he did not talk at all and just looked down as the therapist made various validating remarks ("It's hard talking to someone you don't know," "You're not in here for anything you've done wrong," etc.) or asked questions related to his expectations about counseling (e.g., "What did your mom tell you you were coming for?") or told him about her role ("My job is to talk to kids about things that have happened to them that have been hard to deal with," etc.). No matter what the therapist tried, Billy refused to answer. In the second session, Billy and his sister were together in the session and were more forthcoming, as indicated by the above information they provided about their father, his girl-friend, and their stepfather. Billy was guarded when the therapist brought up the recent sexual abuse and avoided answering any questions, while his sister was willing to discuss it. He denied having bad dreams.

The social worker obtained a release from Mrs. Bronsky to talk to his teacher, who says that in her mind, there is no doubt that Billy has ADHD. "He's classic. He can't sit still. He gets out of his seat if any item attracts his attention. He always has to be fiddling with something. He talks when I'm talking." When asked about oppositional symptoms, she says, "He talks back if I tell him to stop disrupting the class and makes excuses. He glowers at me and folds his arms, refusing to do his work at all at times. The little work he fin-ishes is a mess and full of mistakes. Everyone else is always to blame. He's not accountable, at all."

Directions Part I, Multi-Axial Diagnosis: Given the case information, and your responses to the questions below, prepare the following: a multi-axial diagnosis, the rationale for the diagnosis and GAF score, and additional information you would have wanted to know in order to make a more accurate diagnosis.

Questions to consider when formulating a diagnosis for Billy

1. Has Billy suffered any recent stressors that could account for his symptoms? Did his symptom pattern precede or follow the stressful life events?

2. Do the oppositional behaviors arise out of frustration due to inattention and hyperactivity?

3. Has Billy been exposed to trauma? Could his symptom pattern be indicative of PTSD?

4. Is Billy's enuresis primary (there never was a period that he had a dry bed) or secondary (developed after a period of time when there was a dry bed)?

Multi-Axial Diagnosis

Axis I:

Axis II:

Axis III:

Axis IV:

Axis V:

Rationale and Differential Diagnosis

Additional Information Needed

Biopsychosocial Risk and Resilience Influences

Onset

Many researchers assert that ADHD represents a pattern of cognitive or neuropsychological impairment that is manifested in the person's deficits regarding self-regulation, behavior inhibition, and self-control (Barkley, 2006). Although this conceptualization has not been proved, there is broad support for the fact that child factors, rather than family, neighborhood, and other influences related to socioeconomic status (SES), are responsible for ADHD (Ford, Goodman, & Meltzer, 2004). Risks for vulnerable and oppressed populations are summarized in Figure 5.1.

FIGURE 5.1 Risks for Attention-Deficit Hyperactivity Disorder in Vulnerable and Oppressed Populations.

FEMALES

- Fewer girls tend to be diagnosed with ADHD than their male counterparts partly because they are less likely to demonstrate inattentiveness and hyperactivity, but impairment for girls with ADHD is pervasive.[1,2]

MINORITIES

- Although the incidence of ADHD is similar for African-American and Caucasian populations, African-American children tend to be underdiagnosed and undertreated for the condition.[3]
- Prevalence rates for Hispanics are estimated at 3.3 percent, compared with 6.5 percent for Caucasians; however, the condition may go unrecognized in Hispanics given the lack of population-based studies performed,[4] language barriers, underreporting by mothers due to lack of knowledge of symptoms, cultural differences in developmental expectations by Hispanic mothers, or physician bias.[5]

LOW SES

- Lead exposure increases the risk of ADHD.[6]

BIOLOGICAL INFLUENCES

ADHD is assumed to be an inherited genetic disorder. If a parent has ADHD, there is a 25 to 50 percent chance that the child will have the disorder (Weiss et al., 2000). Thirty to thirty-five percent (30–35 percent) of siblings have the disorder (Faraone & Khan, 2006). Twin studies suggest that genetic factors account for the variance in ADHD by at least 30 percent, and possibly as much as 97 percent (Samudra & Cantwell, 1999; Root & Resnick, 2003). The precise genetic mechanisms that contribute to the onset of ADHD are not known, but dopamine transmitter and receptor genes, as well as several serotonin transporter and receptor genes, have been linked to the disorder (Faraone & Khan, 2006; Levy, Hay, & Bennett, 2006).

Aside from genetics, other biological influences may influence the development of ADHD. Children who are born prematurely are at twice the risk for ADHD as full-term children (Bhutta, Cleves, Casey, Cradock, & Anand, 2002). Maternal smoking and

---

[1]Arnold, 1996.
[2]Hinshaw, Owens, Sami, & Fargeon, 2006.
[3]Bailey & Owens, 2005.
[4]Bloom & Dey, 2006.
[5]Rothe, 2005.
[6]Braun, Kahm, Froehlich, et al., 2006.

drinking during pregnancy may independently act as predisposing influences (Kahn, Khoury, Nichols, & Lanphear, 2003). Research on maternal drug use during pregnancy is limited, although heroin dependence and cocaine use have been associated with ADHD (Samudra & Cantwell, 1999). Variables such as poverty and poor prenatal care may be more significant influences than drug use, however. Lead exposure is also thought to have increased the number of ADHD cases by 290,000 in the United States alone (Braun, Kahm, Froehlich, et al., 2006).

GENDER

ADHD is more prominent among boys by a ratio of approximately 2.5:1 (Centers for Disease Control, 2005), perhaps because boys more often come to the attention of professionals. Because of this gender difference, more research has been done on boys with ADHD than on girls (Rucklidge & Tannock, 2001). A recent landmark study on females with ADHD compared them five years after they had been diagnosed to girls their ages without ADHD (Hinshaw, Owens, Sami, & Fargeon, 2006). Those with ADHD had significantly more impairment across all symptom domains, including externalizing, internalizing, substance use disorders, eating problems, peer relations, and academic performance. At follow-up, they had significantly more impairment across all the symptom domains studied—externalizing, internalizing, substance use disorders, eating problems, peer relations, and academic performance—than did girls who had not been diagnosed with ADHD. These findings indicate the seriousness of ADHD symptoms in girls and the importance of proper diagnosis and treatment. The study also found that the girls with ADHD had experienced more maltreatment (mostly sexual abuse and neglect) at ages five and younger than did the girls in the comparison study (Briscoe-Smith & Hinshaw, 2006). It is uncertain whether the abuse was a causal factor in the ADHD.

SOCIAL INFLUENCES

Although many experts vigorously assert that ADHD is a neuropsychological disorder, others suggest that attachment patterns between parent and child and other family dynamics may contribute to the onset of ADHD (Kreppner, O'Connor, & Rutter, 2001). A recent study found a link between family adversity and ADHD symptoms independent of conduct problems, suggesting that family and social risk influences may be both a cause and consequence of ADHD (Counts, Nigg, Stawicki, et al., 2005).

More recently, Jacobvitz, Hazen, Curran, and Hitchens (2004) reported a study that tracked families with ADHD from ages two through seven, in which family dynamics produced certain symptoms in children. Specifically, hostility in family interactions at age two were predictive of ADHD at age seven. More studies are needed to determine whether the symptoms of ADHD were already present in those toddlers, contributing to the family hostility. For boys, enmeshed family patterns also tended to produce ADHD symptoms in children, replicating the findings of an 11-year longitudinal study by Carlson et al. (1995), in which mothers turned to their children for intimacy with resultant ADHD in boys.

Course and Recovery

Continuance rates from childhood to adulthood ADHD are estimated to be 36 percent in the U.S. population, with 8.1 percent of adults meeting diagnostic criteria (Kessler, Adler, Barkley, et al., 2005, 2006). In a study following hyperactive children into young adulthood, a third (32 percent) had failed to complete high school, and far fewer were enrolled in college compared with the control group (without hyperactivity) (Barkley, 2006). In addition, the young adults with hyperactivity had fewer friends and had more difficulty keeping friends. Sexual risk taking, in terms of both number of partners and unprotected sex, was also indicated. Moreover, adults with ADHD showed impaired work performance, and this effect was particularly evident among blue-collar workers (Kessler et al., 2005). People with ADHD have more car accidents, citations, and speeding tickets than people without ADHD, although they do not perceive themselves as poor drivers (Knouse, Bagwell, Barkley, & Murphy, 2005).

Long-term outcomes for persons with ADHD are influenced by the severity of the disorder; more severe ADHD is more persistent (Kessler, Adler, Barkley, et al., 2005) and is associated with worse outcomes (Barkley et al., 2006). Any parental or family difficulties that contribute to inconsistent, coercive, or decreased efforts at managing the child's behavior may increase problem behaviors in the child with ADHD (Weiss & Hechtman, 1993) and may eventually lead to the development of oppositional defiant disorder (ODD) or conduct disorder (CD), which presents further risk. As noted above, family adversity, particularly marital conflict, is associated with ADHD (Counts, Nigg, Stawicki, et al., 2005). It is unclear whether these factors contribute to or are a consequence of child ADHD.

Another factor identified in families involves household composition. A two-parent home may be a protective influence, because two parents are more likely to manage successfully the stress related to having a child with ADHD (Cuffe et al., 2001).

MINORITY STATUS

While the incidence of ADHD is considered to be similar for African-American and Caucasian populations, fewer African-Americans are diagnosed and treated (Bailey & Owens, 2005). Certain barriers to intervention among African-Americans include characteristics of clients and their families (such as inadequate knowledge of the symptoms, treatment, and consequences of untreated ADHD) and the fear of both overdiagnosis and misdiagnosis. Other barriers are related to limitations in the health care system, such as a lack of culturally competent health care providers, racial stereotyping by professionals, and the failure of clinicians to evaluate the child in multiple settings before diagnosis (Bailey & Owens, 2005).

Few studies of ADHD have been carried out to establish its prevalence among the Hispanic population. One estimate by the National Center for Health Statistics reported a prevalence of 3.3 percent in Hispanics and 6.5 percent in Caucasians (Bloom & Dey, 2006). The incidence of ADHD may truly be lower in Hispanic children, but underdiagnosis may also explain the differential rates (Rothe, 2005). Other explanations for the disparity in these rates include language barriers that interfere with the ability to report ADHD symptoms, the family's degree of acculturation (less acculturated mothers may not recognize symptoms of ADHD), different developmental expectations by Hispanic mothers, or physician bias that may result in failure to address symptoms of concern in the Hispanic population. Of the Hispanics who are diagnosed, many are undertreated. Difficulties with access to care among members of this population may partly explain this inadequacy (Rothe, 2005).

Directions Part II, Biopsychosocial Risk and Resilience Assessment: Formulate a risk and resilience assessment, both for the onset of the disorder and the course of the disorder, including the strengths that you see for this individual.

TABLE 5.1 Biopsychosocial Risk and Resilience Assessment for the Onset of the Disorder

RISK MECHANISMS	RESILIENCE MECHANISMS
Biological	
Psychological	
Social	

TABLE 5.2 Biopsychosocial Risk and Resilience Assessment for the Course of the Disorder

RISK MECHANISMS	RESILIENCE MECHANISMS
Biological	
Psychological	
Social	

What techniques could you use to elicit additional strengths in this client?

Intervention

ADHD is a chronic developmental condition that requires ongoing management and monitoring. Intervention should focus on helping clients learn to cope with, compensate for, and accommodate to symptoms, as well as on reducing additional problems that may arise as a result of these symptoms (Barkley, 2004). Goals formed usually include improved school functioning, peer relationships, and family relationships (Pelham et al., 2005). Children with ADHD and their families often require multimodal interventions such as medication, school-based interventions, and parent training (Conners, Epstein, March, et al., 2001; Multimodal Treatment Study of Children with Attention Deficit/Hyperactivity Disorder Cooperative Group, 1999).

Psychosocial Interventions

Psychosocial interventions may be targeted toward parents, children, and the school system and typically include behavioral and cognitive-behavioral strategies. Family and classroom interventions have been shown to be more effective than individual interventions, although one promising intervention is the use of exercise for youth with symptoms of hyperactivity (Barkley, 2004).

FAMILY INTERVENTIONS

The empirical literature on family intervention for ADHD mainly involves parent training (Barkley & Murphy, 2006). This is a brief treatment model involving about 12 sessions in either individual or group formats. Parents receive information about ADHD, its medications, effective parenting practices, how to reinforce children's coping strategies, and how to manage parental stress. Through positive reinforcements children learn prosocial behavior such as following directions, completing homework, doing household chores, and getting along with siblings. Parents are taught to respond to children's negative behaviors by ignoring or punishing the child so that he or she will suffer negative consequences for engaging in the behavior. Parents are taught these principles through didactic instruction, behavioral rehearsal, modeling, and role playing. Because children with ADHD have problems with schoolwork, other interventions for parents include structuring the home environment so that the child has a place to work relatively free of distractions, regular teacher verification of satisfactory homework completion, and a home-based reinforcement system featuring regular school-home note exchanges (DuPaul & Power, 2000).

A meta-analysis of 16 studies in which parents were involved with their child's treatment was conducted (Corcoran & Dattalo, 2006). Compared to control conditions, parent-involved treatment had a low to moderate effect on ADHD and externalizing symptoms. Given that some of the control conditions themselves involved viable treatments, such as medication and child treatment, it is noteworthy that parent-involved treatment produced overall gains above and beyond these control treatments. Parent-involved treatment had an even higher effect on internalizing symptoms and family functioning. The few studies to date assessing academic performance showed that family treatment may positively benefit academic performance. Children's social skills, on the other hand, were not affected by family treatment, despite the thrust of many programs to improve such skills.

Further support for family involvement was provided by Pelham, the largest treatment study conducted to date on ADHD (Conners et al., 2001). When outcome variables were collapsed, combining behavioral parent training and medication resulted in the largest gains.

SCHOOL INTERVENTIONS

School-based services for children with ADHD rest on a foundation provided by several federal laws (DuPaul & Power, 2000; Root & Resnick, 2003; Tannock & Brown, 2000). These laws prohibit schools from discriminating against people with handicaps; mandate free and appropriate public education for children with ADHD; ensure a multidisciplinary evaluation process toward the development of an IEP; and guarantee reasonable accommodations for persons with a substantial limitation of a major life activity, of which learning is part. Children and adolescent students with ADHD are typically placed in general education classrooms, although these youth may perform better academically in special education classes (Purdie et al., 2002).

A meta-analysis of studies of school-based intervention indicated that contingency management programs and academic interventions are more effective than cognitive-behavioral interventions at improving the classroom behavior of children with ADHD (DuPaul & Eckert, 1997). Academic performance was more difficult to affect, however.

Medication

As a result of the accumulated evidence, stimulants are the first-line treatment for ADHD in both children and adults (McClellan & Werry, 2003; Multimodal Treatment Study of Children with Attention Deficit/Hyperactivity Disorder Cooperative Group, 1999; Weiss & Weiss, 2004). Of concern is the danger of prescribing stimulants for adults with substance use disorders (Faraone, Spencer, Aleardi, Pagano, & Biederman, 2004). The primary psychostimulant drugs used include methylphenidate (71 percent of cases), amphetamines, and pemoline (Bentley & Walsh, 2006). However, when stimulants are compared with one another, few differences have been found in their relative effectiveness (Brown, Amler, Freeman, et al., 2005).

In a review of the randomized trials of the use of stimulants in ADHD, improvement in core symptoms occurred in 65 to 75 percent of consumers compared with 5 to 30 percent of those taking a placebo (McClellan & Werry, 2003). The stimulants also seem to be effective in reducing aggression (Connor, Glatt, Lopez, Jackson, & Melloni, 2002). In addition, the stimulants positively affect social and classroom behavior, although they improve academic achievement only modestly (Brown et al., 2005).

If a child does not respond to an alternative stimulant after the first stimulants are ineffective at therapeutic doses, then the recommendation is to try atomoxetine, a noradrenergic reuptake inhibitor (Pliszka, Crismon, Hughes, et al., 2006). Antidepressants such as bupropion and the tricyclics (but not desipramine, which has been associated with child deaths) are a third option if the above have not been helpful.

Recommendations have also been made for comorbid disorders. In the case of ADHD and depression, medication should initially target the disorder that is most problematic (Pliszka et al., 2006). Therefore, a stimulant should be used if ADHD is the major problem and an antidepressant if the depression is severe. For comorbid anxiety, atomoxetine or an SSRI can be used as a first-line intervention.

> **Directions Part III, Goal Setting and Treatment Planning:** Given your risk and protective factors assessments of the individual, your knowledge of the disorder, and evidence-based practice guidelines, formulate goals and a possible treatment plan for the individual.

Critique

ADHD is considered an inherited neuropsychological disorder, but substantive supporting evidence about its specific nature is lacking (DeGrandpre, 1999). Social influences—for example, attachment patterns, parental stress, and poverty—and other biological contributing factors—for example, maternal smoking—may be underrecognized as risk mechanisms.

ADHD is a problematic diagnosis because both underdiagnosis and overdiagnosis are common, depending upon the geographical area in which the child lives (Purdie, Hattie, & Carroll, 2002). This situation points to the lack of reliability of the diagnostic criteria, with a reliance instead on community standards dictating referral patterns.

A further problem with the diagnosis of ADHD involves the validity of the criteria for females and for adults. Fewer girls tend to be diagnosed with the disorder even controlling for referral bias. Females have a lower base level of inattentiveness and hyperactivity than their male counterparts and must therefore deviate much further from girls without symptoms in order to be diagnosed (Arnold, 1996). As a result, appropriate diagnostic criteria for females are now being discussed, so that girls can be appropriately identified for services (Ohan & Johnston, 2005).

Finally, adults are now being diagnosed with ADHD at higher rates, with such symptoms as "procrastination, overreacting to frustration, poor motivation, insomnia, and difficulty with time management" (Weiss & Weiss, 2004, p. 27). However, these symptoms are not listed in the DSM for ADHD; the diagnostic criteria center on the behaviors of children. Efforts are now under way to institute criteria more relevant for adults. For instance, a note for the symptom of "often runs about or climbs excessively in situations in which it is inappropriate" may state that, for adolescents or adults, this may be translated into subjective feelings of restlessness (APA, 2000, p. 92). Still, criteria for adults must be made uniformly relevant and be empirically validated.

The age-of-onset criterion has been widely debated (Cuffe, McKeown, Jackson, Addy, Abramson, & Garrison, 2001; Loeber et al., 2002; Willoughby, Curran, Costello, & Angold, 2000), especially for adults (Faraone, Biederman, Spencer, et al., 2006). Given the lack of empirical evidence supporting the age-at-onset criterion, as well as difficulties in demonstrating impairment before the age of seven in older adolescents and adults, some have argued that the criterion should be revised to include a broader period of childhood, up to age 12 (Ohan & Johnston, 2005).

Critical Perspective

Directions Part IV, Critical Perspective: Formulate a critique of the diagnosis as it relates to this case example. Questions to consider include: Does this diagnosis represent a valid mental disorder from the social work perspective? Is this diagnosis significantly different from other possible diagnoses? Your critique should be based on the values of the social work profession (which are incongruent in some ways with the medical model) and the validity of the specific diagnostic criteria applied to this case.

CASE 2

Wayne, a 40-year-old Caucasian male, came to see a social worker for counseling after Wendy, his girlfriend of nine months, broke up with him. He described feeling devastated by the breakup (a week ago) and said that he had pleaded with her to take him back. He admitted to calling her constantly since the breakup, to the point where she had changed her phone number. He said he felt nauseated and sick, had problems sleeping, thought about her "all the time," and didn't know what he was going to do without her. He also said he was thinking that he was a "fuck-up" for losing her.

Wayne admitted that he was the reason for the breakup. He said that he couldn't control his temper and that "one little thing" might set him off. He described a recent incident in which he and his girlfriend went rollerblading in a local park. He kept stopping because he felt his shoelaces weren't tight enough. As the more experienced skater, she started to feel frustrated and told him that she would skate on and that they could meet up in half an hour. He flew into a rage, started shouting at her in public, and then stomped off. An hour and a half later, when he had gotten over being mad, he returned to the car, where she was waiting for him. They argued about this incident for the rest of the day. He said, "Why does she have to get so upset? She knows I have a temper and that I'll eventually get over it."

Wayne, who worked as a repairman, also described himself as being very forgetful. For example, he would often leave tools in various apartments where he was working and then waste a lot of time trying to find them. He also left taps running in his own apartment because something else would catch his interest.

He became easily frustrated if he had to deal with too many things at once, such as a lot of work orders. He said Wendy had helped him to get more organized. She had bought a dry-erase board and a calendar to remind him of things that needed to be done. Wayne admitted to having a hard time concentrating on anything other than watching television. That's what had made it hard for him to do well in high school and why he didn't consider college.

In the second session Wayne was accompanied by his ex-girlfriend Wendy, who is college educated and works as a human resources manager. She maintained that they were still apart but that she would consider getting back with him if he made some changes, such as managing his frustration and acting maturely, with the help of counseling. She described Wayne as "like a child." She said it was part of his appeal when she first met him; he seemed so innocent and cute and just blurted out his thoughts. She said her initial attraction to him had been physical. She had been unemployed for a short period and lived in the apartment complex where he was working at the time. She had a lot of work done on her apartment, and he agreed to get her marijuana. After "partying" together, they became sexually involved. She said she was no longer smoking, since she had taken a job at a company that does random drug testing.

She said Wayne would lose his temper over anything, even "stuff that hadn't happened." She described one incident in which she went out with her coworkers for a good-bye dinner for an executive in her company. With the speeches and the various courses, the dinner went on longer than she had expected. By the time she got home, there were ten messages on her answering machine from Wayne. On the final message, he broke up with her. She said it took an hour to convince him that she had been at the work dinner the whole time. Wendy said another problem was his driving. She refused to let him drive with her anymore, because he would drive too fast, switch in and out of lanes, and yell at other drivers. Wayne said he "hates traffic" and feels unbearable frustration when he is stuck behind other drivers.

Wendy realized she had her own "issues" and is working on them in her own therapy. She said that she didn't foresee getting married to Wayne. He said that was fine because he never wanted to get married, but he would eventually like to live with her. He also said he never wanted children, and Wendy revealed that he had physically abused his previous girlfriend's child. He said, "I feel bad about that. He didn't deserve it. I know I'm too much of a kid myself to have kids."

Wendy said she had met Wayne's mother and was surprised she was so nice. Wayne's mother was sympathetic to Wendy's difficulties with him, commenting that, "He's always been like that." She said that he was an exhausting child, and from the time he could walk she ran after him constantly. Wayne didn't mind her, not so much because he was contrary but because he was so distracted; he went with whatever caught his fancy at the moment. Wendy said his mother had told her that Wayne had had some problems after his birth and he had had to stay in the hospital for a week. Wendy didn't know more specifics than that. She said Wayne's mother has never smoked cigarettes or used drugs and drinks alcohol minimally, although Wayne's father reportedly had a problem with alcohol. In the session, Wayne announced that he was thirsty and got up and left the office to use the drinking fountain down the hall. Wendy commented that this was a good example of how he was; if he felt a sensation or had a thought, he would act on it immediately, rather than delaying gratification or thinking things through.

Wayne graduated from high school but got poor grades throughout school. He denied being in any specialized classes ("I'm not a retard." Then he laughed. "At least I don't think I am."). He said he wasn't diagnosed with any learning disorders that he knew of or anything else as a child. He joined the army after high school, served for four years, and was honorably discharged. He said that he was in the army during peacetime, so he saw no combat.

After that he worked as a maintenance man for apartment complexes. He liked the work—moving around all day and figuring out how to fix things rather than being "stuck in an office." He also got a free apartment as part of his job. But he said the pay was "crap" and he didn't have health insurance.

He admitted to having a hard time keeping a job for more than a year. It wasn't so much because he would forget instructions that were given to him. His work was usually good enough for management to overlook that. But he would usually end up "talking back" to management because he wouldn't "take any shit." He said that he had walked away from one job in the past for something that made him mad.

Wayne said he generally got along well with his coworkers and enjoyed talking to people who lived at the apartment complex. He said he had some good friends from the military that he still saw occasionally, although they didn't live in the same town.

Wayne said he did not have a history of trouble with the law, except for traffic and speeding tickets, for which he was jailed once. Then he added that he had been arrested on one occasion for family violence charges against his previous girlfriend (the one before Wendy). He pointed out that in all his other serious relationships (four in all), he had behaved violently only with that one person and said that she was "stupid," "a bitch," and "knew how to get me." He said that she was also violent with him, and the charges were eventually reduced to a class C misdemeanor for both of them. He said she also had a drinking problem and would steal his belongings and pawn them in order to buy beer. She eventually left him after two years for another man.

Wayne said he liked to drink and occasionally smoked marijuana, but not like his past girlfriend and other friends who "couldn't stop." He said that he tended to lose interest after a few beers, and he never missed drinking if he didn't have any money to buy beer. He denied any other drug use, said he "hated coke" because of the way people acted when on it, and commented that he was too "hyper" to take something like that.

As for Wayne's childhood, he didn't remember much. He didn't know his father at all. According to his mother, his father physically abused her, but she didn't leave him until he started physically abusing Wayne and his younger (by two years) brother. Wayne repeated that he did poorly in school and would run around the classroom when he was young. He said he still considered himself a slow reader.

Wayne was seeing the counselor as one of the agency's sliding-scale clients and said that as a result of having to pay the $5 fee, he would be eating macaroni and cheese, potatoes, and peanut butter and jelly sandwiches until the end of the month (a week away) when he got his check. He attributed this problem to the fact that he didn't get paid much, but also admitted to mismanaging his money. He would spend money on something that caught his eye and later not have money for food or bills.

Please go to the Appendix for directions to this case. The following questions will help to guide your thinking about a possible multi-axial diagnosis.

Questions to consider when formulating a diagnosis for Wayne

1. Has Wayne suffered any recent stressors that could account for his symptoms? If so, did his symptom pattern precede or follow the stressful life events?

2. Do Wayne's angry outbursts arise out of frustration due to inattention and hyper-activity?

3. Has Wayne been exposed to trauma in his past? Could his symptom pattern be indicative of PTSD?

4. Was a learning disorder behind Wayne's frustration and inability to complete schoolwork?

5. What techniques would you use to elicit additional strengths for Wayne?

6

— ▼▲▼ —

Oppositional Defiant Disorder and Conduct Disorder

Josie is a 19-year-old Romanian female currently placed at a specialized school for children with developmental disabilities and emotional and behavioral problems. She has attended the program for the past year. Her teacher reports that she often disrupts class, becomes verbally aggressive, has attacked other students, and has difficulty transitioning from one activity to the next. The trigger for these behaviors is typically frustration due to her inability to complete or understand school assignments. She will make disparaging comments about herself ("I'm stupid") before erupting in anger.

Oppositional defiant disorder (ODD) and conduct disorder (CD), both categorized as disruptive disorders of childhood and adolescence, are discussed together in this chapter because they both feature anger, defiance, rebellion, lying, and school problems (Biederman, Faraone, Milberger, Jetton, Chen, et al., 1996; Loeber et al., 2000). Children with ODD are usually younger and do not seriously violate the basic rights of others (APA, 2000), but ODD often precedes CD (Kronenerger & Meyer, 2001).

Prevalence and Comorbidity

ODD is more common than CD, with a lifetime prevalence of 9.5 percent of the U.S. population (Nock, Kazdin, Hiripi, & Kessler, 2006). The median age of onset of CD is 11.6 years. For preschoolers, estimates for the rates of ODD range between 4 to 16.8 percent, and for CD between 0 and 4.6 percent (Egger & Angold, 2006). Males have a higher rate of CD than females (12 percent versus 7.1 percent) (APA, 2000). ODD is more prevalent in males before puberty, but rates appear equal after puberty (APA, 2000).

CD increases the risk of many other mental, emotional, and behavioral disorders (Loeber et al., 2000). The more severe the CD symptoms, the higher the risk of other disorders (Nock et al., 2006). In the majority of cases, CD occurs before mood disorders and substance use disorders, whereas impulse control disorders precede CD. Attention-deficit hyperactivity disorder (ADHD) is common in children with ODD and CD. Anxiety disorders show no particular temporal relationship with CD. For girls with CD, comorbidity with depression is more common than it is with boys and often precedes CD (Ehrensaft, 2005).

Assessment of ODD and CD

Social workers should always engage in a multifaceted approach to ODD and CD, using many informants—the child, parents, and school personnel—to obtain reports and different methods—interview, rating scales, and observations of the child—to formulate their assessment (Alvarez & Ollendick, 2003; Fonagy & Kurtz, 2002; McMahon & Frick, 2005). The DSM criteria require behavior problems in more than one setting. Children also tend to downplay their own symptoms (Loeber et al., 2002). Symptom reports from parents and teachers are preferable, although even these sources have their biases. Teachers are more accurate than mothers at identifying a child's ADHD symptoms, whereas parents are more aware of their children's oppositional behavior. For different assessment tools for conduct problems, see McMahon and Frick (2005).

Figure 6.1 includes additional guidelines for making DSM diagnoses (APA, 2000).

Josie was born in Romania and placed in an orphanage at the age of six weeks, and she was finally adopted by an American couple at the age of eight. Her half sister (one year younger) was also adopted. Three years ago, Josie took the Wechsler Intelligence Scale for Children and was shown to have a verbal IQ of 57, a performance IQ of 65, and an overall IQ of 57. Severe deficits in expressive and receptive language were noted.

Results of the Vineland Adaptive Behavior Scales—Interview Edition indicated that her overall functioning fell into the low, mild deficit range—a level comparable to that of an eight year old. Her communication skills fell at the 10.2 age equivalent, her daily living skills were at a nine-year-old equivalent, and her socialization skills were at 7.11 age equivalent. According to the Ekwall/Shanker Reading Inventory, she was reading at a first-grade level. Overall, results of individually administered, standardized testing in math, reading, and written expression placed her in the first percentile for her age, which was significantly lower than was expected for her IQ.

During the time of testing, Josie was attending a specialized school for students with learning disabilities, where she did well for a while but then began exhibiting aggressive and threatening behaviors to students and staff. She was then referred to another specialized school that offered self-contained classrooms and a much more restrictive program with a clinical team. Her behavior improved at this placement until her grandmother died two years ago, at which time the school also moved to a different building. School reports indicate that she was absent 23 days that year. In the file, school personnel remark on Josie's

FIGURE 6.1 Guidelines for Assessing Oppositional Defiant Disorder and Conduct Disorder.

- Transient oppositional behavior is common in children and adolescents.
- Consider a less severe diagnosis, such as adjustment disorder with disturbance of conduct (when there is a recent stressful life event) or the V-code "child or adolescent antisocial behavior."
- Oppositional behaviors should be distinguished from disruptive behaviors associated with ADHD, which occur in response to frustrations associated with inattention and hyperactivity.
- A diagnosis of ODD or CD should not be made when the symptomatic behavior is protective for a child (for example, one living in an impoverished, high-crime community).
- Symptoms should not occur only in the context of a mood disturbance or symptoms of psychosis.
- Consider whether the oppositional and angry behaviors are part of a symptom pattern indicative of PTSD; irritability and outbursts of anger are listed as symptoms under the hyperarousal criterion for PTSD.
- In cases where the client meets criteria for both ODD and CD, only conduct disorder should be diagnosed.
- When ODD or CD is diagnosed, a separate child and family relational problem (V-code) should not be included.
- CD should be diagnosed in adults older than 18 only if the criteria for antisocial personality disorder are not met.
- See suggested modifications to the DSM criteria for ODD and CD for preschoolers from the Research Diagnostic Criteria-Preschool Age (Task Force on Research Diagnostic Criteria: Infancy and Preschool, 2003) at http://www.infantinstitute.org.

Sources: APA, 2000; Carlson, Tamm, & Gaub, 1997.

poor self-esteem, poor coping skills, difficulty transitioning to new environments and dealing with new people and experiences, tendency to be easily distracted, disruptiveness in class, defiance toward staff, and attention-seeking behaviors. A year and a half ago, Josie carried a pocketknife that was subsequently confiscated. She said she didn't intend to use it but only wanted to show it to her friends. From that point she had to be searched daily.

After that placement Josie was transferred to her current school, where she continues to display disruptive and angry behavior, to the point of attacking other students on occasion. The teacher completed an ADHD rating scale, but neither the score on this test nor the teacher's remarks indicated that Josie had the disorder. However, her reactions when frustrated do tend to have an impulsive and explosive quality.

During the last semester Josie was absent 25 days, with six of those due to school suspension. At that time she had been in detention 66 times for a total of 38 hours for various reasons, including being out of location, throwing objects, disruption, and physical aggression toward staff. In addition to the pocketknife incident, Josie brought matches to the school on two occasions. She again mentioned that she had no intention of hurting anyone; she just wanted to show off. Staff have often had to restrain her while transporting her to locked support. In the hallways, she yells profanities, tears down bulletin boards, pushes other students, and runs away from staff.

In the school environment Josie is said to have positive relationships with one of the assistant teachers and a counselor. One teacher described Josie as helpful in the classroom and showing pride in her accomplishments. Josie has a small group of friends and is particularly close to one other female student in the classroom. They spend a lot of time talking with each other, sometimes disrupting class with their chatter.

Her adoptive mother says that her relationship with Josie is good (which Josie confirms) and that Josie is able to confide in her. According to her mother, Josie also gets along well with her sister. However, her mother reports that Josie has become verbally threatening and abusive to her, although not physically. She says that Josie's temper rises when faced with tasks or chores she doesn't want to do. Josie's mother says that she finds herself giving in to Josie "more than I should" because she just wants to end the conflict.

The family lives in a middle socioeconomic neighborhood, where most of the residents know each other. Josie's father works long hours and travels frequently for business. He is not as involved with his children as his wife is and on weekends typically plays golf. Most of the parenting responsibility falls on Josie's mother, although she claims not to mind this. "All I've ever wanted to do was be a mother." Josie's mother says that she has a circle of friends that she relies on for support, although some of the parents are wary of Josie being around their children. The family regularly attends a Protestant church, and many of her own friends are from her church.

Josie's mother says that when Josie was adopted, she made a good transition, but they soon had her tested, not knowing if some of her difficulties in learning and delays in language were due to cognitive deficits.

Josie denied feelings of depression or sadness at this time with the social work intern, although she did say, "I'm stupid." There has been no change in her eating or sleeping habits. There is also no evidence of manic episodes.

Josie's most recent physical examination was conducted two months ago. No abnormal physical findings were noted. She had successful open-heart surgery while in Romania.

Directions Part I, Multi-Axial Diagnosis: Given the case information and your responses to the questions on the next page, prepare the following: a multi-axial diagnosis, the rationale for the diagnosis and GAF score, and additional information you would have wanted to know in order to make a more accurate diagnosis.

Questions to consider when formulating a diagnosis for Josie's disruptive behaviors

1. How long have Josie's disruptive behaviors been going on?

2. Have stressful events occurred in Josie's life recently? Is an adjustment disorder warranted?

3. Is Josie's frustration related to hyperactivity and inattention?

4. Do Josie's behaviors seem to protect her in living in a high-crime, violent neighborhood?

5. Does she seem to have a mood disorder (either depression or bipolar disorder)? What questions might you ask to determine the presence of mood symptoms?

6. Do Josie's behaviors seem indicative of PTSD? What else would you need to know to consider PTSD?

7. How would you decide if her symptoms are more indicative of ODD or CD?

Questions to consider when formulating a diagnosis for Josie's intellectual and learning disorders

1. Can learning disorders be diagnosed in the presence of mental retardation?

2. Can people with mental retardation exhibit mental health disorders?

Multi-Axial Diagnosis

Axis I:

Axis II:

Axis III:

Axis IV:

Axis V:

Rationale and Differential Diagnosis

Additional Information Needed

Biopsychosocial Risk and Resilience Influences

Onset

More research has been done on risk influences for CD than for ODD, but the disorders share similar influences (Burke et al., 2002), so they will be discussed here together. Overall, the reader should note that familial and social factors predict the diagnosis of CD better than individual characteristics of the child (Dekovic, 1999). The number of risk influences from different domains of functioning (individual, family, and social) also seems critical. In one study 2 percent of youth who had no childhood risk influences showed persistent delinquency in adolescence, compared with 71 percent of youth who had risk influences in five different areas of life (Frick, 2006). The risk and protective influences for CD and ODD in oppressed and vulnerable populations are summarized in Figure 6.2.

FIGURE 6.2 Oppositional Defiant Disorder and Conduct Disorder in Oppressed and Vulnerable Populations.

FEMALES

- The disorders are less prevalent in females than males before puberty, but rates are more equal after puberty,[1] mainly due to girls' involvement with antisocial boyfriends.[2]
- CD may go unrecognized in females because of relational or indirect aggressiveness—for example, exclusion of others; threats of withdrawal from relationships; rumor spreading; and efforts to alienate, ostracize, or defame others.[3]
- Inadequate information exists for treatment for girls because of the lack of gender-specific treatment research.[4]

MINORITIES

- Hispanics are at lower risk for ODD.[5]
- When controlling for SES and neighborhood influences, there is little difference in the prevalence of most conduct problems among African-American, Hispanic, and non-Hispanic white youth. Minority youth, however, are more likely to join gangs (Lahey & Waldman, 2003).
- Physical discipline may not be associated with child aggression among African-American children.[6]
- Insufficient data exist on effective interventions for children who are from minority groups,[7] although minority youth benefit from juvenile offender programs as well as Caucasian youth.[8]

LOW SES

- Living in poor and disadvantaged communities poses substantial risks for antisocial behavior in children in terms of unemployment, community disorganization, availability of drugs, the presence of adults involved in crime, community violence, and racial prejudice.[9]
- Other indirect influences are that parents living in poverty are overwhelmed by stressors, hindering their parenting ability.

BIOLOGICAL INFLUENCES

A meta-analysis of 51 twin and adoption studies found that there are both genetic and environmental influences on antisocial behavior, and determining the relative extent of each influence is difficult (Rhee & Waldman, 2002). The strength of family influences, which

---

[1]APA, 2000.
[2]Burke, Loeber, & Birmaher, 2002; Moffit, Caspi, Rutter, & Silva, 2001.
[3]Ledingham, 1999; Loeber et al., 2000.
[4]Brestan & Eyberg, 1998; Ehrensaft, 2005.
[5]Nock, Kazdin, Hiripi, & Kessler, 2006.
[6]Deater-Deckard & Dodge, 2005.
[7]Brestan & Eyberg, 1998.
[8]Wilson, Lipsey, & Soydan, 2003.
[9]Hill, 2002; Loeber et al., 2000; McGee & Williams, 1999.

include both genetic and shared environmental influences, was greater in twin studies and sibling adoption studies than in parent-offspring studies, suggesting a large role for genetic influences. Another meta-analysis of 12 twin studies and three adoption studies found that genetic effects explained half the children's variance in antisocial behavior, especially for severe antisocial behavior (Mason & Frick, 1994). In addition, early difficult temperament (defined as negative emotionality, intense and reactive responses to stress and frustration, and inflexibility) predicts conduct problems (Nigg & Huang-Pollock, 2003), whereas an inhibited or approach-withdrawal temperament is protective against antisocial behaviors (Burke, Loeber, & Birmaher, 2002; Lahey & Waldman, 2003).

Children with a greater genetic predisposition to conduct problems are, unfortunately, more likely to encounter environments that foster antisocial behavior (Loeber et al., 2002). Children predisposed to CD are likely to be raised by ineffective (and sometimes abusive) parents with histories of antisocial behavior, substance abuse problems, and other psychopathology. With regard to mating, the likelihood of persons with particular characteristics selectively partnering and producing children is substantial for antisocial behavior (Ehrensaft, 2005).

Low IQ, especially verbal deficits, may give rise to the development of antisocial behaviors (Hill, 2002; Nigg & Huang-Pollack, 2003; Wachs, 2000). Children who are unable to identify emotions in themselves and others and cannot reason well verbally may react aggressively rather than by talking about their feelings, seeking comfort, or problem solving.

Male gender is a risk influence for the development of conduct problems. Females may demonstrate more empathy and distress over breaking rules and hurting others at a younger age than boys do (Alvarez & Ollendick, 2003). Girls' communication skills are also more developed at a younger age, as are their social skills. Other reasons for differences in rates of conduct problems may include gender-specific hormone levels, especially testosterone.

PSYCHOLOGICAL INFLUENCES

More severe and chronic conduct problems and poorer treatment outcomes are associated with a number of personality traits, such as lack of guilt, empathy, emotional expression; low harm avoidance; and a preference for novel, exciting, and dangerous activities. These traits are found in about a third of treatment-referred children with early-onset conduct problems (Frick, 2006). However, the dominant personality profile for this type of conduct disorder features impulsivity, low verbal IQ, and a lack of emotional regulation, coupled with higher rates of family problems. Problems with emotional regulation result in impulsive and reactively aggressive behaviors. Other psychological factors conferring risk include hyperactivity (Frick, 2006), early aggression, and (for girls) high stress and poor coping (Burke, Loeber, & Birmaher, 2002).

SOCIAL INFLUENCES

Children who live in poor and disadvantaged communities experience a variety of risks. These include poverty, unemployment, community disorganization, availability of drugs, the presence of adults involved in crime, community violence, racial prejudice, overcrowding, poor and unresponsive schools, and lack of access to services—for example, day care, after-school programs, and health and mental health services (Hankin, Abela, Auberbach, et al., 2005; Hill, 2002; Loeber et al., 2000). These stressors may overwhelm parenting abilities.

Family characteristics and family functioning are strongly implicated in the development of conduct problems. Characteristics of family structure that may give rise to child conduct problems include single-parent families and inconsistent parent figures. Large family size (four or more children) is another risk (Werner, 2000), since in large families financial and parenting resources are often taxed considerably.

Family functioning variables that are risk influences involve parental conflict, separation, violence, and high parental stress (Loeber et al., 1998). Conversely, family stability, stable parental relationships, and parental social support are protective. Any parental psychopathology (depression, substance use problems, antisocial personality disorder, and criminal offending) is also a risk influence (Steinberg, 2000). Further, parental rejection of the child, lack of supervision, and lack of involvement in the child's activities are risk influences for the disruptive disorders. Moreover, child physical abuse and sexual abuse, which often occur in the context of the family, are associated with conduct problems (McGee & Williams, 1999). A large-scale twin study recently established that maltreatment together with the presence of genetic risk increases the rate of conduct problems by 24 percent, whereas maltreatment without such risk increases the rate of conduct problems by only 2 percent (Jaffee, Caspi, & Moffitt, 2005).

Peer relationships can act as either a risk or protective mechanism for the onset of (Hill, 2002) and recovery from conduct problems (Dekovic, 1999). Youth with conduct problems display several distortions in the way they perceive and code their social experiences (Dodge, 2003; Kazdin, 2001). These distortions include an inability to produce a variety of strategies to manage interpersonal problems, difficulty figuring out ways to achieve a particular desired outcome, problems identifying the consequences of a particular action and its effects on others, a tendency to attribute hostile motivations to the actions of others, and failure to understand how others feel. The combination of perceived threat and limited options for managing social situations makes antisocial youth more likely to respond with aggression rather than with prosocial problem-solving strategies. In general, children diagnosed with conduct problems often experience rejection by peers for their aggression and lack of social skills (Miller-Johnson, Coie, Maumary-Gremaud, & Bierman, 2002). As a result, delinquent youth often consort together, further reinforcing their conduct problems.

Deviant peer relationships are a major pathway for adolescent-onset CD (Frick, 2006). In adolescence the rate of ODD in females increases relative to that among boys, most likely because of girls' involvement with antisocial boyfriends (Burke et al., 2002; Moffit, Caspi, Rutter, & Silva, 2001).

Course & Recovery

Approximately 25 percent of youth with ODD later develop CD (Hinshaw & Anderson, 1996), while about 50 percent of children diagnosed with CD overcome their symptoms by adolescence (Lahey et al., 2002). Antisocial personality disorder in adulthood is a possibility for between 25 percent (Lemery & Doelger, 2005) and 50 percent (Burke, Loeber, & Lahey, 2003) of males who had conduct problems as youth, whereas borderline personality disorder may be a risk for girls with antisocial behavior (Ehrensaft, 2005).

Many of the risk and protective mechanisms for recovering from ODD or CD and subsequent social adjustment are the same as those involved with the onset of these disorders. One major factor having to do with the course of the disruptive disorder has to do with the age of onset; compared with the adolescent-onset types, the childhood-onset type results in more severe and chronic problems that persist into adulthood (Moffit, Caspi, Harrington, & Milne, 2002).

For females, continued involvement with deviant partners might lead to a high risk of experiencing intimate partner violence (Maughan & Rutter, 2001). Although conduct problems predict earlier sexual involvement for both boys and girls, the consequences of sexual behavior are more serious for girls because they may become pregnant and drop out of school (Ledingham, 1999). Having children, however, is protective for females with CD in terms of the persistence of the disorder. The transition to motherhood may result in decreased opportunities for the adolescent's deviant behavior and a strengthening of social bonds through the child. Both these developments inhibit the willingness of adolescent girls to engage in antisocial behavior (Ehrensaft, 2005). At the same time, mothers with CD are often harsh disciplinarians (Capaldi & Patterson, 1994; McMahon, 1994). This tendency, along with the effect of assertive mating and consequently increased genetic risk, puts their children at particular risk for the development of antisocial behavior (Ehrensaft, 2005).

Directions Part II, Biopsychosocial Risk and Resilience Assessment: Formulate a risk and resilience assessment, both for the onset of the disorder and the course of the disorder.

TABLE 6.1 Biopsychosocial Risk and Resilience Assessment for the Onset of the Disorder

RISK INFLUENCES	*PROTECTIVE INFLUENCES*
Biological	
Psychological	
Social	

**TABLE 6.2 Biopsychosocial Risk and Resilience Assessment
for the Course of the Disorder**

RISK INFLUENCES	PROTECTIVE INFLUENCES
Biological	
Psychological	
Social	

What techniques could you use to elicit additional strengths in this client?

Interventions for ODD and CD

Psychosocial Interventions

Most studies of treatments for ODD and CD have focused on boys rather than girls (Fonagy & Kurtz, 2002), with males being represented at a 5:1 ratio in one review (Brestan & Eyberg, 1998). Clearly, there is a need for research into gender-specific treatment outcomes, particularly because of the risks to children of antisocial mothers for the development of conduct problems. One treatment implication from a review of conduct problems in females is that priority should be given to stabilizing and structuring the home environment and building trust between clients and their caregivers. Girls with conduct problems are more likely to come from homes characterized by intense emotional conflict and unstable interpersonal relationships (Ehrensaft, 2005).

Along these lines, family interventions have received the most empirical support for the treatment of conduct problems (Brestan & Eyberg, 1998; Latimer, 2001). See Table 6.3 which provides a summary. The most extensively investigated and demonstrably effective model for conduct problems is parent training. Individual treatment for conduct problems is not as effective by itself as family interventions are, except for clients with mild symptoms (Brestan & Eyberg, 1998). Individual treatment may more effectively serve as a component of a broader treatment program targeting several risk domains. At the same time, meta-analyses have shown that short-term cognitive-behavioral individual and group therapy sessions are moderately effective in reducing antisocial behavior (Bennett & Gibbons, 2000) and anger (Sukhodolsky, Kassinove, & Gorman, 2004). In the Sukhodolsky et al. (2004) study, social skills development, problem solving, and their combination were more effective than treatments focusing on feeling identification, self-monitoring of anger symptoms, and relaxation training. Modeling, feedback on role-plays, and the assignment of homework were important aspects of treatment, so these elements should be part of treatment for this population.

Classroom-based contingency management programs, which may be used in conjunction with parent training when school problems are prominent, are effective in controlling the behavior of children, but they have not yet been shown to generalize beyond the classroom or beyond the termination of the program (Heering & Wilder, 2006; McKerchar & Thompson, 2004; Popkin & Skinner, 2003).

Medication

As discussed, many youth with ODD or CD will have comorbid ADHD. Stimulants are effective for reducing aggression with this population (Pappadopulos, Woolston, Chait, et al., 2006). In addition, risperidone reduces aggression substantially in those with CD and below average IQ. Other classes of medication have either not been studied sufficiently or show little evidence of effectiveness. Aggression uncomplicated by ADHD should first be treated with a psychosocial approach, and such an approach should continue even when medications are used.

TABLE 6.3 Family Interventions for ODD/CD

PROGRAM DESCRIPTION	OVERALL RESULTS	LIMITATIONS OF THE APPROACH	EMPIRICALLY VALIDATED MANUALS/ PROGRAMS
Parent training: Parents are taught to specify goals for behavioral change; track target behaviors; positively reinforce prosocial conduct through the use of attention, praise, and point systems; and employ alternative discipline methods.	• Two-thirds of children under age ten improve with parent training.[10] • Strengthening social support for the caretaker enhances effectiveness.[11] • Video training (Webster-Stratton) models are most effective[12] and cost-efficient.[13] • With low SES families, individually delivered parent training is more effective than group delivery. • Adding child therapy may weaken the effect of parent training.	Parent training programs are more effective with persons who[14] 1. Are younger and have mild to moderate problems 2. Do not have comorbid disorders 3. Live in middle to high SES homes 4. Live in two-parent households 5. Live with families with low stress and high social support. Also, these programs do not generalize to school behavior or academics.[15]	*Helping the Noncompliant Child* (ages 3–8) (Forehand & McMahon, 1981), *Living with Children* (ages 3–12) (Patterson & Gullion, 1968), and *The Incredible Years* (ages 2–8) (Webster-Stratton, 2001).

(Continues)

---

[10]Fonagy & Kurtz, 2002.
[11]Behan & Carr, 2000.
[12]Bradley & Mandell, 2005.
[13]Behan & Carr, 2000; Fonagy & Kurtz, 2002.
[14]Fonagy & Kurtz, 2002; Lundahl et al., 2006.
[15]Bradley & Mandell, 2005

TABLE 6.3 Family Interventions for ODD/CD (Continued)

PROGRAM DESCRIPTION	OVERALL RESULTS	LIMITATIONS OF THE APPROACH	EMPIRICALLY VALIDATED MANUALS/ PROGRAMS
Multisystemic Therapy (MST): A manualized, ecologically based family preservation program targeted at juvenile offending.	Has been touted by many sources as a model program.[16] Among programs designed to treat juvenile offenders, the Washington State Institute for Public Policy (1998) claimed MST was the most cost-effective.	A recent meta-analysis indicated that the only outcome affected by the program was arrests[17] and treatment and comparison groups were not always comparable (favoring the treatment group).	(Henggeler, Schoenwald, Borduin, Rowland, & Cunningham, 1998; Henggeler, Schoenwald, Rowland, & Cunningham, 2001).
Functional Family Therapy (FFT): A behavioral-systems family therapy targeted at juvenile offending.	• In controlled studies, FFT has led to greater change than have other treatments and control groups, and change has been maintained at 2.5 years follow-up.[18] • FFT has been found cost-effective.[19]	Few studies have been conducted.	(Alexander & Parsons, 1982; Gordon, Arbuthnot, Gustafson, & McGreen, 1988).

[16]Fonagy & Kurtz, 2002; Weisz, 2004.
[17]Littell, 2005.
[18]Kazdin, 2001.
[19]Aos et al., 1998; Aos et al., 2001.

Directions Part III, Goal Setting and Treatment Planning: Given your risk and resilience assessments of the individual, your knowledge of the disorder, and evidence-based practice guidelines, formulate goals and a possible treatment plan for this individual.

Critical Perspective

The DSM criteria for CD include overt aggression, and as a result of this focus, females with this disorder may be underrecognized. The female presentation of CD tends to be less noticeable, because it involved indirect or relational aggressive behaviors such as the exclusion of others; threats of withdrawal from relationships; efforts to alienate, ostracize, or defame others; and rumor spreading (Ledingham, 1999; Loeber et al., 2000). Some experts have suggested that the diagnostic criteria for CD should be modified for females to include these variables (Loeber et al., 2000; Ohan & Johnston, 2005), although others have argued that there are no gender differences in symptom patterns (Moffit, Caspi, Rutter, & Silva, 2001).

In their critique of the DSM-IV, Kutchins and Kirk (1997) emphasize the importance of distinguishing between behavior as a dysfunction within a person and as a reaction to life stressors. Although it is possible that a client's behaviors signifies internal dysfunction as postulated by the DSM, it is possible that he or she is reacting negatively to environmental circumstances or, more likely, that a combination of these forces is working together. Indeed, the literature on ODD and CD identifies coercive family factors and other social environment variables as key to the development of these disorders. The DSM view of internal dysfunction is therefore not in line with what has been empirically validated as contributing to these disorders.

Directions Part IV, Critical Perspective: Formulate a critique of the diagnosis as it relates to this case example. Questions to consider include: Does this diagnosis represent a valid mental disorder from the social work perspective? Is this diagnosis significantly different from other possible diagnoses? Your critique should be based on the values of the social work profession (which are incongruent in some ways with the medical model) and the validity of the specific diagnostic criteria applied to this case.

CASE 2

Sam is a nine-year-old African-American male who is new to a school that offers educational services for children who can no longer perform in an ordinary school setting. He came from an elementary school where he attended a special education program. He was referred to the specialized school because he continued to exhibit significant behavioral, social, emotional, and academic difficulties.

The prior public elementary school's psychological report stated that Sam spent a majority of his time out of the classroom, either on suspension or in counseling sessions because of his behavior. The report also stated that he required physical restraint on a number of occasions and was recently so aggressive and dangerous that the school filed a complaint with the court asserting that he was out of control both at home and in school. No further information was available about the outcome of this referral to the courts, nor about the specifics of the behavior that warranted such a referral.

Sam lives with his mother, his three-year-old brother, paternal great-grandmother, and uncle in his great-grandmother's home. The family recently moved from the home of Sam's grandmother after a heated argument between Sam's mother and her own mother. This is the third move and Sam's fourth school in just three years. Sam's father was shot to death a year ago (his mother was no longer with him at the time), and he has no contact with his father's family except for his paternal great-grandmother. Sam did have a relationship with his paternal grandmother, but she passed away six months ago.

Sam's mother completed the eleventh grade, is currently unemployed, and collects Supplemental Security Income. It is unclear why Sam's mother receives such assistance. Sam also has a 12-year-old half brother and a 10-year-old half sister. All the children have the same mother but different fathers, and the older children live with their paternal relatives.

Sam's family had home-based services to assist with the difficulties they were experiencing, but the services were terminated several months ago because the agency lost all contact with Sam's mother. The home-based worker stated her belief that his mother may have started a new relationship and that in the past the mother has allowed her relationships with men to take away from her time with her children. The worker also stated that the unstable living situation and mother's mental state (which she believes may be dysthymic disorder) make it difficult to work with the family on a consistent basis. Through the home-based services agency, Sam was connected with mental health counseling, but his attendance and participation were sporadic.

About a year ago Sam took the Woodcock Johnson tests, which indicated that his reading, writing, and math skills were significantly delayed for his age, IQ, and educational level. His academic achievement is poor because of these delays. Because of his refusal to participate in a number of the tests, his IQ score could not be accurately identified, but the examiner estimated it to be in the range of 74 to 87.

Since the beginning of the school year Sam has continued to exhibit aggressive and dangerous behaviors. In a meeting with the behavior staff director of the school, the social work intern learned that Sam will have to be searched daily because of his many threats of bringing a knife or gun to school to kill staff. Sam has had to be physically restrained by staff at least a dozen times. The director stated she would never restrain Sam alone and that it takes two to three staff to do so safely. In this same meeting, the director stated that Sam has attempted to stab staff with pencils and thumbtacks grabbed from hallway bulletin boards.

In locked restraint, Sam will kick the door and scream out obscenities. According to incident reports, Sam has spit at, lunged at, and attacked staff and has even tried biting. He tends to blame others for his behavior ("I'm in support because [staff member] said a bad word to me."). He neither shows remorse for his behavior nor empathy toward people he has been angry with.

Sam's teacher reports that he often has difficulty transitioning from one location to another or from one assignment to another. Sam refuses to complete his school assignments and will not accept redirection from the teacher. He often becomes verbally disrespectful toward her, but she reports he has not yet been physically aggressive. She does report that he will often destroy property (ripping papers, breaking pencils, turning over chairs and desks) when upset and is known for tearing up his school worksheets when he does not want to work on them.

Sam currently spends a significant amount of time out of class because of his behaviors. He is falling behind in class work because of his absence from lessons and his refusal to participate. Not surprisingly, Sam doesn't have friends because other children are scared of his out-of-control behaviors.

Sam's mother is difficult to contact, and she doesn't return telephone calls in a timely manner. She is guarded about sharing personal information. She attended the most recent individualized educational plan (IEP) meeting and reports that since Sam was a young child, she has seen similar behaviors at home. When Sam gets frustrated, he becomes verbally and physically abusive toward her.

Sam's mother states that she has sought outside help to control Sam's behavior. She attempted mental health counseling, but discontinued services because he refused to speak. Sam's mother says she is overwhelmed and has tried every punishment—spanking, sending him to his room, taking away privileges—but that none of her efforts has been successful in changing his behavior. She says that he does not seem depressed to her, just angry. Sam's mother states that she has also called Juvenile Court to relinquish Sam. She was told to come in to complete the intake process but did not do so.

Sam presents as a well-dressed and well-groomed young boy. When he is not upset, he is engaging and very polite. He states that he enjoys coming to the sessions with the social work intern, and he plays games cooperatively, though with high energy, during these times. He shows particular interest in sports, especially basketball. He doesn't bring up his deceased father or other aspects of his family life and shies away from questions about them, although he admits to feeling "sad" about his father's and his grandmother's deaths. He denies, however, that he is sad in general. He says he has not been sexually or physically abused, but says that in the past his mother and a couple of her boyfriends have "whipped" him but not left marks. Sam's most recent physical examination, performed a year ago, confirms that he is in good health and particularly noted that he has a good appetite.

Please go to the Appendix for directions to this case. The following questions will help to guide your thinking about a possible multi-axial diagnosis.

Questions to consider when formulating a diagnosis of Sam's disruptive disorders

1. How long-standing is Sam's pattern of oppositionality?

2. What recent stressors has Sam experienced? Would the stressors warrant a diagnosis of adjustment disorder?

3. Does Sam have a history of trauma? Are his oppositional and conduct problems indicative of hyperarousal as part of a symptom pattern of PTSD?

4. Does Sam's disruptive behavior seem to arise out of frustration because of inattention and hyperactivity?

5. Are Sam's behavioral symptoms protective for him (i.e., does he need to fight in order to protect himself in an impoverished community)?

6. Does Sam display symptoms of depression?

7. How would you determine whether ODD or CD is the appropriate diagnosis in this case?

CASE 3

Nell is a 13-year-old Hispanic-Caucasian female. She is currently detained at the county juvenile detention center for violating the conditions of probation by continuing to run away from home.

Nell previously resided with her mother, stepfather, 15-year-old brother, and 14-year-old sister in a single-family rental in a suburban, working-class neighborhood. Nell also has two older brothers who no longer live at home. The family just moved two months ago after being evicted from their last residence. The landlord told them that the neighbors complained about the police constantly being called to the house for family arguments and Nell's runaway behavior. Nell also admitted that she stole money from a neighbor's home on several occasions. The neighbors eventually confronted her, but the incident was not reported to the police.

Nell stated that she does not get along with her stepfather (he has been in her life for two years) and has a conflicted relationship with her mother. She says that she has a close relationship with her sister. Nell's parents agree that her stepfather is strict and inflexible about rules, while her mother gets in the middle of conflicts between her husband and her daughters. Nell's mother admits that her children take advantage of her. Nell's mother and stepfather claim that their relationship is "all right," but that the arguments over discipline and Nell's behavior in particular exact a toll. Despite Nell's negative behaviors, both her mother and stepfather actively participate in meetings involving treatment planning, academic issues, and court dates. They both stated that they love and care for Nell a great deal but are unsure what they can do to help her.

The family has a low socioeconomic status (SES). Nell's stepfather works in retail, and Nell's mother said that she quit her job as a secretary when she was diagnosed with breast cancer. Her mother stated that she worries that her children do not always have the same clothing and "things" that their peers have. The family does have health insurance.

Nell is in seventh grade and is currently being schooled through the county school system at the juvenile detention center. She does enough, she says, "to get by." According to her parents, Nell was an honor roll student and a member of the safety patrol and the school choir until her behavior changed drastically about a year ago.

In the past year Nell has refused to obey her parents' rules and has run away from home over a dozen times. She often stays out late at night and refuses to tell her parents where she is going or with whom. She often misses school when on the run, and her grades have suffered significantly. Nell has admitted to hanging out with males who are in their twenties, including known gang members but denies personal membership in any gang.

Nell's parents report that any time she does not get her way, she throws temper tantrums and threatens to run away. They state that she went from being a sweet, loving child to being disrespectful and unmanageable. Nell's acting out seemed to start when Nell's older sister disclosed to her mother that their biological father sexually molested her. Nell denies that she witnessed the sexual abuse or that she was sexually abused herself. After the sexual abuse disclosure, Nell's mother was diagnosed with breast cancer. Nell has shared some concern about this, stating, "I don't want my mom to die."

Nell admitted to engaging in sexual activity with at least ten male partners in the past several months. On at least two occasions she had sex with male strangers in laundromats for $5 because she was trying to save up enough money to move to another state. Nell stated that she almost always initiates the sex and cannot seem to control this behavior. She thought she was pregnant on more than one occasion, but stated that tests she took while in shelter care confirmed that she was not pregnant and did not have any sexually transmitted diseases. Nell has previously accused male staff at the shelter and the juvenile detention center of touching her in a sexually inappropriate manner, but all cases have been investigated and deemed unfounded.

Nell stated that she started using various substances about a year ago. Marijuana is her drug of choice, and at the height of her use (four months ago) she smoked every other day. Nell reported last using marijuana one month ago. Additionally, around this time she smoked marijuana laced with cocaine "once or twice" and reported snorting several lines of cocaine on one occasion.

Nell reported that she has also used alcohol, and four months ago her use increased to several times a week. She stated that she can consume five to seven 12 ounce beers before she is intoxicated. Nell reported vomiting on several occasions and experiencing three or four blackouts. She stated that she last consumed alcohol one month ago before she was admitted to the juvenile county detention center.

Nell admitted to dextromethorphan (DXM) use beginning this past year. DXM, the active ingredient found in many over-the-counter cough and cold medications, produces hallucinogenic and stimulant effects in high doses. Seven months ago, because of her running away and substance use, Nell was placed in a county shelter care residential facility. While there, staff reportedly took her to the hospital after she ingested ten tablets of DXM. She stated that she last used DXM four months ago when she ingested 15 pills.

Nell denied experiencing withdrawal symptoms from any substance. She said that she does not see anything wrong with "smoking a little weed and having a few drinks" and was unable to articulate any negative consequences associated with substance use. She admitted that her incidents of sexual activity have been when she is under the influence of one substance or another, even when she has been with adult males unknown to her. She acknowledged that it is illegal for her to drink alcohol and use drugs and knows that it upsets her mother, but she has no intention of stopping. Nell reported that the majority of her friends also use alcohol and drugs. Access is no problem, she claims, because her friends are older and able to obtain marijuana and alcohol.

Nell's mother and stepfather state that they have witnessed her under the influence of substances and believe that a problem exists. Nell's mother says she herself rarely drinks, but Nell's stepfather says he has a "couple of beers" each night when he gets home from work. Both parents deny that he has a problem with alcohol. However, Nell's mother said that Nell's biological father was an "alcoholic," and it was one of the reasons she left him, along with his sporadic employment. Nell has not had contact with her father since the divorce three years ago.

Nell has hypothyroidism, a medical condition in which the thyroid is underactive and does not produce a sufficient amount of thyroid hormones. She reported no other health or medical issues. Nell takes a thyroid hormone medication, Levothyroxine.

Nell ran away from shelter care but was returned there until five months ago, when she used a paper clip to cut her nickname into her forearm. At that point Nell was referred to a psychiatric hospital. Nell denied suicidality in the past or at present.

After her stay at the psychiatric hospital, Nell went home. Soon after, she had a fight with her mother and drank kitchen cleaner. Nell insisted that she drank it to make her mother feel bad and had no desire actually to harm herself. She was then placed in a nonprofit home for at-risk adolescents but ran away on three occasions. She was put on probation for her runaway behaviors.

When reporting on her current mood, Nell states that although at times she feels sad and worried, she believes it is because of her circumstances—being locked up at the juvenile detention center. She is convinced she will feel better once she returns home with her family. While being interviewed, Nell showed little remorse for her actions and their effect on her family or her personal well-being.

Nell has several strengths. She has an engaging personality, is smart, and has an excellent singing voice. She used to be in the school choir, and her goal is to become a professional singer. Nell believes that her problems will be solved when she and her sister are able to get along with their mother and stepfather. Nell does not wish to return home until her relationship with her parents improves and they no longer see the need to criticize her and yell at her.

Please go to the Appendix for directions to this case. The following questions will help to guide your thinking about a possible multi-axial diagnosis.

Questions to consider when formulating a diagnosis of Nell's behavior problems

1. Have stressful life events occurred in Nell's life recently, enabling a less severe diagnosis of adjustment disorder to be considered?

2. Have Nell's symptoms occurred only in the context of a mood disturbance?

3. Are the conduct problems part of a symptom profile that includes trauma exposure and other aspects of PTSD, including reexperiencing, numbing, and hyperarousal?

4. How can ODD and CD be differentiated in this case?

5. Do ADHD symptoms seem to account for Nell's frustration and impulsive behaviors?

Questions to consider when formulating a diagnosis of Nell's substance use

1. How can abuse and dependence be distinguished for each of the substances she used?

2. When three substances are involved, as they are in this case, should the social worker list three separate disorders?

7

— ▼▲▼ —

Alzheimer's Disease

Mrs. Shirley Washington is an 89-year-old African-American female who was admitted to the hospital with a diagnosis of lumbago (the medical term used for general lower back pain), and urinary retention (failure to empty the bladder completely). Mrs. Washington appeared confused and disoriented when the social work intern attempted to assess her. The social work intern then made an appointment with Mrs. Washington's son, who was listed in her chart as the emergency contact.

Mr. Washington appeared relieved when contacted by the social work intern. He reported that he was the primary caretaker of his elderly mother, whom a physician had diagnosed with dementia about one year ago after performing a series of tests. Mr. Washington said that the symptoms were initially not serious. Mrs. Washington would occasionally forget things, but she was able to take care of herself. The son stated, however, that during the last three or four months his mother was becoming more forgetful. She would pick up various personal items and then put them down, becoming frustrated when she was unable to find them. Mr. Washington reported that he kept finding these items, mainly things that belonged to his mother, in random places in and around the house. In addition, Mr. Washington reported that his mother is no longer able to perform certain activities, such as knitting, that she had done throughout her life. Mrs. Washington, he went on to say, often did not recognize her own children or other relatives and friends. She became panicky at such times and would yell at people to leave her alone. These episodes became worse around sunset.

Cognitive disorders are characterized by deficits in a person's thought processes that are due to brain dysfunction and account for a significant decline from the previous level of functioning (APA, 2000). The major classifications of cognitive disorders include *delirium* (a time-limited cognitive disturbance), the *amnestic disorders* (with memory impairment as the only symptom), and the *dementias* (which feature multiple cognitive deficits including, but not limited to, memory impairment). This chapter focuses on Alzheimer's disease (AD), a debilitating cognitive disorder classified as a dementia. About 50 to 60 percent of persons with dementia have AD, the most common form of dementia worldwide (Suh & Shah, 2001). AD involves a progressive decline in the number of functioning neurons in the person's central nervous system (Cummings & Cole, 2002). There are many other dementias that, unlike AD, stem from identifiable medical conditions; for example, vascular dementia is produced by a series of small strokes.

Prevalence and Comorbidity

Old age is often falsely stereotyped as a stage of life that includes high rates of AD. Still, the disease affects as many as four million Americans (Boise, Neal, & Kaye, 2004). More than half of them receive care at home, while the others reside in health care institutions. The prevalence of AD doubles for every age group five years beyond age 65. Some studies indicate that nearly half of all people 85 and older have symptoms of AD (Boise, Neal, & Kaye, 2004). Prevalence estimates range from 1.4 to 1.6 percent for persons aged 65 to 69 years, rising to between 16 and 25 percent for persons over 85 years old. A study sponsored by the National Institute on Aging indicated that the annual number of cases in the United States is expected to double by the middle of the 21st century (Herbert, Beckett, Schurr, & Evans, 2001). This number was 377,000 in 1995 and is expected to reach 959,000 by the year 2050. The proportion of new cases identified after age 85 will increase from 40 percent (in 1995) to 62 percent in 2050, when the youngest "baby boomers" reach that age.

Approximately 40 to 50 percent of persons with AD experience symptoms of anxiety and depression (10 to 20 percent have a major depressive disorder). About 30 to 40 percent have delusions (often persecutory), and 20 to 30 percent experience hallucinations (Altman, 2001).

Assessment Guidelines

AD must be diagnosed by a physician, although there are no medical tests that can positively identify the presence of the disorder; instead, it is diagnosed when other possibilities are ruled out (Altman, 2001). The following guidelines, however, can help differentiate possible AD from other cognitive and DSM disorders (see Figure 7.1):

> Mr. Washington stated that he locked the house at night and took the key to his bedroom because Mrs. Washington would sometimes wander through the house. On several occasions when the key was in the lock, she wandered into the streets and got lost. Fortunately, Mrs. Washington was never injured and was returned home by either neighbors or the police. Mr. Washington mentioned that his mother took medication for the dementia, but the medication caused constipation. She ate prunes every morning and drank milk of magnesia.

FIGURE 7.1 Assessment Guidelines for AD.

- AD is a "rule-out" diagnosis. Rather than being positively identified by medical examination, it is ruled "in" if other possible conditions cannot account for the symptoms.
- Dementia is not diagnosed if the cognitive deficits occur exclusively during a period of delirium, even though delirium can occur in the context of dementia.
- Memory impairment alone is not sufficient to diagnose dementia (it may indicate the presence of an amnestic disorder).
- Other types of dementia are due to identifiable medical causes such as strokes, anemia, brain tumors, hypothyroidism, infections, and metabolic deficiencies.
- Cognitive impairments may occur due to the effects of substance intoxication or withdrawal, so these possible etiologies must be ruled out.
- Dementia differs from the cognitive disorder of schizophrenia in that the latter diagnosis has an earlier age of onset, less severe cognitive impairment, and symptoms that usually include hallucinations and delusions.
- Memory deficits may be present in major depression; these deficits tend to remit with the depression.
- Most older adults experience age-related cognitive impairments, but these are not as severe as the symptoms of dementia; still, it is often difficult to distinguish "normal" cognitive decline from the early stages of dementia.

Sources: First, Francis, & Pincus, 2002; Altman, 2001.

When the social work intern asked Mr. Washington about his mother's substance use, he sighed and said that his mother used to smoke cigarettes. She didn't smoke on a regular basis anymore, but sometimes people would give her cigarettes that she would save and smoke later. Unfortunately, she would often put a lit cigarette down and then forget about it, leading to several small fires in the home. Mrs. Washington also used to drink two bottles of beer every night with dinner until about two months ago, when Mr. Washington started to give his mother nonalcoholic beer as recommended by her primary care physician.

Mr. Washington reported that his mother was still able to take care of most of her activities of daily living (ADLs). However, she did require help with washing and bathing. Because she had difficulty getting in and out of the bathtub, Mr. Washington remodeled the bathroom and installed a tub with a seat and a door on the side. When helping his mother undress for the bath during the past few weeks, Mr. Washington noticed some occasional incontinence.

Mr. Washington reported that the house in which he and his mother live has two levels, with approximately 12 steps between levels. Mrs. Washington had no difficulty climbing the stairs prior to her recent hospitalization. She also did not use a cane or wheelchair or any other durable medical equipment.

Mr. Washington stated that until recently one of his brothers lived in town and helped out with the care of his mother; however, this brother moved out of state several months ago for a work-related reason. Mrs. Washington has two more sons, both of whom live out of state, and various grandchildren scattered throughout the country. Mrs. Washington also has an elderly brother and sister who live in the area. In addition, Mr. Washington has many friends and a few other relatives who live locally and occasionally help out with the care of his mother.

Mr. Washington mentioned that his mother's symptoms of dementia have worsened over the past few months, and it has become increasingly difficult for him to take care of her. He expressed frustration that his mother had recently failed to recognize him on several occasions and had started shouting, believing him to be an intruder. Mr. Washington requested that the social work intern help him place his mother in long-term care because of his inability to continue to provide adequate care. At 70 years of age, he is becoming elderly himself and is experiencing some health problems, including back pain, which make it difficult to help with his mother's ADLs such as washing and bathing. He has never married and said he needs to concentrate on looking after himself.

As for Mrs. Washington's previous life history, she received a high school diploma and spent most of her adult years taking care of her children. She worked for the Census Bureau for about ten years. Mr. Washington indicated that to his knowledge the family had no history of dementia or any other mental health disorders. He admitted that Mrs. Washington followed a high-fat diet for most of her life, eating a lot of fried foods.

Mrs. Washington lacks financial assets; she has no savings and does not own a home. Mr. Washington owns the house they are living in, and he has the financial means to take care of her. Mrs. Washington has health care access through Medicare and a private insurance company from her deceased husband's employment.

Directions Part I, Multi-Axial Diagnosis: Given the case information and your responses to the questions below, prepare the following: a multi-axial diagnosis, the rationale for the diagnosis and GAF score, and additional information you would have wanted to know in order to make a more accurate diagnosis.

Questions to ask when formulating a diagnosis for Mrs. Washington

1. Does Mrs. Washington exhibit memory impairment?

2. Since memory impairment alone is not sufficient to diagnose dementia, what other symptoms of dementia, if any, does Mrs. Washington exhibit?

3. Do Mrs. Washington's symptoms seem to be worsening over time?

4. Could Mrs. Washington's symptoms be related to medical causes or to her use of any substances?

5. How can one differentiate the symptoms that are occurring in Mrs. Washington from schizophrenia?

6. Does Mrs. Washington exhibit symptoms of depression? If so, could her cognitive symptoms be secondary to her depression?

7. Can Mrs. Washington's symptoms be attributed to the normal cognitive decline that occurs with old age?

8. Is Mrs. Washington's condition serious enough to put her at risk for self-harm?

Multi-Axial Diagnosis

Axis I:

Axis II:

Axis III:

Axis IV:

Axis V:

Rationale and Differential Diagnosis

Additional Information Needed

Biopsychosocial Risk and Resilience Influences

Onset

AD may be recorded as *with early onset* (before age 65) or *with late onset*. A minority of AD patients develop the disorder between the ages of 40 and 50, and an earlier onset implies a more rapid course. This form of AD often runs in families (McMurtray, Ringman, & Chao, 2006). In general, AD has a gradual onset and produces a slow, steady decline in the person's cognitive functioning. Risks for AD are heavily weighted toward biological

FIGURE 7.2 Alzheimer's Disease in Vulnerable and Oppressed Populations.

FEMALES

> After age 90, the incidence of AD is higher among women.[1]

DISABILITY

> Individuals with Down syndrome have an increased risk of AD.[2]

SOCIOECONOMIC STATUS

> Persons possessing a low educational background and occupational status appear to be at higher risk of AD (and vascular dementia) because of the following associated risk influences: consumption of high-fat foods; vitamin deficiencies (B-12 and folic acid); elevated levels of homocysteine (linked to circulatory problems), poor exercise habits; cigarette smoking; and ingestion of environmental toxins.[3]

ETHNICITY

> All ethnic minority caregivers report worse physical health than do Caucasian caregivers. African-American caregivers experience lower levels of caregiver burden than do Caucasian caregivers.[4]
>
> Asian-American caregivers tend to be more depressed than do Caucasian caregivers.[5]
>
> Hispanic caregivers experience less depression, lower levels of role captivity, and higher amounts of self-acceptance than do non-Hispanic caregivers.[6]

mechanisms, but there are also some psychological and social influences on its development. See Figure 7.2 for risks associated with vulnerable and oppressed populations.

BIOLOGICAL RISK INFLUENCES

The role of genetics and biology is universally accepted as critical in the etiology and course of AD. A recent analysis of the Swedish Twin Registry reported a 58 to 79 percent biological heritability for AD for both men and women (Gatz, Reynolds, Fratiglioni, Johansson, Mortimer, et al., 2006). Age of onset is significantly more similar for monozygotic than for dizygotic twin pairs, however, indicating an important role for environmental influences.

In people with AD, brain cells in the cortex and hippocampus (areas that are responsible for learning, reasoning, and memory) die after they become clogged with two abnormal structures: *neurofibrillary tangles* (twisted masses of protein fibers), and *plaques* (deposits of a protein called amyloid) (Meeks, Ropacki, & Jeste, 2006). Symptoms begin with changes to the

---

[1]Ruitenberg, Ott, Van Swieten, Hofman, & Breteler, 2001.
[2]Ruitenberg, Ott, Van Swieten, Hofman, & Breteler, 2001.
[3]Lyketsos, Steinberg, Tschanz, Norton, Steffens, & Breitner, 2000.
[4]Morano, 2003.
[5]Jones, Chow, & Getz, 2005.
[6]Morano & Saunders, 2005.

amyloid, which is part of a larger molecule, the amyloid-precursor protein (APP), which extends from a neuron's outer membrane (Ziabreva, Perry, & Perry, 2006). Normally APP is "chopped up" by other enzymes and dissolves after its use. In AD, however, a pair of enzymes (beta and gamma secretase) cleaves APP in the wrong places, leaving behind insoluble amyloid fragments, which then become prone to bind to each other and to other proteins, forming fibrils that make them even less soluble and harder for the body to the clear. These fibrils in turn bind with one another to form plaques. When these substances reach a certain threshold, the brain can no longer function efficiently. Brain neurons slowly die and lower levels of essential neurotransmitters are produced, creating signaling problems among cells.

Specific information about genetic processes in Alzheimer's disease is lacking, but mutations in any of four genes (located on chromosomes 1, 14, 19, and 21) are associated with its development (Nowotny, Smemo, & Goate, 2005). The APOE-2 and -3 proteins appear to protect against AD by strengthening structures vital to nerve cell functioning.

Some biological risk influences for AD are associated with gender and race. There is a gender difference in AD incidence, but it is not significant until the age of 90, after which it is higher among women (Ruitenberg, Ott, Van Swieten, Hofman, & Breteler, 2001). One study of thousands of persons with AD and healthy volunteers revealed that the APOE-4 gene appears to increase the risk of AD for persons in many ethnic groups, but perhaps more consistently for Caucasians (Farrer, Cupples, & Haines, 1997). Persons with Down syndrome, which is related to an extra copy of chromosome 21, have an increased risk of AD. Mothers who deliver such children prior to age 35 also have an increased risk, because they may carry the marker gene. It must be emphasized that AD is a genetically heterogeneous disorder, and advances in the knowledge of the human genome may contribute to more accurate profiles of the development and course of the disorder (Papassotiropoulos, Fountoulakis, Dunckley, Stephan, & Reiman, 2006).

Several biological protective influences have been identified for AD (Jedrziewski, Lee, & Trojanowski, 2005). These include regular exercise, the maintenance of low cholesterol, the use of statins (medications that work to lower cholesterol), and the absence of head trauma.

PSYCHOLOGICAL RISK INFLUENCES

There are no known psychological causes of AD. One meta-analysis has, however, identified depression as a small but significant risk influence (Ownby, Crocco, Acevedo, John, & Loewenstein, 2006). Another five-year study of older adults found that although a history of depression did not predict an onset of AD, depressive symptoms are often an early symptom of AD (Gats, Tyas, St. John, & Montgomery, 2005). When people begin to experience the symptoms of AD, however, depression and anxiety are common. People may exhibit mood swings, become distrustful of others, and show increased stubbornness. Those emotional states and behaviors may be in response to frustration and changes in self-image, but biological reasons have also been offered to explain why depression is often present with AD (Bonavita, Iavarone, & Sorrentino, 2001). Higher rates of depression are found among first- and second-degree relatives of persons with AD, perhaps because the characteristic neurofibrillary tangles are higher in cerebral areas where the pathogenesis of depression takes place; thus the two disorders may share a biological association.

SOCIAL RISK INFLUENCES

Lifestyle factors may contribute to negative health conditions that put some people at greater risk for AD, although the role of these influences is somewhat speculative (Lyketsos, Steinberg, Tschanz, Norton, Steffens, & Breitner, 2000). The prevalence of possible contributing factors, such as infections, nutritional deficiencies, brain injury, endocrine conditions, cerebrovascular diseases, seizure disorders, substance abuse, and brain tumors, varies across cultural groups. Persons with higher risks of these types may have relatively low educational backgrounds and occupational status. They may consume high-fat foods, have low blood levels of folic acid and vitamin B-12, and have elevated levels of homocysteine, an amino acid that has been linked to circulatory problems. Their lifestyles may include poor exercise habits, cigarette smoking, and the ingestion of environmental toxins such as water pollutants.

Protective risk influences for Alzheimer's disease have been identified in one literature review as including high educational level, continued employment, regular engagement in activities that use cognitive functions, and the pursuit of leisure activities (Jedrziewski, Lee, & Trojanowski, 2005).

Course and Recovery

AD cannot be cured or stabilized indefinitely; its downward course is unfortunately unremitting. The duration of its course is unpredictable, but five to ten years is most common. Some mechanisms can either hasten or slow the progression of the disease, however; these are outlined in Table 7.1. These mechanisms are discussed in more detail later in this chapter, but this section centers on family caregiving, as there are positive associations between caregiver coping and patient survival time (McClendon, Smyth, & Neundorfer, 2004), and between dysfunctional coping strategies and caregiver depression and anxiety (Cooper, Katone, Orrell, & Livingston, 2004). Research consistently shows that there is a sensitive psychological balance between patients with AD and their caregivers, and that the patient's agitation is related to caregiver behaviors and attitudes (Lott & Klein, 2003).

Only one-third of persons with dementia in the United States live in nursing homes (Boise, Neal, & Kaye, 2004), which means that families are the primary caregivers for the majority of these individuals. While the symptoms of Alzheimer's disease are distressing for the affected person, the situation may be equally stressful for the caregivers (Phillipe, Lalloue, & Preux, 2006). Behavior problems—perceptual disturbances, mood disturbances, wandering, agitation, sleep disturbances, incontinence, and refusal to eat—are the leading reason family members seek professional intervention on behalf of a person with apparent dementia (Lott & Klein, 2003). Predictors of caregiver burden are the elderly person's behavioral disturbances (especially at night) and hallucinations (Allegri, Sarasola, Serrano, Taragano, Arizana, et al., 2006).

The caregiver faces ongoing challenges in balancing his or her own limits on time, energy, and patience. The stresses experienced by family caregivers may be heightened by their fears of loss, guilt over not being an adequate caregiver, ambivalence about the caregiver role, conflicts with each other, and fears about their own mortality. Caregivers with preexisting symptoms of depression experience these stresses more severely (Lu & Austrom, 2005). Support availability is significantly associated with less stress (Morano, 2003). Many caregivers also develop some degree of resentment toward the client because of the relentless responsibilities associated with client care (Martin-Cook, Remakel-Davis, Svetlick, Hynan, & Weiner, 2003).

There are some differences among caregivers of older adults (not limited to AD) from different ethnic groups with regard to stress, resource availability, and psychological outcomes. A meta-analysis of empirical studies found that minority caregivers were younger, less likely to be a spouse, and more likely to receive informal support (Pinquant & Sorensen, 2006). They provided more care than Caucasian caregivers and felt stronger obligations to do so. Asian-American caregivers used less formal support than Caucasian caregivers and, like Hispanic caregivers, were more depressed than their Caucasian counterparts. One focus group study found that in each of these cultures, families were slower to seek out professional interventions than were their counterparts in Western cultures, being more likely to rely on cultural traditions of family caregiving (Jones, Chow, & Getz, 2005).

TABLE 7.1 Biopsychosocial Risk and Resilience Assessment for the Course (or Quality of Life) of Alzheimer's Disease

RISK INFLUENCES	PROTECTIVE INFLUENCES
Biological Early onset (before age 60) Cerebrovascular disease Poor diet (fatty foods, low blood levels of folic acid and vitamin B-12)	Later onset (after age 60) Good physical health Low-fat diet, high in folic acid and vitamin b-12, high fish diet
Psychological High levels of stress Depression	Lower levels of stress Stable mood
Social Later diagnosis Lack of resource availability Absence of psychosocial interventions	Early detection and intervention Resource availability Interpersonal supports Psychosocial interventions

Directions Part II, Biopsychosocial Risk and Resilience Assessment: Formulate a risk and resilience assessment, both for the onset of the disorder and the course of the disorder, including the strengths that you see for this individual.

TABLE 7.2 Biopsychosocial Risk and Resilience Assessment for the Onset of the Disorder

RISK INFLUENCES	PROTECTIVE INFLUENCES
Biological	
Psychological	
Social	

TABLE 7.3 Biopsychosocial Risk and Resilience Assessment for the Course of the Disorder

RISK INFLUENCES	PROTECTIVE INFLUENCES
Biological	
Psychological	
Social	

What techniques could you use to elicit additional strengths in this client?

Intervention

Goals

Interventions for persons with AD are focused on promoting the client's safety, comfort, and productivity for as long as possible and helping the family or other caregivers be more competent and capable of managing the stresses that accompany their role. A survey of health care professionals in the United Kingdom indicated that early intervention in AD and other forms of dementia is considered important for providing critical support for the client and his or her caregivers (Illife & Manthorpe, 2004). Early assessment and diagnosis can reveal the range of potential problems in need of intervention, help individuals prepare for the future, align them with support groups and other community resources, provide financial and legal referrals for persons and their families (such as information about disability benefits and power of attorney), and initiate ongoing counseling and monitoring.

Psychosocial Interventions

A literature review of evidence-based psychosocial interventions for AD patients found support for group activities, physical activities, activity planning based on an evaluation of an individual's behavior patterns, and sensory interventions such as music interventions and hand massage (Bharani & Snowden, 2005). The psychosocial interventions described below provide examples of these kinds of interventions and are widely accepted by professionals as effective, but it should be kept in mind that there is not yet extensive evidence-based research to support some of them.

Traditional "talk" psychotherapies are not helpful to persons with AD except for their adjustment in the early stages of the disease, when cognitive functioning is largely intact. Both, interpersonal and cognitive therapies have been used with clients in the early stages. In one study brief psychodynamic or interpersonal therapy (six sessions) helped clients to experience less subjective stress but had no effects on cognitive functions (Burns, Guthrie, Marino-Francis, et al., 2005). In another study the use of cognitive interventions (focused on education and problem solving) helped the client and family to become proactive in managing the disease (Claire, Wilson, Carter, Roth, & Hodges, 2004). Cognitive rehabilitation and training, however, are not effective for improving the client's cognitive functioning (Clare, Woods, Moniz-Cook, Orrel, & Spector, 2007).

Many studies suggest that psychosocial interventions are helpful in improving the patient's quality of life (feelings of well-being and comfort). Most of these interventions reflect the types of activities supported in the above meta-analysis. In one study of 201 persons with AD, perceived quality of life improved with regular cognitive stimulation (being encouraged to engage in regular physical activity and discussion), although this did not affect the course of the disorder (Lu, Masterlund, Mulnard, Cotman, Miller, et al., 2006). Another study of residents in a Florida nursing home found that when nursing staff were trained to communicate more often and more substantively with residents, those residents' self-reports of depression diminished (Bourgeois, Dijkstra, & Hickey, 2005). Further, staff gained a greater awareness of the residents' personal lives and cognitive abilities.

There is wide agreement among researchers and practitioners that *behavioral* interventions can be modestly effective in reducing or abolishing certain problem behaviors of clients with AD, including aggression, screaming, poor hygiene, and incontinence (Cohen-Mansfield, 2001; Grassel, Wiltfang, & Kornhuber, 2003). For behavioral interventions to be effective, the social worker needs first to clarify the target behavior and break it down into steps. The social worker next identifies the relevant antecedent and consequent reinforcers of the target behavior as clearly as possible, including the roles of significant others, and then enlists the caregivers to develop environmental conditions that will make the client more likely to exhibit the desired behavior. The social worker should teach caregivers how to reinforce the client's performance of desired behaviors (with praise, hugs, or a special "reward" activity, for example).

Lichtenberg and his colleagues have developed a "well-being" intervention for persons with dementia residing at special care units in nursing homes (Lichtenberg, Kemp-Havican, MacNeill, & Johnson, 2005). This intervention, which emphasizes the empirically validated strategy of increasing clients' activity levels, involves training nursing staff to implement a well-being treatment for individual clients three times weekly for 20 to 30 minutes. Following a brainstorming session with the resident's primary caregivers, the staff implement a series of structured pleasurable activities for the residents on the unit such as bird watching, walking, and small group interactions. The staff member assesses the client's mood and then engages in the activity, which is followed by rating the client's mood again. After a 13-week experimental study involving 20 residents with dementia, members of the experimental group had significantly fewer behavioral problems, even though their levels of depression were unchanged.

Three other types of cognitive and behavioral interventions are commonly associated with older adults, including those with AD: reminiscence, validation, and reality orientation therapies. The reminiscence and validation therapies attempt to improve or maintain the patient's quality of life and self-esteem—and prevent depression, anxiety, and behavior problems—by stimulating the client's memory (Kunz, 2002; Thorgrimsen, Schweitzer, & Orrell, 2002). While commonly used, there is evidence to support the usefulness of reminiscence therapy (Woods, Spector, Jones, Orrell, & Davies, 2007). Some participants experience cognition and mood improvement, and caregivers may experience lower strain. Validation therapy represents a similar intervention, except that the client's erroneous statements and observations are not challenged. The point of the intervention is to relieve the client's negative moods by facilitating emotional expression and conveying empathy (Zeltzer, 2003). Reality orientation, which is used to increase the client's awareness of the present and ability to focus on self-care, also seems to have modest benefits, although these tend not to persist beyond the situation in which they are applied (Metiteri, Zanetti, Geroldi, Frisoni, DeLeo, et al., 2001; Spector, Davies, Woods, & Orrell, 2000). These two interventions include some possible adverse effects, however, among them increased agitation and frustration in clients and stress in caregivers who apply them.

Other therapies have been adapted for use with persons who have AD. The recreational therapies provide stimulation and enrichment for persons with dementia, mobilizing their cognitive processes. These interventions also seem to produce short-term improvements in mood and decreases in behavioral problems (Heyn, 2003; Fitzsimmons & Buettner, 2003; Rovner, Steel, Shmuely, & Folstein, 1996). Art interventions focus on the patient's self-expression through the visual arts, which may help persons with AD tap into memories (Abraham, 2005). One study of persons in the early and middle stages of dementia found that participants demonstrated significantly more interest, sustained pleasure, attention, self-esteem, and normalcy during a creative arts program (Kinney & Rentz, 2005). Still, these persons showed no differences in negative affect or sadness. Studies of music therapy as a means of diminishing behavior and cognitive problems, and improving social and emotional functioning, are also inconclusive (Vink, Birks, Bruinsma, & Scholton, 2007).

Nutritional Interventions

Many persons with Alzheimer's disease gradually lose their interest in eating, which contributes to their health problems. Several studies have considered the effects of interventions on nutritional outcomes. In one study behavioral interventions by nursing staff were successful in keeping residents with AD at their meal tables longer and eating more food (Beattic, Algase, & Song, 2004). The use of nutritional supplements improved weight gain in another experimental study of 91 patients, although their weight gain was not associated with changes in mood or cognitive function (Laque, Arnaud-Battandier, Gillette, Plaze, Andrieu, et al., 2004). Still, nutritional supplements are least likely to enhance energy intake in persons with low body weight (Young, Greenwood, Van Reekum, & Binns, 2004). Diets high in carbohydrates are more favored by persons in the late stage of the disease and thus should be provided for those persons (Young, Greenwood, Van Reekum, & Binns, 2004).

To summarize the psychosocial interventions, empirical evidence shows that clients' quality of life, behavioral symptoms, and the course of the disorder can be positively affected by the consistent application of interventions that encourage the client to be as physically and mentally active as possible (Bharani & Snowden, 2005). The fact that many psychosocial interventions with AD clients have only short-term benefits should not deter the social worker from using them.

Medications

The ideal remedy for AD would slow the production of amyloid by disabling the enzymes that fabricate it (Altman, 2001; Atchley, 2000). Current drug research is focused on the development of *beta secretase* (a type of enzyme that affects the speed of molecular processes in the body), since the earlier gamma blockers (which moderate the activity of a certain brain neurotransmitter) seemed to interfere with normal brain function (Ballard & Howard, 2006). Other drugs are being targeted to prevent the binding of amyloid fragments and to bolster the immune system to ward off development of amyloid (Roberson & Mucke, 2004). New drugs under investigation may mimic the protective actions of APOE-2 or -3, or block the effects of APP-4. Drug therapy may be able to decrease blood levels of APOE-4, remove excess amyloid, and support growth factors that keep brains healthy (Lavretsky, Nguyen, & Goldstein, 2006).

With the above in mind, no known medical treatment exists at the present time to cure AD or stop its progression. At present, drug interventions are limited to those that modify its symptoms and slow its progression (McShane, Areosa-Sastre, & Minakaran, 2007; Lopez & Birks, 2007). The most prominent of these are the cholinesterase inhibitors. The FDA has approved four such drugs since 1994: tactrine, donepezil, rivastigmine, and galantamine (Kalb & Rosenberg, 2004). These medications work by inhibiting the breakdown of a key brain chemical, acetylcholine. A meta-analysis reveals that these medications may improve cognitive function and global level of functioning in persons with mild to moderate AD, but that no solid evidence for drug therapy in severe dementia exists (Birks, Grimley-Evans, Iakovidou, & Tsolaki, 2007; Olsen, Poulsen, & Lubline, 2005). Adverse effects are significant and account for high rates of medication withdrawal (Evans, Wilcock, & Birks, 2004). There is little evidence that any one of the specific drugs is superior to the others in producing these modest effects.

Several claims have been made that the cholinesterase inhibitors (donepezil in particular) can improve the person's responsiveness to psychosocial interventions. One experimental study found that the use of donepezil in combination with a cognitive stimulation program (12 hours of participatory activities involving homework and life-story discussions provided over eight weeks) had greater effects on conversational and functional abilities than the medication alone (Zientz, Rackley, & Chapman, 2007). Another randomized, controlled trial found that reality-orientation interventions by care-givers (engaging the patient in reality-based communication for 30 minutes three times a week) enhanced the effects of donepezil (Onder, Orazio, & Ezio, 2005).

Other types of medications may be effective for treating the symptoms of psychosis, agitation, and depression in persons with AD (Raicu & Workman, 2000). These are mentioned here only briefly, because they are described more fully in other chapters of this book. In general, all of the psychotropic medications are prescribed in lower doses for older clients than for other age groups because of the slower metabolism and rates of clearance through the kidneys typical among the elderly (Bentley & Walsh, 2006). The effectiveness of these medications may be compromised by interactions with other medications the person might be taking. Older adults tend to be more sensitive than younger people to the adverse physical effects of all medications.

Antipsychotic drugs are the only class of medications effective in reducing or eliminating symptoms of psychosis and agitation (Lonergan, Luxenberg, Colford, & Birks, 2007). No differences in effectiveness have been found between the older ("conventional") and newer ("atypical") medications. Still, because of the increased incidence of cerebrovascular events in dementia patients treated with these medications, caution is advised in their use (Ballard & Waite, 2006).

Formal evaluations of the efficacy of antidepressants with dementia clients are lacking. One meta-analysis of controlled studies found very weak support for the contention that antidepressants are an effective intervention for persons with depression and dementia (Bains, Birks, & Dening, 2005). Another review of double-blind, placebo-controlled, randomized trials found that antidepressant drugs improved depression but did not reduce agitation (Franco & Messinger-Rapport, 2005). The newer selective serotonin reuptake inhibitors, which have not yet been studied for this purpose, are generally the first choice of physicians because of their relatively mild side effects. The antianxiety benzodiazepine drugs and anticonvulsant drugs may also be helpful in reducing agitation among persons with dementia (Stahl, 2000).

Interventions for Caregivers

Interventions for caregivers should include both skill-building and coping components. Psychoeducational interventions have been found to be effective for alleviating the stress of caregivers and improving their coping skills (Burns, Nichols, Martindale-Adams, 2003; Gallagher-Thompson et al., 2000; Haupt, Karger, & Janner, 2000; Rivera, 2000; Kuhn & Fulton, 2004; Mittleman, Roth, Haley, & Zarit, 2004; Akkerman & Ostwald, 2004). Even "lay" community consultants may be successfully trained to provide caregivers with support and education, to an extent that caregivers experience less depression, less sense of burden, and diminished reactivity to client behavior (Teri, McCurry, Logsdon, & Gibbons, 2005).

Media-based psychoeducational interventions show promise as well. Caregivers who participated in a 12-month computer-mediated, voice-interactive intervention designed to assist with responding to patient problem behaviors through counseling, access to stress experts, and a voice-mail telephone support group resulted in significantly lower anxiety, depression, and sense of bother about caregiving (Mahoney, Tarlow, & Jones, 2003). A related study demonstrated the utility of a telephone-based intervention for rural caregivers providing information, education, and support on an as-needed basis (Glueckauf, Stine, Bourgeois, Pomedor, Rom, Young, et al., 2005). On a related topic, Teri, McCurry, Logsdon, and Gibbons (2005) found that "lay" community consultants could be successfully trained to provide caregivers with support and education, to the extent that they then experienced less depression, less sense of burden, and diminished reactivity to client behavior.

Directions Part III, Goal Setting and Treatment Planning: Given your risk and resilience assessments of the individual, your knowledge of the disorder, and evidence-based practice guidelines, formulate goals and a possible treatment plan for this individual.

Critical Perspective

Research on Alzheimer's disease overwhelmingly concludes that the disorder results from degenerative biological processes in the brain. There appear to be no significant psychological or social factors that directly affect its onset, although its course may be exacerbated or slowed in the context of certain emotional and social factors. For these reasons AD is universally accepted as a medical disorder. It does not generate much debate within the social work profession about negative labeling, stigma, subjectivity, and the effects of values on diagnosis. In fact, one may wonder why AD is included in the DSM at all, although cognitive disorders related to aging, substance abuse, and injury have been included in the manual since the first edition in 1952. In spite of these points, the specific causes and range of biological characteristics of AD have not been identified, which points to the need for further research before its etiology, symptoms, and course can be specifically identified.

Directions Part IV, Critical Perspective: Formulate a critique of the diagnosis as it relates to this case example. Questions to consider include: Does this diagnosis represent a valid mental disorder from the social work perspective? Is this diagnosis significantly different from other possible diagnoses? Your critique should be based on the values of the social work profession (which are incongruent in some ways with the medical model) and the validity of the specific diagnostic criteria applied to this case.

CASE 2

Paul is a 56-year-old Caucasian male. He was raised by both parents and has one brother, but little is known about his early years or his family's medical history. He was diagnosed with Down syndrome and moderate mental retardation sometime during his youth. He attended a special education program in the public school system until his 18th birthday. Afterwards he remained at home with his parents and did not participate in any day programs for his cognitive impairment. When Paul was 20 years old, his mother died from complications due to diabetes. Paul took her death very hard, secluding himself and rarely leaving his home. His father had a serious stroke when Paul was 33, and they both moved to another state to live with his brother. Paul started working in a sheltered workshop shortly after arriving there. He had a hard time coping with these adjustments and began experiencing depressive symptoms as well as significant anxiety. He also gained almost 50 pounds. He began seeing a therapist and was put on medication for depression and anxiety. Three years later the family moved to yet another state; soon afterwards Paul entered the County Mental Retardation Residential Program and moved into a group home.

Paul thrived in this program. Within two years he lost all of the weight he had gained after his mother's death and no longer needed psychotropic medication. Initially Paul was living in a home with 24-hour supports, but he was so successful there that he was given the opportunity to move into a more independent placement, a town home for four adult males. Daytime supports were in place to help the residents with budgeting, shopping, home maintenance, transportation to medical appointments, and medication administration. Paul was able to perform most other daily living tasks on his own, including showering, dressing himself, cooking simple meals, doing his laundry, and using public transportation. Paul also had no problems communicating with others; he spoke clearly and had a fairly diverse vocabulary. He was never able to read, but he was able to comprehend most of what was read to him and always asked questions about things he didn't understand.

For about the past 15 years Paul worked in a variety of jobs for an employment company that helps find jobs for people with cognitive disabilities. His most recent job was in a hotel, where he worked in the kitchen polishing all of the dinner and banquet ware for the catering department. He enjoyed this job and took pride in bringing home his paychecks. His supervisor said he was an excellent employee, always on task and pleasant.

Paul is a friendly, helpful, and compassionate person. He is always open to new learning experiences and enjoys spending time in the community. He particularly likes live music and theatre, dancing, bowling, and movies. He is well liked by all who know him.

After Paul's father died 20 years ago, he and his brother eventually lost contact. Preceding this, his brother would routinely cancel plans to spend time with him, usually without any notice. Paul also reported that his brother treated him poorly when they did spend time together, calling him stupid, yelling at him, and pushing him around physically. As a result, Paul decided that he no longer wanted to spend any time with his brother. They had no contact for over ten years, until his brother wrote an e-mail to the County Mental Health and Mental Retardation system earlier this year, inquiring about him. Paul received the message and wrote back, but there was no response. His brother visited Paul once when he was in the hospital for ten minutes, but there has been no contact since.

Paul does have some close friends. He has a very close bond with the three men with whom he lived for 15 years, as well as with one housemate's family whom he routinely visits. He also befriended some of the program staff members, maintaining relationships with them long after they worked with him. He often spent the holidays and weekends with these friends.

Over the years Paul has developed a number of health problems. He has alopecia, a disease that caused him to lose all of the hair on his body, and he also has diverticulosis, a growth in the intestinal wall. Until recently he exercised at the local gym several days a week and has been eating healthy foods, so he has suffered few negative effects from these disorders.

About four years ago Paul's residential program underwent some changes. The level of staff support increased as the needs of Paul and his housemates also grew. They now had overnight support to ensure that the men got up and went to work on time during the week. They also had staff for extended hours on the weekends to help transport them to community and recreational activities, as navigating public transportation became harder. Paul was still able to communicate and perform his daily living skills with little assistance until fairly recently.

Two years ago the staff at Paul's group home began noticing changes in his behavior. He was beginning to struggle with signing his name. He also began repeating questions multiple times, for example, "What are we doing today?" When reminded, he would say, "Oh, that's right." Over the next year the staff noticed additional changes, such as Paul's increased apprehension of the unknown and greater fearfulness of walking on grass or any unpaved surfaces due to fear of falling. His repetition of questions also became more frequent. Due to the emergence of these behaviors, and his Down syndrome, his neurologist put him on Aricept, a medication designed to stabilize the symptoms of early cognitive deterioration, one year ago.

Around this time Paul began having a harder time remembering the names of people he knows, but with prompting he was able to recall them. He also began developing behavioral problems, such as incontinence during the night and smearing feces in the bathroom. His emotions became much more intense, and he cried easily whether he was happy, sad, or upset. During the past year Paul began to struggle with tasks such as cooking and laundry that he was previously able to complete. He lost his desire to go outside the home as well. His "lifeline" also appeared to be blurring. He had always talked fondly of his years growing up, but he began talking as if those memories were recent, and to speak about his parents as if they were still alive. He was taken off Aricept six months ago because of concern that it was exacerbating his symptoms. While the smearing ceased, no other changes were noted.

Six months ago there was a marked decline in Paul's appetite and an increase in lethargic behavior. Initially, staff thought this was due to a virus but after two weeks he was unable to overcome it. His doctor did some tests and determined that he was dehydrated. A few days later his energy appeared to be returning, but he then had a seizure at home and was taken to the hospital by ambulance. Since he had no history of seizure activity, doctors ordered both a CAT scan and an MRI. There was no evidence of stroke, but the doctor said that small strokes are rarely evident in such tests, and he suspected that Paul had had several.

After Paul returned from the hospital, his condition deteriorated further. He was no longer able to dress or shower without full assistance. He had frequent accidents with incontinence and began wearing special undergarments. He was unable to complete his duties at work and had to quit his job. After a few weeks he began to sit slumped over and was no longer able to eat solid food, or even feed himself. His communication skills suffered, he had trouble focusing on what people were saying, and he answered questions with only one word. Soon he could walk only with support.

Since his decline during the past month had been so rapid Paul was re-admitted to the hospital. The doctors thought that some of his behaviors could be due to a too-strong dose of antiseizure medications, so these were discontinued. After a few days Paul began to regain some of his faculties. He was able to converse with others, sit up straight, eat on his own (although still only pureed foods), and walk with support. He was introduced to a new anti-seizure medication while still in the hospital, and upon release was referred to a rehabilitation facility for physical and occupational therapy.

Paul did well in his physical and occupational therapy sessions. He became strong enough to walk on his own, and some remnants of his "old self" returned. Still, he was unable to return to the group home, because he required more daily support than the facility was able to provide. He applied for Medicaid and became a resident in another long-term nursing facility.

At the present time Paul's condition fluctuates day by day. He is still able to walk but sometimes has difficulty eating without assistance, often forgetting how to use utensils properly. He recognizes his friends when they visit but is unable to recall their names. Paul is still affectionate and enjoys company, but he generally speaks in one-word phrases, and his responses to questions often seem nonsensical. He can often be found staring into space with a blank expression or playing intently with a small object, such as a straw or piece of paper.

Paul has been hospitalized twice since moving into his present nursing facility. Once he was found lying on the floor of his room with a dangerously low amount of oxygen in his system, and the other time he had another seizure. A friend of his has been appointed his legal guardian to make medical and monetary decisions for him. The guardian is currently trying to transfer him into a group home that offers more intensive support, or to a different nursing home, due to concerns that have arisen in his current placement. His current roommate has pretty much taken control of all extra space and has been heard calling him "stupid" and other similar terms. Paul is also not generally encouraged to use the skills he does have in this facility. For example, staff were transporting him everywhere in a wheelchair, unaware that he could still walk. A similar scenario occurred in regard to his feeding himself.

Please go to the Appendix for directions to this case. The following questions will help to guide your thinking about a possible multi-axial diagnosis.

Questions to consider when formulating a diagnosis for Paul

1. Does Paul show any evidence of memory impairment?

2. Does Paul demonstrate other clinically significant symptoms?

3. Do Paul's symptoms seem to be worsening over time?

4. Has Paul experienced a recent medical crisis (e.g., strokes, anemia, brain tumors, hypothyroidism, infections, and metabolic deficiencies)?

5. Do Paul's cognitive impairments occur because of the effects of substance intoxication or withdrawal?

6. How can one differentiate the symptoms that are occurring in this client from schizophrenia?

7. Is there evidence that Paul's memory deficits are temporarily associated with major depression?

8. Can Paul's symptoms be attributed to the normal cognitive decline that happens in old age?

CASE 3

Mr. Grahm is an 88-year-old Caucasian widower and father of 11 children. After his wife died 21 years ago, Mr. Grahm retired and moved into his daughter's urban home. For 11 years following the move, Mr. Grahm volunteered by coaching at a local high school, filing at one local hospital, and transporting patients around the buildings at another hospital. In addition, Mr. Grahm stayed active by attending church on a daily basis, attending his grandchildren's sports activities, and visiting with family members whenever possible. Mr. Grahm also walked two miles every day to stay healthy.

Beginning 10 years ago, Mr. Grahm's daughter and family noticed that he frequently misplaced his keys, hats, wallet, and other items. Mr. Grahm also started to forget that he had eaten less than an hour after he had had a meal. In addition, his volunteer supervisors reported that Mr. Grahm was found wandering the parking lot, confused about where he was. He made filing errors and asked for assistance at least once a week regarding the filing system that he had initially developed and with which he had been quite conversant. Eight years ago Mr. Grahm began getting lost driving to his volunteer jobs.

Over the next few years Mr. Grahm cut back on his volunteer work because of increasing trouble with the tasks, getting lost, and displaying general confusion. Mr. Grahm's confusion increased at home as well. He lost items more regularly and frequently forgot his daily schedule, whether or not he had eaten, and whether he had turned off the stove. These problems caused Mr. Grahm to become frustrated, agitated, and confrontational with his daughter.

Six years ago Mr. Grahm suffered an atrial fibrillation, a heart rhythm disturbance that caused him to experience a series of minor strokes. He was admitted to the hospital for several days. Upon returning home, Mr. Grahm's family noticed a marked decline in his functioning. Mr. Grahm could not remember card games he had played his whole life. He called family members by the wrong name. He occasionally forgot how to get to church and back.

Shortly after his hospital stay, Mr. Grahm retired from all volunteer activities because his family members took his car away from him. Mr. Grahm also began to worry about intruders at night. He would get up to check the doors, the hallways, and the kitchen. He looked for robbers, and he accused neighbors and family members of spying on him and stealing his money. He hid his personal items and could not find them. Following this, Mr. Grahm could no longer balance his checkbook, remember how to fill out a check, or pay bills.

As the years passed, Mr. Grahm's mental functioning continued to deteriorate, and he became more stubborn and agitated. The family reports that as of four months ago Mr. Grahm rarely remembered where his personal items were, people's names, recent events, what he was doing, or what day it was. He forgot people and would become upset or anxious because he did not know who the people in the house were. Mr. Grahm accused family members of stealing from him daily. He awoke at night wandering around. When asked, he could not remember where he was. At night, Mr. Grahm often believed he was a college student or young husband again; he would deny having children and would insist upon completing his homework or whatever task he needed to complete. He would often think he was in one of his past houses. He slept later into the morning and took naps during the day. He was unable to prepare toast in the morning because he couldn't remember what he was doing long enough to put the bread in the toaster. Mr. Grahm's memory of the past was starting to fade, with the most recent memories vanishing first.

Several months ago, Mr. Grahm was found unconscious in his room and was taken to the hospital, where he remained for one week. The social worker did not have access to the medical reports from this hospital stay. Upon Mr. Grahm's return to the home, he began having auditory hallucinations and became delusional several times a day. He thought that bugs were attacking him. He could not remember most people, even his caregivers, and was suspicious of everyone. Mr. Grahm also began to wet himself. He could no longer follow two-step instructions, because he could not remember each step nor which one came first. Mr. Grahm remains in this state currently.

Regarding his developmental and social history, Mr. Grahm experienced a normal birth. He had three older brothers, one younger brother, and an older sister, and reports having close relationships with his parents and siblings. His younger brother is his only living relative, and this brother suffers from AD. His sister was diagnosed with schizophrenia and lived her adult life in supervised residential facilities. Two of his brothers had alcohol use problems. Mr. Grahm denies any substance abuse or having ever seen a psychologist or psychiatrist.

Mr. Grahm grew up on a farm and his family had lower-middle socioeconomic standing. He completed two years of college and then worked two-blue collar jobs most of his adult life to support his family. Mr. Grahm retired at age 67.

Mr. Grahm had kidney stones removed at age 66. Since then he has undergone two hip replacement surgeries and cataract surgery. He was diagnosed with diabetes mellitus, type II, at age 82, although he made only minor dietary changes to manage this. That same year Mr. Grahm was diagnosed with hypertension and severe rheumatoid arthritis in his neck, shoulder, hands, and hips. Mr. Grahm currently takes eight medications for his various health problems.

Mr. Grahm lives with his youngest and middle daughter and her husband. These three family members provide Mr. Grahm with his basic care. All family members work, so Mr. Grahm is left alone during the day. Three of his other children visit him weekly, and all others visit him twice a month and call him each week. Mr. Grahm reportedly had close relationships with his children and grandchildren.

Mr. Grahm's primary caregivers report being exhausted and on edge. Because of his nightly wandering and hallucinations, at least one of them stays up with him each night. At the same time, his agitation and suspicion cause him to reject their care, and he lashes out at them. The family is concerned about Mr. Grahm's safety during the day and their ability to provide him with proper care.

Mr. Grahm is a practicing Catholic and his faith is a strong support for him. Until this year he attended Mass each morning and had a core group of friends from the church. He still attends Mass and sees his friends on Sundays. Mr. Grahm occasionally speaks with his former coworkers and volunteers, and they have provided him with additional support and conversation when needed.

The family reports that Mr. Grahm functions best at home during the day and when there are a lot of people around. He suffers most at night after a long day of visitors. Mr. Grahm enjoys reminiscing and watching live sports outside. The middle daughter, with whom he lives, most easily calms him. Mr. Grahm is also more alert when he eats regular meals that are low in sugar. He denies suicidal thoughts, although he says that he is lonely and sleeps when he is alone.

Please go to the Appendix for directions to this case. The following questions will help to guide your thinking about a possible multi-axial diagnosis.

Questions to consider when formulating a diagnosis for Mr. Grahm

1. Mr. Grahm experienced many physical problems prior to his observed memory decline. How could these have a bearing on his cognitive functioning?

2. Mr. Graham experienced a serious circulatory disorder after his memory had become impaired. How does this complicate the Axis I diagnosis?

3. To what extent do Mr. Grahm's environmental conditions seem to influence his mental status?

4. Are there any recent stressors that may account for Mr. Grahm's symptom presentation?

5. Is Mr. Grahm under the influence of any substances that may account for the symptoms?

6. Do Mr. Grahm's delusions and hallucinations point to the possibility of a psychotic disorder?

7. Does Mr. Grahm seem at significant risk for self-harm?

8

—▼▲▼—

Substance Use Disorders

Vlad is a 17-year-old Caucasian male court-mandated to attend a six-month residential treatment program at a local juvenile detention center for breaking and entering and unauthorized possession of a firearm. Vlad has unsuccessfully participated in several residential placements in the past few years and has repeatedly had positive urine screens for marijuana use.

Substance use and abuse are both highly prevalent in American society. Social workers often work with clients who have substance-related problems, regardless of their agency settings. This situation arises partly because of the high comorbidity found between substance-related and other disorders, as well as problems such as domestic violence and child abuse. Social workers thus need to be able to assess for substance use disorders and become familiar with their empirically validated treatments. Alcohol-related disorders in adolescence and adulthood are the primary focus of this chapter, although other substances will be mentioned.

The DSM provides general criteria for *substance abuse* and *substance dependence* rather than separate criteria for each substance, of which there are 11 classes (APA, 2000). The defining characteristic of *abuse* involves negative consequences of use, while *dependence* indicates compulsive use despite serious consequences, often accompanied by tolerance and withdrawal. The DSM also describes *substance-induced disorders*, among them intoxication, withdrawal, dementia, amnesia, and psychosis as well as mood, anxiety, sexual dysfunction, and sleep problems.

Prevalence and Comorbidity

Substance abuse disorders are the fourth most diagnosed group of disorders in the United States, and impulse control disorders (Kessler, Chiu, Demler, & Walters, 2005). According to the National Epidemiological Survey on Alcohol and Related Conditions, 8.46 percent of adults, that is, 17.6 million people, met criteria for a past-year alcohol use disorder (Stinson, Grant, Dawson, et al., 2005). Two percent of the population, representing 4.2 million people, met criteria for any drug use disorder. The lifetime prevalence estimate for a substance use disorder is 14.6 percent (Surgeon General, n.d.). The rate was similar among African-Americans and Caucasians (9.5 percent and 9.3 percent, respectively) but lower for Hispanics (Breslau, Kendler, Su, et al., 2005). In older adults, one-month prevalence rates for alcohol use disorders ranged from .9 to 2.2 percent (Surgeon General, 1999). In 2004 the rate of substance dependence or abuse was 8.8 percent for youths aged 12 to 17 (SAMHSA, 2006).

There is a high degree of psychological comorbidity with substance use disorders. Adolescent abusers have a 60 percent likelihood of being diagnosed with another psychiatric disorder, most frequently the disruptive disorders (conduct disorder [CD], oppositional defiant disorder [ODD], and attention-deficit hyperactivity disorder [ADHD]), depression, PTSD (Armstrong & Costello, 2002; Chung & Maisto, 2006). Not surprisingly, alcohol and drug use disorders are highly comorbid with each other. Among individuals with an alcohol use disorder, over half (55.17 percent) also had a drug use disorder (Stinson et al., 2005). People with drug use disorders are at particular risk for concurrent mental illness (Stinson et al., 2005). According to the National Comorbidity Survey, more than half (51.4 percent) of adults with substance use disorders at some point in their lives also had another mental disorder (Kessler, 2004).

Various theories have been postulated to explain high comorbidity between substance use and other mental disorders. Buckley (2006) suggests the following three:

1. People use substances to medicate symptoms of other mental disorders.
2. Substance use may precipitate mental illness.
3. There may be genetic vulnerability to both substance use and mental disorders involving certain neurotransmitter systems.

Unfortunately, substance use in people with mental disorders may lead to destabilization and exacerbation of mental illness symptoms, medication noncompliance, health consequences, and risky behavior such as increased suicidal ideation (Buckley, 2006).

Substance use disorders also have significant medical consequences. Substance dependence (excluding nicotine) in the United States annually accounts for 40 percent of all hospital admissions and 25 percent of mortality rates (500,000 deaths) (SAMHSA, 2006). Medical problems related to drinking include gastrointestinal (gastritis, ulcers, liver problems, and pancreatitis) and cardiovascular (hypertension and cholesterol and subsequent heart disease) conditions (Corrao, Bagnardi, Zambon, & Arico, 1999).

Assessment

Social workers should routinely screen both their clients and clients' family members for alcohol and drug problems (McCrady, 2005). Age bias among health care providers may present particular obstacles to the thorough assessment of older adults (Vinton & Wambach, 2005). Providers may not think of bringing up the issue of substance abuse with older adults, believing that elders cannot benefit from intervention or that their quality of life would not improve. It is also true that elderly self-reports may be unreliable. Recollection or reporting of alcohol problems among older adults may be based on their denial, sense of stigma, inclinations toward social desirability, and memory impairment. It is sometimes difficult to tell whether physical and cognitive problems in the elderly are due to aging or the effects of consumption (Vinton & Wambach, 2005).

Figure 8.1 summarizes assessment guidelines for use with all age groups.

FIGURE 8.1 Assessment of Substance Abuse.

1. Examine patterns of use, including onset, frequency, quantity, drugs of choice, tolerance, or withdrawal symptoms.
2. Examine "triggers" and contexts of use.
3. Review consequences of substance abuse in the physical (might include physical examination), psychological, legal, financial, occupational, and educational realms.
4. Assess motivation for treatment, including the perceived advantages and disadvantages of use.
5. Review major life events that may contribute to substance abuse.
6. Assess the possible coexistence of other disorders, including the relationship between the onset and progression of the other symptoms and their relationship to substance use. Optimally, the assessment of comorbid disorders should take place about three to four weeks after the person has stopped using substances.
7. Consider the client's strengths and coping skills, and inquire about periods of abstinence or reduced use.
8. Assess the client's social support networks.
9. Assess for suicide risk (see Chapter 10 for guidelines on how to conduct such an assessment).

FOR ADOLESCENTS

Interview the adolescent and parent(s) separately. The interview with the parent should be done to gather information about the child but should also address the extent of parental substance use, attitudes toward their child's use, the amount of monitoring and supervision the youth receives, and the level of cohesion in the family (Bukstein, Dunne, Ayres, et al., 1997).

Sources: Bunstein et al., 1997; Graybeal, 2001; Miller & Rollnick, 2001; Riggs & Whitmore, 1999; Bradizza et al., 2006.

Vlad is on probation for breaking and entering until his 18th birthday. He entered a neighbor's house through the window and stole money and electronics. Upon searching his bedroom, police discovered a gun, which resulted in a second charge of unauthorized possession of a firearm. Vlad states that he bought the gun from a friend after being threatened and had no intention of actually using it. After he was arrested and charged, his mother paid his restitution, and he has yet to repay her. He also underwent urine screens as a condition of his probation, which were repeatedly positive for marijuana use.

Vlad has attended but failed to complete several residential placements in the past several years, including a military school, a private alternative school, and a wilderness program. His disobedience of regulations has contributed to his termination from several previous placements. Despite reports of his prior disregard of authority figures, Vlad presents as cooperative, bright, and approachable. His posture and eye contact are appropriate, but he displays a somewhat flat affect. He expresses a desire to improve his relationship with his family and stay out of trouble. He says that the burglary occurred four months prior, and that until he was placed at the residential program he continued to flout the rules his parents had set for him. He recognizes that once he turns 18, the legal repercussions for any crimes he commits will become more severe.

Vlad was adopted at age seven from an orphanage in Russia. His biological parents were alcoholics, and his father was physically abusive toward his mother. It is unknown whether or not Vlad was abused, but his father literally threw him out on the street when he was five years old. He was discovered by the Russian police wandering the streets with frozen nasal passages and frostbite due to the extreme cold. Parental custody was rescinded, and Vlad was placed in an orphanage.

Vlad's two younger biological brothers were adopted by a family in the United States. When this family discovered that the two boys had an older brother still in Russia, Vlad was adopted by a relative of this family. Prior to his incarceration, Vlad lived with his adoptive parents, Mr. and Mrs. Meyers, and two younger adopted sisters. Vlad also has three much older stepbrothers from Mr. Meyers's first marriage. Mr. and Mrs. Meyers are both officers in the United States military. Mr. Meyer is now retired and lives with the two girls; Mrs. Meyers is currently stationed overseas. Despite the physical distance between them, Mr. Meyers claims that he and his wife are close. The family is well off financially, and the parents appear to be invested in their children's well-being. Mr. Meyers says the family's main support is their extended family out of state.

Vlad states that his most important relationships are with his adoptive sisters and his biological brothers, all of whom live out of state. However, Mrs. Meyers says that even when given the opportunity to visit with his biological brothers, he has chosen to stay at home rather than travel to visit them. Vlad's relationship with his father is beginning to improve, but he expresses an immense amount of anger and resentment toward his adoptive mother. Both his adoptive mother and father state that Vlad does not have close attachments to other people. According to his adoptive parents, he has always preferred to be alone in his room and shies away from physical affection.

Of his early childhood in Russia, Vlad recalls little, unsure whether his memories are "real or dreams." Mr. Meyers attends the bi-weekly family therapy sessions and reports that Vlad was a "wonderful, happy little boy." Both Vlad and Mr. Meyers deny a history of significant illnesses or injuries and state that Vlad is in excellent physical health. He does have some residual sinus problems and is susceptible to allergies as a result of his early childhood experience. It is unknown whether there is a history of mental illness in Vlad's biological family other than his parents' alcoholism.

Vlad has a history of unsuccessfully treated mental health issues. He has received psychological evaluations and counseling at most of his past placements. He says that at age 11, he took Adderal to treat ADHD, but he is not currently taking any medications. Vlad adamantly denies a history of cruelty toward animals or fire setting. He states that he gets into fights only when antagonized by others.

Vlad has a history of frequent and persistent alcohol and marijuana use beginning at age 11 or 12. Vlad admits to smoking daily "as long as me or my friends had some." He reports evidence of tolerance to marijuana, both increasing the amount to achieve the desired effect and reduced feelings of intoxication with continued use. Despite a significant history of negative consequences—criminal involvement, academic problems, and interpersonal conflicts—he has not been successful in controlling or limiting his marijuana use. He says he experiences cravings for marijuana every day and admits that he would still be using if he had access. He says that he used alcohol more infrequently ("a few times a week, mostly beer"), but more often when marijuana wasn't available. He said he was able to control or stop his alcohol consumption "when I tried, although I didn't usually want to." He said he doesn't miss alcohol as much as he does marijuana. He admits that he tried PCP on two occasions but found the effects dysphoric and unpleasant; he denies use of any other substances.

Vlad does not display empathy for the victims of his crime nor express guilt for the strain he has caused his family. He is aware, however, that the majority of his problems stem from his substance use and involvement with undesirable peers. He admits that he has a problem with substances and would probably be using if he had access to drugs and alcohol.

Vlad has had two heterosexual relationships. He reports that he felt a strong attachment to his first girlfriend but believes that his parents sabotaged the relationship. He admits that on two occasions he hit his last girlfriend during arguments while he was under the influence of alcohol and marijuana. He claims that she sustained no injuries as a result of his abuse.

Beginning around age 11, Vlad began to associate with a group of undesirable peers. Even after the family relocated to a new neighborhood at age 14, Vlad continued to select unsuitable friends, and his behavior worsened.

He repeatedly disobeyed his curfew, and on several occasions would run away overnight when his parents attempted to ground him. He started skipping classes at school, and his academic performance began to suffer, although he had received good grades before this time. He was also unable to play basketball, a sport at which he excelled, given the school policy requiring a minimum grade point average to play sports.

Vlad attended school at the detention center and was able to earn his GED with minimal preparation. His father reports that Vlad has always been a talented artist. He initially had some difficulty processing his feelings verbally and was given the option of using a therapeutic journal and mandala circle drawings as an outlet for his emotions. Vlad used both the journal and the mandala drawings effectively and produced some creative works depicting both positive and negative feelings he experienced over the course of therapy. Vlad can be stubborn at times, but because of this trait he tends to work hard at an assignment or project until it is satisfactorily completed. For example, he was given an art assignment when he was first placed in the detention center and spent a month working on the drawing. He created a beautiful final product of which he was extremely proud.

Vlad expresses interest in attending a trade school or community college where he can study to become a car mechanic or electrician, as he is "good at fixing things." Mr. Meyers says he will support Vlad in whatever educational and occupational decisions he makes. Vlad is athletic and hopes to resume playing basketball in the future. The Meyers family regularly attends a Catholic church, and Mr. Meyers has a close relationship with the priest. Vlad identifies as Catholic and previously attended a church youth group.

While in the program Vlad has been sharing living quarters with up to 14 other adolescents and is well liked by his peers. His peers describe Vlad as funny, athletic, competitive, and helpful on the unit. Vlad denies any feelings of depression or sadness or any suicidal intent. He also denies experiencing any manic symptoms or episodes when these were described to him. He says the main feeling he struggles with is anger. He admits that he has difficulty controlling himself when he is mad, and he typically yells and throws things.

Vlad views his biggest problems as his negative relationship with his parents and his marijuana use. He states that he would know his problems were solved when he could communicate with his parents if he had problems involving work, friends, or school. Vlad would like to be able to ask his parents questions about his birth family and adoption and hopes to feel close enough to them to have a conversation about his early life. Once he gets out of the residential treatment program, he would like to start eating dinner with his family on a regular basis and playing basketball with his dad and his sisters.

Vlad hopes that one day he will no longer feel the urge to get high and thinks this will happen when he does not feel so angry all of the time. He recognizes that for his situation to change he would have to stop feeling so angry toward his parents, become more capable of effectively managing his anger, and feel more connected to his family and peers. Rather than reacting to angry feelings by yelling or throwing something, Vlad hopes to be able to walk away from a situation and address whatever made him angry when he is feeling calmer. Vlad said that he would know his situation has changed for the better when his parents stop criticizing him for his friends and choices. When asked what he would be doing when they accept him, Vlad admitted that he would have to be making better choices. Vlad says that if he is busy with school, work, and other positive activities, he will no longer struggle with boredom, which he identified as a trigger for his drug use.

When asked the miracle question ("What would you experience if you woke up one day and your life was the way you want it to be?"), Vlad states that he would be enrolled in college and getting good grades, working at a part-time job that pays well, have a girlfriend who does not use drugs, and enjoy a close relationship with his family.

Directions Part I, Multi-Axial Diagnosis: Given the case information and your responses to the questions below, prepare the following: a multi-axial diagnosis, the rationale for the diagnosis and GAF score, and additional information you would have wanted to know in order to make a more accurate diagnosis.

Questions to consider when formulating a diagnosis for Vlad's disruptive behaviors

1. How long-standing is Vlad's pattern of disruptive behaviors?

2. What recent stressors has Vlad experienced? Would these stressors warrant a diagnosis of adjustment disorder?

3. Does Vlad have a history of trauma? Are his disruptive behaviors indicative of hyperarousal as part of a symptom pattern of post-traumatic stress disorder? Is there another disorder that can more appropriately account for his early childhood adversity?

4. Do Vlad's disruptive behaviors seem to arise out of frustration because of his inattention and hyperactivity?

5. Are Vlad's behavioral symptoms protective for him? For example, does he need to fight in order to protect himself in an impoverished, high-crime community?

6. Do Vlad's behaviors occur only during a depressive, psychotic, or manic episode?

7. How do you determine if ODD or CD is the appropriate diagnosis in this case?

8. Would you consider an Axis II disorder for this client?

Questions to consider when formulating a diagnosis for Vlad's substance use

1. How long has Vlad's problematic substance use been occurring?

2. Does Vlad experience negative consequences from his use of substances?

3. Does Vlad show tolerance and withdrawal symptoms for any drug?

Multi-Axial Diagnosis

Axis I:

Axis II:

Axis III:

Axis IV:

Axis V:

Rationale and Differential Diagnosis

Additional Information Needed

Biopsychosocial Risk and Resilience Influences

Onset

Substance use disorders usually begin in late adolescence or early adulthood, with a median age of 20 years (Kessler, Berglund, Demler, et al., 2005). Various risk and protective processes for the onset of adolescent substance use have been delineated, although these are less evident for abuse and dependence. Many of these risk and protective factors overlap with those that have been outlined for ODD and CD (see Chapter 6) (French, Finkbiner, & Duhamel, 2002; Kaplow et al., 2002; Martin et al., 2002). Aside from the influences stated for ODD and CD, other risk mechanisms specific to substance abuse and dependence for adolescents include early onset of drinking (defined as before 14) (Hingson, Hereen, & Winter, 2006), early externalizing problems (Siebenbruner, Englund,

Egeland, & Hudson, 2006), and the presence of adverse family processes due to both the family environment and heredity (Hopfer, Stallings, Hewitt, & Crowley, 2003). Problem alcohol use seems to be moderately heritable (Young, Rhee, Stallings, et al., 2006). Family risk is particularly related to lack of parental monitoring (Siebenbruner, Englund, Egeland, & Hudson, 2006). Protective mechanisms include parental warnings about alcohol and having abstinent friends. At the community level, the availability of drugs and alcohol offers risk, while community prohibitions against such use are protective.

For the onset of substance use disorders in adults, genetic mechanisms have received much attention, but one meta-analysis established that heritability is actually quite low, though stronger for males (Walters, 2002). One factor that protects against the development of substance use disorders is not having a mental disorder (Armstrong & Costello, 2002). Disorders that often precede substance use are depression in females and antisocial personality disorder in males (Lynch, Roth, & Carrol, 2002). Many females with substance use problems have a history of physical or sexual abuse, both as children and adults (Orwin, Maranda, & Brady, 2001). At the social level, peers who use substances place an individual at risk, whereas friends who do not support such use are protective against the development of alcohol and drug problems. Finally, the availability of drugs in a particular neighborhood confers risk for those who live there.

Course and Recovery

Several characteristics of clients, their substance use patterns, and their environments influence the course of recovery (Chung & Maisto, 2006; Conner, Sorenson, & Leonard, 2005; Karageorge & Wisdom, 2001; McKay, 1999; Orwin, Maranda, & Brady, 2001; SAMHSA, 2006; Bond, Kaskutas, & Weisner, 2003) and many of these involve special populations (see Figure 8.2).

Patterns of use that present risk include high levels of pretreatment use, substance use during treatment, and use the year after treatment. Abstinence lasting two years is a protective influence. Protective client characteristics include client motivation and the absence of a comorbid mental health problem. PTSD may put a client at risk for worse outcomes (Bradizza, Stasiewicz, & Paas, 2006). For this reason, clients with PTSD should receive treatment for this disorder soon after receiving substance use treatment. Social workers should also be aware that people with depression may be slower to benefit from treatment (Conner, Sorenson, & Leonard, 2005). For adolescents, conduct problems, depression, and ADHD present risk for relapse (Chung & Maisto, 2006).

Socially, a lack of family support for sobriety and substance abusing family members, socializing with substance abusing peers (especially for teenagers), low socioeconomic status, and life events featuring physical or sexual victimization are risk influences. Protective mechanisms include family support for sobriety, nonsubstance using peers, the ability to develop new relationships, AA attendance, and interventions that attend to culturally relevant beliefs.

Some gender differences in relapse also appear. In general, women tend to benefit more than men in treatment for alcohol use disorders (though not necessarily for drug disorders) despite greater pretreatment risks (Walitzer & Dearing, 2006). Negative mood

FIGURE 8.2 Substance Use Disorders Among Oppressed and Vulnerable Populations.

YOUTH

- Children born to addicted mothers are at risk for health problems, including fetal alcohol syndrome, low birth weight, complications of postnatal withdrawal, and HIV infection.[1]

RACIAL AND ETHNIC MINORITIES

- The rate of substance dependence or abuse among Hispanics is lower than for Caucasians.[2]
- African-Americans have a higher death rate from alcohol-related medical problems than their Caucasian counterparts, although prevalence rates of substance use disorders are similar.[3]
- The rate of substance abuse or dependence is highest among Native Americans and Alaska Natives.[4]
- The second-highest rate of substance abuse or dependence (13 percent) is among biracial persons.[5]
- Being Asian offers protection against substance use disorders—the annual prevalence rate among Asians is 4.2 percent[6]—possibly because of the negative physiological response ("flushing") found in many Asian groups (Japanese, Chinese, and Koreans).
- Ethnic minorities are less likely to have access to services.[7]
- While it is recommended that intervention should integrate culturally relevant beliefs and healing practices, such guidelines have tended to be nonspecific and have not yet been subjected to empirical testing.[8]

SOCIOECONOMIC STATUS (SES)

- People with lower education and low SES are at higher risk for drug abuse and dependence.[9]
- People of low SES have limited access to affordable treatment.[10]

GAY AND LESBIAN PERSONS

- Homosexuals are at increased risk for substance abuse[11] for the following possible reasons: limited social venues where alcohol is not a feature of the environment; limited access to societal institutions that provide protection against substance abuse (i.e., marriage); lack of social support; coping with grief over loss of gay peers through disease and death; coping with discrimination.

WOMEN

- Males have a higher risk of having substance use disorders, except for younger cohorts. In 2004, males aged 12 or older were twice as likely as females to be classified with substance dependence or abuse problems (12.7 percent versus 6.2 percent), but among youths aged 12 to 17 the rate of substance dependence or abuse was similar (8.7 to 9.0 percent).[12]

- Women are more susceptible than men to rapid onset of addiction and health problems once they begin drinking;[13] this disparity may be partly due to women's higher fat and lower water ratios, which may impair their ability to metabolize alcohol.[14]
- In treatment, females have more health problems than males, including respiratory, gynecological, heart, and digestive conditions.[15]
- Depression often precedes substance use in females, so use seems to be a coping response.
- Many females with substance use problems have a history of physical or sexual abuse (both as children and adults),[16] and a history of victimization is associated with a worse outcome.
- Financial barriers such as lack of money, health insurance, child care, and transportation, as well as the fear of social stigma associated with substance abuse, may contribute to women's underrepresentation in treatment[17]
- Women often develop substance use problems in the context of relationships with substance abusing male partners.[18]

OLDER ADULTS

- Age bias among health care providers may present obstacles to assessment of substance use disorders in the elderly,[19] as providers may not believe that elders can benefit from intervention or that their quality of life would improve as a result.

states and depression, overall, play a greater role for adults than teenagers, whose main risk typically involves a social context (Chung & Maisto, 2006). Negative mood is a particular risk for women, while positive mood is associated with relapse for men.

Other gender differences in relapse involve marital and interpersonal conflict for women; for men, being unmarried or alone presents risk (Walitzer & Dearing, 2006). Being married may not be protective for women because they are often partnered with men who have substance use problems.

---

[1]Abbot, 1994; Nelson-Zlupko et al., 1995.
[2]Breslau, Kendler, Su, et al., 2005.
[3]Mirin et al., 2002; Corrao, Bagnardi, Zambon, & Arico, 1999.
[4]Surgeon General, 1999; Huang et al., 2006.
[5]Surgeon General, 1999.
[6]Mirin et al., 2002.
[7]Wells, Klap, Koike, & Sherbourne, 2001.
[8]Castro, Proescholdbell, Abeita, & Rodriquez, 1999.
[9]Huang et al., 2006; Stinson et al., 2005.
[10]SAMHSA, 2006.
[11]Beatty, Geckle, Huggins, et al., 1999.
[12]SAMHSA, 2006.
[13]Abbot, 1994; Nelson-Zlupko, Kauffman, & Dore, 1995.
[14]Abbott, 1994.
[15]Wechsberg, Craddock, & Hubbard, 1998.
[16]Orwin, Maranda, & Brady, 2001.
[17]Nelson-Zlupko, Kauffman, & Dore, 1995.
[18]Ashley, Marsden, & Brady, 2003.
[19]Vinton & Wambach, 2005.

For adolescents, among pretreatment, treatment, and post-treatment factors, it was the latter, including participation in aftercare and AA meetings, a lack of substance- using peers, involvement in a variety of non-substance-related activities, use of coping strategies learned in treatment, and motivation to continue sobriety, that had the most influence on outcomes (Chung & Maisto, 2006).

Directions Part II, Biopsychosocial Risk and Resilience Assessment: Formulate a risk and resilience assessment, both for the onset of the disorder and the course of the disorder, including the strengths that you see for this individual.

TABLE 8.1 Biopsychosocial Risk and Resilience Assessment for the Onset of the Disorder

RISK INFLUENCES	PROTECTIVE INFLUENCES
Biological	
Psychological	
Social	

TABLE 8.2 Biopsychosocial Risk and Resilience Assessment for the Course of the Disorder

Risk Influences	*Protective Influences*
Biological	
Psychological	
Social	

What techniques could you use to elicit additional strengths in this client?

Intervention Goals

Intervention goals for clients who abuse substances are summarized in Figure 8.3. Generally speaking, permanent abstinence is the major goal of intervention. Whether adult clients can manage controlled drinking is a controversial topic. Abstinence is always recommended for adolescents (Bukstein et al., 1997), but controlled alcohol use may be a possibility for some adults (Weinberg et al., 1998). Controlled drinking may also be an interim goal for some people or may be appropriate in the early stages of alcohol abuse (Mirin et al., 2002). Walters (2002) conducted a meta-analysis of 17 studies on behavioral self-control training, an intervention used to help people control their drinking, and concluded that it showed effectiveness comparable to abstinence-based programs. Such self-control techniques include spacing out drinks, prolonging the duration of drinks, switching to lower-proof drinks, avoiding high-risk situations, and self-monitoring.

Intervention

About half of those with a substance use disorder will eventually make treatment contact (Wang, Berglund, Olfson, et al., 2005), although past-year treatment seeking is low: 6 percent for people with alcohol use disorders, 16 percent for people with drug use disorders, and 22 percent for people with both alcohol and drug use disorders (Stinson et al., 2005). Commonly available treatment settings include (in order of usage) outpatient rehabilitation facilities, inpatient rehabilitation facilities, inpatient hospitals, and outpatient mental

FIGURE 8.3 Intervention Goals.

1. Reduce or eliminate substance use.
2. Improve psychological and social functioning by mending disrupted relationships, reducing impulsivity, building social and vocational skills, and maintaining employment.
3. Prevent relapse by discussing the client's ambivalence about sobriety, identifying the emotional and environmental triggers of craving, developing coping strategies to deal with internal or external stressors, exploring the chain of decisions leading to the resumption of substance use, and learning from brief relapse episodes (slips) about triggers leading to relapse so as to develop effective techniques for early intervention.

FOR ADOLESCENTS
1. Improve family communication.
2. Train parents to provide proper guidance and limit setting for the youth.
3. Recognize and, if possible, treat addiction patterns in the parents.
4. Help adolescents and their families to develop alcohol- and drug-free lifestyles.

Sources: Larimer, Palmer, & Marlatt, 1999; Bukstein et al., 1997.

health centers (SAMHSA, 2006). Some programs are specifically designed for adolescents, pregnant or postpartum women, and women with young children. Many people receive intervention from locations that are not specialized for the treatment of these disorders, including self-help groups, private doctors' offices, emergency rooms, and prisons or jails (SAMHSA, 2006).

Client characteristics that influence decision making about the most appropriate treatment setting include the perceived potential harm of withdrawal, the severity of comorbid health and mental health concerns, the level of previous treatment response, and the extent of environmental support for the client's sobriety (Mirin et al., 2002). These risks need to be addressed in treatment with either a high degree of community support or temporary removal from those circumstances through residential treatment. Regardless of the treatment site or modalities utilized, positive outcomes are associated with the frequency, intensity, and duration of treatment participation (Mirin et al., 2002; Prendergast, Podus, & Change, 2000).

Psychosocial Treatments

Although Alcoholics Anonymous (AA) models of recovery have tended to dominate the substance abuse field (Fuller & Hiller-Sturmhofel, 1999; Kelly, Myers, & Brown, 2002; Sheehan & Owen, 1999), social workers should be aware of alternatives for people who need help with substance use disorders. Here, we will talk about AA, alternative self-help groups, motivational interviewing, cognitive behavioral treatment, and family interventions. In AA self-help groups, the participant reaches and maintains abstinence by moving through a series of 12 steps with the assistance of a support group and sponsor. AA and NA (Narcotics Anonymous) self-help groups have been shown to increase abstinence, self-efficacy, and social functioning for those who attend, especially when they engage in outside activities with people they meet at AA (Humphreys, Wing, McCarty, et al., 2004). However, self-help groups should probably not act as a substitute for professional intervention, especially for those who are mandated to attend treatment; nonvoluntary clients typically do not stop drinking when attending AA (Kownacki & Shadish, 1999). AA treatment models have also been developed as a treatment modality. In one large-scale study called Project MATCH, such a treatment was as effective as other treatments, especially for those who initially showed severe dependence and for those whose social networks supported drinking (Longabaugh et al., 1998; Project MATCH Research Group, 1997).

The reader should be aware that, in addition to 12-step groups, there are alternative self-help groups available to clients. These include Secular Organization for Sobriety, SMART Recovery, Women for Sobriety, & Moderation Management (Humphreys, Wing, McCarty, et al., 2004).

As the reader may know, many people who present to treatment are not willing to change and maintain they do not have a problem. One treatment approach, motivational interviewing, has been designed for such nonvoluntary clients. Motivational interviewing focuses on exploring and resolving the ambivalence people have about changing (Miller &

Rollnick, 2002; Walitzer, Dermen, & Conners, 1999). It can be used as a stand-alone intervention or as a way to engage clients in other interventions. The benefits of motivational interviewing are that it can be implemented in a brief fashion, it has proven validity (Burke, Arkowitz, & Dunn, 2002), and it can be effective with clients who demonstrate high levels of anger (Longabaugh et al., 1998; Project MATCH Research Group, 1997).

Cognitive behavioral therapy can also be targeted at substance use problems (McCrady, 2005). It focuses on altering thought processes that lead to maladaptive substance use, intervening in the behavioral chain of events that led to substance use, helping clients deal successfully with craving, and promoting the development of social skills and behaviors compatible with remaining sober. Other cognitive-behavioral treatments that are part of family intervention are described below.

Families have tremendous potential impact on either perpetuating or ameliorating the substance abuse problems of a family member, including the abuser's ability and willingness to comply with intervention (Mirin et al., 2002). Studies have consistently found a higher rate of improvement when families were involved in treatment than when they were not (Edwards & Steinglass, 1995). In addition, most family interventions were superior to alternative conditions in terms of the client's length of time in treatment and reduced drug use (Stanton & Shadish, 1997). Family therapy approaches have received the most attention for adolescent substance use disorders (Weinberg et al., 1998) and are the treatment of choice for adolescents. Such therapy models include brief strategic family therapy (Szapocznik & Williams, 2000), functional family therapy (Alexander & Parsons, 1982), multidimensional family therapy (Liddle, Dakof, & Parker, 2001), and multisystemic therapy (Henggeler, Schoenwald, Borduin, et al., 1998).

For the partners of people with addictions, Al-Anon has been a widely used intervention approach. However, unilateral therapy (Thomas, Santa, Bronson, & Oyserman, 1987), also referred to as reinforcement training (Sisson & Azrin, 1986), "Pressures to Change" (Barber & Gilbertson, 1996), and coping skills training (Rychtarik & McGillicuddy, 2005), may be effective for those who want to reduce their partner's drinking. In these interventions, family members are trained on how to exert influence on the drinker so that the person may develop motivation to change. The research shows that these approaches have resulted in the person with substance use entering treatment at a significantly higher rate and with reduced drinking than in the comparison conditions. An additional advantage of the coping skills training approach was that it reduced both violence and drinking in partners who were violent (Rychtarik & McGillicuddy, 2005).

Couples intervention may be indicated when there is marital conflict along with substance abuse and both partners are motivated to participate. These interventions are cognitive-behavioral in nature and involve building communication skills, planning family activities, initiating caring behaviors, and expressing feelings (McCrady, Noel, Abrams, Stout, Nelson, et al., 1986). The interventions are typically brief (15 sessions or fewer), and even briefer forms of the treatment have recently been developed (Fals-Stewart, O'Farrell, & Birchler, 2005). Results from three decades of research with married

FIGURE 8.4 Guidelines for the Treatment of Co-Occurring Mental Health and Substance Use Disorders.

1. Concrete needs, such as shelter and physical health, must be a priority (Rosenthal & Westreich, 1999).
2. The mental disorder should first be stabilized.
3. Motivational interviewing may help people comply with mental health treatment and substance use treatment.
4. Confrontation, a common approach in many substance abuse treatment settings, may not be effective for clients who are psychotic or potentially suicidal, and a supportive approach is suggested instead.
5. For clients with depression and anxiety, cognitive-behavioral therapy can address both the psychiatric and substance use concerns.
6. The initial phase of substance abuse treatment may be crucial to successful engagement and retention, so developing interventions that focus on improving early success in clients who are depressed may be beneficial (Conner, Sorensen, & Leonard, 2005).

Sources: Petrakis et al., 2002; Martino, Carroll, Kostas, et al., 2002.

or cohabiting men with substance use disorders have found that this intervention offers many advantages over individual treatment, among them reduced substance use, fewer arrests, fewer hospitalizations, improved relationship satisfaction, reduced family violence, improved adjustment in children living in the home, and better cost-benefit and cost-effectiveness (Fals-Stewart, O'Farrell, & Birchler, 2005). Research in this area has focused mainly on males with substance use disorders and their spouses or cohabiting partners.

As discussed, other mental health problems often coexist with substance use disorders. Some guidelines have been developed for the treatment of people with co-occurring psychiatric and substance use disorders (Petrakis et al., 2002), as summarized in Figure 8.4.

Pharmacologic Interventions

Two types of medications are currently used in substance abuse treatment, including aversive medications (such as Antabuse), designed to deter client drinking, and anticraving medications (known as the antidipsotropics), which purport to reduce the desire to drink (Fuller & Hiller-Sturmhoffel, 1999). Studies of Antabuse have shown that compliance is associated with abstinence (Fuller & Hiller-Sturmhofel, 1999). Although meta-analyses of the anticraving medications, naltrexone and acamprosate, have shown small effects (Kranzler & Van Kirk, 2001; Mann, Lehert, & Morgan, 2004; Streeton & Whelan, 2001), a large-scale study of over 1,300 people with alcohol dependence showed that naltrexone alone (but not acamprosate) was effective in reducing drinking (Anton, O'Malley, Ciraulo, et al., 2006).

Directions Part III, Goal Setting and Treatment Planning: Given your risk and resilience assessments of the individual, your knowledge of the disorder, and evidence-based practice guidelines, formulate goals and a possible treatment plan for this individual.

Critical Perspective

A major problem with the DSM criteria for substance-related disorders is their differential relevance to persons of different age groups. One criterion for dependence, for example, is the person's increased tolerance to the effects of the substance, resulting in increased consumption over time. For older adults, changes related to physiology and the effects of prescription drugs may alter their drug tolerance (Surgeon General, 1999). They may decrease consumption with no reduction in intoxication. Further, diagnostic criteria that relate to the impact of drug use on typical tasks of young and middle adulthood may be largely irrelevant to older adults. For these reasons abuse and dependence among older adults may be underestimated.

Additionally, DSM criteria for negative consequences may not be applicable to adolescents who do not face immediate adverse consequences. For substance use dependence, the required symptoms—craving, tolerance, and withdrawal—have not been established for adolescents (Bukstein & Kaminer, 1994). Therefore, it has been suggested that criteria should be developed specific to adolescence.

Finally, for adolescents substance use may be part of a constellation of conduct problems. For example, in one study of 1,774 adolescents detained in the juvenile justice system, almost half had at least one substance use disorder (McClelland, Elkington, Teplin, & Abram, 2004). In addition, in 2003 more than half (53 percent) of adolescent admissions were referred to treatment through the criminal justice system (SAMHSA, 2006). Indeed, the risk and protective influences for the development of conduct problems and substance use are very similar. It is not that one problem causes another, but that they co-occur (Wei, Loeber, & White, 2004). A recommendation to deal with the diagnosis of adolescent substance use, therefore, is to subsume diagnostic criteria under conduct disorders (Bukstein & Kaminer, 1994).

Directions Part IV, Critical Perspective: Formulate a critique of the diagnosis as it relates to this case example. Questions to consider include: Does this diagnosis represent a valid mental disorder from the social work perspective? Is this diagnosis significantly different from other possible diagnoses? Your critique should be based on the values of the social work profession (which are incongruent in some ways with the medical model) and the validity of the specific diagnostic criteria applied to this case.

CASE 2

Janelle is a 53-year-old widowed Caucasian female who began individual therapy three months ago in a women's outpatient substance abuse program as a self-referral. She wants to quit drinking once and for all, and also to get help for a deepening depression. She reports having been "depressed" since the death of her second husband four years ago (of a heart attack), but this has gotten worse in the past six months as she has tried to stop drinking.

Janelle has abused alcohol on and off since she was 15. She takes no other drugs. Janelle's father and one of her uncles were alcohol abusers, and her adult daughter (age 29) drinks heavily.

When Janelle began individual therapy, she reported having drunk approximately ten beers a day during a previous nine-month time span, which ended six months ago (after which her depression began to worsen). During that time, she drank in larger and larger amounts to achieve the desired effect, despite the fact that she was aware of the possible negative effects on her health. Janelle states that her impulse to drink was strong whenever she tried to stop, and that she experienced spells of shaking when she went without alcohol. Janelle reports having abused alcohol for many years before that, but not on a daily basis. She was more of a "binge drinker," drinking mixed drinks in bars and at home to the point of passing out, alone or with friends, once every week or two. Janelle currently reports having abstained from alcohol for the past six months, except for two episodes of binge drinking since she began treatment one month ago. These episodes were related to being alone and feeling lonely.

Janelle admits that she feels "terrible" about herself, since she continues to drink so much at times. "I must be a real weakling to have to rely on alcohol and not be able to quit. I'm certainly not very attractive in this condition." In addition to the issues related to her drinking, Janelle reports experiencing intense feelings of loneliness that she attributes to a long-term sadness due to the loss of her second husband.

Janelle also has a serious physical condition. She was diagnosed with type II diabetes eight years ago and currently adheres to a special diet to control that illness. She reports several past hospitalizations due to dehydration, which frequently occurs in persons with type II diabetes. Janelle reports that she must be sure to drink enough liquids and watch out for symptoms such as dizziness and feeling weak. Janelle has also experienced episodes of nausea and vomiting since undergoing stomach surgery for an ulcer four months ago. Her doctor had told her to expect periods of nausea related to her stomach condition. Janelle reports that she used to "love food," but since the stomach surgery she has experienced a decreased appetite and general lack of interest in food. She finds this very frustrating and admits that "now and then" she "forgets" about her diet and just eats what she wants, even though she may feel ill afterward. She has been warned by physicians that drinking alcohol is hard on her stomach, and while this serves as a motivator for her to stop, she still can't "just do it." She sees her medical doctor regularly but cannot sustain the treatment plans he initiates with her.

Janelle is currently working as a clerk at a coffee shop. She seems to have a strong work ethic and has had a variety of jobs throughout her adolescent and adult life. They are all unskilled jobs, as Janelle has only a high school diploma and never "sets out to work in one place for too long, because my kids have always needed me." Her three children are adults now, but she is highly involved in the lives of her two grandchildren, often caring for them. Janelle misses work occasionally due to oversleeping or being hung over, but she has never lost a job due to this behavior. She states that she is considered to be "likable" and a "good worker." She adds that "working has been especially helpful since my husband died," because it keeps her mind off her sadness. She admits that if she doesn't have to go to work in the morning, she tends to lie in bed alone for many hours, feeling preoccupied with her sadness and crying about her lack of "purpose" in life.

Janelle currently lives alone in an apartment. She is in regular contact with her children. Although her family relationships provide her with support, they are also sources of stress in Janelle's life. Her children make frequent and last-minute demands on her time for child care and financial assistance. Janelle currently has a romantic partner, who is separated but still involved with his wife. She views this relationship as shallow and temporary, and she wonders if she will ever again be close to a man. In addition to still grieving the loss of her second husband, she is also mourning the recent death of a good friend. Janelle currently has few friends, and while her church community is a possible source of support, she is not currently very involved with it. Janelle does not have regular transportation and must rely on friends and family in order to meet this need.

Despite her current stresses she enjoys some activities, most notably fishing and cooking. She greatly values her role as a grandmother. Janelle also maintains a sense of humor about her physical health, her often stressful relationships with her children, and her overall life situation.

Janelle grew up in a rural community in the mountains of Virginia. She was raised and continues to identify as Baptist. She considers herself a religious person, and she attended church regularly in the past.

Janelle also grew up in a household that featured emotional and physical family violence. Her father was alcohol-dependent and physically and emotionally abusive toward Janelle, her two brothers, and her mother. Janelle identifies using alcohol as one way she learned to cope with the trauma and stress of her family situation. Alcohol was easily obtained in her community, even by adolescents, and Janelle states that she began to enjoy the "buzz" from whisky and wine very quickly after she began drinking. She and her friends often drank in each other's homes and in the nearby woods and were rarely caught or confronted about their activity.

Shortly after graduating from high school, Janelle married a man she believed would be a "good provider." She states that her attraction to the man, whom she never knew "too well," abated after a year or so, but she stayed in that emotionally abusive marriage for the next 20 years, because "I had kids then." He berated her as a wife, parent, and person. Janelle worked a series of unskilled part-time jobs during those years and says she was never happy. She saw her life as "all stress and all work." She was prone to spells of extreme hopelessness in which she stayed in bed, wished that she could die, and wondered why there was nothing "pleasurable" in her life. Janelle reports that in the past six months, and at several other times in her life, she experienced symptoms such as low mood, fatigue, feelings of worthlessness, excessive guilt, and trouble falling asleep.

Please go to the Appendix for directions to this case. The following questions will help to guide your thinking about a possible multi-axial diagnosis.

Questions to consider when formulating a response to a diagnosis for Janelle

1. What range of problems does Janelle herself believe she is experiencing?

2. How long has Janelle's problematic substance use been occurring?

3. Does Janelle experience negative consequences from her use of substances?

4. Does Janelle show tolerance for and withdrawal symptoms from alcohol?

5. How long have Janelle's low moods been occurring?

6. What recent stressors has Janelle experienced? Would these stressors warrant a diagnosis of adjustment disorder?

7. Do Janelle's drinking behaviors occur only in certain mood states? What is the relationship between Janelle's drinking and her moods?

CASE 3

Larry is a 27-year-old Caucasian male who lost his driver's license six months ago after his third DUI offense; he is required to complete a substance abuse program in order to have the license reinstated. He kept drinking on the first two occasions he was placed in the program and refused to attend the required weekly AA meetings. This is the last opportunity the agency will give him to comply with the program requirements before they close his case. Larry came to the interview at the treatment facility well dressed and spoke articulately. He was somewhat fidgety, constantly wringing his hands and shifting in his seat. He also had some difficulty keeping his train of thought as he spoke about his situation, stating that he felt "distracted."

Larry started using marijuana when he was 14 and drinking when he was 16. He was arrested for several drug- and alcohol-related offenses in his youth, and spent time in a juvenile justice facility as a result. He was diagnosed with ADHD when he was in elementary school and struggled with all academic subjects, especially math. He was on Ritalin for several years but is no longer taking it. He dropped out of school during his senior year because he was making so much money dealing drugs that he did not see the need to continue struggling in school. He later completed his GED while serving a jail sentence for dealing.

Larry is now working as a realtor, but his business is suffering because he cannot drive. While he seems motivated to complete the program so that he can get his license back, he believes he has learned to "control" his drinking and sees no problem with his regular marijuana use. When asked what he means by "controlling" his drinking, he said that the three DUIs got his attention and he doesn't want to get into further legal trouble. He now drinks only "a couple of beers" on weekdays; on weekends, he consumes a six pack each night. He no longer drinks at bars since he can't drive and can't afford to buy drinks. He says he is not seeing much of his friends lately because of his transportation problems. Another reason he views his alcohol use as not being a problem is that his friends tend to drink more than he does. In contrast, he sees himself as only a social drinker.

In sum, Larry does not think he should be in a substance abuse program. He also thinks he should be given credit for the few weeks he attended the program in the past, so that his current requirements could be shortened. Larry is disgusted that he is required to attend AA, stating that he is "not like those people" and asking, "How am I supposed to attend all these meetings and groups if I can't drive?"

Larry is the older of two boys. His parents divorced when he was 11, leaving his family to struggle financially. He is close to his mother. Larry considers his mother his strongest support and often turns to her for help. He says she is sympathetic to his driving prohibition, and she sometimes takes him places he needs to go. She supports his need to seek treatment so that he can get his license back, but according to Larry, "she doesn't think I have a problem either." Larry has not kept in touch with his father, and his relationship with his brother is somewhat strained. Larry claims that his brother is the source of much of his stress and that he has a lot of resentment toward him. It seems that Larry and his brother started a business together that is not working out, and Larry feels his brother is to blame. Members of Larry's paternal family (an uncle and grandfather) have a history of alcohol use disorders.

Larry is currently living with his girlfriend of 18 months and their three-month-old daughter in an apartment. His relationship with his girlfriend has been a major source of stress for the last six months. They were engaged to be married but have broken the engagement, as Larry wants to "move on." Though they still live together, they are not getting along, and Larry is having a hard time dealing with the tension. He says they argue about his inadequate earnings, his drinking and marijuana use, and his children from the previous marriage. Larry admits he gets so frustrated with the situation that he has been violent with his girlfriend, usually when drinking. She has called the police, and Larry has been arrested twice for family violence. When questioned about these episodes, Larry says, "I've never hit her." He does, however, admit to once pinning her against the wall and "getting in her face." He also shoved her out of the way when she blocked his way out of a room, which on at least one occasion resulted in her being knocked to the floor.

Larry has three children from a previous marriage whom he cares for every other weekend. His relationship with his ex-wife is acrimonious according to his description. His oldest child, who is six, was diagnosed with leukemia three years ago. During that time, Larry was taking antidepressants to help him deal with "that gut-wrenching situation." The child's cancer is now in remission, and Larry is no longer taking the medication. When asked, he said that he did not notice if his distractibility and fidgeting were any better on antidepressants as "I had other things on my mind." He says that he does not feel depressed currently but is "stressed out."

Larry says he smokes marijuana to help him relax, and that it is the only thing that helps him in this way. He has used it at least twice a week for several years in the evening. He finds using marijuana preferable to being on medication. He does not report tolerance, saying that he has always smoked one joint "to get high" and this amount has not changed in years.

Larry considers himself in excellent health and reports that "everything checked out fine" at a physical examination about a year ago. He suffers from asthma, but keeps it under control by using an inhaler before he exercises. He is not currently taking any other medications. He tries to work out every day and notices that he is having an easier time working out since he quit smoking last month.

Larry states that he has problems sleeping. It is not hard for him to fall asleep, but he wakes frequently and has trouble getting back to sleep. He feels that he does not get enough "deep sleep" to feel refreshed in the morning. Larry also complains that he feels anxious all the time and cannot remember when he has not felt that way. He worries about his children, his relationship with his girlfriend, his job, and his need to complete this program. He feels this anxiety in his stomach and in his head and neck.

Given his visible symptoms of distractibility and hyperactivity and the fact that Larry was diagnosed with ADHD as a child, the social work intern asked about other symptoms of inattention, hyperactivity, and impulsivity. In regard to inattention, Larry admitted to avoiding tasks that take a lot of mental energy and having difficulty keeping his attention on paperwork. He says that he would probably make more money if he were better organized. He says that his girlfriend complains about his forgetfulness and inattentiveness to her, even when she speaks to him directly. With regard to hyperactivity, Larry fidgets, but he denies any of the other symptoms when asked about them. However, he admits to "feeling restless" if he does not drink or smoke marijuana in the evenings.

Please go to the Appendix for directions to this case. The following questions will help to guide your thinking about a possible multi-axial diagnosis.

Questions to consider when formulating a diagnosis for Larry

1. How do you differentiate between Larry's substance use as abuse or dependence?

2. Since Larry admits to drinking and smoking marijuana regularly, how do you know whether to attribute his other symptoms to his substance use or to decide if they warrant a diagnosis of their own?

3. Could some of Larry's other symptoms (restlessness, stress) be caused by his substance use?

4. How do you account for Larry's symptoms of restlessness, fidgeting, and anxiety?

5. Larry was diagnosed with ADHD as a child; does he still seem to warrant this diagnosis?

6. Has Larry experienced recent stressors? Can they be accounted for in a diagnosis?

7. Of obvious concern are Larry's family violence episodes with his girlfriend. How can you account for these in a diagnosis?

9

— ▾▲▾ —

Schizophrenia

Anna Yannucci is a 26-year-old single Caucasian female who was referred to the outpatient mental health facility following a two-week stay at a psychiatric unit of a local hospital. A report from the hospital indicated that her father, Thomas Yannucci, took Anna to the hospital from an apartment where she had been staying for two weeks with a 45-year-old man. Her father believed that this man was a drug user and barely knew his daughter. Mr. Yannucci had learned where Anna was staying when she called him one day to ask for money. He came to the apartment immediately and found that his daughter was apparently not eating well, not changing or washing her clothes, not going outside, and not communicating coherently. When her father arrived, Anna was sitting still and remained quiet, watching television absently. When spoken to, she replied in polite but short phrases and rarely initiated conversation. She seemed "lost in her own little world." Mr. Yannucci brought Anna home from the apartment and later that day drove her to the emergency services unit of the hospital. Mr. Yannucci stated that his daughter "behaves like this much of the time" but he thought that she had lately become even more difficult to communicate with. He added that she always "sat around, spaced out" when she was in her own apartment.

Schizophrenia is a mental disorder characterized by a person's abnormal patterns of thought and perception. It is a *psychotic* disorder, that is, a mental state in which the person's thoughts and perceptions are severely impaired. Schizophrenia includes two types of symptoms (APA, 2000). *Positive symptoms represent exaggerations of normal behavior* and include hallucinations, delusions, disorganized thinking, and tendencies toward agitation. *Negative* symptoms represent the absence of what would be considered normal behavior and include flat affect (the absence of expression), social withdrawal, noncommunication, passivity, and ambivalence in decision making.

Prevalence and Comorbidity

Schizophrenia has a worldwide prevalence of approximately 1 percent (Murray, Jones, & Susser, 2003). Data from the National Institute of Mental Health-sponsored Epidemiological Catchment Area research project noted the lifetime prevalence of schizophrenia to be 1.3 percent in the United States (APA, 2000). Schizophrenia tends to be diagnosed among African-American persons more frequently than among Caucasians. This imbalance may result because practitioners attribute and weigh particular symptoms differently for clients of different races (Trierweiler, Neighbors, Munday, Thompson, Binion, et al., 2000). Clinicians of Caucasian origin tend to interpret the suspicious attitudes of African-Americans as symptomatic of schizophrenia, representing delusions or negative symptoms, when these attitudes may in fact be protective in situations of perceived discrimination.

Persons with schizophrenia have a high rate of comorbidity for other DSM disorders. A recent national comorbidity study found that 79.4 percent of persons with lifetime nonaffective psychosis (most often schizophrenia) meet the criteria for one or more other disorders (Kessler, Birnbaum, Demler, Falloon, Gagnon, et al., 2005). These include a mood disorder (most often major depression) (52.6 percent), anxiety disorders (especially the phobias, post-traumatic stress disorder [PTSD], and panic disorder) (62.9 percent), and substance abuse (26.8 percent). A recent meta-analysis found that persons with schizophrenia who abuse substances experience fewer negative symptoms than those who are abstinent (Potvin, Sepehry, & Strip, 2006). This suggests either that substance abuse relieves negative symptoms or that persons with fewer negative symptoms are more prone to substance use. Along these same lines, several studies have found that nicotine use helps to alleviate psychotic symptoms in some persons with schizophrenia (Punnoose & Belgamwar, 2006).

Assessment

The clinical assessment of schizophrenia is done through client interviews, interviews with significant others, and history gathering. There are no tests currently available that conclusively determine when schizophrenia is present. See Figure 9.1 for assessment guidelines.

The admission report stated that Anna had been living with her younger sister in a condominium owned by her father for the past six months. She met the man with whom she was most recently staying at a fast-food restaurant. He had bought her lunch and then invited her to his apartment, where he lived alone. Mr. Yannucci did not know why Anna would accept the invitation, but he added that, "she does crazy things sometimes." He thought that the man wanted to take advantage of his daughter financially.

Doctors at the hospital ordered a variety of neurological tests to rule out physical causes of Anna's symptoms. A toxicology screen found no traces of drugs in her system. While at the hospital Anna was cooperative, except that

FIGURE 9.1 Assessment of Schizophrenia.

ADULTS

- Criterion A for schizophrenia requires two of the following symptoms: delusions, hallucinations, disorganized speech, grossly disorganized or catatonic behavior, and negative symptoms for a period of one month.
- Assess for the duration of active symptoms, which may rule out brief reactive psychosis or schizophreniform disorder.
- Refer client for medical evaluation to rule out any medical conditions that may be contributing to symptom development.
- Assess whether the client abuses substances or is currently under the influence of a drug that may be causing symptoms.
- Assess for psychosocial stressors that may be contributing to symptom development.
- Assess for psychotic or mood disorders among relatives.
- Assess the family system for the possibility of stresses that may precipitate an onset of psychotic symptoms.
- Assess for mood swings at present or in the client's history that may indicate a schizoaffective, major depressive, or bipolar disorder.
- Assess for premorbid functioning to determine the presence of a possible schizoptypal, schizoid, or paranoid personality disorder.
- The practitioner must be careful to rule out the possibility of organic, major affective, pervasive developmental, obsessive-compulsive, and substance use disorders.

CHILDHOOD

- In cases of childhood psychosis, rule out the presence or influence of developmental, anxiety, and mood disorders.
- Visual hallucinations and disorganized speech may be more common than delusions and hallucinations.

she refused to consider taking medications. When asked for her reasons, she replied simply, "I just don't want to." Staff efforts to help the client elaborate on any of her thoughts and feelings were not successful. In fact, Anna seemed to become mildly irritable when asked questions, always saying, rather politely but in a monotone, "I just don't have a lot to talk about right now." She rarely made direct eye contact with staff but tended to stare blankly. Anna did seem to enjoy walking about the unit, and the nursing staff reported that she often appeared to be talking to herself. Her mood was quite consistent, but as one nurse wrote, "the patient doesn't seem to be feeling anything."

Anna's condominium was located one mile from the mental health agency. She walked to her first appointment alone, arriving on time and with the card in her hand. Her father met her there, coming from his job at a bakery. Anna was dressed appropriately but appeared not to have changed her clothes or bathed in the recent past. She exuded such a strong, disagreeable odor that support staff at the agency complained to the director about her presence in the waiting room. Anna seemed oblivious to this condition. Upon questioning, she denied hearing voices but seemed highly distracted at times, as if her attention were focused on somewhere far away. She minimized the issues of her personal hygiene, saying that she eats "something good every day" and bathes "when I need to." Her answers to all questions were brief. She seemed preoccupied but not upset about being at the agency.

Anna stated that she spent most of her time at home but added, "I like to take walks for exercise." When asked to elaborate, she said that she took walks every day to nearby fast-food restaurants or the bank to deposit and withdraw money. She did not have a job, did not attend school, and was not involved in any recreational activities. When asked about her goals in these areas, she said, "I'd like to have a job someday when I'm ready." When asked about any friends, she said, "I'd like to have friends someday," but about the present, she said, "People can't be trusted." Anna stated that she got along with her sister, but that "we don't really talk much." Thirty minutes into the interview Anna said, "It's nice meeting you, but I should go now." The social worker asked if she would mind waiting in the room or outside on the porch while he talked with her father. She agreed, and walked outside. Throughout this interview Anna had maintained the same blank look on her face, revealing no emotional content.

Mr. Yannucci remained for another half hour and provided much background information. He is a 50-year-old Italian-American who came to the United States when he was ten years old. He has worked successfully in the restaurant business for the past 30 years, always maintaining strong ties to the Italian community in his city. The welfare of his family is paramount to him. He clearly does not understand what might be "wrong" with his daughter, and he tends to see her behavior as "willful misbehaving." Yet he tried hard to understand her as he told the story of her background.

"I have to be responsible for my daughter. It is a father's responsibility to care for his family. But I do not understand why she does not try harder. Anna's mother and I never got along. I was the breadwinner and she was the mother, and she became very strange not long after we married. She stayed home all the time and sometimes did not come out of her room. She cried often for no good reason and did not do enough to take care of Anna, her sister, and me. She talked about crazy things and never made sense. Sometimes she walked away from home and did not return for days. Sometimes the hospital would call me—or the police would. She was always wandering around looking for Lord knows what, finally getting into trouble when she stole food and objects out of people's yards. I did my best to help her get more rest and get outside more with good people, but it did not work. Her behavior became worse as the years went on. Finally, she left me for good. I don't know where she is, but she lives here in town. A few times she comes to get money from me, but that's all.

"Anna was a good girl growing up. She wanted to be a nurse, and she got good grades in school. Every day she came home from school and went to her room and studied. But she was not a sociable girl. She never had a boyfriend. That was good, because I didn't want her with dangerous boys. She stayed home and studied and helped take care of me and her sister Beth. She never talked much, but she behaved well and was respectful."

When asked for details about Anna's functioning as a child and adolescent, Mr. Yannucci stated, "She did not ever seem to be happy, but that's only because she was serious, which is a good thing. She didn't have friends, but that was fine, too, because she was busy at home. She never wanted to go out and play in the neighborhood, even as a young girl. Like I said, she kept to herself and studied. She didn't need much help from her mother or me. She was independent.

"I didn't want her going to college, but Anna was determined. She lived at home and went to the university, but she did not do well. She stopped going to school and started staying in her room more. She was still helping out around the house, but not as much, and it got worse. After about a year she started to loaf all the time and sat in the television room alone. She started having bad dreams, because I could hear her screaming many nights in her bedroom. Many times I would notice her talking to herself, but when I asked what she was doing she got quiet and said, 'Nothing.'

"Two years ago I met my current wife, Margaret, and she did not care for Anna's behavior at all. Margaret thought that Anna was 'crazy,' which is a terrible thing to say about someone. She thought that Anna should be forced to move away or go to school again, and leave us to our new life. But my wife is a good person. She thought that I was babying Anna, and that I should make her live on her own. But I can't do that. So as a compromise I got a condominium for Anna and her sister. Margaret told me that she would not marry me unless I did that. I go and see them every day! I plead with Anna to get a job and to get busy, but she will not do it. She stays home and does nothing. She is a nice girl, so why would she not want to be busy and have friends? I don't understand her. And lately she has started wandering off, just like her mother."

At this point, the interview ended. Anna returned to the room for a few minutes and politely declined an offer to see a physician for a medication evaluation. She did agree to come back to the agency in two days to meet with the social worker again. "It wouldn't hurt anything" was her response to the invitation.

Directions Part I, Multi-Axial Diagnosis: Given the case information and your responses to the questions below, prepare the following: a multi-axial diagnosis, the rationale for the diagnosis and GAF score, and additional information you would have wanted to know in order to make a more accurate diagnosis.

Questions to consider when formulating a diagnosis for Anna

1. What symptoms of problematic thinking, feeling, and behavior does Anna present?

2. Are any of the above symptoms clearly psychotic?

3. Is it possible that Anna has, or has had, a mood or schizoaffective disorder?

4. How does Anna's poor communication complicate the process of her assessment and diagnosis?

5. Is there evidence of a premorbid personality disorder in this client?

6. How would you characterize Anna's childhood and adolescent functioning, given the information presented?

Additional Information Needed

Multi-Axial Diagnosis

Axis I:

Axis II:

Axis III:

Axis IV:

Axis V:

Rationale and Differential Diagnosis

Biopsychosocial Risk and Resilience Influences

Onset

The specific causes of schizophrenia are not known. Its onset and course are likely due to a mix of biological, psychological, and perhaps some social influences (Cardno & Murray, 2003). Many persons who develop schizophrenia display what is called *premorbid* or "early warning" signs. These include social withdrawal, a loss of interest in life activities, deterioration in self-care, and a variety of "odd" behaviors. The signs can exist for many years, but even when present they do *not* guarantee the eventual onset of schizophrenia. The *stress/diathesis theory* holds that schizophrenia results from a mix of heritability and biological influences (perhaps 70 percent) and environmental and stress factors (approximately 30 percent) (Cardno & Murray, 2003), which may include insults to the brain, threatening physical environments, emotionally intrusive or demanding experiences, and emotional deprivation.

See Figure 9.2 for a summary of issues related to the diagnosis of schizophrenia in special populations.

BIOLOGICAL INFLUENCES

Biological theories of schizophrenia implicate the brain's limbic system (center of emotional activity), frontal cortex (governing personality, emotion, and reasoning), and basal ganglia (regulating muscle and skeletal movement) as primary sites of malfunction (Conklin & Iacono, 2003). People with schizophrenia are believed to have a relatively high concentration of the neurotransmitter dopamine in nerve cell pathways extending into the cortex and limbic system. Dopamine levels are not considered causal for the disorder, however, and other neurotransmitters, including serotonin and norepinephrine, have also been proposed as risk influences (Stahl, 2000). Whether symptoms result from abnormal development or deterioration of function is not clear.

Some researchers are beginning to study the influences of certain chromosomes on molecular pathways in the brain as causal mechanisms for schizophrenia (e.g., Detera-Wadleigh & McMahon, 2006), but this work remains speculative. Still, its genetic transmission is supported by the higher-than-average risk mechanisms among family members of persons with the disorder (Cardno & Murray, 2003). An identical twin of a person with schizophrenia has a 47 percent chance of developing the disorder. A non-identical twin has only a 12 percent likelihood, which is the same probability as for a child with one parent who has schizophrenia. Other risk factors include a maternal history of schizophrenia and affective disorder (Byrne, Agerbo, & Mortensen, 2002). The age of onset for a child tends to be earlier when the mother has schizophrenia. Further, negative symptoms are frequently seen among nonpsychotic first-degree relatives of people with schizophrenia.

It has also been hypothesized that a variety of neurodevelopmental phenomena account for the onset of schizophrenia (Meinecke, 2001). These include central nervous

FIGURE 9.2 Schizophrenia in Vulnerable and Oppressed Populations.

CHILDREN
- Schizophrenia is rare prior to adolescence, with only 10 percent of persons experiencing its onset by that time.[1]

WOMEN
- Men have an earlier onset (ages 18 to 26) compared with women (26 to 40 years).[2]
- Women tend to have higher levels of premorbid (prepsychotic) functioning and more positive symptoms than men do; women also have a better prognosis with regard to their social functioning potential and response to intervention.[3]

MINORITIES
- African-Americans are more frequently diagnosed with schizophrenia than are Caucasians, possibly due to clinician interpretation of culturally appropriate suspicion within the African-American community as a negative symptom, rather than a learned attitude.[4]

LOW SES
- The prevalence of schizophrenia is twice as high in lower than in higher socio-economic classes for the following three reasons:[5] increased stressors due to living in low SES may contribute to the onset of schizophrenia; persons who develop schizophrenia lose occupational and social skills and fall into the lower classes; and others never develop skills to establish themselves in stable social roles.

OLDER ADULTS
- Older adults have not been studied as extensively with regard to antipsychotic medications effects, so at present there is little data to guide decisions about which medications to prescribe for them.[6]
- There is no clear evidence that any particular psychosocial interventions are suited to older adult clients.[7]

system development, the quality of nerve cell connections, the manner in which nerve cell activity influences the formation of circuits underlying brain functions, and the development of the dopamine system. The brain volumes of persons with schizophrenia appear to be less that those of persons without the disorder. A recent literature

[1]Fonagy, Target, Cottrell, & Phillips, 2002.
[2]Seeman, 2003.
[3]Seeman, 2003.
[4]Trierweiler et al., 2000.
[5]Mulvany, O'Callaghan, Takei, Byrne, & Fearon, 2001.
[6]Marriott, Neil, & Waddingham, 2006.
[7]Van Citters, Pratt, Barters, & Jeste, 2005.

review found that the whole-brain and hippocampus volumes of most study participants were reduced, while ventricular volume was increased (Steen, Mull, McClure,
Hamer, & Lieberman, 2006). In genetically predisposed subjects, the change from vulnerability to developing psychosis may be marked by a reduced size and impaired
function of the temporal lobe (Crow, Honea, Passingham, & Mackay, 2005), although
some researchers do not agree that a reduction in size of the temporal lobe or amygdala
is inevitable (Vita, Silenzi, & Dieci, 2006). Traumatic brain injury, often cited as a contributing cause of the disorder, increases the chances of schizophrenia in families, but
only when there is already a genetic loading (Malapsia, Goetz, Friedman, Kaufmann,
Faraone, et al., 2001).

Brain trauma from birth complications has been postulated as one of the pathways
to the disorder (Prasad, Shirts, & Yolken, 2007), and obstetrical complications are related
to earlier age of onset (Kirkpatrick, Herrera Catanedo, & Vazquez-Barquero, 2002). Post-
mortem studies show brain abnormalities indicative of developmental problems in the
second or third trimester of pregnancy, such as altered cell migration in the hippocampus
and prefrontal cortex. Other postulated (but debated) causes of these abnormalities could
be the higher-than-expected frequencies of prenatal exposure to influenza viruses and
infections (urinary and respiratory) in persons who later develop schizophrenia (Kesha-
van, Gilbert, & Diwadkar, 2006). People with schizophrenia tend to be born in winter
or early spring, which means that their mothers were pregnant during a time of year
when viruses are more prevalent (Reid & Zborowski, 2006). There is some evidence
that persons with schizophrenia who were born in summer months have more negative
than positive symptoms (Kirkpatrick et al., 2002). Also, older men are more likely
than younger men to father sons with schizophrenia, (Harlap, 2001). While the risk
influence is not clear, it could be due to a mild biological degeneration in the father's
reproductive system.

Biological characteristics that are protective of a person's developing schizophrenia
include the absence of a family history of the disorder, normal prenatal development,
and a normally developed central nervous system. Protective environmental influences include being born during the late spring, summer, or fall, and an absence of
physically traumatic events during childhood and adolescence (Geanellos, 2005; Jobe &
Harrow, 2005).

PSYCHOSOCIAL INFLUENCES

There are no known psychological influences of specific stress events, on the development of schizophrenia, although many years ago they were considered the likely dominant causes (Phillips, Francey, Edwards, & McMurray, 2007). There are, however, some
possible social risk influences for schizophrenia. These include living in an urban versus
a rural environment, being born into a relatively low socioeconomic status (SES), and
having migrated into a new culture (Selten, Cantor-Craae, & Kahn, 2007). Conversely, living in a rural environment, being of middle- or upper-class SES, and geographic stability
would be protective.

Course and Outcome

Schizophrenia tends to be a chronic disorder (Perkins, Miller-Anderson, & Lieberman, 2006) and complete remission is uncommon (Jobe & Harrow, 2005). Its course, however, is variable. Suicide is unfortunately the number one cause of premature death in schizophrenia, 20 to 40 percent of persons attempt suicide at some point in their lives and 9 to 13 percent succeed (Pinikahana, Happel, & Keks, 2003). Persons most at risk for suicidal ideation during the early stages of the disorder are young white males who are depressed, unmarried, unemployed, socially isolated, functionally impaired, and lacking external support (Pinikahana, Happell, & Keks, 2003). The average life span of persons with schizophrenia is approximately ten years less than the national average in the United States, although this reduced life expectancy is not only due to suicide but also lifestyle factors such as high rates of smoking, medication use, side effects of medication, substance use, diet, poor access to health care, and other risks related to poverty (Brown, Birtwistle, Roe, & Thompson, 1999; Goff, Sullivan, McEvoy, et al., 2005).

While the causes of schizophrenia are uncertain, clues are available to differentiate a better or worse prognosis. These are listed in Table 9.1.

TABLE 9.1 Risk and Resilience Assessment

RISK MECHANISMS	*PROTECTIVE MECHANISMS*
Biological Gradual symptom onset Prominence of negative symptoms Repeated relapses of active symptoms Medication absence or noncompliance	Biological Later age of onset Brief duration of active phases Good interepisode functioning (with minimal residual symptoms) Absence of brain structure abnormalities Family history of mood disorder
Psychological Poor insight into the disorder Delay in intervention	Psychological Insight into the disorder Early and ongoing intervention
Social Significant family expressed emotion Poor social adjustment prior to the onset of schizophrenia Noncompliance with, or absence of, psychosocial interventions Absence of a support system Living in an urban area	Social Development of social skills prior to onset of the disorder Family participation in intervention Interest in independent living Participation in a range of psychosocial interventions Presence of support systems Living in a non-urban area

Sources: Andreasen, Carpenter, Kane, Lasser, Marder, & Weinberger, 2005; Butzlaff & Hooley, 1998; Chambless, Bryan, Aiken, Steketee, & Hooley, 1999; Ferdinandi, Yoottanasumpun, Pollack, & Bermanzohn, 1998; Lenoir, Dingemans, Schene, Hart, & Linszen, 2002; Pharoah, Rathbone, Marl, & Streiner, 2003.

Directions Part II, Biopsychosocial Risk and Resilience Assessment: Formulate a risk and resilience assessment, both for the onset of the disorder and the course of the disorder, including the strengths that you see for this individual.

TABLE 9.2 Biopsychosocial Risk and Resilience Assessment for the Onset of the Disorder

RISK MECHANISMS	PROTECTIVE MECHANISMS
Biological	
Psychological	
Social	

TABLE 9.3 Biopsychosocial Risk and Resilience Assessment for the Course of the Disorder

RISK MECHANISMS	PROTECTIVE MECHANISMS
Biological	
Psychological	
Social	

What techniques could you use to elicit additional strengths in this client?

Intervention

While strong empirical research support for many interventions is lacking, there is a consensus that the treatment of schizophrenia should be multimodal and should include interventions targeted at specific symptoms as well as the social and educational needs of the client and family (McClellan & Werry, 2000). In this section we will review medication, individual therapy, group intervention, family intervention, assertive community treatment, case management interventions, hospitalization, vocational rehabilitation, and early intervention. A literature review established that client satisfaction with interventions for schizophrenia and other psychotic disorders is influenced by multiple factors, including an absence of significant drug side effects, participation in treatment planning and decision making, and the involvement of family members in the intervention plan (Chue, 2006).

Medications

Medication is the primary intervention modality for persons with schizophrenia. It cannot "cure" a person of the disorder but can be effective in eliminating or reducing some of the symptoms. The first generation of antipsychotic drugs, most popular from the 1950s through the 1980s, act primarily by binding to dopamine receptors and blocking their transmission (Leonard, 2003). These medications act on all dopamine sites in the brain, although only those in the forebrain contribute to the symptoms of schizophrenia. A reduction in dopamine in other areas (extending from the midbrain to basal ganglia) causes adverse effects of akathisia (restlessness and agitation), dystonia (muscle spasms), parkinsonism (muscle stiffness and tremor), and tardive dyskinesia (involuntary muscle movements of the face and limbs). Anticholinergic medications are often prescribed to combat these effects, although they in turn have their own adverse effects of blurred vision, dry mouth, and constipation.

The "second-generation" antipsychotic medications, available in the United States since the late 1980s, act differently from those developed earlier (Julien, 2001). Clozapine, the first of these, acts selectively on dopamine receptors (Wahlbeck, Cheine, & Essali, 1999). Their sites of action are the limbic forebrain and the frontal cortex, and thus they do not carry the risk of adverse effects for the muscular system. The fact that they block receptors for serotonin suggests that this neurotransmitter also has a role in the production of symptoms. Risperidone, introduced in 1994, has fewer adverse effects than the first-generation drugs and is at present the most widely prescribed antipsychotic drug (Jayram, Hosalli, & Stroup, 2006; Hunter, Joy, Kennedy, Gilbody, & Song, 2003). Olanzapine, sertindole, ziprasidone, quetiapine, and amisulpride are other newer medications on the market (Mota-Net, Lima, & Soares, 2002; Schatzberg & Nemeroff, 2001). Their somewhat greater alleviation of negative symptoms suggests that serotonin antagonist activity is significant in this regard.

Both the first- and second-generation medications continue to be used to treat persons with schizophrenia (Essock, 2002). Prescribing practices depend on the physician's preferences and the client's family history and financial status (the older medications are less expensive). The effects of antipsychotic medications on older adults have not been studied as extensively, so at present there is little data to guide decisions about which medications to prescribe for them (Marriott, Neil, & Waddingham, 2006). There is some evidence that the newer atypical antipsychotic medications are more effective for older adults than the first-generation drugs (Van Citters, Pratt, Barters, & Jeste, 2005).

While almost all physicians recommend antipsychotic medication for persons with schizophrenia, their relative risks and benefits with regard to the patient's physical and emotional well-being are subject to debate (Cohen, 2002). Studies of drug effectiveness for schizophrenia symptoms consistently show that many clients discontinue their medication for a variety of reasons, such as perceived ineffectiveness and adverse side effects. One large-scale study found that the first-generation medications were as effective as the newer medications, but discontinuation rates over an 18-month period for all medications were alarmingly high, at 74 percent (Lieberman, Stroup, McEvoy, Swarts, Rosenheck, et al., 2005). Up until this study, it was assumed that the lesser adverse side effects of the newer medications would be associated with increased compliance.

Nonadherence is best predicted by recent illicit drug or alcohol use and medication-related cognitive impairment (Ascher-Svanum, Faries, Zhu, Ernst, et al., 2006). Fortunately, clinical practices such as counseling, written information, and occasional phone calls can increase medication adherence, at least in the short term (Hanes, Yao, Degani, Kripalini, Garb, & McDonald, 2005). Despite the issues of adverse effects and limited effectiveness, medication nonadherence is significantly associated with poorer outcomes in schizophrenia. A multisite study of 1,900 consumers found that client nonadherence was associated with greater risks of hospitalization, use of emergency services, arrests, violence, victimization, poorer mental functioning, greater substance abuse, and alcohol-related problems (Ascher-Svanum, Faries, Zho, Ernst, Swartz, & Swanson, 2006).

Other types of medication are occasionally prescribed for persons who have schizophrenia, usually along with the antipsychotic drugs. These include antidepressants (Whitehead, Moss, Cardno, & Lewis, 2002), benzodiazepines (Gillies, Beck, McCloud, & Rathbone, 2005), and carbamazepine (Leucht, McGrath, White, & Kissling, 2002). There is no clear evidence that these medications help alleviate symptoms of depression or control psychotic symptoms, however.

Electroconvulsive therapy (the induction of a seizure by administering an electrical shock to the scalp) is an intervention that has been used for more than 50 years with persons who have schizophrenia. While controversial, several dozen studies have shown that it can be an effective short-term option for alleviating symptoms, especially when the client has not responded to medication or rapid improvement is sought (Tharyan & Adams, 2005).

Psychosocial Interventions

INDIVIDUAL PSYCHOTHERAPY

Research on psychodynamic intervention with schizophrenia has limited empirical support. Malmberg and Fenton (2005) concluded that individual psychodynamic treatment is not effective in leading to the outcome criteria of symptom reduction, reduced hospitalizations, and improved community adjustment. One positive aspect of this type of intervention, however, is that it alerts the practitioner to the importance of the worker-client relationship. Persons with schizophrenia are often initially distrustful of service providers, so no matter what type of intervention is provided, the practitioner must take care to develop a positive working alliance with the client over time.

Cognitive-behavioral therapy (CBT) is increasingly being used to treat persons with schizophrenia (Kuipers, Garety, & Fowler, 2006). This is based on the premise that current beliefs and attitudes mediate much of the person's affect and behavior. CBT focuses first on a review of the client's core beliefs regarding self-worth, the ability to create changes in his or her life, and realistic short- and long-term goals. If the client appears to be thinking "irrationally" in any of these core areas (that is, drawing conclusions that are insufficiently based on external evidence), the social worker can work toward the client's acquisition of more "rational" thinking. Clients are thus helped to (1) modify their assumptions about the self, the world, and the future; (2) improve coping responses to stressful events and life challenges; (3) relabel some psychotic experiences as symptoms rather than external reality; and (4) improve their social skills. It is important to emphasize that while clients with schizophrenia engage in psychotic thinking about some or many issues in their lives, some aspects of their thinking are either "rational" or amenable to change.

A recent meta-analysis of research on the efficacy of CBT for schizophrenia indicates that it is an effective adjunct to medication (Pfammatter, Junghan, & Brenner, 2006). Despite these encouraging findings, it is not yet clear what are the specific ingredients of effective psychosocial intervention or which interventions are most effective in particular settings. Further, CBT does not affect social behavior and overall cognitive functioning (Hayes & McGrath, 2000). Another group of researchers reviewed clinical trials and concluded that while CBT showed promise, more research was needed to demonstrate their effectiveness relative to "supportive" therapies (Jones, Cormac, da Mota Neto, & Campbell, 2004).

Social skills training (SST) is a type of CBT that addresses deficits in interpersonal relations, which are common among persons with schizophrenia. SST promotes the client's acquisition of social skills and leads to short-term improvements in cognitive functioning (Pfammatter, Junghan, & Brenner, 2006). These benefits are accompanied by small improvements in social functioning. Still, in studies that compare randomized control groups with other interventions, there is no clear evidence that SST yields any benefits in relation to relapse rate, global adjustment, quality of life, or adherence to other interventions (Pilling, Bebbington, Kuipers, Garety, Geddes, et al., 2002).

Recently, an intervention model known as "personal therapy" has received attention because of an outcome study using randomized control group design (Hogarty, 2002; Hogarty, Greenwald, et al., 1997; Hogarty, Kornblith, et al., 1997). The main assumption of personal therapy is that stress worsens the symptoms of schizophrenia. Initially, the focus of the study was on teaching clients to notice their physical and emotional stress reactions and to manage these reactions with improved coping skills. After at least a year of weekly sessions, clients learned how to engage more actively in work and other community settings. The intervention seemed to improve vocational and social functioning at two-year follow-up for those who lived with their families. However, people who resided apart from a family setting had more severe symptoms initially, and they had difficulty securing basic needs such as housing, food, and clothing. For these people, the intervention of personal therapy may have acted as an additional stressor rather than helping them.

GROUP INTERVENTIONS

Group interventions include insight-oriented, supportive, and behavioral modalities. They are often used in conjunction with other interventions such as medication and CBT. There are few controlled studies of group therapy. In his review of the descriptive literature on both inpatient and outpatient groups, Kanas (2000) concluded that for persons with schizophrenia, groups focused on increased social interaction were more effective than insight-oriented groups. Group interventions are widely used in inpatient settings, but there is little evidence of their effectiveness in helping to stabilize persons who are recently highly symptomatic. Regarding outpatient groups, a meta-analysis of control-group studies produced only modest evidence that group therapy results in reduced symptom severity and increased social and vocational skills (Huxley, Rendall, & Sederer, 2000).

FAMILY INTERVENTIONS

Family participation in the client's intervention is a protective influence (Pharoah, Rathbone, Mari, & Streiner, 2003). When a person has schizophrenia, a chronic emotional burden develops that is shared by all family members. Their common reactions include stress, anxiety, resentment of the impaired member, grief, and depression (Hatfield, 1993). The concept of family (or caregiver) expressed emotion (EE) has been prominent in the schizophrenia literature for the past 30 years. EE can be defined as the negative behaviors of close relatives toward a family member with schizophrenia, including emotional over-involvement and expressions of criticism and hostility. The concept is not used to blame family members for the course of a relative's illness, but to affirm that families need support in coping with it. In a meta-analysis by Butzlaff and Hooley (1998) of 27 studies, EE was consistently shown to correlate with symptom relapse, especially for clients with a more chronic disorder. Family environments with low EE are associated with fewer symptom relapses and rehospitalizations than those with high EE environments are.

Therefore, family interventions in schizophrenia usually focus in part on producing a more positive atmosphere for all members, which in turn contributes to the ill relative's adjustment. Piling et al. (2002) conducted a meta-analysis of all randomized clinical studies done on single- and multiple-family intervention (conducted in groups) and found that these interventions were more effective at 12 months than the comparison conditions, which usually included some form of "standard care" (such as medication alone). Single-family interventions reduced readmission rates in the first year. After two years all 18 family interventions lowered the relapse and readmission rates of the ill relative and increased medication compliance. Another review of the literature on EE showed that family interventions designed to reduce expressed levels of criticism, hostility, or overinvolvement do tend to decrease relapse and increase medication compliance, although families are still left with a significant burden (Pharoah, Rathbone, Mari, & Streiner, 2005).

ASSERTIVE COMMUNITY TREATMENT AND CASE MANAGEMENT INTERVENTIONS

Case management is a term used to describe a variety of community-based intervention modalities designed to help clients receive a full range of support and rehabilitation services in a timely, appropriate fashion (Rubin, 1992). Case management interventions are usually carried out in the context of large, community-based programs. The most famous of these, assertive community treatment (ACT), was developed by Stein and Test (1980) in Wisconsin and has since been replicated in many other sites around the world. By 1996 there were 397 such programs in the United States (Mueser, Bond, Drake, & Resnick, 1998). The core characteristics of the ACT model of service delivery are assertive engagement, service delivery in the client's natural environment, a multidisciplinary team approach, staff continuity over time, low staff-to-client ratios, and frequent client contacts. Services are provided in the client's home or wherever the client feels comfortable and focus on everyday needs. Frequency of contact is variable, depending on assessed client need. Other kinds of case management programs share some, but not all, characteristics of the ACT model.

In a recent review of 75 studies, Marshall and Lockwood (2003) found that both ACT and case management were more effective than other forms of intervention in helping clients stay in contact with services, spend fewer days in the hospital, secure employment, and express life satisfaction. There were no clear differences, however, in measures of mental status and social functioning. ACT was superior to case management in client use of hospitalization, but differences on the other measures were not clear. Although ACT does promote greater client acceptance of interventions (Tyrer, Coid, Simmonds, Joseph, & Marriot, 1998), another comprehensive review indicated that the programs vary considerably with regard to staffing, types of clients, and resources; comparisons are thus difficult to make (Mueser et al., 1998). Further, efforts to make interventions compulsory are not effective in engaging clients (Kisely, Campbell, & Preston, 2005). That being said, the reviewers found that client gains persist only as long as comprehensive services are continued. This raises the question of whether clients are acquiring skills and resources that promote permanent improvement or are showing short-term gains that reflect intensive support.

HOSPITALIZATION

It is widely believed that inpatient hospitalization is an expensive, ineffective, and socially undesirable treatment setting for persons with schizophrenia. Hospitalization is primarily used now to stabilize persons who are a danger to themselves and others, rather than providing active and ongoing interventions. Five randomized controlled trials showed that a planned short-term stay does not encourage a revolving door pattern of admission for people with serious mental illnesses (Johnstone & Zolese, 2005). Still, the use of clubhouses and other partial or day hospitalization programs is effective in reducing inpatient admission and improving outcomes (Marshall, Crowthier, Almaraz-Serrano, Creed,

Sledge, et al., 2006). Partial or day hospital programs are staff-run, structured, psychosocial rehabilitation programs for persons with schizophrenia who have the capacity to live in the community. Clubhouses are vocational rehabilitation programs in which members work side by side with staff to complete the work of the facility (for example, cooking lunch, keeping records, managing a member bank, and answering phones). Members and staff engage equally in all aspects of clubhouse operations. Members are not paid for their participation, but an employment specialist helps to place members in community jobs.

VOCATIONAL REHABILITATION

Vocational rehabilitation is work-related activity that provides clients with pay and the experience of participating in productive social activity. The goals of vocational programs may be full-time competitive employment, any paid or volunteer job, the development of job-related skills, and job satisfaction. Twamley, Jeste, and Lehman (2003) conducted a meta-analysis of randomized controlled trials of vocational rehabilitation that focused on both client placement and support (with training, placement, and occasional contact) or supported employment (more intensive participation by the case manager in the client's job functions). Programs have a positive influence on promoting work-related activities such as paid employment, job starts, duration of employment, and earnings. Supportive employment programs tend to be more effective than pre-vocational training (Crowter, Marshall, Bond, & Huxley, 2001). Unfortunately, a diagnosis of schizophrenia is negatively related to the attainment and maintenance of employment when compared with other diagnoses.

Bond (2004) conducted another meta-analysis of the effectiveness of supported employment for people with severe mental illness. He found that in 13 studies, 40 to 60 percent of clients obtain competitive employment, versus 20 percent of those not enrolled. Interestingly, while clients who hold jobs for an extended period of time show benefits such as improved self-esteem and symptom control, their employment does not correlate with outcomes such as prevention of hospitalization and quality of life.

EARLY INTERVENTION

Early intervention refers to efforts to detect schizophrenia in its early stages and then provide those persons with phase-specific treatment. Several such programs have been initiated in the United States, Europe, and Australia (Marshall & Lockwood, 2003). Data regarding the risks and benefits of early detection and intervention remain sparse, and the evidence is not sufficient to justify pre-onset treatment as a standard practice (McGlashan, Miller, & Woods, 2001). There are also ethical issues involved in primary prevention efforts, including clinical priorities, screening ethics, stigma, confidentiality, and informed consent (Rosen, 2000).

Directions Part III, Goal Setting and Treatment Planning: Given your risk and protective factors assessments of the individual, your knowledge of the disorder, and evidence-based practice guidelines, formulate goals and a possible treatment plan for this individual.

Critical Perspective

Schizophrenia remains an enigma. While it is among the most disabling of all mental disorders, researchers and clinical practitioners are not able to describe exactly what it is, how it is caused, or how it can be effectively prevented or treated (Cardno & Murray, 2003). There is a consensus, however, that its primary causes are biological or hereditary (although the extent of those influences is debated), and that family and social environments are more significant to its course than to its onset. There is also a general worldwide agreement on its basic symptom profile. Schizophrenia thus appears to be recognized as a valid mental disorder.

A major problem with the diagnosis of schizophrenia is that its causal influences are inferred from the hypothesized actions of antipsychotic medications (Conklin & Iacono, 2003; Stahl, 2000). As more information about the condition's neurobiology is developed, professionals may become able to articulate its core features. As described earlier, the limited effectiveness of these medications casts some doubt on the validity of the presumed "nature" of schizophrenia. Still, because the pharmaceutical industry and psychiatric profession are so heavily invested in drug marketing (Moncrieff, Hopker, & Thomas, 2005), relatively little research currently focuses on the psychosocial influences of the disorder.

Directions Part IV, Critical Perspective: Formulate a critique of the diagnosis as it relates to this case example. Questions to consider include: Does this diagnosis represent a vallid mental disorder from the social work perspective? Is this diagnosis significantly different from other possible diagnoses? Your critique should be based on the values of the social work profession (which are incongruent in some way with the medical model) and the validity of the specific diagnostic criteria applied to this case.

CASE 2

Donald is a 23-year-old Caucasian male who presents as quiet and polite, with a flat affect. At age 20, he was in church with his family when he started spinning his body around, feeling that something was pushing him. After returning home, he felt restless and randomly moved items and furniture around the house. Over a short period of time, his parents noticed that his speech was becoming disorganized and his behavior more erratic. He would sit outside in cold weather with light clothing, sleep in the backyard, and live in his car. At one point Donald felt he was possessed by demons and needed to purify his body by not eating. He thought that if he lost weight, the demons would have to leave. From the initial onset of his symptoms until early last year, Donald was hospitalized 14 times as a result of aggressive behavior toward his family. His aggression was usually characterized by shouting and shoving his parents. Once he punched his father in the face. At times Donald is bothered by his aggressive thoughts and has sufficient insight to recognize that his illness impacts his life.

Donald is currently receiving treatment from a county mental health agency as an outpatient. He is seen regularly by a social worker and by the psychiatrist who monitors Donald's medication and coordinates treatment with his primary care physician. Donald is also attempting to become more involved with a day treatment program, but is finding it difficult. Initially, he liked the idea of participating in group activities and having the chance to develop social relationships. Over time it became stressful for him, and at one point he said he felt the program was "evil" so he stopped attending. He is trying to attend again, but initially he would go out on the grounds and stay behind the trees. Donald has progressed to being able to come out from behind the trees and sometimes enter the building, but he is still not able to engage in any kind of social interaction. He has been known to wear earplugs during his entire time at the day program to protect himself from perceived ridicule.

When at home, Donald spends the vast majority of his time in his room. He no longer watches television or listens to music, activities he previously enjoyed doing. His parents encourage Donald to eat dinner with the family several times a week to foster the social interaction he otherwise lacks. He is notably distracted by his internal stimuli and often talks and laughs to himself. He paces, goes in and out of the house, and picks up and examines items that are not there. His speech is often tangential.

Donald is currently obsessed with children and their safety. He mistrusts his father and fathers in general, although abuse by his father has been ruled out. He mistrusts the Catholic church because of reports of child abuse by priests. He often misinterprets parental behavior as child abuse. On a recent visit to a fast-food restaurant, Donald saw a father holding a fussy child. He thought the child was crying because the father was holding the child "in a perverted way," and he demanded that the father put the child down.

At his intake for the day treatment program, Donald told the doctor that his parents and siblings had murdered his friend. In truth, the friend had died of a heroin overdose. He also reported that he hears a voice that is "nasty" in tone. He stated that the voices "do cruel jokes" on him, and he laughs or talks back to them. He tries to control the voices by praying. Donald also talks about "a presence touching me." He described it as a sharp jolt of terror, as if someone was in the room with him, touching him. This presence comes and goes, and Donald thinks it may be Satan. He also thinks that people are reading his mind and making fun of him.

Recently, Donald has had problems sleeping and is becoming increasingly agitated over the need to organize protests against abortion. His father contacted Donald's social worker and requested that both the social worker and the doctor see Donald to reevaluate his medication. When Donald was informed of this appointment, he became extremely annoyed and threatened to cut the doctor's throat. He left the house on foot, returning several hours later at 2:00 A.M., cold, tired, and wet from the rain. He agreed to be hospitalized the next day.

Over the course of his illness Donald has continued to experience periods of depression. During these periods, which last for several weeks, he will sleep at least 12 to 14 hours and has a great deal of difficulty waking. By his parents' report, he eats less, is more withdrawn, more isolated, and less active than at other times. His depressed moods are noted by his mother, his social worker, and the psychiatrist. He has described other moods in which he feels like "doing a lot of things," but these episodes were short-lived and do not meet the criteria for manic or hypomanic states. According to both Donald and his family members, he does not smoke or use drugs or alcohol.

Despite his psychotic and depressive symptoms, there are times (at most a few days at a time) when he is oriented to reality and does exhibit some insight regarding his illness. However, he continues to experience "voices" (while understanding that these are not real) and flat affect and withdrawal, even during these periods.

Donald is the youngest of three children. His mother reported that she had a normal pregnancy and delivery with Donald. He was born in February. Donald's older brother is 34 and his sister is 26. His mother works as a nurse, and his father is an engineer. There is a family history of mental and mood disorders. Donald's mother is taking antidepressants, and her brother has bipolar disorder with manic episodes marked by psychosis and a substance use disorder. There is also a history of attempted suicides in Donald's mother's family, and a paternal great-uncle had "a breakdown."

Donald's parents describe him as a shy child who did well in school. He was diagnosed with depression at age 13 and took antidepressants until he was 20. At age 15 he had his first suicidal ideation but made no attempt to take his life. He also reported thoughts of suicide when he was 19 and 20, but never made any attempts.

Donald graduated from high school with a 3.6 GPA. He attended college for three semesters, earning a 3.1 GPA in his studies. During high school and college Donald held several jobs. He worked in a veterinarian's office for nine months. He was also employed in retail and as a waiter in several eating establishments, but was unable to stay employed at any of these places more than a few weeks.

The medications Donald currently takes are a cause for concern. His illness has not responded well to medications, even though he is taking many of them. These include Depakote, Zyprexa, Abilify, Geodon, and Risperdal. He is experiencing several undesirable side effects, most notably tremors of his hands, arms, and feet. The health care providers treating Donald would like to have him try clozapine, described by his social worker as a drug of last resort. This is an unlikely possibility, however, as transitioning medications requires a person to be hospitalized. The patient is then monitored twice weekly during the first six months and weekly for the following six months. Donald has not been particularly compliant with medication and treatment but is especially reluctant to be hospitalized, feeling that hospitals are "evil."

Please go to the Appendix for directions to this case. The following questions will help to guide your thinking about a possible multi-axial diagnosis.

Questions to consider when formulating a diagnosis for Donald

1. What symptoms of psychosis does Donald display, and how long have these symptoms been evident?

2. The diagnosis of schizophrenia also requires impairment. Is impairment evident in this case?

3. Are psychotic or mood disorders present among relatives?

4. Does Donald have a history of depression or mood swings that might indicate a schizoaffective, major depressive, or bipolar disorder?

5. Are there any medical conditions that may be contributing to Donald's symptom development?

6. Is the client's use of substances or medications causing symptoms?

7. Are there psychosocial stressors that might be contributing to Donald's symptom development?

8. What was Donald's premorbid functioning like?

CASE 3

Emma is a 59-year-old African-American woman, born in July, who presents with a well-groomed appearance but flat affect. Her medical chart shows that her weight is in the normal range for her height, and she has a medical diagnosis of hypertension. Emma is an inpatient resident at a mental health facility, where she has resided since her admission one year ago.

Emma believes that she still owns a house in another city, in spite of having been shown the deed of sale from 13 years ago. She says her son has been replaced by an impostor who came from a seedpod. Emma also states that she was shot while at work but went home because she didn't bleed. She denies that she has siblings, saying they were just people who were put in her parents' house to be raised. She says she doesn't want contact with them, and they don't attempt to contact her. When questioned about some of these beliefs, Emma states that she was instructed by a secret group, of which she is part, not to give out further information. When staff challenge her beliefs, she says it hurts her feelings and responds to them in anger.

Emma has been observed responding to internal stimuli. She also reported in rounds that while in her room, she heard her psychiatrist's voice telling her she was released. Emma does not believe herself to have a mental illness or hypertension, and states that she takes her medication only because the nurses give it to her. She is currently being treated with Haldol (a first-generation antipsychotic), the dosage of which was recently increased due to persistent delusions. A previous medication, Zyprexa (a second-generation antipsychotic), was recently discontinued due to lack of efficacy.

This is Emma's third admission to an inpatient mental health facility. Emma is pleasant when approached. She attends scheduled treatment groups independently. Her records show her to be Protestant, but she does not attend any spiritual services at this time. She participates in occasional outings if prompted.

Prior to admission, Emma was living with her son in a large urban area where she was noncompliant with medication and reportedly caused problems in the home. She was originally placed with her son 14 years ago after becoming unable to care for herself in her home, which was located in another city where she had lived for ten years. At the time she was removed, she had no electricity and no running water. Her son was appointed legal guardian and payee at that time. At his house, her son stated she would sit in front of the television with no sound and get up only to go outside to smoke. She was reported as being aggressive toward her grandchild and attempted to return to the home she no longer owns. On one occasion she had to be removed from her son's house by the police for aggressive behavior toward him. On another occasion she had to be removed by the police from a bank, where she erroneously insisted that she had an account. Emma is now estranged from her son. He says he is "worn out from dealing with her."

Emma has a history of noncompliance with outpatient treatment. She has no history of drug or alcohol abuse but does smoke about half a pack of cigarettes per day. Neither does she have a history of depressive or manic episodes. Her son said there was no family history of schizophrenia that he knew of, and he didn't think that his mother had suffered from traumatic events as a child. He said that his mother's parents were strict and would give out "whippings" for misbehavior. Emma came from a poor background, and when she married, the family could have been classified as "working poor."

When Emma was going through a divorce in her 40s, she told her son that she'd bought him a car and that he should go to the dealer and pick it up. When he spoke with the car dealer, he discovered that his mother had had a number of confused conversations with the dealer, telling him the bank would provide the necessary money. She had not, in fact, bought a car. He soon found out that his mother had also not paid his college tuition bill, which she denied.

Emma was recently evaluated by the occupational therapy department using the Kohlman Evaluation of Living Skills (KELS) and the Allen Cognitive Level Screen (ACLS). Emma was reported to be friendly and cooperative during this 90-minute evaluation. Emma's KELS score showed her as able to accomplish some tasks independently but having poor judgment in other areas. She was unable to identify her current source of income but stated that the bank gives money to people who need it. She has not been employed for over 20 years but states that after her release from the mental health facility, her prior employer will find her and send her to France to a government school. Emma's ACLS results showed weakness in the areas of problem solving, insight, and judgment. Overall, her scores, KELS/fair and ACLS/4.4, demonstrate her need to live in a 24-hour supervised environment.

Please go to the Appendix for directions to this case. The following questions will help to guide your thinking about a possible multi-axial diagnosis.

Questions to consider when formulating a diagnosis for Emma

1. What symptoms of psychosis does Emma display?

2. The diagnosis of schizophrenia also requires impairment. Is impairment evident in this case?

3. Part of the diagnostic process is to assign a subtype for schizophrenia. What subtype seems evident based on Emma's symptoms?

4. Schizophrenia requires coding of the course of illness, which can be classified only after one year. How would you code Emma's disorder?

5. Are there any medical conditions that may be contributing to Emma's symptom development?

6. Is the client's use of substances or medications causing symptoms?

7. Are there psychosocial stressors that might be contributing to Emma's symptom development?

8. Are psychotic or mood disorders present among Emma's relatives?

9. Does Emma have a history of depression or mood swings that might indicate a schizoaffective, major depressive, or bipolar disorder?

10. What was Emma's premorbid functioning like (to determine the presence of a possible schizoptypal, schizoid, or paranoid personality disorder)?

10

▼▲▼

Depressive Disorders

Tammy is a 44-year-old African-American female who was diagnosed with multiple sclerosis (MS), a degenerative autoimmune disease, nearly 15 years ago. The disease has progressed to the point where she walks with two canes, one in each hand, when she leaves her house, although she is able to use only one cane around the house. Tammy is unable to hold a job because of her disability and receives about $500 in Supplemental Security Income (SSI) each month. In addition, she receives food stamps and Medicaid.

Tammy first sought assistance from the social work department a month ago because of her housing situation. She has lived with a friend in her basement bedroom for the past 18 months. The friend's grown son, who does not live with them, owns the house. The friend also has two other sons who live in the house. Tammy pays them $200 in rent each month and uses her food stamps to buy food for the entire household. The situation is causing her great stress, as the two young men make her feel unwanted. They are loud and harass her (they "get on me") and make it difficult to sleep. She is unable to use the shower because it is not big enough to put in her safety seat, and she has fallen a few times while using it. She takes sponge baths in her room instead.

The stress of her living situation is worrying her, and she is afraid that she'll have another attack of MS and require hospitalization. She has been hospitalized once since moving in with this friend. In addition, she has checked herself into a psychiatric hospital twice since living with her friend. Now, for the past several weeks, she has found herself crying every day, feeling hopeless, and wanting to hurt herself. She has never actually attempted self-harm, however. She stays in her bed, either sleeping or watching television, most days, except for the times she has her physical therapy appointments. She describes feeling "incredibly tired" and also says that she wants to stay out of the way of her roommates so that they won't bother her.

Prevalence and Comorbidity of Depression

Out of all disorders that may be experienced in one's lifetime, depression is the most common. Indeed, 16.6 percent of people in the United States will experience a major depressive disorder in their lifetime (Kessler, Berglund, Demler, Jin, & Walters, 2005). A *major depression* is a period of two weeks or longer during which a person experiences a depressed mood or loss of interest in nearly all life activities. In a given year, 1.5 percent of the adult population will suffer from dysthymic disorder (Kessler, Chiu, Demler, & Walters, 2005). *Dysthymic disorder* represents a general personality style featuring symptoms that are similar to, but less intense than, those of major depression.

Lifetime prevalence rates for adolescent depression range from 15 to 20 percent (Birmaher, Ryan, Williamson, et al., 1996; Lewinsohn & Essau, 2002), and rates for dysthymia range from 2 to 5 percent (Birmaher et al., 1996; Cottrell, Fonagy, Kurtz, Phillips, & Target, 2002). Subthreshold cases (those in which the client does not meet full criteria for the diagnosis) may produce as much impairment as those that meet full criteria (Gonzalez-Tejara, Canino, Ramirez, et al., 2005). For older adults, DSM-IV diagnosable depression rates range from 0.8 to 8 percent (Kraaij, Arensman, & Spinhoven, 2002).

Depression is consistently found to be about twice as common in women as in men in all studies (Kovacs, 2001). This gender gap, which emerges by age 14, is found internationally (Canada, Great Britain, and the United States) (Wade, Cairney, & Pevalin, 2002) and persists across the life span (Kessler, 2003).

The lifetime rate of comorbidity for adults with major depressive disorder is nearly three-fourths (72.1 percent) (Kessler, Berglund, Demler, et al., 2005). The most common comorbid disorders by far are the anxiety disorders (59.2 percent), followed by impulse control disorders and then substance use disorders.

Comorbid disorders in youth with depression are also likely (40 to 70 percent) (Cottrell et al., 2002; Waslick et al., 2002). Dysthymia (with major depression) and anxiety disorders are the most common comorbid conditions (Birmaher et al., 1996), followed by the disruptive disorders (oppositional defiant disorder, conduct disorder, or attention deficit/hyperactivity disorder) (Cottrell et al., 2002). Other concurrent conditions include substance abuse problems, eating disorders, learning disabilities, and medical problems (Waslick et al., 2002).

Assessment

Many people, particularly the elderly, do not see depression as a health problem that can be treated but rather as a character weakness or a sign of being "crazy" (Laidlow, Thompson, Gallagher, et al., 2003). Other elders may view depression as a normal event in older age. It is important that depression is identified and treated, not only to reduce suffering but also because health care costs are higher for people with depression (AHCPR, 1993), and untreated depression can lead to disability, worsen other physical illnesses, and result in premature mortality from medical conditions and suicide (AHCPR, 1993).

Figure 10.1 provides general assessment guidelines for clients who may have depression. Figure 10.2 lists risks for depression among vulnerable and oppressed populations.

> Tammy has been a patient at the rehabilitation hospital for most of the course of her disease. She sometimes has what she calls "attacks" in which her MS symptoms worsen and she needs to be hospitalized. She recognizes that this usually happens when she is under great stress. Currently she is seen in the outpatient clinic and attends physical therapy twice a week. She hopes to become strong enough to need only one cane while out in public, and none at home. Her therapist believes that she is making good progress and that her goal is attainable.
>
> Tammy's family situation is marked by conflict and estrangement. Tammy is divorced and has two daughters and a son, all grown. Her son is in jail. Her younger daughter is pregnant, and her older daughter just moved into a subsidized apartment. She says her relationship with her older daughter is strained, but they do speak. Her ex-husband died a few years ago while in prison. She has a sister who lives in a shelter in a neighboring county, but they also are not on speaking terms. Tammy says this is because while she was still married, her sister had an affair with her ex-husband. All her brothers are in jail, and she is not close to any other relatives.

FIGURE 10.1 Assessment Guidelines for Depression.

- Assess the recent occurrence of any stressors that may account for the client's symptoms of depression, to consider the possibility of an adjustment disorder.
- Determine whether the client is under the influence of any substances that may account for the depressive symptoms.
- Assess the client for symptoms of mania, to rule out bipolar disorder.
- With children and adolescents, seek collateral reports from parents and teachers, given many adolescents' reluctance to disclose their feelings. When they do communicate, adolescents tend to be accurate reporters of their emotions. Count a symptom as present if *either* the parent or the child reports it.
- Older adults do not typically complain of sadness, anxiety, or hopelessness but speak instead of physical (weight loss, insomnia, and fatigue) and cognitive (such as memory and concentration impairment) signs of depression.
- For all clients, especially older adults, symptoms of depression are common to many medical conditions and can be brought on by medications taken for physical disorders.
- For resources on standardized assessment instruments for depression, see Joiner, Walker, Pettit, et al. (2005) for adults and Klein, Dougherty, and Olino (2005) for children and adolescents.

Sources: AHCPR, 1993; Alexopoulos et al., 2001; Bird & Parslow, 2002; Birmaher et al., 1996; Kotlyar, Dysken, & Adson, 2005; Waslick, Kandel, & Kakouros, 2002.

FIGURE 10.2 Depression in Vulnerable and Oppressed Populations.

YOUTH

- Teens, especially girls, are at increased vulnerability for depression,[1] which may place an individual at risk for future episodes and other mental disorders into adulthood.[2]

OLDER ADULTS

- Depressive symptoms can be precipitated by common ailments at this stage of life, such as Alzheimer's disease, stroke, Parkinson's disease, heart disease, cancer, and arthritis;[3] however, prolonged and unresolved grief, dependence upon others, and the accumulation of negative life events[4] may also contribute to depression.
- Elderly people who live in low-SES neighborhoods and are receiving treatment for depression tend to respond less well to treatment than their counterparts residing in middle-income tracts.[5]
- Other factors inhibiting treatment response in elders are an accumulation of negative life events, prolonged or unresolved grief, problems related to becoming dependent on others, role transitions associated with old age, and social isolation.[6]
- Being older than 59 is associated with lack of appropriate treatment for depression.[7]
- The elderly may not participate in psychotherapy because of out-of-pocket payments required, lack of referrals from health care providers, or the lack of availability of local psychotherapy providers.[8]

WOMEN

- Rates of depression for women are twice that of men,[9] beginning by age 14, and persisting through the life span.[10] A number of reasons may account for the disparity: female hormonal changes,[11] rumination as a coping strategy,[12] higher rates of sexual abuse,[13] greater interpersonal stress,[14] lower appreciation and pay for women's work, and role overload.[15]

(continues)

---

[1]Kovacs, 2001.

[2]Fergusson, Horwood, & Lynskey, 1996.

[3]Alexopoulos, Katz, Reynolds, et al., 2001; Shanmugham et al., 2005.

[4]AHCPR, 1993; Cole, 2005.

[5]Cohen, Houck, Szanto, et al., 2006.

[6]AHCPR, 1993.

[7]Young et al., 2001.

[8]Wei, Sambamoorthi, Olfson, et al., 2005.

[9]Kovacs, 2001.

[10]Kessler, 2003.

[11]Desai & Jann, 2000.

[12]Nolen-Hoeksema, 2002.

[13]Bolen & Scannapieco, 1999.

[14]Girgus & Nolen-Hoeksema, 2006.

[15]Le et al., 2003.

FIGURE 10.2 Depression in Vulnerable and Oppressed Populations (*continued*).

PEOPLE WITH DISABILITIES
- Medical conditions and disabilities increase the risk of depression.[16]

MINORITIES
- Being African-American is associated with lack of appropriate treatment for depression.[17]
- African-American women have the lowest rates of suicide.[18]
- American Indian and Alaskan Natives have the highest rate of suicide among these aged 15 to 24.[19]

Tammy is not eligible for public housing. She used to live in a Section 8 apartment, but was evicted. Her children were responsible for paying her bills, and she did not realize that they were not paying her rent until she owed over $2,000. She is ineligible to get back on the public housing list until she has paid back this money. She has worked with the Center for Independent Living to try to find alternatives, but the cheapest apartments they have been able to find her have rents higher than her monthly income.

Tammy says she does not take beta interferon, a medication used to treat MS symptoms that has a suspected connection to the development of depression (Arnett & Randolph, 2006). On her most recent admission, eight months ago, the psychiatrist prescribed an antidepressant medication and recommended psychotherapy when she left the hospital. Tammy said she went to only one psychotherapy appointment and stopped taking the antidepressants when she began feeling better. She now reports that she is starting to wonder if she should go back to the psychiatric hospital, but she is afraid that if she leaves her friend's house this time, the friend will not let her move back in once she leaves the hospital. She would rather work on easing the stress in her life.

One method Tammy uses to cope with her feelings is smoking marijuana. She started smoking it to relieve the symptoms of her MS, but in the past few months she admits she has been using it more to cope with psychological stresses. She said she smokes approximately every other day and gets marijuana from the young men with whom she lives.

Tammy does not have many outside social activities. She used to belong to a church, but when she was evicted and moved in with her friend it was too far to walk, so she stopped attending. She does have a strong faith in God and believes that despite all the troubles she is having, things could be much

---

[16]Ciesla & Roberts, 2001; Karasu et al., 2002.

[17]Young et al., 2001.

[18]Tondo, Albert, & Baldessarini, 2006.

[19]CDC, 2004.

worse. She is grateful that she has housing for the moment and is able to receive the medical care she needs.

Tammy has a tenth-grade education. She said she used to smoke crack cocaine in her "younger days," but after her then husband went to prison for drugs 20 years ago, she stopped. She said that it wasn't that difficult when she "made up her mind to do it." She said that both her parents drank too much and fought with each other verbally and physically when she was growing up. She said both her parents died when she was a young adult—her father from emphysema and her mother from cancer.

Directions Part I, Multi-Axial Diagnosis: Given the case information and your responses to the questions below, prepare the following: a multi-axial diagnosis, the rationale for the diagnosis and GAF score, and additional information you would have wanted to know in order to make a more accurate diagnosis.

Questions to consider when formulating a diagnosis for Tammy

1. Has the client experienced episodes of major depression in the past?

2. Are there recent stressors that could account for the depressive symptoms? In that case, could a social worker give a diagnosis of adjustment disorder with depressed mood?

3. Could substances account for the depressive symptoms?

4. Could Tammy's MS medication be contributing to the depression?

5. Could Tammy's medical condition be responsible for the depressive symptoms?

6. Are symptoms of mania or hypomania evident currently, or were they in the past?

7. Is a substance-related diagnosis warranted in this case? How could one determine if abuse or dependence is the more appropriate diagnosis?

8. How can a clinician account for Tammy's failure to follow through with the recommendations for treatment after her last inpatient hospitalization?

Multi-Axial Diagnosis

Axis I:

Axis II:

Axis III:

Axis IV:

Axis V:

Rationale and Differential Diagnosis

Additional Information Needed

Biopsychosocial Risk and Resilience Influences

Onset

BIOLOGICAL INFLUENCES

The fact that major depression tends to run in families partially supports the notion of a process of genetic transmission. The heritability for major depression ranges from 31 to 42 percent (Sullivan et al., 2000). The genetic potential for depression may be transmitted as an affective temperament that makes one susceptible to a mood disorder depending on other internal and external mechanisms.

As discussed in Chapter 2, biological theories of depression have been formulated largely from the hypothesized actions of antidepressant drugs. Many types of depression are thought to be associated with deficiencies of certain neurotransmitters in the limbic area of the brain, which controls emotions. Although no genes linked to depression have been found to have more than small effects (Ebmeier, Donaghey, & Steele, 2006), a large longitudinal study of a birth cohort in the United States found that a variation in the serotonin transporter gene appears to moderate the influence of life events on depression (Caspi, Sudgen, Moffit, Taylor, Craig, et al., 2003). The researchers concluded that this finding supports the notion of a gene-environment interaction in the production of depression. Sher (2003) reported that an increase in the secretion of the cortical enzyme caused by stress contributes to vulnerability to mood disorders. The author asserts that there is a genetic component to variability in cortical secretion.

Various biological and psychosocial reasons have been postulated for the gender gap in depression. Biological theories consider the hormonal shifts females experience during premenses, pregnancy, postpartum, and menopause (Desai & Jann, 2000). One set of researchers studied the pubertal development of 100 Caucasian girls between the ages of 10 and 14 and found that early puberty predicted higher levels of emotional arousal, which in turn predicted increased depressive affect (Graber, Brooks-Gunn, & Warren, 2006). In this sample negative life events and attention difficulties appeared to stimulate the production of certain biochemicals associated with depression and aggression.

In adulthood, almost one-fifth of women who give birth (19.2 percent) have a major depressive episode during the first three months postpartum (Gavin, Gaynes, Lohr, et al., 2005). The specific mechanisms by which hormones exert their influence have not been delineated (Le, Munoz, Ippen, & Stoddard, 2003), although it has been thought that they relate to the increased presence of gonadal hormones such as estrogen, which control the coding of serotonin, during women's childbearing years (Steiner, Dunn, & Born, 2003). However, it may be that instead hormonal changes interact with genetic vulnerabilities and psychosocial influences. For example, depression may result when a genetically vulnerable person undergoes role changes related to reproductive events in societies that devalue women's roles.

MEDICAL PROBLEMS

While depression can be detrimental to physical health, involving activity restriction, illnesses, increased health care use, and mortality (Rugulies, 2002; Shanmugham, Karp, Drayer, et al., 2005), medical conditions such as heart attack, cancer, stroke, multiple sclerosis, HIV, and diabetes in turn increase the risk of depression (Ciesla & Roberts, 2001; Karasu et al., 2002). In older adults, symptoms of depression can be precipitated by illnesses common at that stage of life, including Alzheimer's disease, stroke, Parkinson's disease, heart disease, cancer, and arthritis (Alexopoulos, Katz, Reynolds, et al., 2001; Shanmugham et al., 2005). Untreated depression can also be a risk influence for the recovery of health. It can increase overall levels of impairment, interfere with healing, and impede an individual's motivation and ability to follow through with prescribed treatment.

PSYCHOLOGICAL INFLUENCES

One of the reasons that teens are more vulnerable to depression is that adolescence is a period when young people develop formal operational thinking and can reflect upon causality for events in their lives. They may develop a negative attribution style, attributing negative events to internal, stable, and global attributions ("He broke up with me because

I'm no good") (Abramson, Seligman, & Teasdale, 1978). Positive outcomes are ascribed to external, transient, and specific reasons ("She likes me because she has no one else to talk to in that class"). Adolescence is also a time when future orientation develops, and a person in distress may experience hopelessness about the future (Abela, Brozina, & Haigh, 2002).

At the psychological level, depression is also related to distorted and rigid beliefs and thoughts. These typically involve the "cognitive triad" of depression (thoughts about the self as worthless, the world as unfair, and the future as hopeless) (Beck, Rush, Shaw, & Emery, 1979). Coping style is another psychological variable associated with the onset of depression. Coping methods that are more active in nature, such as problem solving, have the potential to ward off depression. However, avoidant coping styles, such as evading situations and indulging in ruminative thinking (the tendency to focus on the symptoms of a distressed mood in an incessant and passive way, rather than in an active, problem-solving manner) (Nolen-Hoeksema, 2002), present risk. Females may be more likely than males to display ruminative thinking rather than active, problem-solving coping, which may partly explain the gender gap in depression (Dekovic, 1999; Nolen-Hoeksema, 2002).

SOCIAL INFLUENCES

Family factors can influence the development and maintenance of depression in youth. Families with a depressed adolescent often show some of the following characteristics (Diamond, Reis, Diamond, Siqueland, & Isaacs, 2002): weak attachment bonds (Sund & Wichstrom, 2002); parental criticism and hostility; parental psychopathology; ineffective parenting; enmeshed family relationships (Jewel & Stark, 2003); and greater overall family stress (Asarnow, Jaycox, & Tompson, 2001).

Depression in mothers is a particular risk mechanism for youth anxiety and depression both when children are young and when they mature into adulthood. A 20-year longitudinal study found that as adults, children of depressed parents had three times the rate of anxiety disorders, major depression, and substance dependence as did those with non-depressed parents (Weissman, Wickramaratne, & Yoko, 2006; Pilowsky, Wickramaratne, Rush, et al., 2006). The association of parental depression with increased rates of depression in their children may be accounted for by genetics, impaired parenting, modeling, and its link to parental marital problems (Goodman & Gotlib, 1999).

A number of studies have indicated a significant relationship between depression and childhood physical abuse and sexual abuse (Penza, Heim, & Nemeroff, 2006). Of all types of maltreatment, sexual abuse poses the greatest risk for depression and suicide attempts (Fergusson, Beautrais, & Horwood, 2003). The rate of sexual abuse is higher in females (Bolen & Scannapieco, 1996), which may also partly explain the gender gap in the diagnosis of depression.

Social support may mitigate harsh early family circumstances and the stressful life events that people with depression are prone to experience (deBeurs, Beekman, Geerlings, Deeg, Van Dyck, & Van Tilburg, 2001; Kraaij, Arensman, & Spinhoven, 2002). Friends can provide support and enable people to self-disclose in a safe setting. Having positive peers is associated with less depression in adolescence (Gutman & Sameroff, 2004).

For teenage girls, interpersonal stress may contribute to the onset of depression. Adolescent females invest more than boys in relationships. They may "exhibit a heightened concern about what others think of them and a greater dependence on the approval of others . . . (which may or may not be forthcoming) for their own sense of self-worth" (Girgus & Nolen-Hoeksema, 2006). These tendencies lead to greater sensitivity and reactivity to interpersonal stress (Rudolph, 2002). The emotional distress girls may experience seems then to put them at risk for further problems in relationships, thus creating a cycle of distress that may result in depressive symptoms.

For adults, supportive, intimate relationships are a protective influence, whereas marital problems pose a risk for depression (Uebelacker & Whisman, 2006). In terms of the wider social environment, neighborhood cohesiveness acts as a protective influence for adolescent females, whereas neighborhood problems pose risk (Gutman & Sameroff, 2004).

Course and Adjustment

Depressive disorders are associated with high rates of relapse (Brodaty, Luscombe, Peisah, Anstey, & Andrews, 2001; Klein, Shankman, & Rose, 2006) and put people at risk for suicide. For example, suicide is the third leading cause of death among young people ages 15 to 24 (Centers for Disease Control, 2004). However, the course of depression is variable, depending on the balance of risk and protective influences (see Table 10.1).

TABLE 10.1 Biopsychosocial Risk and Resilience Influences for the Course of Depression

RISK INFLUENCES	PROTECTIVE INFLUENCES
Features of the disorder Higher levels of depression Prior depressive episodes Presence of residual symptoms Early onset A longer depressive episode prior to assessment	*Features of the disorder* Lower levels of depression No prior episodes No residual symptoms Later onset Early assessment
Biology Female gender Medical conditions or poor general health Attention problems	*Biology* Male gender Good health
Psychological Comorbid disorders Cognitive distortions Sense of hopelessness More daily hassles	*Psychological* Lack of comorbid disorder General sense of hope Relatively few daily stressors

(Continues)

TABLE 10.1   Biopsychosocial Risk and Resilience Influences for the Course of Depression (Continued)

Social	*Social*
Weak family relationships	Strong family relations
Family conflict	Lack of mental health disorders in parents
Parental psychopathology	
Maternal depression	
Being unmarried	
Stressful life events	
Low SES	Middle to high SES
School problems (suspensions) for children and adolescents	Satisfactory school functioning

Sources: Barnett, Sirey, Bruce, et al., 2002; Birmaher, Ryan, Williamson, et al., 1996; Bockting, Spinhoven, & Koeter, 2006; Brent, Kolko, Birmaher, et al., 1998; Kaminski & Garber, 2002; Kovacs et al., 1997; Mueller, Leon, Keller, et al., 1999; Rushton, Forcier, & Schectman, 2002.

Directions Part II, Biopsychosocial Risk and Resilience Assessment: Formulate a risk and protective mechanisms assessment both for the onset of the disorder and the course of the disorder, including the strengths that you see for this individual.

TABLE 10.2 Biopsychosocial Risk and Resilience Assessment for the Onset of the Disorder

RISK INFLUENCES	PROTECTIVE INFLUENCES
Biological	
Psychological	
Social	

TABLE 10.3 Biopsychosocial Risk and Resilience Assessment for the Course of the Disorder

RISK INFLUENCES	PROTECTIVE INFLUENCES
Biological	
Psychological	
Social	

What techniques could you use to elicit additional strengths in this client?

Intervention

People with depression tend to seek help for their disorder only about six to eight years after onset (Wang, Berglund, Olfson, et al., 2005). This delay is seen as an increase in time to treatment from the past and is most likely due to national public awareness campaigns, the marketing of medications directly to consumers, and expanded insurance coverage. Many people with depression seek help only from primary care providers, and only about 19 percent of them receive appropriate care, defined as using medication or counseling in ways that are consistent with empirically validated treatment guidelines (Young, Klap, Sherbourne, & Wells, 2001). In addition, the lack of appropriate care for depression is associated with being male, African-American, uneducated, younger than 30, or older than 59 (Young et al., 2001). Therefore, social workers should be able to assess clients for depression, especially those particularly at risk of not receiving appropriate care, and either provide them with referrals that will ensure validated treatment or administer the treatment themselves.

The initial stage of intervention for persons who are depressed is to assess for suicidal risk, which is associated with the following factors (Borges, Angst, Nock, et al., 2006; Fawcett, 2006):

- Presence of suicidal or homicidal ideation, with intent or plans
- History and seriousness of previous attempts (a key factor)
- Access to lethal means for committing suicide
- Presence of psychotic symptoms
- Presence of severe anxiety
- Presence of substance use
- Presence of conduct problems
- Family history of or recent exposure to suicide

Some social factors involved with suicide attempts include young age, low socioeconomic status, divorce (Borges et al., 2006), and cultural and religious beliefs that promote suicide—for instance, that suicide is a noble way to handle difficulties (Department of Health and Human Services, 2001).

The social worker can also ask a number of strengths-based questions when doing a suicide risk assessment, such as the following (Bertolino & O'Hanlon, 2002):

- Have you had thoughts about hurting yourself in the past? What did you do to get past that point?
- Things sounded really hard then. How did you manage? How did you stop things from getting even worse?
- What needs to happen now so that you feel a bit better? What will that look like?

If the practitioner concludes that the risk of suicidal behavior is considerable, inpatient treatment should be considered. Inpatient intervention is especially indicated if the client is psychotic, severely hopeless, demonstrates suicidal or homicidal ideation with significant substance abuse, has strong impulses or plans to act on these ideas, has inadequate social supports for effective outpatient treatment, and has a complicating psychiatric or medical condition that makes outpatient medication treatment unsafe (Fawcett, 2006). Outpatient intervention is indicated if the client is free of psychosis, not abusing substances, and maintaining control over suicidal thoughts.

If a client with suicidal ideation is seen on an outpatient basis, the social worker should take certain precautions (Fawcett, 2006). He or she should provide education about the symptoms of depression and the effectiveness of treatment; develop a "no harm" contract; advise abstinence from substances, as these may increase symptoms and impulsive behaviors; see the client at least weekly to monitor suicidal ideation, hopelessness, and substance abuse; explain to family members how to respond to suicidal ideas; and remove any firearms from the house.

Psychotherapy

Interventions for persons with depression may include psychotherapy and medication. The psychotherapies described here include cognitive-behavioral therapy (CBT), interpersonal therapy, family therapy, and bibliotherapy.

The benefits of psychotherapy are that many clients prefer it to medication; it is appropriate with clients who have mild, moderate, or chronic depression; and the person learns to cope with or avoid factors that precipitate the depressive episodes (Karasu et al., 2002). Psychotherapy is particularly indicated when the person's life is characterized by psychosocial stress, difficulty coping, and interpersonal problems. Sometimes psychotherapy is not indicated, however, at least not by itself—for example, if the person is severely depressed or at risk of not completing the course of treatment. Further, sessions may be time-consuming, and it may not be easy to find high-quality treatment and practitioners.

For both adolescents and adults, CBT or interpersonal psychotherapy is considered a first-line psychotherapy due to its greater efficacy relative to medication, lack of side effects, and cost-effectiveness (Antonuccio, Thomas, & Danton, 1997; Wampold, Minami, Baskin, & Tierney, 2002). If psychotherapy is not successful, medication can be used as a supplement.

Interpersonal therapy (IPT) is a relatively brief intervention (approximately 12 sessions) focusing on how current interpersonal relationships have contributed to the person's depression. This perspective considers interpersonal conflicts to be a major source of depression. The social worker's goal is to help the client repair these conflicts (Swartz & Markowitz, 1995). Intervention focuses on significant role transitions, grief processes, and interpersonal disputes or deficits; it has also been adapted for use with adolescents (Moreau, Mufson, Weissman, & Klerman, 1991).

CBT involves *behavioral* models that focus on the development of coping skills, especially in the domains of social skills and pleasant daily activities, so that the person receives more reinforcement from his or her environment. *Cognitive* models include assessing and changing the distorted thinking that people with depression exhibit.

Much more research has been conducted on CBT, however, than on interpersonal therapy. Meta-analyses (including over 80 controlled studies) have shown CBT to be more effective than either no-treatment control groups or medication (Sanderson & McGinn, 2001), even for chronic depression (DeRubeis, Gelfand, Tang, & Simons, 1999). CBT has also been used to treat depression successfully in older adults (Arean & Cook, 2002). "Nevertheless, there are insufficient data on the efficacy of CBT for minority elderly, frail elderly, and older adults with mild cognitive impairment" (Mackin & Arean, 2005, p. 812).

A meta-analysis has indicated that group treatment for depression is as helpful as individual treatment (McDermut, Miller, & Brown, 2001). Since group treatment is generally more cost-effective, social workers may consider delivering treatment through groups for this population.

Another modality studied for the administration of CBT has been telephone delivery for people who are incapacitated by illness (such as MS) (Mohr, Hart, & Julian, 2005). This method may be viable and cost-effective for people who have difficulties with mobility, transportation, and child care. Yet another modality used for CBT is computer-assisted technology (Wright, Wright, Albano, et al., 2005); outcomes are similar to the standard delivery of CBT.

For adolescents, meta-analyses (Cuijpers, 1998; Reinecke, Ryan, & Dubois, 1998) have indicated positive outcomes for CBT in terms of reduction of symptoms for up to two years. Another major review, however, found that none of the studies on CBT met the criteria for well-established treatments (Kaslow & Thompson, 1998). Key components of well-supported, efficacious treatments include an offering of manualized treatment that has produced superior results over comparison conditions in at least two randomized, controlled trials. However, the work of Stark and colleagues (Stark, Reynolds, & Kaslow, 1987; Stark, Rouse, & Livingston, 1991) merited the standard of a "probably efficacious treatment" for children (grades three to eight), and the work of the research team of Lewinsohn and colleagues (Clarke, Hawkins, Murphy, Sheeber, Lewinsohn, & Seeley, 1995; Lewinsohn, Clarke, Hops, & Andrews, 1990; Lewinsohn, Clarke, Rhode, Hops, & Seeley, 1996) merited the standard of "probably efficacious treatment" for adolescents.

Despite the amount of research support for CBT, not everyone is suited to CBT, however. Characteristics associated with positive response include employment, female gender, an absence of comorbidity, and functional attitudes (Karasu et al., 2002).

As discussed, family influences play a large role in the development of depression in adolescents. However, based on the available evidence, *family therapy* for adolescents does not seem to offer any particular advantages over individual therapy (Klein, Dougherty, & Olino, 2005).

For adults, when depression arises in an interpersonal context, cognitive-behavioral marital therapy may be indicated (Beach & Jones, 2002). This skill-building approach follows the principles of social learning, cognitive techniques, and behavioral exchange to enhance marital support and intimacy and reduce marital stress and negative expectancies. However, the few studies conducted have been primarily with white, middle-class, married couples seen in outpatient settings.

Apart from studies on couples, family work has not been a focus of research. However, among severely depressed individuals the addition of a brief course of family therapy (average five sessions) to medication improved outcomes following hospitalization (Miller, Keitner, Ryan, et al., 2005).

Bibliotherapy is an intervention technique in which a client reads books related to overcoming or managing depression more effectively (Cuijpers, 1997; Floyd, 2003; Scogin, Hanson, & Welsh, 2003). Bibliotherapy can be administered as an adjunct to other psychotherapies (the practitioner recommends a book to be read between visits) or as a self-administered treatment without other interventions. Bibliotherapy tends to work best for clients with mild to moderate levels of depression. The benefits are that the client can work at his or her own pace at home, it is cost-effective for those who cannot afford medication or psychotherapy, and it provides skills for coping after the intervention has ended. Limitations include its lack of appropriateness for clients with severe depression or low motivation, low reading ability, cognitive impairments, or a history of unsuccessful individual therapy.

Bibliotherapy has been empirically evaluated in several published studies (Scogin, Hanson, & Welsh, 2003; Floyd, 2003; Smith, Floyd, Jamison, & Scogin, 1997; Cuijpers, 1997). These researchers evaluated the effectiveness of both Dr. David Burns's *Feeling Good* and Dr. Peter Lewinsohn's *Control Your Depression* as self-administered treatments for depression. The investigators concluded that the books were as effective as either a full course of individual psychotherapy or treatment with antidepressant drugs. Positive gains were noted for adults and elders for a three-year follow-up period.

Medication

Patterns of intervention with adolescents have changed over the years, with less focus on psychotherapy and a greater use of medication (Olfson, Marcus, Druss, et al., 2002). Social workers should thus be prepared to educate clients and their families about the benefits and limitations of medication. The prescribing physician should see clients often (every one to two weeks) in the initial treatment phase. Close monitoring produces greater treatment adherence and more opportunities for education and also enables clinicians (including social workers) to assess clients for potential worsening of symptoms, the emergence of suicidal thinking, and other complicating factors.

Concerns have been raised about the use of medication with youngsters. For children, cardiac problems may be associated with the tricyclic medications (Silva, Gabbay, & Minami, 2005). Indeed, the older antidepressants are not recommended for children, given the lack of evidence to support their use (Hazell, O'Connell, & Heathcote, 2003). In the United Kingdom, due to concerns about suicidality, even the selective serotonin reuptake inhibitors (SSRIs) are banned for people under age 18.

In this country SSRIs are used with adolescents and have shown greater therapeutic effectiveness and fewer adverse effects than the older tricyclic drugs. A systematic review of SSRIs with youth aged five to 18 found that only fluoxetine (Prozac) showed favorable risk-to-benefit profiles (Whittington, Kendall, Fonagy, et al., 2004). A more recent meta-analysis indicated that Prozac, as well as other antidepressants, although having only a modest effect on depression, has benefits greater than the risks from suicidal ideation or attempts in teenagers (Bridge, Iyengar, Salary, et al., 2007). However, only Prozac outperformed placebo in children younger than 12. Therefore, social workers should be aware that other SSRIs are not indicated for the treatment of depression in children.

According to the results of a recent large-scale, multisite study, a combined approach offering both medication (in the study Prozac was given) and CBT over 36 weeks was found most effective, resulting in gains for a majority of youth in that condition (71 percent) (Treatment for Adolescents with Depression, 2004). Prozac alone was next in effectiveness, improving depression in 61 percent of participants. The CBT group performed only slightly better than placebo (with 43 percent versus 35 percent improving).

Along with antidepressants, antipsychotics are being prescribed, for a significant number of youth. The reader should note that there are no controlled studies on the use of either antipsychotics or antidepressant and antipsychotic combinations for the treatment of depression in youth (Olfson, Blanco, Liu, Moreno, & Laje, 2006).

Because of its perceived cost-effectiveness, medication is increasingly prescribed as a first-line treatment for depression in adults by managed care health organizations. However, in a study of the cost-effectiveness of fluoxetine (Prozac) versus CBT and their combination, medication involved a 33 percent higher cost than CBT alone over a two-year period (Antonuccio et al., 1997). Higher costs were related to the increased rate of relapse with medication; the side effects experienced; and, most seriously, suicide.

There is a common perception that the newer SSRIs are more effective than the older tricyclic antidepressants, but a meta-analysis of 102 randomized controlled trials found no overall difference in efficacy between the two classes of drugs (Anderson, 2000). The exception is that the tricyclic drugs appear more effective in inpatient settings. The SSRI drugs are better tolerated, however, with significantly lower rates of treatment discontinuation. Further, studies have shown that the effects of antidepressants are not substantially greater than placebo effects. A comprehensive review of studies on medication efficacy indicated that medication might be only 25 percent more effective than inactive placebos (placebos without side effects) (Antonuccio, Burns, Danton, et al., 2000). More recently, a meta-analysis comparing tricyclic antidepressants with active placebos (those that mimic the side effects of medication) indicated that the tricyclics performed only "slightly better" than the active placebos (Moncrieff, Wessely, & Hardy, 2004).

A recent large-scale study showed that an eight-week dose of citalopram (Celexa) produced remission rates (defined as the absence of symptoms) of 28 percent and response rates (a reduction of about half in symptom levels) of 47 percent (Trivedi, Rush, Wisniewski, et al., 2006). As discussed in the risk and protective influences, remission is a desirable outcome because residual symptoms after treatment put people at risk for relapse. The Trivedi et al. (2006) study results demonstrate that a majority of people (over 70 percent) do not meet the desired goal of medication, and fewer than half even show a response.

A common practice, if there is lack of response with one antidepressant, is to try another. For instance, in a continuation of the study described above, remission rates were examined for those who initially lacked response to Celexa (Rush, Trivedi, Wisniewski, et al., 2006). Apparently, there was little difference in performance between the various SSRIs or SNRIs, with remission rates ranging between 17.6 percent and 24.8 percent. This study also shows the generally comparable efficacy of the various antidepressants commonly prescribed. Another practice, if there is lack of response to medication, is to augment with another antidepressant. Referring again to the same study above, Trivedi, Fava, Wisniewski, et al. (2006) found that adding bupropion (Wellbutrin) to Celexa resulted in remission rates of nearly 30 percent.

A nationally representative sample indicated that a significant proportion of clients (40 percent) discontinue taking medication during the first 30 days of treatment (Olfson, Marcus, Tedeschi, & Wan, 2006). Individuals who were of low SES and of Hispanic origin were particularly at risk for stopping the use of medication. Clients treated with SSRIs or SNRIs were more likely to continue medication than those treated with the older medications. The use of psychotherapy was positively related to drug adherence in this review.

For older adults, a majority (72 percent) of 18 placebo-controlled trials indicated statistically significant favorable results for medication use versus placebos (Taylor & Doraiswamy, 2004). Still, the authors warn that a significant number of clients will not respond to medication.

To summarize, the use of medication to treat depression has certain indications and contraindications (Karusu et al., 2002; AHCPR, 1993). Medications may be indicated if the client has severe depression, prefers the option of medication, has a personal or a first-degree relative history of prior positive response, is likely to adhere to a medication regime, and can work with an experienced physician. Medication may also be indicated when psychotherapy alone has not been successful (Antonuccio et al., 1997). Medication may not be indicated if there are cost considerations or if the client has a medical illness or takes other medications that make its use risky. The benefits of medication are that it is easily administered, may be effective for all severity levels of depression, and can produce a relatively rapid response (four to six weeks). Its limitations are the need for monitoring, the possibility of adverse effects, potential use in suicide attempts, and the possibility of nonadherence. Further, it is difficult to predict how a certain person will react to a particular medication. The process of finding a medication and appropriate dosage that helps improve mood is one of trial and error (Healy, 2002).

Older Adults

For major depression in elders, first-line evidence supports use of an antidepressant, either alone or in combination with psychotherapy (Shanmugham et al., 2005). As with younger adults, about 50 percent of older people will experience treatment response, which is defined as a reduction of half their symptoms, from a course of antidepressants. Because of changes in physiology in older adults, clinicians should increase doses more slowly than in younger clients and monitor them closely for side effects and medication interactions, to which older adults tend to be more sensitive (Alexopoulos et al., 2001).

Although nearly all older adults in the United States have basic health coverage through Medicare, fee-for-service reimbursements currently cover only 50 percent of mental health care costs (Wei, Sambamoorthi, Olfson, et al., 2005). Depressed older adults are often unwilling to seek treatment when they have to pay out of pocket. Further, primary care physicians may not refer older adults to psychotherapy because of a lack of awareness of its possible clinical efficacy. A national survey of community-dwelling Medicare beneficiaries aged 65 and older found that the use of psychotherapy was associated with relatively younger age, a college education, and the availability of psychotherapists (Wei et al., 2005). Even when psychotherapy was used, only a minority (33 percent) included clients who remained in consistent treatment, defined as extending for at least two-thirds of the episode of depression. The availability of local providers correlated positively with consistent psychotherapy use. One implication of this study is that for older adults with less formal education, social workers may need to provide education on how psychotherapy works and to respond to an individual's concerns about therapy.

In addition to CBT, discussed earlier, reminiscence and life review therapies may be effective for older adults, according to a meta-analysis of 24 studies (Bohlmeijer, Smit, & Cuijpers, 2003). A strong effect was shown for these interventions, especially for those with severe depression. Most of the studies were conducted in noninstitutionalized settings, however, so the results may not generalize to the elderly in nursing home and extended care facilities.

Directions Part III, Goal Setting and Treatment Planning: Given your risk and protective factors assessments of the individual, your knowledge of the disorder, and evidence-based practice guidelines, formulate goals and a possible treatment plan for this individual.

Critical Perspective

As major depressive disorder criteria stemmed mainly from clinical consensus, Zimmerman, McGlinchey, Young, and Chelminski (2006) conducted an empirical analysis and found that the weight change and indecisiveness criteria could be eliminated from the diagnosis. This modification would result in more streamlined criteria and would include subthreshold cases (those that currently do not meet all the necessary criteria), in which there is often significant impairment.

It must also be acknowledged that the criteria for depression, focusing on affective and cognitive symptoms, comprise a view that is particular to industrialized, Western nations (Marecek, 2006, p. 289). Other cultures describe different ways of understanding depressive suffering. For example, in many Asian cultures, somatic complaints are foremost. The DSM criteria fail to capture these culture-bound experiences.

The chief limitation of the psychiatric view of depression is the assumption underlying the diagnosis, namely, that it is due to internal dysfunction. This assumption can be seen in the widespread acceptability of biological theories of depression and the use of medication as treatment. The focus on medication, which furthers the interest of the pharmaceutical companies, has also been criticized as a method aimed at providing only symptom relief rather than targeting broader social changes (Marecek, 2006).

Directions Part IV, Critical Perspective: Formulate a critique of the diagnosis as it relates to this case example. Question to coonsider include: Does this diagnosis represent a valid mental disorder from the social work perspective? Is this diagnosis significantly different from other possible diagnoses? your critique should be based on the valuues of the social work profession (which are incongruent in some way with the medical model) and the validity of the specific diagnostic ccriteria applied to this case.

CASE 2

Note: While the following clinical illustration is intended to focus on Axis I disorders, the client in this case also experiences *mental retardation*, an Axis II disorder that is not covered in this book. Mental retardation is a developmental disability, presumed to be lifelong. It is characterized by an IQ below 70 that creates significant impairments in two or more of the following areas: self-care, communication, home living, social and interpersonal skills, use of community resources, self-direction, functional academic skills, work, leisure, health, and safety. It is important to emphasize that the diagnosis is made not on the basis of IQ alone but on the interaction of IQ with the person's environment, which together affect the client's ability to function. Mental retardation may be mild (IQ of 50–55 to 70), moderate (IQ of 30–35 to 50–55), severe (IQ of 20–25 to 35–40), or profound (IQ less than 20–25).

Indira is a 23-year-old female who, after a long waiting period, was accepted to live in a group home for people with mental retardation. Twelve individuals live in the group home, which is located in a middle-class neighborhood. The home is split up into three apartments, with four residents each.

Prior to her move to the group home, which occurred four months ago, Indira lived with her parents and younger brother in a private home. Her parents came to this country from India before Indira and her brother were born. Her father is a computer analyst, and her mother never worked outside the home. Indira was the first child; she was born prematurely and with the umbilical cord wrapped around her neck. According to Indira's mother, the doctors did not believe that Indira would survive, and she spent many months in the hospital before her parents were allowed to take her home.

During her childhood Indira was tested and found to have an IQ of about 15; she is also blind and suffers from a seizure disorder. Indira cannot walk more than a few steps and only when she can hold onto someone with both hands. She is wheelchair-bound and overweight. Indira cannot communicate verbally but understands the English language. She conveys "yes" and "no" by nodding or shaking her head. She can follow simple commands. Indira can't complete any activities of daily living by herself. For example, she is incontinent. She can feed herself with a spoon, but only messily, and she has to wear a bib. She can drink with a straw but cannot lift a cup. She can rattle toys and put them in her mouth.

When she was a child, Indira attended a school for children with severe disabilities, autism, and mental retardation. After graduating from this school, Indira participated in a day program for adults with mental handicaps. At the day program, participants typically watch television, do puzzles, and color.

According to Indira's mother, there is no history of mental illness in either her or her husband's family, and she has never suffered from depression, although she is very sad about Indira's current plight. She denies that Indira has ever suffered from depression.

The relationship between her parents appears to be loving. Indira's brother enjoyed a healthy childhood and is now a senior in high school. Indira's primary caregiver has always been her mother. However, after 23 years of caring for her handicapped and overweight child, her mother started to experience health problems, especially backaches. The family decided that they could no longer adequately care for Indira and asked a social worker for help in finding a suitable placement.

After several visits to the group home, Indira was accepted and she was moved in. She had one staff member assigned to her in the morning and a different one in the evening, and she appeared to connect well with both of them. She smiled and responded to games and outings that were initiated by staff. Two weeks after Indira moved into the group home, however, management changed and several permanent staff quit their job. The result was that Indira now had relief staff caring for her, meaning different voices on a daily basis. Especially during the weekends, Indira did not have much to do. She got up late and then spent most of her day in the living room, where the television was on. Outings were rare due to the unstable staff situation, and relief staff did not want to take the responsibility of taking residents into the community.

Indira started to become less active; she did not smile anymore and was easily annoyed and distracted, making her feelings known through nonverbal sounds and body position. She refused to eat most meals except for desserts and started losing weight. Indira's refusal to eat might have been caused by the different food. Her mother usually cooked Indian food, with lots of rice, spiced vegetables, and fruits. Since the cow is sacred for Hindus, Indira had never eaten beef before. The cook in the group home was not able to reproduce these foods and prepared standard American meals, such as hamburger, macaroni and cheese, tuna helper, and so on.

At night staff would often hear her crying for a long time until she fell asleep. Indira then had a difficult time getting up in the mornings. She used to be cooperative and help staff by moving her body into the right position for washing and dressing but refused to do so after a while. She appeared to become more withdrawn and closed her eyes more often during the day. When staff tried to engage her in an activity, Indira would bury her face in her hands and rock herself back and forth as if to comfort herself, while making noises that sounded as if she were crying—even though no tears streamed down her face.

Indira's parents became very concerned for their daughter; they visited her two to three times a week, but Indira did not change her behavior when they were around. She rejected the hands of her mother and did not hug her as she used to do.

Indira's behavior changed gradually at first and became more severe after several weeks. In the meantime, the staff situation in the group home did not stabilize; Indira continued to have different caregivers. Indira exhibited the same behavior in her day placement, and her counselor consistently reported

that Indira was not eating her lunch and was not participating in group activities as she used to. The nurse at the group home eventually became concerned enough to schedule a complete physical exam and visit with the psychiatrist for Indira, even though when her doctors saw her just prior to her move into the group home, everything had seemed fine.

Please go to the Appendix for directions to this case: The following questions will help to guide your thinking about a possible multi-axial diagnosis.

Questions to consider when formulating a diagnosis for Indira

1. What are Indira's primary symptoms?

2. Is there a clearly identifiable environmental or interpersonal stressor or stressors that immediately preceded Indira's symptoms? If so, what is it (or are they)?

3. Has Indira suffered from major depression in the past?

4. Are there any aspects of Indira's personality (as much as we know of it) that put her at risk for the symptoms she displays?

5. Are there any environmental stressors prior to the current one(s) that may have put Indira at risk for her symptoms?

6. What strengths are evident in Indira, her family, and her residential setting that may help to resolve the problem situation?

CASE 3

Mrs. Elizabeth Cuthbert is an 81-year-old Caucasian female. She has been diagnosed with syncope (fainting spells), hypertension, and chronic obstructive pulmonary disease. For the last four months she has resided in a nursing facility and receives skilled nursing services. Mrs. Cuthbert's move to the facility occurred as a result of repeated syncope and falls. Her condition has been exacerbated by the recent development of a foot drop, a weakening of the structures in her ankle that allows the foot to dangle when walking. This ailment has increased her risk of falling. Mrs. Cuthbert has been fitted with an ankle foot orthosis (AFO) and provided with a walker, but she claims these aids make her feel "weak." Mrs. Cuthbert receives physical therapy for her balance and occupational therapy for her tasks of daily living. Her discharge plan involves placement in an assisted living apartment once she has developed the safety and ambulation skills that will allow her to live without constant monitoring.

Mrs. Cuthbert's medications for the last six months include therapeutic aspirin, blood pressure medication, and Tylenol for pain relief from her fall and osteoarthritis. She is compliant with her medications.

Mrs. Cuthbert was widowed 20 years ago and has lived alone in her home of 35 years since that time. Her immediate family includes two adult children, who live in the area, and three grandchildren, who visit and send her letters. Family members visit frequently, at least twice a week.

Mrs. Cuthbert expresses a negative attitude toward the aged in comments during unrelated discussions. For instance, when the social work intern first met her, she cast aspersions on an "old dog" who lived in the unit, and then went on to make negative comments about her own appearance, saying she looked like "an old hag." She received the social worker's supportive comments positively, but the change in attitude appears transitory.

The results of a mini-mental status examination conducted on Mrs. Cuthbert indicated that she was aware of person, time, and place. Mrs. Cuthbert was also evaluated using a mood scale to determine her risk for depression. She scored 7 out of 15 (a score higher than 5 is indicative of depression). Her response to the mood-scale questions revealed feelings of worthlessness, low energy, insomnia, and diminished interest in pleasurable activities. Mrs. Cuthbert evidences no symptoms of mania.

Mrs. Cuthbert is undergoing significant change in her social support system as a result of her recent move to the nursing facility. She no longer has the neighbors whom she visited each day as she went about retrieving her newspaper, checking on her garden, and watering her outdoor plants. She has lost the use of her car and feels that she should give up driving permanently to prevent possible accidents. She also no longer has the option of walking to her place of worship because of her current condition.

An additional problem for Mrs. Cuthbert is her reluctance to make safety changes that will allow her to move to an assisted living apartment in a nearby community where several lifelong friends reside. She has been very reluctant to adopt the walker or the AFO and has been refusing the majority of her physical and occupational therapy treatments because she is "tired."

During her care plan meeting Mrs. Cuthbert expressed surprise that the entire interdisciplinary team had gathered to discuss her case with her and her family. She asked, "Why are all of you interested in me?" She stated that she wanted to move to assisted living because she would be able to visit with her friends there once she did so. When told that she could not move until she addressed the safety and ambulation deficits she is experiencing, she expressed interest in cooperating with the various therapists and counselors.

According to Mrs. Cuthbert's daughter, Barbara, until her current health problems and the move to the nursing facility, Mrs. Cuthbert was a relatively contented person. She crocheted, enjoyed crossword puzzles, called on friends, assisted two shut-ins whom she has known for years, and had her grandchildren over for weekend visits. Since her admission to the nursing home, it has become difficult for her to accomplish several of her old activities, and simply not feasible to continue others. However, she has also discontinued the activities that were appropriate for her while at the nursing home, except for doing crossword puzzles. Barbara noted that her mother was not interested in going out for meals as she had been before her fall. Her daughter speculated that her mother might not want to be seen in public with the AFO and walker, but noted that she also refused take-out meals offered as well. When asked, Barbara was unaware of any history of mood disorders or other mental illness in her mother's background, but said that her mother wouldn't typically speak of such things anyway.

Mrs. Cuthbert's financial situation is sound. She owns her own house and collects pensions from both her own employment as a secretary and her husband's work.

Please go to the Appendix for directions to this case: The following questions will help to guide your thinking about a possible multi-axial diagnosis.

Questions to consider when formulating a diagnosis for Mrs. Cuthbert

1. What are Mrs. Cuthbert's primary symptoms?

2. Is there a clearly identifiable environmental or interpersonal stressor or stressors that immediately preceded Mrs. Cuthbert's symptoms? If so, what is it (or are they)?

3. Are there any episodes of major depression in Mrs. Cuthbert's history?

4. Are there any aspects of Mrs. Cuthbert's personality (as much as we know of it) that put her at risk for the symptoms she displays?

5. Are there any environmental stressors prior to the nursing home placement that may have put Mrs. Cuthbert at risk for her symptoms?

6. What strengths are evident in Mrs. Cuthbert, her family, and her residential setting that may help to resolve the problem situation?

11

— ▾▲▾ —

Bipolar Disorder

Catherine is a 38-year-old married Mexican-American female with no children who lives in a rural county. She was court-ordered to attend an outpatient mental health clinic for individual and group anger management services. Two months ago she was charged with assault by her husband, after stabbing him in the shoulder with a steak knife during an argument at a local restaurant. Catherine is also currently awaiting incarceration for an arrest in which she was recklessly driving a vehicle without a license. She has in fact been jailed on five occasions, for offenses ranging from disturbing the peace to assault. The social worker met with Catherine on four occasions over five weeks. Catherine is separated from her husband but is open to possibly reuniting with him after she receives professional help.

Catherine is in generally good physical health and reports that she is in regular contact with her family physician. She broke her arm two years ago in a saloon fight, however, and has diminished strength in that arm. She also reports having ankle pain due to possible arthritis, which moderately decreases her physical mobility. Still, Catherine has kept a full-time job at the Post Office for the last 15 years, working primarily as a mail sorter but occasionally as a deliverer.

Catherine reports that she has had irritable and "up and down" moods for most of her adult life. She describes extended periods of time when she becomes "hyperactive" and easily annoyed by people around her. Catherine says she has "incredible energy" at those times and "gets a lot of things done." At those times she likes delivering the mail, working out at the local recreation center, eating out in restaurants, and going to bars. She rests primarily with "short naps" during her energy bursts. Catherine drinks alcohol (only beer) regularly and makes no apologies for it. "It's fun. Who says girls can't hold their liquor like the guys?" Upon further questioning, she admits that she only drinks "enough to get drunk" when she is in a "high energy" phase. Otherwise she limits herself to a few beers on the weekends.

Catherine admits that she "wears herself out" after about a month of this hyperactivity, becoming "shaky" and "disoriented" from a lack of sleep. When she is in a manic episode, she is apt to lose her temper and will argue with "almost anyone" who gets in the way of her activities. She gets into physical fights frequently, often with strangers, but sees this as acceptable behavior. "I was raised to take care of myself. No one is going to push me around." Despite her erratic behaviors, Catherine is well known and "accepted for who I am" in her small community. The culture of her Mexican-American family of origin features high levels of emotional expressiveness, and Catherine is comfortable acting in this way too. Following her arrests, she is typically released from jail after a few days to the custody of her husband, with the charges dropped.

Bipolar disorder is a mood disorder in which a person experiences one or more manic episodes that usually alternate with episodes of major depression (APA, 2000). Depressive episodes are described in Chapter 10. A manic episode is a period in which a person's mood is elevated and expansive to such a degree that he or she experiences serious functional impairment in all areas of life. Manic episodes may be characterized by unrealistically inflated self-esteem, a decreased need for sleep, pressured speech, racing thoughts, distractibility, an increase in unrealistic goal-directed activity, and involvement in activities with a high potential for painful consequences. Manic episodes develop rapidly and may persist for a few days or up to several months.

Another feature associated with bipolar disorder is the *hypomanic* episode (APA, 2000), a person's gradual escalation over a period of days or weeks from a stable mood to a manic state. In this mild form of mania the person experiences higher self-esteem, a decreased need for sleep, a higher energy level, an increase in overall productivity, and more intensive involvement in pleasurable activities. Its related behaviors may be socially acceptable, but the danger is that the bipolar person's decreased insight may lead him or her to believe that the disorder has permanently remitted and that there is no need for ongoing interventions. In fact, poor insight is a prominent characteristic of the active phases of bipolar disorder (Grant, Hasin, Stinson, Dawson, Chou, et al., 2005).

There are two types of bipolar disorders (APA, 2000): *Bipolar I* disorder is characterized by one or more manic episodes, usually accompanied by a major depressive episode. *Bipolar II* disorder is characterized by one or more major depressive episodes accompanied by at least one hypomanic episode.

Prevalence and Comorbidity

Estimates of the overall prevalence of bipolar disorder have increased in recent years and range from 0.5 to 5 percent (Matza, Rajagopalan, Thompson, & Lissovoy, 2005). The estimated prevalence in the most recent National Comorbidity Survey was 2.1 percent (Merikangas, Akiskal, Angst, Creenberg, & Hirschfeld, et al., 2007).

The lifetime prevalence of bipolar I disorder is equal in men and women (close to 1 percent), although bipolar II disorder is more common in women (up to 5 percent) (Barnes & Mitchell, 2005). In men the number of manic episodes equals or exceeds the number of depressive episodes, while in women depressive episodes predominate.

Bipolar I disorder is often comorbid with substance use, anxiety, and personality disorders (Grant, Stinson, Hasin, Dawson, Chou, et al., 2005). The highest rates of comorbidity are 71 percent for anxiety disorders, 56 percent for a substance use disorder, 49 percent for alcohol abuse disorder, 47 percent for social phobia, and 36 percent for a personality disorder (Marangell, Kupfer, Sachs, & Swann, 2006). One study of 500 clients in a bipolar disorder treatment program noted an earlier age of onset (15.6 versus 19.4 years) and an increased presence of suicidal ideation in persons with comorbid anxiety disorders (Simon, Otto, Wisniewski, Fossey, Sagduyu, et al., 2004). Another study concluded that bipolar disorder is more often accompanied by cluster B personality disorders (antisocial, borderline, narcissistic, and histrionic) than by a major depressive disorder (Mantere, Melartin, Suominen, Rytsala, Valtonen, et al., 2006). Further, a one-year prospective study of 539 outpatients revealed that persons with rapid-cycling bipolar disorder have higher rates of lifetime substance abuse (45.4 percent versus 36.4 percent) and anxiety disorders (50.2 percent versus 30.7 percent) (Kupka, Luckenbaugh, & Post, 2005). Bipolar disorder is also modestly associated with medical illnesses in adulthood, for example, cardiovascular, cerebrovascular, and respiratory diseases (Krishnan, 2005).

Bipolar women are 2.7 times more likely than men to have a comorbid disorder. Women with bipolar disorder have a premature mortality rate, which may be related to metabolic changes that increase their risk of diabetes and vascular disease (Taylor & MacQueen, 2006). Women are also at greater risk for anxiety disorders and thyroid problems. Women have an increased risk of developing episodes of bipolar I disorder in the postpartum period. Bipolar men have a greater prevalence of alcoholism than women do (Barnes & Mitchell, 2005).

Given this information about comorbid disorders, it is important to note that substance abuse and the presence of another comorbid disorder are two major risk influences for suicidal ideation and behavior among persons with bipolar disorder (Hawton, Sutton, Haw, Sinclair, & Harris, 2005). Other risk influences identified in this meta-analysis include a family history of suicide, an early onset of bipolar disorder, high levels of depression, severity of the affective episodes, the "mixed" type of the disorder, and the presence of rapid cycling.

Catherine says that she doesn't know why these energy bursts come and go. "I don't know, it's all about biorhythms, isn't it?" She admits to getting "dark, really dark" for extended periods of time as well, sometimes for several months. She is barely able to get her work done when depressed, admitting that her boss complains about her "laziness." When she is not in a "hyper" or "down" mood, Catherine's moods tend to change throughout any given day. She reports the following symptoms on a daily basis at those times: forgetfulness, shifting ideas, distractibility, cycling between not sleeping at all and sleeping too much, bursts of energy, feelings of elation, decreased interest in most of her daily activities, fatigue, feelings of sadness, and impulsivity.

When asked whether it has ever been suggested that she had a mental problem, Catherine sighs. "My doctor thinks I should take medicine for my moods, but I don't want to do that. I'm not a doper. I like to drink, but I'm not a doper." When pressed on this point, Catherine adds, "I'm usually pretty calm when I see my doctor. I don't go to him when I'm hyper." Surprisingly, Catherine does not recall that many people in her community have suggested professional intervention to her. "I can take care of myself. All of us had to learn to do that where I came from." Regarding her drinking, Catherine does not exhibit signs of tolerance or withdrawal. She experiences no physical symptoms when she does not drink for weeks at a time, and she has not increased her overall alcohol intake over the years.

Catherine was born and raised in a midwestern state and moved to the mid-Atlantic region when she was six years old. Her mother was a homemaker who was considered "odd" by her siblings. "She stayed home most of the time and seemed sad. She never had any fun. She was pretty, though, but I think Dad married her because he got her pregnant." She says her mother was nice but not very active and that she drank too much. Her father, a military veteran, was a "great man" whom she loved very much. He "worked all the time" but played with Catherine and her younger brother, to whom she has never been close.

When Catherine was 16 years old, her father died. She reports that her father was the most important person in her life. She remembers always being an active child but that she got "out of control" at about that time. Her mother died of breast cancer when she was 29 years old, though she reports that her mother's passing was more manageable for her.

Catherine has been married for 15 years to a seemingly supportive husband. "We met at community college. He's a good man, a calm man, and he taught me to get more focused about my life." Carl, a manager at a local manufacturing plant, reports that he loves his wife and repeatedly states, "She is my heart and my life." Catherine and her husband both report having frequent financial difficulties, requiring her husband to work long hours and leaving Catherine at home alone many evenings.

Catherine says she has some friends but inconsistent contact with the people in the community. "I'm friendly with everyone, but nobody in particular." She stated that she is eager for her mandated treatment to end so that she could resume her work routines without interruption. When asked about her possible sentencing to more time in jail, she shrugged. "I'm sorry for acting out like I do. I hope the judge knows that. My husband is OK with me now. I'm a good person."

Assessment of Bipolar Disorder

Because of its presumed biological influences, social workers need to participate in a multidisciplinary assessment of persons with possible bipolar disorder. A meta-analysis of 17 studies revealed that most persons with bipolar disorder were able to identify symptoms in advance of their first episode, the most common of which is sleep disturbance (77 percent median prevalence) (Jackson, Cavanaugh, & Scott, 2003). Adults with bipolar disorder are sometimes misdiagnosed with borderline personality disorder, and as noted earlier, the two disorders are sometimes comorbid (Zanarini, Frankenburg, & Hennen, 2004). There is much symptom overlap between them, as both types of clients may experience dramatic mood swings, alternating periods of depression and elation, and transient psychotic symptoms. The disorders are distinct, however. With the personality disorder, the mood changes are related to environmental influences and chronic feelings of insecurity, whereas bipolar disorder features more biologically patterned mood changes (Stone, 2006). Further, the client with bipolar disorder may function very well when stable, while the client with a personality disorder tends to be continuously labile. Other general assessment guidelines are summarized in Figure 11.1 (First, Francis, & Pincus, 2002).

Social workers must be extremely cautious in their diagnoses of children, since there is controversy about appropriate criteria with that population. Most researchers agree that bipolar disorder can occur in childhood and adolescence, but that it

FIGURE 11.1 Assessment Guidelines for Bipolar Disorder.

- Assess family history for the presence of bipolar disorder, other mood disorders, or substance use disorders.
- Assess the client's social history for evidence of any significant mood problems.
- Facilitate a medical examination to rule out any medical conditions that may be responsible for the symptoms.
- Make sure the symptoms are not the result of the direct physiological effects of substance abuse.
- Rule out major depression, which would be the diagnosis in the absence of any manic or hypomanic episodes.
- Rule out cyclothymic disorder, which is characterized by the presence of hypomanic episodes and episodes of depression that do not meet criteria for that disorder.
- Rule out psychotic disorders, which are characterized by psychotic symptoms in the absence of a mood disorder.
- Assess for suicidal ideation.
- Assess the quality of the client's social supports.
- Evaluate the client's insight into the disorder.

presents differently in those age groups (Birmaher, Axelson, Strober, Gill, Valeri, et al., 2006). Symptoms that are most specific to childhood bipolar disorder include elevated mood, pressured speech, racing thoughts, and hypersensitivity (Youngstrom, Findling, Youngstrom, & Calabrese, 2005). The child typically engages in reckless behavior, but this must be distinguished from either normal behavior or that which may also be associated with other disorders. In one recent literature review it was found that 15 to 28 percent of adults with bipolar disorder experienced the onset of their disorder before age 13 (Post & Kowatch, 2006). The valid diagnosis of bipolar disorder in children can be facilitated with the use of a screening instrument such as the Child Behavior Checklist (Youngstrom, Finding, Youngstrom, & Calabrese, 2005).

Directions Part I, Multi-Axial Diagnosis: Given the case information and your responses to the questions below, prepare the following: a multi-axial diagnosis, the rationale for the diagnosis and GAF score, and additional information you would have wanted to know in order to make a more accurate diagnosis.

Questions to consider when formulating a diagnosis for Catherine

1. What range of symptoms does Catherine present relative to her mental, emotional, and behavioral functioning?

2. How does Catherine describe her movement between high and low moods?

3. Do Catherine's temper outbursts seem to be related to environmental influences?

4. Does Catherine demonstrate symptoms of a personality disorder?

5. How are Catherine's physical problems significant in relation to her mental status?

6. What are Catherine's primary coping mechanisms? Do they seem to be serving her well?

Multi-Axial Diagnosis

Axis I:

Axis II:

Axis III:

Axis IV:

Axis V:

Rationale and Differential Diagnosis

Additional Information Needed

Biopsychosocial Risk and Resilience Influences

Onset

The etiology of bipolar disorder is primarily biological, although certain psychological and social stresses may contribute to the first episode of mania or depression. The discussion below focuses on genetic and biological mechanisms.

GENETIC AND BIOLOGICAL INFLUENCES

Family history studies indicate a higher-than-average aggregation of bipolar disorder in families. Children with a bipolar parent are at increased risk for mental disorders in general, and their chances of developing bipolar disorder are between 2 and 10 percent (Youngstrom, Findling, Youngstrom, & Calabrese, 2005). Persons who have a first-degree relative with a mood disorder are more likely to have an earlier age of onset than persons without a familial pattern. Twin studies further support the heritability of the disorder. A study of identical and fraternal twins in which one member of the pair had bipolar disorder showed a concordance rate of 85 percent (McGuffin, Rijsdijk, Andrew, Sham, Katz, et al., 2003).

Researchers once speculated that the potential for bipolar disorder emanated from a single gene, but studies are now focusing on polygenic models of transmission (Ryan, Lockstone, & Huffaker, 2006). While genetic research remains promising, the "core" of bipolar disorder remains elusive, because no brain-imaging techniques exist yet that might provide details about its causes.

There are various proposed sites of dysfunction in the brain for all the mood disorders. Four areas under study include the role of neurotransmitters, the endocrine system, physical biorhythms, and physical complications during the mother's pregnancy and childbirth (Swann, 2006). The amount and activity of norepinephrine, serotonin, gamma-aminobutyric acid (GABA), and perhaps other nerve tract messengers are abnormal in persons with bipolar disorder, although the causes of these imbalances are unknown. Some theories focus on the actions of the thyroid and other endocrine glands to account for nervous system changes that contribute to manic and depressive episodes. Biorhythms, or the body's natural sleep and wake cycles, are erratic in some bipolar clients and may account for, or result from, chemical imbalances that trigger manic episodes. Finally, a few studies have associated obstetrical complications with early-onset and severe bipolar disorder (Scott, McNeil, & Cavanaugh, 2006).

PSYCHOSOCIAL INFLUENCES

Stressful life events may play an activating role in early episodes of bipolar disorder, with subsequent episodes arising more in the absence of clear external precipitants (Newman, 2006). Persons with bipolar disorder who have a history of extreme early-life adversity (such as physical or sexual abuse) show an earlier age of onset; faster and more frequent cycling; increased suicidality; and more comorbid conditions, including alcohol and substance abuse (Post, Leverich, King, & Weiss, 2001). Most clients can recognize that a depressive or manic episode is coming two to three weeks in advance (Marangell, Kupfer, Sachs, & Swann, 2006). Such symptoms include changes in motivation, sleep cycle disturbances, impulsive behavior (for mania), and changing interpersonal behavior. While such insight is usually fleeting, the client may avoid a full manic or depressive episode if he or she receives intervention during this time.

Course and Outcome

Bipolar I disorder is highly recurrent, with 90 percent of persons who have a manic episode developing future episodes (Evans, 2000). The number of episodes tends to average four in 10 years (APA, 2000). Approximately 50 percent of persons with bipolar disorder move through alternating manic and depressed cycles (Tyrer, 2006). About 10 percent experience rapid cycling (APA, 2000), which implies a poorer long-term outcome, since such persons are at a higher risk for both relapse and suicidal ideation (75 percent have contemplated suicide) (Mackinnon, Potash, McMahon, & Simpson, 2005). It is estimated that 40 percent have a "mixed" type of the disorder, in which a prolonged depressive episode features short bursts of mania. Women are at risk for an episode of bipolar disorder in the postpartum stage, and they experience rapid cycling more than men do, possibly because of hormonal differences and natural changes in thyroid function (Barnes & Mitchell, 2005). A majority of those affected (70 to 90 percent) return to a stable mood and functioning capacity between episodes. Between 5 and 15 percent of those with bipolar II disorder develop a manic episode within five years, which means that their diagnosis must be changed to bipolar I disorder (APA, 2000).

A recent meta-analysis of the literature has summarized the predictors of relapse in bipolar disorder (Altman, Haeri, & Cohen, 2006). Major predictors include the number of previous manic or depressive episodes, a history of anxiety, a persistence of affective symptoms even when the mood is relatively stable, and the occurrence of stressful life events. Other predictors include poor occupational functioning, a lack of social support, high levels of expressed emotion in the family, and the personality characteristics of introversion and obsessionality. We will elaborate on many of these predictors below.

Persons with bipolar disorder tend to experience serious occupational and social problems (Marangell, Kupfer, Sachs, & Swann, 2006). One study indicated a stable working capacity in only 45 percent of clients, and 28 percent experienced a steady decline in job status and performance (Hirschfeld, Lewis, & Vornik, 2003). Missed work, poor work quality, and conflicts with coworkers all contribute to the downward trend for clients who cannot maintain mood stability. From 30 to 60 percent fail to regain full function between episodes with regard to vocational and social performance. A meta-analysis by Quraishi and Frangou (2002) suggests that while general intellectual function is preserved in persons with bipolar disorder who have stabilized, there may be some negative effects related to verbal memory and attention capacity.

An adolescent who develops bipolar disorder may experience an arrest in psychological development, thus developing self-efficacy and dependency problems that endure into adulthood (Floersch, 2003). A study of 263 children and adolescents with the disorder highlighted some issues related to course (Birmaher, Axelson, Strober, Gill, Valeri, et al., 2006). Approximately 70 percent of the subjects recovered from their first episodes and 50 percent showed at least one recurrence, most often with a depressive episode. Figure 11.2 summarizes other risk influences for bipolar disorder among members of vulnerable populations.

Clients who experience high levels of life stress *after* the onset of bipolar disorder are four times more likely to have a relapse than clients with low levels of life stress (Tyrer, 2006). Events that can cause these episodes include disruptions in social and family

FIGURE 11.2 Bipolar Disorder in Vulnerable and Oppressed Populations.

FEMALES

- Women are at greater risk of developing bipolar II disorder, which is characterized by symptoms of major depression.[1]
- Women have an increased risk of developing subsequent episodes of bipolar I disorder during the postpartum period.[2]
- Rapid-cycling bipolar disorder is more common.[3]
- Women with bipolar disorder are more likely than men to have a comorbid disorder.
- Women with bipolar disorder are more likely to die earlier than women without the disorder.
- Women are also more at risk for anxiety disorders and thyroid problems.

YOUTH

- Extreme early-life adversity may place one at more risk of developing bipolar disorder. This experience may also predetermine an earlier age of onset, faster and more frequent cycling, increased suicidality, and more comorbid conditions (including alcohol and substance abuse).[4]

supports and changes in daily routines or sleep-wake cycles, such as air travel and changes in work schedules.

One study found that relapse risk was related to both the lingering presence of symptoms of mania and also to harsh comments from relatives (Rosenfarb, Miklowitz, Goldstein, et al., 2001). Clients from families that are high in expressed emotion (critical comments) were likely to suffer a relapse during a nine-month follow-up period. Another study of 360 persons with bipolar disorder indicated that family interactions had some impact on the one-year course of the disorder (Miklowitz, Wisniewski, Otto, & Sachs, 2005). Clients who were more distressed by their relatives' criticisms had more severe depressive and manic symptoms than persons who were less distressed. Further, relatives who became more upset by the client's criticisms had less severe depressive symptoms at follow-up.

Directions Part II, Biopsychosocial Risk and Protective Factors Assessment: Formulate a risk and protective factors assessment, both for the onset of the disorder and the course of the disorder, including the strengths that you see for this individual.

---

[1]Hilty, Brady, & Hales, 1999.
[2]Hilty, Brady, & Hales, 1999.
[3]Hilty, Brady, & Hales, 1999.
[4]Post, Leverich, King, & Weiss, 2001.

TABLE 11.1 Biopsychosocial Risk and Resilience Assessment for the Onset of the Disorder

RISK INFLUENCES	PROTECTIVE INFLUENCES
Biological	
Psychological	
Social	

TABLE 11.2 Biopsychosocial Risk and Resilience Assessment for the Course of the Disorder

RISK INFLUENCES	PROTECTIVE INFLUENCES
Biological	
Psychological	
Social	

What techniques could you use to elicit additional strengths in this client?

Intervention

The National Comorbidity Study indicates that 80.1 percent of all persons with bipolar disorder have received any intervention (Merikangas et al., 2007). In another study, more than half (53.9 percent) of those who sought treatment attended a mental health facility, although 38.3 percent received services from general medical providers and 20.9 percent received treatment from non–health care providers (percentages are overlapping) (Wang, Lane, Olfson, Pincus, Wells, et al., 2005). These statistics are significant in that medication is always recommended as a primary intervention for bipolar disorder, so clients will likely benefit from seeing psychiatrists. Psychosocial interventions can be helpful for controlling the course of the disorder. A recent literature review found that service providers prefer first to stabilize the client's mental status and then introduce psychosocial interventions (Fava, Ruini, & Rafanelli, 2005).

Medications

The Food and Drug Administration (FDA) has approved a number of medications for the treatment of bipolar disorder (Bowden, Ketter, Sachs, & Thase, 2005). These are summarized in Table 11.3. Most physicians recommend that clients take medication even after their moods stabilize to reduce the risk of recurrence of another mood

TABLE 11.3 FDA-Approved Medications Used to Treat Bipolar Disorder

SYMPTOMS	MEDICATION
For acute mania	Lithium, carbamazepine, divalproex, risperidone, olanzapine, quetiapine, ziprasidone, and aripiprazole
For maintenance of stable mood following an acute phase	Lithium, olanzapine, lamotrigine, and aripiprazole
For long-term treatment of bipolar disorder	Lithium, lamotrigine, and olanzapine
For acute bipolar depression	The combination of olanzapine and fluoxetine

episode. It must be emphasized that while older adults may benefit from the same medications as younger populations, they are more susceptible to adverse effects (Young, 2005).

Lithium is the best studied of the mood-stabilizing drugs. It is effective for stabilizing both manic and depressive episodes in bipolar disorder, although it takes several weeks to take effect and it is more effective for treating manic than mixed or rapid cycling episodes (Burgess, Geddes, Hawton, Townsend, Jamison, et al., 2001). As a maintenance drug, lithium has been shown in a meta-analysis to be effective in preventing all types of relapses, but it is most effective with manic relapses (Geddes, Burgess, Hawton, Jamison, & Goodwin, 2004). Lithium also has a positive effect on clients' suicidal ideation and attempts. A meta-analysis documented an 80 percent decrease in such episodes for consumers who have used the drug for 18 months (Baldessarini, Tondo, Davis, Pompil, Goodwin, et al., 2006). Another meta-analysis demonstrated that lithium, compared to both placebo and other medications, is effective in the prevention of suicide or deliberate self-harm (with 80 percent fewer episodes) and death from all causes (55 percent fewer episodes) in persons with mood disorders (Cipriani, Pretty, Hawton, & Geddes, 2005).

The difference between therapeutic and toxic levels of lithium is not great, so monitoring blood levels is important. Most of the common side effects of lithium are transient and benign, but lithium toxicity is characterized by severe diarrhea, dizziness, nausea and fatigue, slurred speech, and spastic muscle movements. Lithium should not be prescribed for women during pregnancy, as it is associated with fetal heart problems (Bowden, 2000), and it should not be used by breast-feeding women because it is excreted in breast milk. Lithium seems to have an anti-aggression effect on children and adolescents (Carlson, 2002). It is not advised for children under age eight, as its effects on them have not been adequately studied. Adolescents appear to tolerate long-term lithium use well, but there are concerns about its accumulation in bone tissue and effects on thyroid and kidney function. The decreased kidney clearance rates of older adults put them at a higher risk for toxic blood levels (Schatzberg & Nemeroff, 2001).

Another class of medications, the anticonvulsants, is also effective for the treatment of bipolar disorder, although like lithium they are not effective in treating mania in its early stages. Still, the medications offer an advantage over lithium in that they usually begin to stabilize a person's mood in two to five days. Results across studies demonstrate that 60 to 70 percent of clients show significant recovery from a manic episode with the anticonvulsants, with an average response rate of 32 percent for depression (Sachs, Printz, Kahn, Carpenter, & Docherty, 2000).

Valproate is the most thoroughly tested of the anticonvulsants. Carbamazepine is a leading alternative to lithium and valproate, but its side effects tend to be more discomfiting than those of the other drugs, and only about 50 percent of clients who use the medication are still taking it one year later (Nemeroff, 2000). A third anticonvulsant drug, lamotrigine, is used less often to treat manic episodes, but according to a large randomized trial, it is the only drug that is effective for bipolar depression (Bowden, Ketter, Sachs, & Thase, 2005).

The anticonvulsant drugs are all used in the treatment of children with bipolar disorder, but few studies have been done to establish long-term safety (McIntosh & Trotter, 2006). The same qualifications that apply to lithium for pregnant women, children, and older adults also apply to the anticonvulsant medications. Carbamazepine is used more cautiously with children, as it can precipitate aggression (Ginsberg, 2006), and it has also been associated with developmental and cranial defects in newborns (Swann & Ginsberg, 2004).

Antidepressant medications (usually the selective serotonin reuptake inhibitors) are not generally used for the treatment of bipolar I disorder. They have been shown to induce mania in as many as one-third of all clients, and one-fourth of consumers experience the activation of a rapid-cycling course (Gijsman, Geddes, & Rendell, 2004). In bipolar II disorder, however, the antidepressants may be used along with an antimania drug for mood stabilization. After a first episode of bipolar depression, antidepressant therapy should be tapered in two to six months to minimize the possibility of the development of a manic episode.

Many clients are prescribed antipsychotic medications on a short-term basis to control the agitation and psychotic symptoms that may accompany their mood episodes. Approximately one-third of persons with bipolar disorder use small doses of these drugs during the maintenance phase of treatment as well, because they tend to experience periods of intense agitation (Faravelli, Rosi, & Scarpato, 2006). Among the newer antipsychotic medications, aripriprazole, olanzapine, risperidone, quetiapine, and zoprasidone have been tested as treatment adjuncts. In a meta-analysis of 18 studies, all of these drugs were superior to placebo in treating bipolar mania, with no significant differences in effectiveness among them (Perlis, Welge, Vornik, Hirschfeld, & Keck, 2006). These medications may be effective for acute bipolar depression as well.

Two alternative methods of mood stabilization are available for persons with bipolar disorder who do not respond positively to medication. One is electroconvulsive therapy (ECT), in which electrical shocks are given to the client, usually in a series over several weeks. While this form of treatment seems overly invasive to some professionals, it is a demonstrated safe and effective method of stabilizing a client's mood (Rush, Sackeim, & Marangell, 2005). Vagus nerve stimulation, provided far less often than ECT, relies on an implanted stimulator that sends electrical impulses to the left vagus nerve in the neck through a lead implanted under the skin. Even more invasive than ECT, it has been shown to be effective in people who experience severe depression with bipolar disorder (Fink, 2006).

Psychosocial Interventions

There is no evidence that psychotherapy without medication can eliminate the risk of bipolar disorder in persons with other predisposing factors. However, psychosocial interventions have an important role in educating the client about the illness and its repercussions so that it can be controlled (Miklowitz, Otto, & Frank, 2007). Teaching clients to identify early warning signs of a manic or depressive episode can significantly reduce their frequency of recurrence (Altman, Haeri, & Cohen, 2006). Clients' feelings and beliefs about their illness greatly affect their medication adherence. In addition, many people with bipolar disorder continue to have problems in their work and social environments despite medication use; therefore, psychosocial intervention can help improve functioning in these areas and build social support (Miklowitz & Otto, 2006). Further, psychosocial treatment can help people with bipolar disorder to develop a regular schedule for their daily living activities (sleep, meals, exercise, and work) to prevent disrupted rhythms or stressful life events from triggering a bipolar episode.

Although studies have been few, a review has indicated empirical support for four types of interventions incorporating the above elements (Miklowitz & Otto, 2006):

- Interpersonal and social rhythm therapy is based on the assumption that interpersonal conflicts are a major source of depression for clients, including those with bipolar disorder (Frank, Kupfer, Ehlers, et al., 1994). It also targets the person's regular scheduling of daily activities (Frank & Novick, 2002).
- CBT interventions challenge a client's cognitions that may activate episodes of mania or depression (such as "I have no control over my moods"), and they can also target cognitions related to medication compliance (Basco & Rush, 2005). CBT further incorporates client education (to help the client overcome cognitive deficits) and systematic problem-solving strategies for clients.
- Family-focused therapy trains family members in communication and problem-solving skills.
- Group psychoeducation may be a more cost-effective modality of treatment.

Directions Part III, Goal Setting and Treatment Planning: Given your risk and protective factors assessments of the individual, your knowledge of the disorder, and evidence-based practice guidelines, formulate goals and a possible treatment plan for this individual.

Critical Perspective

The onset of bipolar disorder appears to result from a complex set of genetic, biological, and psychosocial factors. Research overwhelmingly suggests that biological factors are predominant, while other factors may account more for the timing and course of the disorder. For this reason bipolar disorder has legitimacy within the social work value system as a mental disorder. Still, there are several controversial aspects to the diagnosis of bipolar disorder. First, the disorder has been diagnosed more often in children and adolescents in the past 20 years, and there is much disagreement about the appropriate symptom profile in this age group, raising concerns about its validity. In facts, the DSM criteria for diagnosing bipolar disorder are essentially abandoned when diagnosing children (Birmaher, Axelson, Strober, Gill, Valen, et al., 2006). Among young people there is much symptom overlap with the disruptive behavior disorders.

Another issue related to diagnostic validity is the relationship among bipolar I disorder, bipolar II disorder, and major depression. These distinctions were not established until the publication of DSM-IV, and questions have been raised about whether the disorders are truly distinct from one another. One pair of researchers studied whether the mood disorders might exist on a continuum, based on the observation that manic-type symptoms are present to a variable degree in all mood disorders (Serretti & Olgiati, 2005). They found that when compared with bipolar II disorder, persons with bipolar I disorder had a higher prevalence of reckless activity, distractibility, psychomotor agitation, irritable mood, and increased self-esteem. Still, one or two manic symptoms were observed in more than 30 percent of persons with a major depressive disorder, with psychomotor agitation being the most frequent. Given that excitatory manic signs and symptoms are present to a decreasing degree in bipolar I, bipolar II, and major depressive disorders, the authors concluded that they can be proposed to lie along a dimensional model.

Directions Part IV, Critical Perspective: Formulate a critique of the diagnosis as it relates to this case example. Questions to consider include: Does this diagnosis represent a valid mental disorder from the social work perspective? Is this diagnosis significantly different from other possible diagnoses? Your critique should be based on the values of the social work profession (which are incongruent in some ways with the medical model) and the validity of the specific diagnostic criteria applied to this case.

CASE 2

Ms. Daniels is a 76-year-old Caucasian woman residing in a publicly run assisted living facility (ALF) for the last seven months. For three years prior to moving into this facility she was a resident in another ALF. While there, Ms. Daniels suffered a myocardial infarction that required hospitalization. She subsequently lost her bed and was forced to find a new residence, bringing her to the new ALF. While at the previous ALF, Ms. Daniels was deemed incompetent to care for her financial affairs for reasons of mental illness and was granted a guardian, a former friend. Prior to her stay at the first ALF, she had lived alone in a rented townhouse for 18 years.

Ms. Daniels reports that she is a retired pediatrician, has never been married, and has no children. Ms. Daniels says that during college, she would have periods in which she thought that she could accomplish anything and that everybody loved her. But then she would slide into a depression for several months at a time when a "blackness" would be upon her. Despite these mood swings, she functioned with some success and graduated with honors.

She next went to a prestigious university to undertake her premed coursework and attend medical school. Throughout these years Ms. Daniels felt at times, usually when depressed, that the "authorities" watched her closely for instability. She kept herself in "close check" because they were always looking for reasons to throw her out. During medical school Ms. Daniels sought psychiatric help but was considered to be a "diagnostic puzzle" (in her words). She recalls being given medication for her "anxieties," but she does not recall what these were.

Ms. Daniels's depression and mood swings continued into her medical residency, immediately following which she promptly took $5,000 from her father's savings account without permission and traveled to Europe, where she claims she met "the most interesting people" of her life. Ms. Daniels remembers being "very talkative" at this time and sleeping little, usually on the beach or the street. She had sexual relations with a man the day after they met, and they became engaged two days later. During that time, she wrote a 200-page treatise on how to cure cancer that she still has today. During her three-week stay she spent all the money before receiving a medical escort home at her father's expense. Ms. Daniels was briefly hospitalized upon her return. She was stabilized with anti-anxiety medication and shortly thereafter began her career in pediatric public health.

Her mood swings, which were primarily characterized by depressive episodes, continued until about ten years ago. Her depressive episodes lasted between two weeks and six months. She states that her illness features impulsive and reckless acts, but she can give no other examples of these. Ms. Daniels denies that she was ever hospitalized again, yet over the next 20 years she held 15 different medical positions. She attributes the volatility of her career to her mental illness. She retired from medical practice about 15 years ago and complains about the lack of money she had accumulated at retirement.

It was not until ten years ago that Ms. Daniels started receiving psychotropic medication (lithium) that helped to control her symptoms. The social worker asked Ms. Daniels what that was like and she said, "It was as if the blinders had been taken off, the shades had been lifted, and my eyes had been dusted. Everything seemed so bright it hurt to look around. I felt a huge weight had been lifted from my back that I had been carrying for a long time and I could walk upright with a spring to my step. Even my chest felt clearer and I could take deep breaths again. I did not know what to do with myself. I had spent so much of my time depressed; I no longer knew how to be happy." When asked how often she experienced these feelings, Ms. Daniels said, tearfully, "only a few times."

For the last three months Ms. Daniels has felt useless and that she is not accomplishing anything. She lacks the ability to concentrate, often thinks "black thoughts," and is unsure she wants to continue living. Ms. Daniels feels she cannot safely eat or sleep during her "dark" periods, because she wonders if she is "being watched."

Ms. Daniels's medical diagnoses include glaucoma, peripheral vascular disease, hypertension, osteoporosis, hypothyroidism, allergic rhinitis, gastroenteritis reflux disease, and osteoarthritis. While these conditions are serious, they are being controlled with medical care and do not incapacitate her. Ms. Daniels ambulates throughout the ALF with the aid of a walker. Her sleep is within normal limits.

Although Ms. Daniels has no difficulty making friends currently, keeping them is more of a challenge to her. After a few weeks of friendship, Ms. Daniels suggests that her new friend has some incurable disease and needs a nursing home or hospice care. The same scenarios play out with her ALF roommates, and three of them have asked for transfers. Ms. Daniels has two outside friends. One is 45 years old, on dialysis, and calls Ms. Daniels every night. This friend has told the nursing staff that she is in acute renal failure and is not expected to live more than a couple of months. The second friend is 62 years old and in good health, and she seems to take Ms. Daniels's pronouncements in stride. When Ms. Daniels was asked how she could predict the ends of people's lives, she responded that it was because she is a doctor.

Ms. Daniels reports that she had a distant relationship with her parents because she was a girl and had older, high-achieving brothers. Her father died when she was 39, and her mother died when she was 50. Neither death triggered a worsening of her symptoms. Her two brothers, aged 86 and 82, both live in the vicinity but are frail and have infrequent contact with her. When asked about her relationships with her brothers, Ms. Daniels stated, "They would be great if their money-grubbing wives would just die."

Four mini-mental status exams have been performed since Ms. Daniels has been at this ALF, and she has scored 30/30 on each one. Prior to her latest depressive episode, she participated in activities at the ALF, including a book club, arts and crafts, walks, resident council, political group, and recreational outings. She now participates in only a few activities. At the end of the interview, she said, "I think there'll be a time when I'm going to feel desperate. I don't think I'm going to kill myself, but I just feel trapped. I don't have enough money to live anywhere else, and I don't want to live here. There's not enough for me here. I'm not being challenged or stimulated, and I don't know what to do."

Regarding strengths, Ms. Daniels is intelligent, well educated, and capable of interacting coherently with others; she maintains a high activity level some of the time, has several friends, does not have life-threatening health problems, can verbalize her needs, and adheres to her medication regimen.

Please go to the Appendix for directions to this case: The following questions will help to guide your thinking about a possible multi-axial diagnosis.

Questions to consider when formulating a diagnosis for Ms. Daniels

1. What is the client's history of mood fluctuations since receiving medication ten years ago?

2. Is there a history of mental illness in Ms. Daniels's family?

3. Are any of Ms. Daniels's emotional states and behaviors normal reactions to the aging process?

4. Are any of Ms. Daniels's emotional states and behaviors related to environmental conditions?

5. How do Ms. Daniels's physical problems affect her mental functioning?

6. Does Ms. Daniels exhibit any problematic patterns in her relationships with others?

7. Are Ms. Daniels's symptoms the result of the direct physiological effects of substance abuse?

CASE 3

Vanessa is a 16-year-old African-American female who was referred to an acute psychiatric care facility by her social worker at Child Protective Services (CPS). Vanessa has been living in a group home with seven other behaviorally challenged adolescent girls for the past year and has increasingly been displaying oppositional behaviors that threaten her ability to continue living there. She is loud, argumentative with staff and peers, and prone to angry outbursts when frustrated in a social or school situation. She is reportedly experiencing periods of alternating listlessness and out-of-control activity during which she becomes disruptive to the lives of the other residents and requires almost full-time supervision by the staff. At these times Vanessa talks constantly, cannot focus on a specific topic for more than a few minutes, stays up much of the night listening to music, and argues when asked by staff to respect the privacy of other residents. She says, "Everyone is bothering me again, not letting me get on with the business of my life. I need to be free, to be able to get away." Given her current mood, she is not a reliable self-informant. Much of the information provided here comes from her social worker at CPS and in the form of a letter from her outpatient psychiatrist.

Despite her young age, Vanessa has a six-year history of periods of suicidal ideation and depression that at times seem to be precipitated by feelings of loneliness but at other times seem unpredictable to her professional providers. She has not been able to maintain friendships or any other relationships for more than a few months, as she seems to get bored with other people. Vanessa states at times that she believes she is "like Rosa Parks," that is, a seemingly ordinary woman who will change the world one day with her "special gifts for bringing people together." Because of these symptoms and behaviors, which include threats to harm foster parents when she is being disciplined ("I'll make you pay for this, sometime when you're asleep or not looking"), Vanessa has had four short-term psychiatric stays at three different regional hospitals over five years. "There are times when I have to just relax and get a grip on myself," she says, adding, "I know when it's time to leave, but the stupid nurses don't understand reality." There is no evidence of psychotic symptoms at this time. She is reported to have heard voices when she is either highly elated or extremely depressed. When she is manic, she hears the voices of "angels encouraging me to help my friends," and when depressed, she hears the voice of her grandmother "berating me for being lazy and self-centered." Vanessa says now, "I don't think anyone is really talking to me, but sometimes it seems real." Sometimes Vanessa writes letters to her group home peers, which is unusual in itself; she often includes jokes and riddles that she insists the recipients will understand, but they do not. Several girls at the group home have complained to staff that Vanessa is sending them "crazy" mail. None of it is threatening.

Vanessa has been given a number of diagnoses in the past, including schizoaffective disorder, major depression, oppositional defiant disorder, attention-deficit hyperactivity disorder (ADHD), dysthymia, and several learning disorders. Her IQ has measured in the low-average range. Over the past few years a psychiatrist has conducted her monthly medical and psychiatric evaluations and has prescribed psychostimulant, antimanic, and antipsychotic medications for her. Currently, Vanessa is taking Depakote (an antibipolar drug) and a low dose of an antipsychotic medication (to control her agitation). "I take it because they make me," she says, referring to her physician and the group home staff, "but it's just poison. Fortunately, I can transcend it. I'm stronger than the medication." When asked about her periods of "sadness," Vanessa comments, "That's not me. I'm only like that when my morale is low. It's hard having good morale all the time with what I've been through. But this is the real me." Staff have noted that Vanessa experiences many relatively "calm" periods that can last for many weeks, in which she "listens better" and is more able to attend to her schoolwork and household responsibilities satisfactorily. When asked about her goals, she responds "I want to learn to live on my own, since I don't have a family to return to. I need to make my own way in the world."

Regarding her physical functioning, Vanessa is relatively healthy but has chronic constipation for which she is taking laxatives and stool softeners. She has recently seen a dermatologist for acne on her face and is taking medication to help with skin irritation. Vanessa denies being sexually active, but the staff suspects that she is. When in her high-energy moods, Vanessa is quite flirtatious with boys and is attractive to them.

CPS removed Vanessa and her two older siblings from their original home nine years ago due to parental abuse and neglect. They had lived with their mother, a single parent, who was away from the house a lot, tending to her work but also her active social life. The children were left unattended overnight on many occasions, and it was determined that their mother was not providing the family with either material or emotional support in a satisfactory manner. Worse, her mother openly admitted to the CPS workers that "since I'm alone, the kids are just a bother" and "I'd rather take care of myself, without them." Vanessa admits that she and her siblings were "always arguing" with their mother. "She was mean to us, just criticizing us all the time, and it got so we gave it to her as good as we got it." Vanessa says, "She didn't hit us much, just once in a while. But she was always on us to stay home, and when she found out we'd left, we'd argue." When asked how it felt to live in that household, Vanessa says "We felt terrible. At least I did. She made us feel like crap. I guess she thought that if we felt bad enough, we wouldn't leave the house." Vanessa adds that "She smacked us around some. But my friends got smacked around by their parents too."

CPS records indicate that Vanessa was quite temperamental in their early work with her but add that this is typical for a young girl who has experienced such neglect. One note emphasizes that the client repeatedly said she felt "lost." Staff have noted that Vanessa often speaks in a self-derogatory manner ("I wish I was likable" and "I don't have much of anything going for me") when her mood is relatively stable, which occurs every few weeks and persists for several more weeks.

Her mother's parental rights were terminated five years ago because she would never agree to a reconciliation plan; her present whereabouts are unknown. Vanessa has been separated from her older siblings for many years and has had several foster care and group home placements. She currently resides in the group home where she was placed one year ago. She has no contact at all with her brothers. "Someday we'll be together again," she says. "It will be up to me to make it all happen. I know how to make things happen." Neither of her brothers has a diagnosed mental disorder, but they have been in trouble with the police for antisocial behaviors, including public fighting and—in one brother's case—an armed robbery.

Since coming to the attention of CPS, Vanessa has had an extensive history of defying authority at school and in residential settings and being uncontrollable in terms of doing what she wants, including skipping school to meet with old friends, not doing her assigned housekeeping tasks, and breaking curfews to (she claims) take walks or ride her bicycle. She does not behave like this all the time, however, as she also has periods of being relatively quiet and compliant. Staff are not sure what prompts these "stable" periods.

The staff at the group home report that they have been having a difficult time managing her behavior for approximately five months. Specifically, Vanessa has been engaging in arguments and verbal outbursts with staff and her peers, making disrespectful comments to them, and continuing to have significant difficulties focusing on and completing tasks such as schoolwork. She frequently becomes oppositional with staff when directed and redirected for behavior. The staff notes that Vanessa has periods of several weeks' duration in which she becomes very difficult to manage due to disruptive behaviors. On two occasions she has run away from the home for several days, staying with old friends. She also has periods of several months, however, in which she is rather withdrawn and seems sad. At those times she is quiet, stays in the residence, sits alone in the kitchen, absently watches television, and generally avoids conversing with her peers. In neither state does Vanessa manage her responsibilities adequately, that is, complete her assigned housekeeping tasks or do her homework. Vanessa's daily routine often appears disrupted, since she will at times stay up all night and sleep for much of the day.

Vanessa already receives much professional intervention. At her group home Vanessa attends a psychoeducational group for behavior management and social skills training seven times a week. She also receives recreational therapy and independent living skills training, all of which, according to staff, are difficult to deliver due to her defiant behavior. In addition to the afore-mentioned services Vanessa receives individual and group therapy once a week delivered by a clinical social worker through her group home. She has a good relationship with her social worker, appearing to relax in her presence and to have faith in her desire to be helpful. To help Vanessa with her social skills, an independent contractor provides mentoring services approximately eight hours a week. Vanessa also has a positive relationship with the mentor, who, she says, "is trying hard to help me be able to love myself." She keeps her monthly physician's appointments, but these seem limited to medication evaluations. "I've met some nice staff. Sometimes they have good sugges-tions for me. Just as often I have good suggestions for them, too."

Vanessa is in the eleventh grade at the Education Development Center (EDC). Like the staff at the home where she resides, the staff at EDC report that Vanessa is argumentative, disrespectful, easily distracted and extremely hard to redirect. She has been an "average" student throughout her primary, middle, and high school years, able to pass each grade. At times she has been active on sports teams and is a good gymnast. She is also considered to have good leadership qualities when she can stay on task. In addition, Vanessa has served on the student council during the past two years. She is, however, often in trouble at school for disruptive classroom behaviors, mostly for argu-ing with her teachers and peers.

Vanessa has attended church with different caregivers sporadically throughout the years. Presently, Vanessa attends church with her mentor, and while she enjoys going, she does not appear to miss church when she is not able to attend. Vanessa appears to know a lot about the Bible and will often cite verses or create pictures that depict verses from the Bible. "God has a plan for me. God knows the good things I can do. He will give me courage to put up with the people around me who try to keep me down." When asked what she wants in life, Vanessa replies quickly, "I want all the wars in the world to stop."

> **Please go to the Appendix for directions to this case.** The following questions will help to guide your thinking about a possible multi-axial diagnosis.

Questions to consider when formulating a diagnosis for Vanessa

1. How frequently, and in what circumstances, does Vanessa exhibit psychotic symptoms?

2. How frequently, and in what circumstances, does Vanessa exhibit her disruptive behaviors?

3. What symptoms of ADHD does Vanessa demonstrate?

4. Could Vanessa's presentation be evidence of a reactive attachment disorder or post-traumatic stress disorder (PTSD)?

5. Are Vanessa's thoughts, feelings, and behaviors related to environmental circumstances?

6. How might Vanessa's IQ affect her behavior and capacity to cope with her living situation?

7. What seems to be the nature of Vanessa's problematic patterns in her relationships with others?

12

— ▾▲▾ —

Anxiety Disorders

Andrew is a 15-year-old Argentinian male currently enrolled in the ninth grade. His mother contacted an outpatient mental health agency because of her son's extreme fears of going to school and stated that he has not been able to attend a single day of class since the academic year started two months ago.

At intake, Andrew said he was nervous and was also sweating profusely, but he came across as friendly and mature. He smiled a lot, even when discussing painful subjects. He sustained minimal eye contact, however, and focused instead on the floor.

Andrew explained that he tried to go to school at the beginning of the year but could not get out of his mother's car because he was "so scared." Specifically, he feared "the larger class sizes in high school and "the large crowds of people looking at me and laughing." He realized that "people are probably not saying anything," but he couldn't stop worrying about it. He described physical symptoms such as sweating and a racing heart. He said that he does not have friends at this school and does not know which students from his middle school are now in his high school classes. Andrew mentioned that he does have a small social network outside school. These friends are three years older and primarily his brother's friends. Andrew describes these individuals as "part of the Argentinian community," and "people who have known me for a long time." Andrew also reported difficulty in other areas such as sleeping and eating. He stated that he tries to go to sleep before midnight but sometimes cannot fall asleep until three o'clock in the morning. Sometimes he will lie in bed and "just wait to sleep"; at other times he will go to the kitchen and consume large quantities of food because "I'm so hungry." He reported that he does not eat for the rest of the day because he does not feel hungry then. He maintained that his weight has not changed; he does not feel guilty or bad about his eating habits but does think they are "strange."

Anxiety disorders are characterized by intense, almost unbearable fears that disrupt a person's capacity for social functioning. The DSM chapter on anxiety disorders includes 11 such disorders, and separation anxiety disorder is included with the disorders of infancy and childhood. Brief descriptions of the anxiety disorders, which are differentiated by the nature of the anxious response or feared stimulus (Hagopian & Ollendick, 1997), are offered in Table 12.1, along with their prevalence and recurrence rates (when available). This chapter discusses anxiety disorders in general terms, although at times it will focus on specific anxiety disorders, most notably post-traumatic stress disorder (PTSD).

TABLE 12.1 Anxiety Disorders and Their Prevalence

DISORDER AND DESCRIPTION	PREVALENCE	COURSE (IF AVAILABLE)
Separation anxiety disorder describes excessive anxiety about separating from a major attachment figure.	Lifetime prevalence in children is 4.1 percent and is 6.6 percent higher in children living in single-parent and low-income households.	One-third (36 percent) of childhood cases persist into adulthood.
Panic disorders involve unpredictable anxiety attacks. In panic disorder with agoraphobia, the panic attacks arise from anxiety about being in places or circumstances where escape might be difficult or embarrassing.	Adult lifetime prevalence is 1.1 percent.	Panic disorder without agoraphobia has a 0.82 probability of recovery and a 0.56 recurrence rate. Panic disorder with agoraphobia has a 0.48 recovery rate and a 0.58 recurrence rate.
In panic disorder without agoraphobia, attacks are not associated with particular situations but are characterized by fears of losing self-control.	Adult lifetime prevalence is 3.7 percent.	
In agoraphobia without history of panic disorder, panic symptoms are experienced in places or situations from which escape might be difficult.	Adult lifetime prevalence is 0.8 percent.	
Phobia is anxiety triggered by a specific object or situation and impedes the person's functioning or results in considerable distress.	Lifetime prevalence rates range from 10 percent to 11.3 percent. 12-month prevalence is 8 percent. The majority of those diagnosed are female.	

(continues)

TABLE 12.1 Anxiety Disorders and Their Prevalence (*continued*)

DISORDER AND DESCRIPTION	PREVALENCE	COURSE (IF AVAILABLE)
Social phobia is anxiety related to social situations. Fear of negative evaluation from others is the overwhelming worry.	Both 12-month and lifetime prevalence are 5 percent in the United States. Risk influences include being Native American and of low income.	The probability of recovery is 0.37; mean duration is 16.3 years.
Generalized anxiety disorder is persistent, excessive worry that lasts for at least six months, occurring more days than not, and accompanied by at least three of the following symptoms: restlessness, fatigue, difficulty concentrating, irritability, muscle tension, and disturbed sleep.	A lifetime prevalence of 4.1 percent.	The recovery rate is 0.58 with the probability of recurrence 0.45.
OCD describes recurring thoughts that cause marked anxiety, and compulsive behaviors that temporarily serve to neutralize the anxiety.	Lifetime prevalence rates are approximately 2.5 percent in the community overall, and 1 to 3.6 percent for adolescents. Childhood rates are about 1 percent.	
PTSD is characterized by symptoms of anxiety that follow exposure to a traumatic stressor (APA, 2000). Three major symptom categories include reexperiencing the trauma, avoidance and numbing, and increased arousal.	1 to 14 percent, lifetime prevalence rate of 6.8 percent, of youth exposed to traumatic events, 36 percent have PTSD.	Symptoms in 90 percent of individuals with PTSD persisted longer than three months; for over 70 percent, the disorder lasted longer than a year; more than one-third of people never fully recovered.

Sources: Bruce et al., 2005; Cronk, Slutske, Madden, Bucholz, & Heath, 2004; Fletcher, 1996; Gorman et al., 2002; Grant, Hasin, Blanco, et al., 2005; Kessler, Berglund, Demler, et al., 2005; Kessler et al., 2006. Schnurr et al., 2002; Shear et al., 2006.

Prevalence and Comorbidity

Anxiety disorders are the most common mental health disorders in the United States, with a lifetime prevalence of 28.8 percent (Kessler, Berglund, Demler, et al., 2005). Their prevalence among children and adolescents varies considerably between studies (Cartwright-Hatton, McNicol, & Doubleday, 2006; Velting et al., 2004). On average, one in 30 elementary school-age children will fill diagnostic criteria for an anxiety disorder (Cartwright-Hatton et al., 2006). Information about the prevalence of anxiety disorders among special populations is included in Figure 12.1.

FIGURE 12.1 Anxiety Disorders and Oppressed and Vulnerable Populations.

WOMEN

- Girls present with more fears than boys and generally have higher rates of anxiety disorders, starting during adolescence and continuing through the life span; whether the gender difference is due to biological factors, social factors (such as increased rates of sexual abuse), or a combination of the two, is unknown.[1]

ELDERLY

- Clinical trials that track the effectiveness of standard medications or psychosocial treatments in the elderly are lacking.[2]
- Prevalence rates for PTSD are unknown, although rates for anxiety disorders in general range from 3.5 to 10.2 percent.[3]

MINORITIES

- Although African-Americans have lower rates of anxiety disorders than Caucasians,[4] their anxiety disorders are more likely to persist.[5]
- African-Americans are more likely to report somatic symptoms and to seek medical attention rather than mental health care, which may result in misdiagnosis.[6]
- High rates of PTSD have been found among Asian-Americans and Hispanic-Americans who have been exposed to trauma prior to immigration.[7]

SOCIOECONOMIC STATES

- Middle to upper SES is a protective factor against the development of PTSD, while poverty presents risk.[8]
- People of low SES are less likely to receive treatment.[9]

---

[1]Hagopian & Ollendick, 1997; Ozer et al., 2003.
[2]Gorman et al., 2002.
[3]Wetherell, Lenze, & Stanley, 2005.
[4]Breslau, Kendler, Su, et al., 2005.
[5]Breslau et al., 2005.
[6]Gorman et al., 2002.
[7]U.S. Department of Health and Human Services, 1999.
[8]Horowitz, McKay, & Marshall, 2005.
[9]Fonagy et al., 2002; Warshaw et al., 1997.

Anxiety disorders in general are comorbid with one another and with depression. Substance use disorders are also highly comorbid with anxiety disorders (Kolodziej, Griffin, & Najavits, 2005). In fact, substance use and anxiety disorders serve as risk influences for one another (Goodwin, Fergusson, & Horwood, 2004; Kushner, Sher, & Erickson, 1999; Zimmermann, Wittchen, Hofler, Pfister, Kessler, et al., 2003). Axis II disorders afflict about 50 percent of people with panic disorder (Gorman et al., 2002). The most common of these are the avoidant, dependent, and obsessive-compulsive types.

One-third of children with an anxiety disorder have two or more other disorders (Bernstein & Shaw, 1997). Comorbid major depression is most common, and ADHD is also associated with the anxiety disorders. In children, PTSD frequently presents in conjunction with mood disorders, anxiety disorders, ADHD, conduct disorder, and enuresis (Saigh et al., 1999).

Certain anxiety disorders are associated with the co-occurrence of specific physical impairments (Sareen, Cox, Clara, & Asmundson, 2005). Panic attacks and agoraphobia are related to cardiovascular disease, generalized anxiety disorder is associated with gastrointestinal illness, and social phobia correlates with metabolic and autoimmune disorders such as diabetes, thyroid disease, and lupus (Sareen et al., 2005). The temporal relationship (in other words, which one comes first, or do they occur together?) is not always known, but when anxiety and physical disorders co-occur, they result in greater physical impairment and disability.

Assessment of the Anxiety Disorders

The clinical assessment of anxiety should include a variety of focus areas (Bernstein & Shaw, 1997; Gorman et al., 2002). Figure 12.2 provides a summary of these.

When the client is a child, separate interviews with parents and child are recommended (Velting et al., 2004). Children frequently report fewer symptoms than their parents and tend to be less reliable than parents in reporting details about the onset and duration of anxiety symptoms. For standardized assessment instruments for anxiety disorders, see Martin, Orsillo, and Roemer (2001) for adults, and for children and adolescents, see Fonseca and Perrin (2001).

Assessment Concerns Specific to PTSD

The fact that a person reexperiences trauma and anxiety symptoms alone following exposure to an extreme stressor is insufficient for a diagnosis of PTSD (Cohen, 1998). Avoidance and numbing, as well as increased arousal (hypervigilance, insomnia, inability to concentrate, and an elevated startle response) are necessary for the diagnosis.

Although parent reporting is critical for diagnosing PTSD in children, parents often have a tendency to minimize symptoms (Cohen, 1998; Scheeringa et al., 1995). On the other hand, when parents have experienced trauma, they may be biased toward seeing more symptoms in their children. Of course, children whose parents have been traumatized may experience impairments in their own adjustment to trauma (Scheeringa, Peebles, Cook, &

FIGURE 12.2 Areas of Assessment for the Anxiety Disorders.

- History of the onset, development, frequency, and nature of the anxiety symptoms.
- Family history of anxiety.
- Any coexisting psychiatric disorders, including substance abuse.
- A general medical history and review of a person's medications, including a physical examination to search for a possible physical basis for the anxiety. This is especially critical for older adults. If there is a physical basis for the symptoms, the appropriate diagnosis is anxiety disorder due to a general medical condition. For medication or substance-induced anxiety, the appropriate diagnosis is substance-induced anxiety disorder.
- The client's response to life transitions, major life events, and stressors.
- Social, school, and occupational history.
- An investigation of times when the anxiety symptoms are not present or are more manageable, and what is different about those times.

Zeanah, 2001). Also with children, the social worker must make a careful distinction between attention-deficit hyperactivity disorder (ADHD) and PTSD (Perrin et al., 2000; Weinstein, Staffelbach, & Biaggo, 2000). Trauma may attenuate already existing ADHD symptoms, chronic hyperarousal and other symptoms of trauma can look like hyperactivity and poor impulse control, and intrusive thoughts can interfere with attention and concentration.

Other differential diagnoses to consider when assessing for PTSD in children or adults include the following (Perrin et al., 2000):

- Acute stress disorder, which resolves within four weeks of the traumatic event.
- Adjustment disorder with anxiety, in which the number of symptoms is not sufficient for PTSD.
- Psychotic disorders, in which the illusions, hallucinations, and other perceptual disturbances are unrelated to exposure to an extreme stressor. When psychotic symptoms accompany PTSD, however, the disorder can be characterized as severe (Sareen, Cox, Goodwin, & Admundson, 2005).
- Bereavement, which involves the nontraumatic (anticipated) death of a loved one and is characterized by negative feelings and recollections of the loved one.
- Other diagnoses, such as a mood disorder or another anxiety disorder, should be considered if the trauma did not precede the PTSD symptoms (Cohen, 1998).

Andrew mentioned that he has felt sad and lonely for a long time. He described intermittent suicidal ideation, but has no intention or plan of hurting himself. He said that he does not talk to anyone about these feelings but occasionally cries and "stays under the covers." He added that his friends "don't even know the truth about why I don't go to school—they just think I'm being a slacker." When asked what he does during the day while he is not in school, Andrew said that he "does nothing except watch Argentinian soap operas on the dish and do homework," which a family friend brings to the home on a biweekly basis.

Andrew's inability to attend school is a great concern for both him and his mother. Andrew wants to become an architect, so he knows it's important to keep up with his schoolwork. They, along with the family friend, have had numerous meetings with the school regarding this difficulty. The school has tried to make Andrew feel comfortable by showing him around the campus after school hours and introducing him to teachers. However, Andrew reported that he did not find this helpful. Currently, his family is looking for the county to provide him with home tutoring until he can return to class. Andrew maintains that his fear of school and other social situations began the previous year while he was in middle school. He denied any negative experiences at school or with his peers and could not identify possible causes of this change. He reported that he missed approximately two to three days per week for about seven months during eighth grade because he was so nervous about going to school. At that time he also began to avoid answering the door and the telephone because he worried about "saying something stupid or wrong." Additionally, he began to avoid social situations, such as going to the mall, going to concerts, and taking public transportation because he didn't like people looking at him. He stated that he sometimes wishes that he were invisible. Andrew said that he believed that if people looked at him it was because of something negative, but described himself as "normal looking." He explained that he will occasionally go to small parties where he knows the people, but only after he asks the host to list everyone who is expected to attend. If he does not know the people, he will not go. Even when he knows the people, Andrew still feels "nervous" and drinks two to three beers to make himself feel better. He reported that he drinks only in social situations and denied ever using drugs or smoking.

Andrew's mother believes that her son started to change following her divorce from Andrew's father three years ago. The mother, who speaks Spanish, explained in broken English and through Andrew's translation that Andrew became more withdrawn after his father left the house. Andrew stated that he and his brother have infrequent contact with his father, who currently resides out of state with a girlfriend. Andrew didn't think his father could be helpful or supportive with his current struggles.

Andrew expressed anger with his father for moving the family to the United States and then "dumping us" to be with another woman. Andrew's mother explained that the family had moved to the United States to improve their economic situation five years ago. Currently, Andrew resides with his older brother and his mother in a rented house. Andrew stated that his older brother works at a shop and that his mother "is in business." When asked to describe the type of business, Andrew turned bright red, looked down, and answered that "she cleans houses." Andrew mentioned that his mother is currently dating someone but could not remember his name. He said that the family was better off financially when their father was around. He said that his father paints houses for a living and doesn't give his mother money now that they are divorced. The family does not have health insurance.

Andrew's mother indicated that she did not know a lot about her family's mental health history but stated that she cried a lot when she was pregnant with Andrew. She reported a normal family medical history. She mentioned that Andrew developed normally and has been fairly healthy except for strep throat approximately six months ago. Andrew's goals for therapy include going back to school and feeling like "the happy kid I used to be when I lived in Argentina." When asked to be more specific, Andrew said he used to enjoy drawing and going out with friends.

Directions Part I, Multi-Axial Diagnosis: Given the case information and your responses to the questions below, prepare the following: a multi-axial diagnosis, the rationale for the diagnosis and GAF score, and additional information you would have wanted to know in order to make a more accurate and comprehensive diagnosis.

Questions to consider when formulating a diagnosis for Andrew

1. What anxiety symptoms does Andrew display? In what types of situations do the anxiety symptoms show themselves?

2. Can Andrew's symptoms be explained by an adjustment disorder?

3. In addition to anxiety, what other clinically significant symptoms does Andrew show?

4. How are Andrew's cultural traditions affecting his symptoms?

Multi-Axial Diagnosis

Axis I:

Axis II:

Axis III:

Axis IV:

Axis V:

Rationale and Differential Diagnosis

Additional Information Needed

Biopsychosocial Risk and Resilience Influences

Onset

GENETIC AND BIOLOGICAL INFLUENCES

A predisposition to anxiety is genetically based (Gorman et al., 2002) but modestly so, accounting for 30 to 40 percent of the etiology (Hettema, Neale, & Kendler, 2001). Risk influences related to one's temperament involve *anxiety sensitivity* (the tendency to respond fearfully to anxiety symptoms), *temperamental sensitivity* (including a range of emotional reactions toward negativity, such as fear, sadness, self-dissatisfaction, hostility, and worry), and *behavioral inhibition* (timidity, shyness, emotional restraint, and withdrawal from unfamiliar situations) (Bosquet & Egeland, 2006; Kagan et al., 1988, as cited in Donovan & Spence, 2000). Conversely, an extroverted temperament exerts a protective influence (Bosquet & Egeland, 2006).

Other biological processes have been associated with the occurrence of anxiety disorders (Knapp, 2006). People with PTSD tend to have abnormal levels of some key hormones that are involved in their response to stress. Their cortisol levels are lower than normal, and their norepinephrine and epinephrine levels are higher than average. Scientists have also found that people with PTSD experience alterations in the function of the thyroid gland and in neurotransmitter activity involving serotonin and the opiates (Yehuda, 2006). When people are in danger, they naturally produce high levels of opiates, which temporarily mask emotional pain, but people with PTSD continue to produce those higher levels even after the danger has passed. This may lead to the blunted emotions associated with the condition. Scientists once believed that people who dissociate themselves from a traumatic experience were showing a healthy response, but it is now suspected that these persons may be more prone to PTSD.

Brain-imaging studies show that the hippocampus (a part of the brain critical to emotion-laden memories) appears to be smaller in persons with PTSD (Jatzko, Rothenhofer, & Schmitt, 2006). Changes in the hippocampus are thought to be responsible for the intrusive memories and flashbacks that occur in people with the disorder, and scientists are investigating whether this symptom is related to short-term memory problems. The extent to which these processes are risk influences for PTSD or result from the person's experiencing certain types of traumatic events is unknown.

PSYCHOLOGICAL INFLUENCES

Psychological theories about the development of anxiety are dominated by the concept of *conditioning*, which is the process of developing patterns of behavior through responses to certain environmental stimuli or behavioral consequences (Kazdin, 2001). An initially neutral stimulus comes to produce a conditioned response after being paired repeatedly with a conditioned stimulus. For example, surviving a traffic accident may evoke overwhelming anxiety when the person passes by an intersection similar to the one where the accident occurred. Although a client's initial symptoms may be directly caused by the trauma, ongoing symptoms may result from avoiding contact with a feared situation (in this example, avoidance of driving), which paradoxically may reinforce the occurrence of the anxiety through negative reinforcement (Foa et al., 2000).

Along with avoidance as a poor coping method, the coping method of dissociation after a trauma puts a person at risk for the development of PTSD (Ozer et al., 2003). In general, problem-solving coping methods are protective against anxiety disorders (Hino, Takeuchi, & Yamanouchi, 2002).

Certain mental disorders put a person at risk for the development of anxiety disorders in adulthood. For example, a history of separation anxiety disorder as a child could predispose an individual to later anxiety problems (Hayword et al., 2004). In addition, major depression often precedes an anxiety disorder, and comorbid depression further increases the risk of the chronicity of anxiety disorders (Bruce et al., 2005). Substance use disorders are also a risk influence for the development of problems with anxiety.

SOCIAL INFLUENCES

Two meta-analyses conducted to determine predictors for the onset of PTSD both found that social influences, involving trauma severity and lack of social support, posed the largest risks (Brewin, Andrews, & Valentine, 2000; Ozer, Best, Lipsey, & Weiss, 2003). In addition to severity, other features of the traumatic experience linked to PTSD involve the degree of exposure to the trauma (intensity, duration, and frequency) and the person's subjective sense of danger (Ford, Stockton, & Kaltman, 2006). Certain types of traumatic events may also predispose to PTSD; these include war-related events (including refugee and immigration status), criminal victimization, and exposure to natural disasters (Mineka & Zinbarg, 2006). Additional social stressors after the traumatic experience, such as homelessness, may lead to PTSD (Creamer, McFarlane, & Burgess, 2005).

Family-related influences for the onset of anxiety disorders include stressful, negative, or traumatic life events, including disruptions of relationships (Bandelow,

Spath, Tichauer, et al., 2002; Phillips, Hammen, Brennan, et al., 2005). Anxious attachment patterns in children are another family-related risk factor. Anxious attachment is characterized by an infant's becoming distressed and frantically seeking comfort from the attachment figure through clinging and crying when faced with something the child fears (Hanklin, Kassel, & Abela, 2005). Subsequent contact with the caregiver, however, does not seem to help the child experience a sense of security or reduce the anxiety. In a study that tracked children from infancy to adolescence, youth with an anxious attachment pattern were more likely to suffer from an anxiety disorder as teenagers than those who were securely attached or showed avoidant attachment (Warren, Huston, Egeland, & Sroufe, 1997). The way insecure attachment history exerts its influence on adolescent anxiety appeared to be related to negative representations of the relationship that are internalized by the child (Bosquet & Egeland, 2006).

A number of other interpersonal patterns are seen in families of children with anxiety disorders, such as parental overcontrol, overprotection, and criticism (Donovan & Spence, 2000). Children of anxious parents may be more likely to observe anxiety in their parents and to have fearful behavior reinforced by their parents (Bandelow et al., 2002; Hagopian & Ollendick, 1997), as well as having a genetic risk.

Course and Recovery

Anxiety disorders are common, but many cases go untreated, causing lasting impairments (Fonagy, Target, Cottrell, et al., 2002). In a 12-year longitudinal study it was found that these disorders tend to be chronic, with low rates of recovery and high probabilities of recurrence (Bruce, Yonkers, Otto, et al., 2005). For example, the mean duration of social anxiety is 15.1 years (Grant, Hasin, Blanco, et al., 2005). Most cases of PTSD are long-term (Schnurr et al., 2002). PTSD is also the only anxiety disorder associated not only with suicidal ideation but also with suicide attempts (Sareen, Houlahah, Cox, & Asmundson, 2005).

Few factors have been identified that indicate recovery from anxiety disorders, but comorbid disorders—including parental psychopathology for children with anxiety, low social support, and low socioeconomic status (SES)—have been indicated as risk influences (Fonagy et al., 2002; Warshaw et al., 1997). In addition, people who seek help from the mental health rather than the general health system receive better care (Wang et al., 2005).

Directions Part II, Biopsychosocial Risk and Protective Influences Assessment: Formulate a risk and protective influences assessment, both for the onset of the disorder and the course of the disorder, including the strengths that you see for this individual.

TABLE 12.2 Biopsychosocial Risk and Resilience Assessment for the Onset of the Disorder

RISK INFLUENCES	PROTECTIVE INFLUENCES
Biological	
Psychological	
Social	

TABLE 12.3 Biopsychosocial Risk and Resilience Assessment for the Course of the Disorder

RISK INFLUENCES	PROTECTIVE INFLUENCES
Biological	
Psychological	
Social	

What techniques could you use to elicit additional strengths in this client?

Intervention

Psychosocial Interventions

People with anxiety disorders tend to delay seeking treatment, sometimes for up to 23 years after onset (Wang, Berglund, Olfson, et al., 2005), and they tend to seek help from the health rather than the mental health system (Young, Klap, Sherbourne, & Wells, 2001). One group of researchers found that only one-fourth of clients received appropriate medication, and few (8.5 percent) received referrals for intervention that fit the empirically validated treatment models described here (Stein, Sherbourne, Craske, et al., 2004). Young et al. (2001) found that lack of appropriate care for anxiety was associated with being male, African-American, uneducated, younger than 30, or older than 59.

The evidence-based approach to treating anxiety disorders is cognitive-behavioral treatment (CBT) featuring exposure, for both children and adults (Velting et al., 2004). See Figure 12.3. Brief (i.e., 12-session) protocols have been described with individual, group, and family (for children) formats equally effective (Gorman et al., 2002; Soler & Weatherall, 2005). Still, CBT is only effective in about 50 percent of child and adolescent cases (Soler & Weatherall, 2005), and for elders, CBT may not out-perform other psychosocial treatment alternatives (Wetherell, Lenze, & Stanley, 2005).

For PTSD, interventions with a direct focus on the trauma are most effective (Bisson & Andrew, 2005). Imaginal exposure, a process in which clients confront their memories of the traumatic event, is often used for treating PTSD (Johnson & Lubin, 2006). For

FIGURE 12.3 Components of Cognitive-Behavioral Treatment (CBT) for Anxiety Disorders.

Psychoeducation: providing information about the nature of anxiety and how it can be controlled.

Monitoring anxiety symptoms: their frequency, duration, and triggers.

Cognitive restructuring: identifying, challenging, and replacing maladaptive belief systems that contribute to anxiety.

Breathing retraining: to distract clients from anxiety symptoms and provide a sense of control over them.

Progressive muscle relaxation: to reduce tension in anxiety-provoking situations by alternately tightening and relaxing certain muscle groups.

Problem solving: for generating a variety of practical solutions to life challenges, and exposure.

Exposure: a process in which the client learns to face the feared object until the anxiety dissipates. Typically conducted in a graduated fashion, the practitioner helps the client construct a hierarchy of situations from least to most feared and then work through these in order, conquering smaller fears before going on to bigger ones. There are several variants of exposure: symbolic (through the use of pictures or props), simulated (through role playing), imaginal (the client imagines the feared situation), and in vivo, the preferred method (contact with the real situation/stimulus).

Sources: Gorman et al., 2002; Velting et al., 2004.

example, an initial exposure exercise might consist of the client's writing a detailed account of the trauma and reading it in a therapy session and also at home.

Children who suffer from PTSD are encouraged through desensitization procedures to describe the traumatic event and its aftermath in a manner that diminishes arousal and distressing emotions (Cohen, 2005). Stress management techniques—for example, progressive muscle relaxation, thought stopping, positive imagery, and deep breathing—should be taught to the child prior to detailed discussions of the trauma. The social worker should be aware that intervention for children with PTSD involves direct exploration of the trauma. Although nondirective play therapy is a popular treatment approach (Cohen, Mannarino, & Rogal, 2001), it has not stood up well to CBT in studies (e.g., Cohen & Mannarino, 1996).

A meta-analysis of 26 studies of intervention for PTSD (offered at an average of 15.64 hours, which can be considered brief) found that most strategies involved exposure or eye movement desensitization and reprocessing (described below). Overall, most people who complete treatment (67 percent) no longer meet diagnostic criteria for PTSD (Bradley, Greene, Russ, Dutra, & Westen, 2005). The percentage drops to 56 percent for all people who start treatment, whether or not they finish the course of therapy. Unfortunately, recovery rates over time (after the treatment has ended) are unknown. Although the post-treatment results are encouraging, particularly since PTSD is considered a chronic condition, typically about 30 percent of people selected for study are not eligible for inclusion in the research because they are either suicidal, substance abusing, or psychotic. Therefore, generalizability of these results to clinic populations, who may have one or all of these conditions, may be limited. Combat-related PTSD appears to fare the worst in treatment. This may be due to the greater severity of pathology of veterans who seek treatment at Veterans Administration hospitals, their tendency to limit disclosure upon returning home (which limits opportunities for both exposure and social support), and the potential for secondary gain (disability-based income may depend on remaining symptomatic) (Bradley et al., 2005).

A meta-analysis has also been specifically conducted on eye movement desensitization and reprocessing (EMDR). Shapiro outlined the method in a book (Shapiro, 1995) and has created a training program for clinicians. In a meta-analysis that examined 34 studies for the effectiveness of EMDR (Davidson & Parker, 2001), the major finding was that EMDR was as effective as other exposure techniques, and thus it is empirically validated. Some consider EMDR a form of exposure treatment, since clients are asked to keep a traumatic memory in their minds as the clinician elicits the eye movements. However, the meta-analysis found no evidence that the eye movements were necessary. Further, there were no significant differences between studies in which the clinicians had participated in approved training and those in which they had not.

For obsessive-compulsive disorder (OCD), CBT features exposure and *response prevention*, in which the client refrains from avoiding the stimulus or engaging in the ritualistic behavior (King et al., 1998). For example, if a person has an obsession about organizing soup cans in the kitchen cupboard, he/she is blocked from "straightening up" the cans and may be helped to spend time in a grocery store, observing but not touching the soup cans. In order to help the individual cope during this period, anxiety management skills, such as relaxation training, breathing-control training, and cognitive training, are taught. A support person is usually enlisted to help the client, since the processes are so difficult to complete otherwise. Treatment is usually intensive in nature (four to five hours per day) with a minimum of three sessions per week (Abramowitz, Bridigi, & Roche, 2001; Riggs & Foa, 1993). In general, research on interventions with OCD has found that behaviorally oriented treatments such as those described above are more effective than a purely cognitive approach, such as cognitive restructuring (Eddy, Dutra, Bradley, & Westen, 2004). In contrast to the extensive literature on adults, the empirical evidence supporting CBT for children is inconclusive.

According to Velting et al.'s (2004) review, the most widely disseminated CBT protocol for childhood anxiety is Kendall's Coping Cat program (Kendall, Kane, Howard, & Siqueland, 1990). This protocol is appropriate for 7- to 16-year-old youth with generalized anxiety disorder, social phobia, or separation anxiety disorder. Individual and group treatment manuals are available, with adaptations for greater involvement of family members. In one study of the program, participants were evaluated with a seven-year follow-up after 16 weeks of intervention (Kendall, Safford, Flannery-Schroeder, & Webb, 2004). The favorable gains measured following the test were maintained at follow-up. Youth who were successfully treated also showed reduced substance use compared with those who did not receive the treatment.

Parent-child interventions may include helping parents to encourage the child to face new situations rather than withdraw, to refrain from excessive criticism and intrusiveness, to respond more directly to the child's needs, and to encourage the child to engage in activities despite anxiety. A recent pilot study showed that parents who attended a group-only intervention (their children were not treated) were able to improve their child's anxiety symptoms, particularly when they themselves also had anxiety disorders (Thienemann, Moore, & Tompkins, 2006). On the other hand, if a teenager presents for treatment but has generally good functioning and no comorbid disorder, less parental involvement is indicated. This approach helps the teen to address the developmental task of assuming self-responsibility. For the treatment of child PTSD, parental involvement is recommended (Cohen, 1998; Perrin et al., 2000). Empirical evidence shows that parental emotional reaction to the child's traumatic experience and parental support of the child are powerful mediators of the child's symptoms.

Some general practitioners encourage client use of self-help treatment manuals (Jorm & Griffiths, 2006). One review of self-help treatment manuals administered in general practitioner settings was conducted, and the approach proved promising; the more time a facilitator spent on guidance in the use of materials, however, the more helpful the intervention (van Boeijen, van Balkom, van Oppen, et al., 2005).

Medications

A meta-analysis of treatments for anxiety disorders found that exposure treatment, medications, and combined exposure and medications were equally effective (Kobak et al., 1998). The advantages of medications include their ready availability and the fact that less effort is required of the client (Gorman et al., 2002). Of course, side effects are a potential disadvantage of medication. For many years the benzodiazepines were the first-line treatment for anxiety, but they are no longer the drug of choice because of the risk of physical addiction with continuous use (DeVane, Chiao, Franklin, & Kru, 2005). Benzodiazepines may be used preferentially in situations where rapid symptom control is critical (e.g., the client is about to quit school or lose a job) (Gorman et al., 2002).

The past ten years have seen an increased use of medications initially developed as antidepressants to treat anxiety disorders. In a meta-analysis of 43 studies the selective serotonin reuptake inhibitors (SSRIs) and tricyclics (TCAs) were found to be equally effective in reducing symptoms of panic, agoraphobic avoidance, depression, and general anxiety (Bakker, van Balkom, & Spinhoven, 2002). The number of dropouts, however, was significantly lower in the clients treated with SSRIs (18 percent versus 31 percent), which suggests that these are tolerated better with regard to adverse effects. The side effects of TCAs include dry mouth, constipation, and blurred vision. With PTSD in adults, several controlled trials have shown that SSRIs produce positive effects (Stein, Zungu-Dirwayi, van der Linden, & Seedat, 2003).

If a medication has been used effectively, a trial of discontinuation may be attempted after 12 to 18 months. Many clients (between 30 and 45 percent) partially or fully relapse when medication is discontinued (Gorman et al., 2002). Clients who show no improvement within 6 to 8 weeks with a particular medication should be reevaluated with regard to the need for either a different medication or a combined drug and psychosocial treatment approach.

Because of the physical and psychological dangers of prescribing any psychotropic drugs for children and adolescents, psychosocial interventions should always be used in conjunction with medication, with the exception of OCD (Bernstein & Shaw, 1997). There is a dearth of studies evaluating the effectiveness of psychotropic medications for treating PTSD in children, although physicians prescribe a variety of medications for the disorder (Cohen, 2005).

Few clinical trials have documented the effectiveness of standard medications or psychosocial treatments for older adults (Gorman et al., 2002), although the available evidence suggests the value of pharmacological treatment (Wetherell, Lenze, & Stanley, 2005). If medication is used, the required dose is generally lower than that for younger persons, and any increases should be more gradual than with younger adults.

Directions Part III, Goal Setting and Treatment Planning: Given your risk and protective factors assessments of the individual, your knowledge of the disorder, and evidence-based practice guidelines, formulate goals and a possible treatment plan for this individual.

Critical Perspective

Some have argued that the expanded classification of disorders in the DSM-IV has furthered the purposes of pharmaceutical companies (Angell, 2004). As more constellations of behaviors are considered mental disorders, they become reimbursable and treatable through medication. For instance, in a critique of the DSM, Kutchins and Kirk (1997) discuss social phobia as an example of what could be considered a normal behavior (shyness) now being construed as a mental disorder. The National Comorbidity Survey Replication indicates that 12.1 percent of the U.S. population suffers from social phobia in their lifetime (Kessler, Berglund, Demler, et al., 2005), and it is the second-highest disorder reported in the last 12 months (Kessler, Chiu, Demler, & Walters, 2005). Paxil, one of the SSRI drugs, is now marketed specifically for the treatment of social phobia, even though its actions are no different from other antidepressants of its class.

Several other critiques pertain to PTSD specifically. PTSD is one of the disorders in the DSM that is conceptualized in terms of problematic functioning in the person-environment system because a traumatic event has occurred (Bradshaw & Thomlison, 1996). However, PTSD is not a unique outcome of trauma; depression is as common a response, as are other anxiety disorders, substance use disorders, and eating disorders (Romano, 2004). In addition, in a majority of cases PTSD is accompanied by another disorder. Symptom overlap among diagnostic categories helps to explain the high likelihood of lifetime comorbid disorders seen in PTSD. These facts indicate that diagnostic clarity is lacking for the disorder. In addition, the validity of PTSD in children can be questioned. Some of the DSM criteria may not be relevant to young children—for example, visual flashbacks, dissociation, numbing, and traumatic amnesia (Cohen, 1998). Further, clinician observations and interactions with children may not be extensive enough to garner valid information about symptoms. The extent to which trauma may be experienced differently in children is also unknown. The diagnostic criteria permit a great deal of latitude in determining whether a particular stressor is "extreme" (Perrin et al., 2000), and whether a liberal or strict threshold is used to define "persistent" symptoms (McHugo, Mooney, Racusin, Ford, & Fleischer, 2000).

Directions Part IV, Critical Perspective: Formulate a critique of the diagnosis as it relates to this case example. Questions to consider include: Does this diagnosis represent a valid mental disorder from the social work perspective? Is this diagnosis significantly different from other possible diagnoses? Your critique should be based on the values of the social work profession (which are incongruent in some ways with the medical model) and the validity of the specific diagnostic criteria applied to this case.

CASE 2

Tracy Lo is a 30-year-old married Asian-American woman with two young children. Her parents were born in China but moved to the United States before Tracy was born. She was raised largely with Chinese cultural traditions but married a Caucasian man when she was 22 years old. She was very happy, although her parents were disappointed that she married a "Westerner." Tracy's family situation is stable and her parents, to whom she remained close, have lived nearby since she got married. Tracy and her family lived in apartments until two years ago, when they were finally able to afford their first house in the suburban neighborhood of their large city. Tracy works part-time at a nearby bank, and her husband is a chemist at a plant that develops petroleum products. Their two children are in primary school.

One September the remnants of a hurricane passed through her city. This storm had been predicted as dangerous, and the Lo family took every reasonable precaution to prepare for it. However, a large tree from their backyard was blown over into the house and cut a large hole in the roof. The damage would take several months to repair, and many other homes in the area were also damaged.

Tracy and her family were forced to move temporarily into her parents' three-bedroom apartment. The extended family did its best to accommodate the situation, but space was cramped. It was the first time the extended family had lived together, and the situation was one that understandably resulted in a lack of privacy, frequent shortages of food and clean clothes, and some disagreements about parenting responsibilities. Tracy left her children in the care of her parents, who tended to be stricter than Tracy and her husband had been. Her parents complained that Tracy's husband was not providing the children with strong traditional values.

From the time of the storm, Tracy began to feel increasingly stressed with regard to the tasks of working, caring for her husband, mediating household conflicts, raising her children, and managing the home repair process. She became anxious (experiencing heart palpitations and feelings of unease in her abdomen), began to be irritable with her children, and showed some signs of depression (inability to sleep and concentrate on her work, feelings of overwhelming sadness). Tracy had not experienced symptoms of this type in the past, and in fact she had always functioned effectively and assertively. Her new feelings of helplessness were unfamiliar, and they frightened her. At the suggestion of a coworker, Tracy came to the emergency services unit of a nearby mental health center to ask for help, so that she would not "lose her mind." She did not tell her husband or children about this visit, because she did not want to appear "weak" in their eyes. Her parents in particular would not have approved her going outside the family for help.

Please go to the Appendix for directions to this case: The following questions will help to guide your thinking about a possible multi-axial diagnosis.

Questions to consider when formulating a diagnosis for Tracy Lo

1. What are Tracy's primary symptoms?

2. Is there a clearly identifiable environmental or interpersonal stressor or stressors that immediately preceded Tracy's symptoms? If so, what is it (or are they)?

3. Are there any aspects of Tracy's personality (as much as we know of it) that put her at risk for the symptoms she displays?

4. Are there any environmental stressors prior to the hurricane that may have put Tracy at risk for her symptoms?

5. What strengths are evident in the client, her family, and her community that may serve to help her resolve the problem situation?

CASE 3

Ashley is a 16-year-old, biracial female currently in the legal custody of the city Department of Social Services (DSS). Ashley was originally taken into DSS custody three years ago after revealing that she had been sexually abused by her mother's boyfriend. At the time of her report Ashley attempted to overdose on her antidepressant medication, saying later that she was afraid of what might happen to her. According to Ashley, her mother's live-in boyfriend had fondled her genitalia "every few weeks or so" for four years when her mother was away. Ashley had always been very upset about these physical intrusions but was afraid to tell anyone until she saw an educational movie at her school about sexual abuse. At the hospital she told staff that she did not feel safe at home, even if her mother's boyfriend was gone, and that if she went back she would try to commit suicide again. She added that a 17-year-old stepbrother "taunted" her frequently and struck her across the face "several times, just to be mean."

Ashley's mother seemed angry about Ashley's allegations and did not believe her. Her boyfriend eventually admitted to some of the acts and was sent to prison. Before the hearing, Ashley (then 13 years old) entered foster care through a temporary custody order. Her mother later filed a special petition that placed Ashley in full DSS custody. She supported her boyfriend, stating that he had "bad judgment" but now realized his mistakes.

Ashley stayed in her first foster home for one month before being transferred to a second one, where she lived for only five months. In both instances her foster parents said they could not keep Ashley any longer because she was quick to anger, used profane language, fought physically at times with the other children, and isolated herself in her room for several days at a time. Her foster parents suspected that her behavior represented misplaced anger toward her nuclear family. Ashley was next placed in a small (12-bed) group home but moved after one year because the facility closed. At that time Ashley was placed at her current residential center, which serves about 30 adolescent girls; she has lived there for the past 18 months. Ashley's mother has not participated in treatment that would enable Ashley to return to their home, so at this point, Ashley's foster care goal is to achieve independent living.

Ashley has had three short-term psychiatric hospitalizations in three years for suicidal threats (each of them was less than four days). The first of these occurred when she was living with her mother (at age ten) and being abused by the boyfriend. The second and third hospitalizations occurred while Ashley was in foster care, at ages 11 and 12. Her caseworkers thought that she was both angry and depressed, and that the hospitalizations were related to fears that she would be displaced from those homes. Ashley has twice cut her wrists superficially at the residential center when she became angry about "my stupid life." Staff monitor her closely during these times because her mood seems so low. She once stated that she didn't want to live because she was too frightened of being out in the world. She does not seem to like institutional living, based on her frequently disparaging remarks about other residents and "this stupid program," although she does feel "safe" there, seemingly because she can always isolate herself in her room when in a "bad mood." Staff perceive her threats against staff and other residents as "cries for help." She has been seeing therapists since her first hospitalization and has not been taking antidepressant medication since the first overdose.

Ashley's father is deceased. She does not know the circumstances of his death, and he has been out of her life since Ashley was an infant. She has nine siblings on her father's side and three siblings on her mother's side. Prior to entering CPS custody Ashley lived with her mother (Tanya), her mother's live-in boyfriend (Adam), and two younger siblings. Ashley reports that Adam was also physically abusive at times when angry with her (for no clear reason she could perceive) and would bend her hands back and choke her.

Ashley's problem behaviors in the current facility are described as a tendency to become argumentative and physically threatening when upset, but she also has a pleasant demeanor some of the time. Her aggressive behaviors have subsided at the current facility in the past few months. Although she complains about the program structure, it appears that she benefits from it, in that she can organize her time in such a way as to limit her interpersonal interactions. She is intelligent but considered "lazy" by the teachers, who often try to challenge her to work harder, with some success. Still, she has received failing grades at times, perhaps because she has changed schools as well as residences over the past three years.

Ashley manifests a general "numbing" of emotion when discussing with staff the sexual abuse she has experienced. Her affect becomes blunted, and she uses matter-of-fact, detached responses when discussing her mother's boyfriend and other troubling matters. For example, she described an incident in which she threatened to kill a cat in the presence of her mother but added matter-of-factly that it was a way of frightening her mother and getting her to "back off" on a day when her mother had been verbally abusive toward her. Ashley still has occasional "sharp memories" of her stepbrother striking her across the face and her stepfather choking her.

Ashley frequently appears to be suspicious about what is going on around her, for example, questioning what her peers "are up to" when she sees them in small groups. She always pauses to scan any room that she enters, and she tends to stay out of enclosed public spaces such as bathrooms. Her relationships with the other girls are volatile at times, as Ashley tends to become tense when she is "crowded into" small groups or feels that others are "picking on" her.

While she was growing up, Ashley had "one or two friends" at a time, but none consistently. She spent time with these friends and their acquaintances but says she was not close to any of them. She was "an angry kid" but "usually took it out on [her]" by cutting on her arms (when especially angry with other people) or berating herself "inside." Ashley has never had a boyfriend ("I don't like boys; they're always so pushy") and has apparently had no sexual experiences.

Ashley reports a history of disturbing nightmares in which she is lost and alone on a cold night. Her sleep problems began at age 12 and lasted until just prior to her release from the previous residential treatment facility six months ago. She had trouble falling asleep and would awaken after about an hour and remain awake for the rest of the night. Ashley reports that it has been several months since she has experienced nightmares and difficulty sleeping. She reports that she has been sleeping fairly well since being placed at the current facility, because the "surroundings are more peaceful," but her roommate reports that she says "weird" things during her sleep.

Though Ashley's nightmares and sleeping problems appear to have remitted, she continues to seem tense, constantly shifting her body in her seat and admitting that she feels "uncomfortable" and becomes easily frightened. At a recent Halloween outing to a Haunted House, Ashley became extremely disturbed, started crying, and had to leave the activity. Also, when looking at pictures from a Halloween party, she cried out when shown pictures of peers in scary costumes and turned her back until the pictures were taken away.

Ashley was once trapped for two hours in an elevator with a pregnant lady. Since then she refuses to ride in elevators and becomes shaky and nauseated near them. She also reports that she feels the same about escalators, because her brothers used to tell her frightening stories about people being sucked into escalators by their shoestrings. She takes the stairs whenever she has to go anywhere.

Ashley has no remarkable history of physical illness. She is 5 feet 2 inches tall and weighs 110 pounds. She is an attractive girl and had a recent exam that confirmed her physical health. She reports that she has gained 15 pounds over the past year and a half, and she is concerned about her weight, saying that she wants to look "fit." Ashley indicated that she is trying to prevent further weight gain by not eating between meals. Her weight concerns seem realistic, and there is no evidence that she has an eating disorder.

School records indicate that Ashley is of average intelligence and is currently attaining Bs at the high school she attends. Ashley claims that she is "content" at the residential facility because she has more freedom now. That is, her foster family had been very strict and now the adults are not "watching all the time." She is capable of positively interacting with adults and staff at times, even though her affect is usually flat. Ashley has had some trouble, however, integrating with the other girls in her home, but she does occasionally talk to a few of them. Reports from her previous group home and residential treatment facility indicate that Ashley was often irritable and depressed and that she had a tendency to lie to others. She made cuts on her arms and wrists prior to her current admission, saying later that she was "terrified" of another move and wanted to feel relief.

Ashley does possess a number of strengths. She enjoys scrapbooking to document her activities and to remember supportive friends and memories. Another one of Ashley's strengths is that she is very personable and verbal at times. She has a sense of humor, and can sometimes be observed joking with peers. She also appears to have some measure of self-confidence at times, responding to questioning in an even, steady voice and without hesitation.

Please go to the Appendix for directions to this case. The following questions will help to guide your thinking about a possible multi-axial diagnosis.

Questions to consider when formulating a diagnosis for Ashley

1. Has Ashley been exposed to traumatic events? If so, how much is known about them?

2. What other stressful life events has Ashley experienced?

3. Does Ashley appear to have significant and pervasive interpersonal problems?

4. What symptoms of depression does Ashley demonstrate?

5. How would you describe Ashley's general coping style?

13

— ▾▲▾ —

Eating Disorders

Nikki, an 18-year-old Caucasian female, came to the university counseling center at the behest of her dormitory floor's residential adviser, who was concerned about Nikki's weight loss. Nikki admitted that she was "not happy" about coming to the center, but she liked the residential adviser and didn't want to "alienate" her. When she came to her initial session, Nikki appeared visibly emaciated and was wearing a long, oversized sweater and baggy sweatpants. At the beginning of the interview, she was guarded and answered questions with only a few words. But when she realized that the social worker "was not going to tell me I needed to gain weight like everyone else," she began to open up, although she spoke in a flat, matter-of-fact tone, even about painful subjects.

Nikki said she had begun to lose weight the summer of her senior year of high school, though her concerns about her weight had begun at age 13. Before that time she had been a "skinny kid," and that's how she wanted to stay. She admitted that she didn't want to grow up and thought that staying thin was a way to achieve this. She said she admired little girls' bodies (even girls as young as three and four), and thought they looked great.

During that summer, Nikki said that she was bored because there were no jobs for high school students in the midsized city where she lived. Losing weight gave her "something to do." Every day, she ate only two meals and jumped rope for 30 minutes. If she didn't exercise daily, she felt "fat" and "disgusted" with herself. Nikki said that before the summer, she didn't have the discipline to cut back on her food intake. At the same time, she said she had exercised and weighed herself almost every day since she was 14 years old. At 5 feet, four inches, she has never weighed more than 105 pounds.

Nikki admitted with embarrassment that she did lose control of her eating on occasion, usually with sweet food (ice cream, brownies, cake) but more recently peanut butter; she could eat an entire jar at one sitting. She said that this happened "maybe once a month" and that she would atone for it by eating even less afterward. She denied using any methods of purging.

When asked how she was feeling during the summer after she finished high school, other than "bored" at the prospect of leaving for college, she seemed surprised by the question and answered, "How did I feel? I didn't feel anything."

Since entering college three and a half months ago Nikki has eaten only two meals a day, subsisting on salad, yogurt, popcorn, and Diet Coke, and has lost an additional 10 pounds (she now weighs 85 pounds). She said that she doesn't feel hungry and that the weight loss has been easy. She has also stopped exercising.

Nikki admitted she hadn't menstruated in seven months and was losing her hair. She didn't mind the lack of menstruation because she had always hated her period, a clear marker that she was a woman. Her hair loss bothered her, however, and she showered only every other day because too much hair fell out when she washed it. She said that occasionally she felt her heart rate "slow down and then speed up." On the one hand, this scared her; on the other hand, she would sometimes think, "Maybe I'll just die of a heart attack, and all this will be over." Despite these physical concerns, she had not been to a doctor.

Nikki said that in one sense she knew she was too thin and wore baggy clothes to disguise the fact, but she still felt "fat inside," recognizing that no amount of weight loss would help her feel different. Yet she didn't know anymore what normal eating was and became panicky when people pressured her about gaining weight. She denied having anorexia to anyone who pushed her about it, saying that she had read the criteria and she hadn't lost 15 percent of her body weight; therefore, she couldn't have it. If she ever got fat, she said, she would be totally worthless.

Eating disorders are characterized by disturbances in a person's eating behaviors and perceptions of body weight and shape (APA, 2000). Pathological fears of becoming overweight lead those with eating disorders to enact extreme, potentially damaging behaviors to lose weight and keep it off. *Anorexia nervosa* and *bulimia nervosa*, the two primary eating disorders, are the focus of this chapter. A third diagnostic category, *eating disorder not otherwise specified*, is a residual category at present. It is often used to diagnose persons who engage in chronic overeating and seek help for that problem.

Prevalence and Comorbidity

In the National Comorbidity Survey Replication, bulimia nervosa was found among 1.5 percent of the U.S. female population and 0.5 percent of the male population (Hudson, Hiripi, Pope, & Kessler, 2006). The lifetime prevalence of bulimia nervosa is 1 percent of the population. The prevalence of anorexia is 0.9 persent of females and 0.3 percent of men. The lifetime prevalence is 0.6 percent of the U.S. population. Bulimia nervosa, in particular, has increased during the second half of the twentieth century (Hudson et al., 2006).

Most people with eating disorders, especially those with bulimia nervosa, have another psychiatric disorder. Indeed, three or more diagnoses is the most common comorbidity pattern among both anorexic (33.8 percent) and bulimic (64.4 percent) clients (Hudson et al., 2006). The most common comorbid diagnoses are (in order of occurrence) anxiety disorders, impulse control disorders (oppositional defiant disorder, conduct disorder, attention-deficit hyperactivity disorder, intermittent explosive disorder), and substance use disorders (Hudson et al., 2006; Franko, Dorer, Keel, et al., 2005). Depression is also common, but may be a consequence of malnutrition among those with anorexia (Godart, Perdereau, Rein, et al., 2007).

Personality disorders are often present with eating disorders, with estimates ranging from low to 58 percent of the time (Cassin & von Ranson, 2005). People with bulimia typically suffer from cluster B (borderline) and C personality disorders (avoidant), while cluster C disorders (avoidant and obsessive-compulsive) personality disorders are associated with anorexia.

General health complications, as well as mental health problems, also occur among those with eating disorders (Rome & Ammerman, 2003). Specific to bulimia are enlarged salivary glands, the erosion of dental enamel, and electrolyte imbalances, which in turn increase the likelihood of cardiac arrhythmia and renal failure. Anorexia is associated with starvation and malnutrition, amenorrhea, metabolic abnormalities, electrolyte imbalances, irregular heart rate, low body temperature, low blood pressure, heart failure, anemia, and the growth of hair over the body.

Assessment

People with eating disorders are underdiagnosed and undertreated. This is especially true for minority (Mexican-American and African-American) women (Cachelin & Striegel-Moore, 2006; Fairburn, Agras, Walsh, et al., 2004). Although some clients are treated for comorbid emotional problems, they do not receive intervention for the eating disorder (Hudson et al., 2006). One recommendation, therefore, is for clinicians to screen clients for eating problems, even if these were not included among their presenting complaint. Assessment guidelines are delineated in Figure 13.1.

Nikki readily admitted to "feeling depressed" since she started high school. She said she sometimes wished she wasn't alive but wouldn't kill herself because of what it would do to her mother. She said she still felt depressed most days, and that everything tended to look dark, "like the color is sucked out of everything. The dorm, all the old buildings around campus, everything looks dreary and grey."

She studied constantly, even though she found it sheer drudgery, because she wanted to get all As and felt guilty when she didn't study. If she didn't get all As, then she would be worthless. Despite all her studying, Nikki had no career plans and was undecided about a major. Therefore, all this

FIGURE 13.1 Assessment of Eating Disorders.

The assessment of a suspected eating disorder optimally involves the following components (Mizes & Palermo, 1997):

1. Clinical interview.
2. Medical evaluation that, in addition to a routine checkup, assesses for problems due to weight loss and amenorrhea, tests for electrolyte imbalance, and refers individuals with bulimia to a dentist for the examination of problems due to enamel erosion.
3. Questionnaire measures of eating disorders, body image, and related problems (see Corcoran & Walsh, 2006).
4. Assessment of concurrent psychiatric disorders.
5. Risk and resilience assessment.
6. Emphasis on times when an individual feels better about herself/her body, and times when eating disorder symptoms have not been present or are lessened.
7. Motivation to overcome the disorder.

Goals (Yager et al., 2002):

1. Restore healthy weight.
2. Reduce or eliminate binge-eating and purging behaviors.
3. Provide education on nutrition and healthy eating and exercise patterns.
4. Treat physical complications.
5. Correct core maladaptive thoughts, attitudes, and feelings related to the eating disorder.
6. Treat comorbid disorders.
7. Build coping skills and problem-solving abilities.
8. Address themes that may underlie eating disorder behaviors (developmental conflicts, identity formation, body-image concerns, self-esteem, sexual and aggressive difficulties, mood regulation, gender role expectations, and family dysfunction).
9. Enlist family support and provide family therapy where appropriate.
10. Improve interpersonal and social functioning.
11. Prevent relapse.

studying "lacked meaning." She said she couldn't see a future for herself and didn't want to be married or have children.

Nikki also didn't have any other activities that she enjoyed, except for meeting boys. She was surprised that boys seemed attracted to her because she didn't think she looked sexually appealing at her current weight. She was asked out on a lot of dates and accepted these invitations, but didn't feel serious about anyone.

Nikki said her concentration was good, although she incessantly thought about food and not eating. She never went to sleep before two o'clock in the morning, because that was when her dorm hall finally quieted down. She would wake up naturally at seven in the morning. She denied feeling tired, although she slept only five hours a night.

When asked about other symptoms of depression before the present time, she said she had had chronic insomnia since becoming a teenager. She had difficulty falling asleep some nights and often woke up at five in the morning. She said that beginning in her teenage years her appetite increased, and one of her few pleasures was food and eating. That was why she had become concerned about her weight; she wanted to eat so much because it made her feel better. Another thing that had made her feel better about herself in high school was male attention. When a boy she liked didn't return the feeling or something went wrong in a relationship, she felt suicidal, although she never acted on those feelings. Nikki couldn't remember a time since she was 14 when these symptoms had lifted for more than a few days at a time. She said she had never been referred for treatment, and because she followed the rules and got good grades, no one really noticed anything unusual about her.

One of her roommates in the dorm was a friend, Alice, whom she had known in high school. Her other roommate, Megan, was a "total partier," who drank a 12-pack when she went out drinking and hung around a coke dealer, "so that must mean she's doing coke, right?" According to Nikki, Megan had some kind of eating disorder. She was thin and would eat only salad and drink alcohol. Nikki said it was hard having Megan as a roommate because she stayed up all night and would come in and out of the room at all hours, disrupting Nikki's sleep. She didn't clean up after herself and constantly left the door unlocked, even though both Nikki and Alice had talked to her numerous times about this.

Nikki said that her parents didn't seem to love or even like each other, and that her mother was always afraid of her father leaving and not providing for them. He would retreat into distant silence if she challenged him, sometimes for days, until she begged forgiveness. When he was mad at her mother, he would take his anger out on the whole family and speak to no one. He typically worked 12-hour days, and also went to work on Saturdays.

Her mother, who was slightly overweight and was always talking about how fat and ugly she was, didn't work outside the home. Nikki said she thought her mother was depressed, although her mother never said so. Nikki said, "I could just feel it in the atmosphere" at home. Nikki said she knew her mother loved her, but she was "insane" and "paranoid." When asked what this meant, she said her mother thought people, such as their neighbors, were "out to get her" and wouldn't answer the phone or the door. She also "would get lost in her own world, and even if we jumped up and down and shouted her name, we couldn't get her attention."

Ever since Nikki was a child, her mother would sometimes tell Nikki she was the "best girl in the world," but at other times she would say that Nikki was "bad," "cold-blooded," "a user of people," and "selfish," and was critical of

Nikki's schoolwork, even though Nikki received all As. Nikki feared that her mother was right about her. When asked, Nikki said her mother displayed this pattern toward other people as well. She would "feel deeply about other people's pain," but if they did something wrong in her mother's eyes, she would "write them off completely." She had cut herself off from her own family of origin as a young adult and had not had contact with them for 20 years.

Nikki had two sisters, both still in high school. The older one was a junior, and she and Nikki were close, but her other sister, a sophomore, was "spoiled" and "impossible for anyone to get along with." Nikki said that due to her father's corporate job, the family had moved around a lot so that he could "move up the ladder." The last move was in the middle of her junior year of high school.

Nikki said she had been brought up going to (Episcopalian) church every Sunday and still went to church by herself now that she was in college. She didn't get much out of going to services but did so because she was "supposed to." She reported that her parents had never considered that she go to counseling because "they didn't believe in it and thought that people should solve their own problems." She said her mother would also say that "only your family can help, not anyone on the outside."

Nikki said she hadn't made any new friends since starting college. She had moved around so much that she didn't feel like making the effort, and no one interested her. Despite this attitude, she went to all the dorm parties on the weekends because "it was something to do." She sometimes drank and felt the effects easily because of her low weight. She said she had started drinking during her junior year in high school, at times to the point of blacking out. She denied any drug use. Several of her paternal relatives (an uncle and a great-uncle) were known to the family as alcoholics.

Directions Part I, Multi-Axial Diagnosis: Given the case information and your responses to the questions below, prepare the following: a multi-axial diagnosis and a rationale, as well as additional information you would have wanted to know in order to make a more accurate diagnosis.

Questions to consider when formulating a diagnosis for Nikki

1. What clinically significant symptoms is Nikki displaying at this time with regard to eating and body shape? What eating disorder encapsulates these symptoms?

2. What other symptoms does Nikki display outside her eating symptoms? What diagnosis encapsulates these symptoms?

3. Has Nikki experienced prior episodes of major depression?

4. Has Nikki experienced recent stressors that could account for her symptoms?

Multi-Axial Diagnosis

Axis I:

Axis II:

Axis III:

Axis IV:

Axis V:

Rationale and Differential Diagnosis

Additional Information

Biopsychosocial Risk and Resilience Influences

Onset

For the purposes of examining the risk and protective mechanisms for the onset of eating disorders, anorexia and bulimia will be considered together, as they share overlapping risk factors, symptoms, and causes (White, 2000). However, influences on each disorder's course will be explored separately, as sufficient evidence has been gathered on each one. Figure 13.2 further describes the relationship to eating disorders and risks for various vulnerable and oppressed populations.

BIOLOGY

Biological influences on eating disorders include heritability, obstetrical complications, early puberty, obesity, and dieting. Anorexia is moderately heritable (Bulik, Sullivan, Tozzi, et al., 2006), and more so than bulimia (Fonagy et al., 2002), although family members of individuals with eating disorders have an increased vulnerability both for eating disorders (Bulik et al., 2006) and for mood disorders (APA, 2000). Specific to bulimia, relatives are vulnerable to substance use disorders and obesity (APA, 2000; Fairburn et al., 1999).

Preterm birth and pregnancy complications are associated with anorexia nervosa. A study conducted in Italy found that certain obstetrical complications, such as

FIGURE 13.2 Eating Disorders and Vulnerable and Oppressed Populations.

FEMALES
- Although eating disorders are more prevalent in females, about 25 percent of cases are represented by males.[1]

GAY AND LESBIAN
- Homosexual males may be at risk for eating disorders.[2]

MINORITIES
- In Western countries, Asians have a similar risk to Caucasians, if not higher.[3]
- Although Caucasian women in Western countries do not have higher rates of diagnosable eating disorders than do non-Caucasian women, they do have higher rates of body dissatisfaction and eating disturbance; this latter effect is especially noticeable among Caucasians and African-Americans.[4]
- Lack of existing research on eating disorders as they pertain to Hispanic, Native American, East Indian, and eastern European women.[5]
- Mexican-American and African-American women are underdiagnosed and undertreated.[6]

[1]Hudson et al., 2006.
[2]Muise, Stein, & Arbess, 2003.
[3]Wildes & Emery, 2001.
[4]Wildes & Emery, 2001.
[5]O'Neill, 2003.
[6]Cachelin & Striegel-Moore, 2006; Fairburn, Agras, Walsh, et al., 2004.

maternal anemia, diabetes, and preeclampsia (a hypertensive disorder), were associated with the development of anorexia, while others, such as placental infarction, early eating difficulties, and low birth weight for gestational age, were associated with bulimia (Favaro, Tenconi, & Santonastaso, 2006). The total number of obstetrical complications was predictive of the development of anorexia. The authors concluded that neurodevelopmental impairments could be associated with the etiology of eating disorders.

Adolescence is clearly a developmental stage that makes females vulnerable to eating disorders. The mean age of onset is 18.9 years for anorexia nervosa and 19.7 for bulimia nervosa (Hudson et al., 2006). Anorexia tends to have an earlier age of onset than bulimia (Lewinsohn et al., 2000). The tension between the cultural ideal of female beauty and the physical reality of the female body after puberty is magnified by female gender role expectations. That is, female identity is defined in relational terms, and beauty is a core aspect of female identity (Striegel-Moore, 1993).

Early onset of puberty (prior to age 11) confers particular risk for the development of eating disorders; conversely, later-onset menarche (age 14 and over) is protective. Interestingly, one review indicated that earlier maturation is related to increased life stress in childhood (DeRose, Wright, & Brooks-Gunn, 2006), although the mechanisms by which this happens are not well understood. Early-maturing females tend to be shorter and heavier; therefore, their body type strays further from the current body ideal (Mizes & Palmero, 1997; Striegel-Moore, 1993). In fact, a lean body build presents protection from eating disorders because this body type matches the contemporary standard. People often tease early-maturing girls for their development; they may also be exposed to experiences for which they are not psychologically prepared, such as dating and sexual pressure.

Childhood obesity poses a risk for bulimia (Stice, 2002), perhaps because of its damaging effect on body image (Striegel-Moore & Cachelin, 1999). Dieting is also a risk (Lowe & Timko, 2004; Patton, Selzer, Coffey, Carlin, & Wolfe, 1999). "Unrealistically rigid standards of dietary restraint coupled with a sense of deprivation may leave dieters vulnerable to loss of control after perceived or actual transgression of their diet. A lapse leads to an 'all-or-nothing' cognitive reaction.... Dieting can also be associated with different conditioning processes that may predispose a person to binge eating. For example, it may increase the appeal of 'forbidden' or 'binge' foods (typically those high in fat and sugar)..." (Lowe, 2002, pp. 96–97). At the same time, dieting alone will not cause an eating disorder, as dieting is fairly normative among adolescent and adult women. Among dieters, more disturbed eating habits and attitudes are associated with the development of eating disorders (Fairburn, Cooper, Doll, & Davies, 2005).

PSYCHOLOGY

Body dissatisfaction and distortion, negative affect, perfectionism, impulsivity, and substance use are risk factors for eating disorders (Stice, 2002). As discussed in the comorbidity section, having a mental disorder puts one at risk for the development of an eating disorder. Protective factors in the psychological domain include high self-esteem, a strong sense of identity, well-developed social and coping skills, and a positive temperament (Striegel-Moore & Cachelin, 1999).

SOCIAL INFLUENCES

Family influences on eating disorders have been noted, but whether the link is due to genetic mechanisms, childhood experiences, family concerns about weight, family psychopathology, or transaction patterns is unknown (Cooper, 1995; Wilson, Heffernan, & Black, 1996). In addition, specific patterns have not been delineated, but families in which eating disorders develop tend to be dysfunctional in various ways (Mizes & Palermo, 1997). A small significant relationship exists between sexual abuse, which often occurs within the context of the family, and eating disorders (Smolak & Murnen, 2002). On the protective side, families that foster parent-child attachment and have effective discipline skills, healthy cohesion, and positive communication help buffer their children against eating disorders (Striegel-Moore & Cachelin, 1999).

Another family process involves the extent to which parents transmit societal values having to do with weight and appearance (Striegel-Moore & Cachelin, 1999). When parents focus excessively on their own or their children's shape and size, children may feel pressure to lose weight (Kotler et al., 2001; Mizes & Palermo, 1997). Teasing by family members about a child's weight is particularly detrimental.

Aside from family influences, other social mechanisms include social support, extracurricular activities, societal values, and socioeconomic status (Striegel-Moore & Cachelin, 1999). A poor social support system may evolve from social isolation, social anxiety, and public self-consciousness and increase risk of eating disorders. Conversely, protective mechanisms include social skills, social connections, and social support (Stice, 2002).

Involvement in certain extracurricular activities that emphasize very low body fat, such as sports and dance, puts an individual at risk for eating disorders (Striegel-Moore & Cachelin, 1999). Activities that emphasize health and fitness protect against the development of eating disorders), as well as activities that presumably involve other aspects of the individual aside from appearance and weight.

Societal overemphasis on thinness for females has resulted in widespread dissatisfaction among females concerning their body image (Mizes & Palmero, 1997). Exposure to images in the media of extremely thin women is associated with dissatisfaction concerning body image (Groesz, Levine, & Murnen, 2002). Finally, products involving weight and appearance targeted at females are big business, creating strong incentives for corporations to boost markets for products that address females' supposed flaws.

Unlike many other mental disorders, high socioeconomic status (SES) does not confer protection against the development of eating disorders (Striegel-Moore & Cachelin,

1999). Females of middle and upper SES may indeed be more vulnerable due to increased demands in terms of social compliance and perfectionism.

Course and Recovery

Studies that follow clients over time reveal wide variations in the course of eating disorders. According to a review of these studies in relation to anorexia, although 50 percent recover (defined by restoration of weight and menses), about 20 percent of individuals are still significantly impaired at follow-up (Fonagy et al., 2002). Many with good outcomes may still show persistent symptoms of depression, anxiety, and/or substance use (Yager et al., 2002). Two-thirds continue to suffer from food and weight preoccupation, and about 40 percent engage in bulimic behaviors. A small proportion of people may die from starvation, heart failure, or suicide (APA, 2000). Suicide is the major cause of death, and suicide rates for those with anorexia are greater than in the normal population (Pompili, Mancinelli, Girardi, et al., 2004). A recent 12-year longitudinal study of German women who had been in inpatient facilities found that 27.5 percent had a good outcome, 25.3 percent had an intermediate outcome, 39.6 percent had a poor outcome, and 7.7 percent unfortunately had died (Fichter, Quadflieg, & Hedlund, 2006).

For bulimia nervosa, a review of 88 studies indicated that 50 percent of women had recovered at five- to ten-year follow up (Keel & Mitchell, 1997), while 30 percent showed bulimic symptoms and 20 percent continued to meet full criteria. The risk of relapse abated after four years.

Suicide attempts are common (i.e., 25–35 percent of those with bulimia) (Franko & Keel, 2006).

Another finding is that the "crossover" rate between anorexia and bulimia is high. Among persons with an initial diagnosis of restricting-type anorexia, 36 percent developed bulimia, while 27 percent of those with an initial diagnosis of bulimia developed anorexia (Tozzi, Thornton, Klump, et al., 2005). The majority of the crossover patterns occurred within the first five years of the disorder.

Following the onset of an eating disorder, a similar combination of risk and protective mechanisms is thought to maintain the condition, determine whether a person recovers, or predict responses to particular interventions (Gowers & Bryant-Waugh, 2004). Table 13.1 and Table 13.2 provide the risk and resilience factors influencing the course of anorexia nervosa and bulimia nervosa, respectively.

TABLE 13.1 Risk and Resilience Factors Influencing the Course of Anorexia Nervosa

RISK	PROTECTIVE
Features of the disorder • initially lower minimum weight • long duration of eating disorder	• shorter duration of illness before treatment
Developmental stage • adults	• adolescent (with younger adolescents having better outcome than older adolescents)
Psychological • greater body-image disturbance • comorbid psychological disorders, such as anxiety disorders (especially OCD), depression, and substance abuse • resistance and denial • sexual problems • impulsivity	
Social • disturbed family relationships before onset of the disorder • impaired social functioning	• support and empathic relationships, whether professional or nonprofessional
Treatment factors • failure to respond to previous treatment	

Sources: Bell, 2003; Berkman et al., 2007; Gowers & Bryant-Waugh, 2004; Keel, Dorer, Franko, et al., 2005; Yager et al., 2002.

TABLE 13.2 Risk and Resilience Factors Influencing the Course of Bulimia Nervosa

RISK	PROTECTIVE
Features of the disorder • high baseline frequencies of bingeing and vomiting • precoccupation and ritualization of eating • long duration of symptoms	• milder symptoms • shorter duration of illness

(Continues)

TABLE 13.2 Risk and Resilience Factors Influencing the Course of Bulimia Nervosa (Continued)

RISK	*PROTECTIVE*
Psychological • substance use disorder • depression • personality disorder • impulsivity • greater body-image disturbance • lower motivation for change • high initial perfectionism	
Social	• support and empathic relationships, whether professional or nonprofessional
Treatment factors • short abstinence period • only reduction in bulimic behaviors at end of treatment	• early change in purging frequency • complete abstinence at end of treatment

Sources: Bell, 2003; Berkman et al., 2007; Fonagy et al., 2002; Gowers & Bryant-Waugh, 2004; Keel, Dorer, Franko, et al., 2005; Keel & Mitchell, 1997; Wilson et al., 1999; Yager et al., 2002.

Directions Part II, Biopsychosocial Risk and Protective Factors Assessment: Formulate a risk and protective factors assessment, both for the onset of the disorder and the course of the disorder, including the strengths that you see for this individual.

TABLE 13.3 Biopsychosocial Risk and Resilience Assessment for the Onset of the Disorder

RISK FACTORS	*PROTECTIVE FACTORS*
Biological	
Psychological	

TABLE 13.3 Biopsychosocial Risk and Resilience Assessment for the Onset of the Disorder   (Continued)

Social	

TABLE 13.4 Biopsychosocial Risk and Resilience Assessment for the Course of the Disorder

RISK FACTORS	*PROTECTIVE FACTORS*
Biological	
Psychological	
Social	

Intervention

A major problem with treatment for eating disorders is that mental health providers tend not to follow evidence-based methods. For example, a survey of Canadian professionals who treated eating disorders found that more than half used addiction-based (12-step) approaches at least sometimes (von Ranson & Robinson, 2006), although an addictions conceptualization of eating disorders has been discounted for anorexia and bulimia (Wilson, 1999). Another problem with the eating disorders treatment arena is that evidence for how to treat anorexia nervosa, in particular, has not been strong. Finally, studies usually do not focus on adolescents, which is unfortunate for a condition that commonly arises in adolescence (Gowers & Bryan-Waugh, 2004).

The goals of intervention with clients who have eating disorders should focus, of course, on aspects of their weight and eating behaviors. However, interventions that attend to weight alone are associated with client dissatisfaction (Bell, 2003), and dietary advice as the only intervention seems particularly onerous to women (Hay, Bacaltchuk, Claudino, et al., 2003).

Treatment Settings

While outcome studies of inpatient treatment of bulimia are lacking, in the vast majority of cases (95 percent) outpatient treatment is sufficient (Fonagy et al., 2002). Inpatient hospitalization for anorexia is indicated in the presence of the following (Foreyt et al., 1998; Golden, Katzman, Kreipe, et al., 2003): (1) serious physical complications (malnutrition, dehydration, electrolyte disturbances, cardiac dysrhythmia, arrested growth); (2) extremely low body weight; (3) suicide risk; (4) lack of response to outpatient treatment; (5) lack of available outpatient treatment; (6) comorbid disorders that interfere with outpatient treatment (i.e., severe depression, obsessive-compulsive disorder); and (7) a need to be separated from the current living situation.

Inpatient treatment usually involves multidisciplinary services comprising psychiatry, psychology, nursing, dietetics, occupational therapy, physical therapy, social services, and general medical services (Foreyt, Poston, Winebarger, & McGavin, 1998). Hospitals typically rely on behavioral systems in which client privileges, such as time out of bed, are linked to weight gain (Yager et al., 2002).

Hospital stays have shortened in recent years due to changes imposed by managed care. Shorter stays make it harder for the client to achieve optimal weight, as weight should be restored at a rate of only one to three pounds per week. If the client is released before reaching optimal weight,[1] he or she may be unable to maintain the weight, which might necessitate rehospitalization (Mizes & Palmero, 1997). In addition, individuals benefit from having some control over the process and pace of intervention (Bell, 2003). Those who are resistant to weight gain may need to gain weight more slowly and have a period of weight maintenance, thus requiring a longer hospital stay (Willer, Thuras, & Crow, 2005). Still, due to patterns of insurance reimbursement, the outpatient care of anorexia will increasingly be the norm.

Psychosocial Interventions

For bulimia, two major psychosocial interventions, both delivered in a brief format (e.g., 16 sessions) have received empirical validation: cognitive-behavioral treatment (CBT) and interpersonal therapy. A review of psychotherapy studies showed that about 40 percent of those who complete treatment recover (this percentage is reduced to 32.6 percent when including dropouts from treatment) (Thompson-Brenner, Glass, & Westen, 2003).

CBT includes a "package" of strategies, among them self-monitoring, social skills training, assertiveness training, problem solving, and cognitive restructuring. A review of

---

[1] 90 percent of normal weight, so that menstruation can resume.

studies found that about one-half of women with bulimia recover with a course of CBT (Hay & Bacaltchuk, 2003), which generally achieves a superior effect to medication (Whittal, Agras, & Gould, 1999).

Individual therapy seems more effective than group modalities (Thompson-Brenner et al., 2003). In addition, a self-help format is a promising approach (Hay & Bacaltchuk, 2003). These intervention procedures have been clearly outlined in treatment manuals (Fonagy et al., 2002). (See Fairburn, Marcus, & Wilson [1993] for an example of a treatment manual.) Despite these advantages, many experienced clinicians do not find CBT as useful as described by researchers (Yager et al., 2002). This disparity may be due to lack of training, discomfort with the methods, or differences between clients seen in the community and those who participate as research subjects. In randomized controlled trials (the gold standard of intervention research), individuals with substance use disorders, bipolar disorder, or suicidality are screened out from research (Thompson-Brenner et al., 2003). Therefore, the results of such trials may not generalize to clients who are seen in clinical settings for bulimia.

Individual interpersonal therapy is another empirically validated approach for bulimia (e.g., Fairburn, Jones, Peveler, et al., 1991; Fairburn, Norman, Welch, et al., 1995), which has been adapted from the treatment of depression. (See Chapter 10.) CBT and interpersonal therapy compare favorably with each other, although interpersonal therapy may take longer to achieve its outcomes.

Unfortunately, these empirically validated interventions have not typically been tested with adolescents. It seems that developmentally appropriate modifications, including a degree of parental involvement and addressing age-related motivational issues, would be necessary (Gowers & Bryant-Waugh, 2004).

A great deal of ambivalence about staying thin and getting better is typically present with eating disorders, and motivational interviewing may be necessary to engage people in treatment and to restore healthy eating patterns. Motivational interviewing, which originated in response to substance abuse (see Chapter 8), has been adapted for eating disorders (Killick & Allen, 1997; Tantillo, Bitter, & Adams, 2001; Treasure & Ward, 1997). Preliminary evidence suggests that motivational interviewing compares favorably with CBT for reducing bulimic symptoms (Treasure, Katzman, Schmidt, Troop, Todd, & de Silva, 1999).

As discussed, certain risk influences involve the family. Although there is consensus among practitioners that family involvement should be part of the treatment plan, at least for younger adolescents with anorexia (Crisp et al., 1991; Robin et al., 1995; Robin, Siegel, Moye, et al., 1999), methodologically strong studies have been few.

Empirical support for psychosocial treatment of anorexia nervosa is lacking. Long-term psychodynamic therapy is most often used for the outpatient treatment of anorexia, although results have not typically been examined empirically (Mizes & Palermo, 1997). A recent randomized, controlled trial comparing CBT, interpersonal therapy, and nonspecific supportive clinical management found that the supportive condition was more effective than interpersonal therapy, a finding that was contrary to the hypothesis (McIntosh, Jordan, Carter, et al., 2005). The majority of people in the study (70 percent) either dropped out or showed few gains. In a more promising vein, CBT was offered as a post-hospitalization treatment for anorexia nervosa in adults and was found more effective than nutritional counseling in improving outcome and preventing relapse (Pike, Walsh, Vitousek, et al., 2003). In a review of individual outpatient psychotherapies aimed at adults with anorexia, Hay, Bacaltchuk, Claudino, et al. (2003) concluded from the six controlled trials that had been conducted to date that no specific treatment was consistently superior to any other one.

Medication

Although psychotropic medications should not stand as the primary treatment of eating disorders (Bacaltchuk, Hay, & Trefiglio, 2001; Gowers & Bryant-Waugh, 2004; Nakash-Eisikovitz, Dierberger, & Westen, 2002), selective serotonin reuptake inhibitors (SSRIs), particularly fluoxetine (Prozac), have been used to treat bulimia. For those who are eligible to participate in research (excluding those who are suicidal and with substance use problems), recovery with SSRIs reaches about 25 percent (Nakash-Eisikovitz et al., 2002). A therapeutic dose of 60 mg fluoxetine has a moderate effect on both bingeing and purging. In addition, the average client still meets criteria for bulimia nervosa after a course of antidepressant drugs. Dropout rates also tend to be high for those treated with medication (Bacaltchuk & Hay, 2003).

Medication does not seem to have much impact on anorexia (Claudino, Hay, Lima, et al., 2006; Gowers & Bryant-Waugh, 2004). When medications are used, it is usually because of comorbid depression or anxiety. People being treated for eating disorders, especially those with anorexia, report psychological interventions as being more helpful than medication (Bell, 2003).

Directions Part III, Goal Setting and Treatment Planning: Given your risk and protective factors assessments of the individual, your knowledge of the disorder, and evidence-based practice guidelines, formulate goals and a possible treatment plan for this individual.

Critical Perspective

A major critique of the diagnosis of eating disorders that is central to the social work perspective is that it focuses on the internal deficits of those with eating disorders, rather than emphasizing social and cultural attitudes (Pratt & Woolfenden, 2003). Both anorexia and bulimia have increased throughout recent decades because of cultural standards of thinness (Keel & Klump, 2003). One of the challenges faced by those involved in prevention efforts is the difficulty of changing the dieting and weight preoccupations that are so culturally pervasive (Mizes & Palmero, 1997).

Another class of critiques has to do with the narrowness of the diagnostic criteria for anorexia and bulimia. As a result, many individuals with serious eating-related problems escape diagnosis and thus the possibility of help. Some researchers recommend more relaxed criteria (e.g., Kotler, Cohen, Davies, Pine, & Walsh, 2001), and several rationales are offered to support such a change (Lewinsohn, Striegel-Moore, & Seeley, 2000). First, a considerable proportion of those seeking treatment for eating disorders are subthreshold cases, meaning that they do not meet enough criteria for formal diagnosis (e.g., Striegel-Moore, Franko, Thompson, et al., 2005). As a result, "eating disorder not otherwise specified" is a commonly used diagnosis, given to nearly 50 percent of clients, particularly adolescents (Yager et al., 2002). In addition, research comparing full-syndrome with subthreshold cases reveals few differences in terms of clinical and psychosocial characteristics, including levels of comorbid depression, suicide attempts, impaired global functioning, and prior treatment. Further, some women who have subthreshold cases eventually develop a full-blown disorder. For adolescents, even subclinical cases may result in impaired health (Lewinsohn, Striegel-Moore, & Seeley, 2000). Finally, "by developing treatments exclusively for anorexia nervosa and bulimia nervosa, the needs of a large population of patients have been ignored" (Fairburn & Walsh, 2004, p. 176).

Several problems related to the criteria for bulimia and anorexia will be explored here; if some of these criteria were modified, a significant number of cases from the "eating disorder not otherwise specified" category would be absorbed. One problem with the criteria for bulimia is the term "excessive exercise" for inappropriate compensating behavior. "Excessive" implies a large amount of time dedicated to exercise, yet it is not the quantity of physical activity that is salient, but its compulsive quality (Adkins & Keel, 2005). It has been suggested that the word "compulsive" be substituted for "excessive." Another way to define the criterion as excessive is to ask the client if the postponement of exercise results in intense guilt or whether it is undertaken solely to influence weight or shape (Mond, Hay, Rodgers, & Owen, 2006).

Other critiques concerning the diagnosis for bulimia involve the duration of binges, the amount of food consumed during binges, and the frequency criterion for bulimia. Although the criterion requires that the binge eating happen "in a discrete period of time," no evidence indicates that discrete binges offer any more clinical utility than episodes that occur over an extended period of time (Franko et al., 2004). The binge is required to be "an amount that is definitely larger than what most people would eat." However, many women report subjective binge episodes and then feel compelled to purge but perhaps would not meet the criterion because their binges are not sufficiently large (Franko et al., 2004). Better indicators of a binge episode might be the level of mood disturbance involved or the sense of loss of control (Herzog & Delinsky, 2001, as cited in Franko et al., 2004). Finally, the DSM requires that the bingeing and purging episodes must occur at least twice a week for a three-month period. However, the decision for this minimum frequency was not based on empirical evidence, and bulimic behaviors less frequent than this may still involve a clinically significant problem (Franko et al., 2004).

Issues particular to anorexia involve the validity of including "amenorrhea" as a criterion; some women who are seriously underweight continue to menstruate (Striegel-Moore et al., 2005). Also, the criterion lacks relevance for prepubescent girls and for males (Franko, Wonderlich, Little, & Herzog, 2004). Another problem with the diagnosis for anorexia is the weight criterion—85 percent ideal body weight—and it is suggested that it should be replaced by a criterion with more latitude, such as "substantial weight loss" (Anderson, Bowers, & Watson, 2001).

A final critique involves the subtyping of anorexia (whether binge eating and purging or restricting) and bulimia (purging or nonpurging). Questions have been generated "as to the utility and validity of these subtypes" (Franko et al., 2004, p. 61). For example, anorexia binge eating-purging type may be more like bulimia than restricting anorexia, which may represent a discrete type of eating disorder. Additionally, the bulimia subtypes may not involve a true distinction.

Directions Part IV, Critical Perspective: Formulate a critique of the diagnosis as it relates to this case example. Questions to consider include: Does this diagnosis represent a valid mental disorder from the social work perspective? Is this diagnosis significantly different from other possible diagnoses? Your critique should be based on the values of the social work profession (which are incongruent in some ways with the medical model) and the validity of the specific diagnostic criteria applied to this case.

CASE 2

Kelly is a 28-year-old married white female whose chief complaint is, "I can't stop eating." She loves foods rich in carbohydrates, such as sugar and flour, and claims that once she starts eating refined foods, she cannot stop (i.e., she loses the ability to control the size of her food portions). Her belief is that once she takes a bite of something that is sugary, "the bite takes me and I'm off to the races." She admits to eating when she is not hungry and reports that she eats quickly, "stuffing it into my face."

Kelly has struggled with food since she was nine years old. Kelly was always "overweight as a child"; she is presently 5 feet 6 inches tall and weighs 200 pounds. She constantly obsesses about food, planning each day what she will eat and where she will obtain food. Often (at least four days a week) she will buy large quantities of ice cream and cake from the store, binge, and then sleep. When she wakes up, she feels depressed, guilty, and full of self-loathing. She often has crying jags because she feels so bad. When questioned, she denied any regular purging, but said that she resorted to laxatives "about once every two weeks."

In the past Kelly has attempted to lose weight. For example, when she was ten years old she joined a recreational track team and was moderately successful in losing weight. However, while her weight began to normalize according to body mass index figures, Kelly would still binge on certain foods, such as pizza, pasta, and desserts. This pattern of behavior continued later during cross-country and cheerleading seasons. She recalls that despite the binge episodes, she would maintain a normal weight and sometimes would even weigh less than was considered healthy for her height and frame, although she never met the criteria for anorexia. During off-seasons, when she was not participating in sports activities, however, her binge eating would result in significant weight gains.

Since her teenage years, Kelly has made multiple attempts to deal with her eating disorder. These include a "healthy" diet devised by a nutritionist; behavioral modifications designed to moderate and control her intake of carbohydrate-rich foods; psychodynamically oriented psychotherapy to explore the causes that led to her binge eating; and CBT to examine her faulty thinking concerning food, body shape, and size. In her mid-20s she also admitted herself to a residential program that specialized in women and empowerment, and attended Overeaters Anonymous (OA), a 12-step support group for compulsive eaters.

There is a strong history of addiction-related disorders in Kelly's family, including alcoholism on the paternal side, and eating disorders, primarily binge eating, on the maternal side. Kelly's mother is a first-generation Italian immigrant who believes that food can be an "emotional comfort." Further, Kelly's mother suffered from bulimia herself; she exercised for weight compensation, even running marathons. Kelly's mother was also sexually abused by an uncle when she was a child.

Kelly has two sisters and three brothers, all of whom are obese. She is close to her sisters and less close to her brothers. All of the brothers exhibit alcoholism to varying degrees, as does her father. Additionally, some of the males in the extended paternal side of the family are described as "gutter" alcoholics.

Kelly's parents had an antagonistic relationship with each other during Kelly's formative years, in which Kelly's father physically and sexually abused Kelly's mother; Kelly witnessed this abuse. Kelly's father works for the Post Office, while Kelly's mother is a school bus driver, placing the family as lower middle class. They are Catholic and attend Mass regularly.

Upon graduating from high school, Kelly attended college, but after the first year, she switched to a community college in order to live at home. She told her family about her eating disorder and was able to derive some emotional support from her sisters and mother. She also attended OA meetings with her mother. Because she had to move to another state to attend graduate school, Kelly was lonely and would use both food and men to fill her emotional void. She also stopped going to OA.

As a result of meeting a man through a personal ad, she married within the year. She admitted that she didn't know him well because they had lived in different areas and had not spent much time together. After the wedding, Kelly discovered that her husband was controlling and verbally abusive. He ordered her around, wanted her to cater to his needs, and called her "fat" and "lazy with no willpower." Although Kelly admits that her husband "pushed and shoved her around" physically, when asked about physical abuse, Kelly became silent and repeatedly avoided talking about the subject.

Kelly recently learned that she was six weeks pregnant. In an attempt to abort the baby *in utero*, she repeatedly punched herself in the stomach (this was not successful) and used ipecac (an over-the-counter emetic often used by bulimic individuals) to purge after binge eating. She also felt suicidal. One day, she wrote a suicide note; placed the note beside her on the car seat in the garage, which was closed; and started the engine in an attempt to commit suicide through carbon monoxide poisoning. However, she then called one of her sisters, who was able to talk her out of the attempt.

Kelly is adamant about wanting a divorce but is concerned about her financial status. Although she has successfully completed graduate school, she has been unable to find a job. She admits that she feels too disgusted with herself even to try. "Who's going to want me when I look like this?" She feels incredibly ashamed of her appearance and her unsuccessful marriage.

Kelly made no friends at graduate school, and the phone contact she maintains with her family members is inadequate to meet her needs for social and emotional support. Kelly presents as a tearful, poorly groomed individual (her hair is not brushed, and she attended initial therapy sessions in baggy pants and inside-out sweatshirt), with suicidal ideation because of her binge eating and deteriorating marital situation.

> **Please go to the Appendix for directions to this case.** The following questions will help to guide your thinking about a possible multi-axial diagnosis.

Questions to consider when formulating a diagnosis for Kelly

1. What clinically significant symptoms does Kelly display in regard to eating and body shape? What eating disorder encapsulates these symptoms?

2. Are there recent stressors that may account for Kelly's symptoms? Do these symptoms warrant an adjustment disorder?

3. Describe Kelly's mood symptoms both now and in the past. Is a major depression diagnosis warranted?

CASE 3

Tina, a 14-year-old biracial Asian-American girl, was brought to outpatient therapy after her discharge from a two-week stay in an inpatient eating disorders unit. Six months previously, she had begun to restrict sweets and fats and drastically increased her exercise regimen (running an hour a day on average). In total, Tina lost 15 pounds from her unusually small 4-feet, 11-inch frame, bringing her weight down to 82 pounds. She had stopped menstruating for three months and had a low heart rate before her hospitalization, during which she was placed on a feeding tube and treated with an SSRI. During her hospital stay she gained 10 pounds.

Other symptoms that had developed prior to and after her hospitalization were a preoccupation with her hygiene and morning routine; she took an average of 90 minutes each morning to get ready, constantly redoing her hair and makeup. She denied that this preoccupation was due to a defect in her appearance; she just wanted to look "perfect." She didn't view these behaviors as excessive and said that all the girls at school spent a lot of time getting ready if they wanted to look good.

Additionally, if she didn't get straight As, she felt like a failure, became angry with herself, and withdrew into her room. She regularly stayed up until two o'clock in the morning doing her schoolwork until it was "perfect" or memorizing for exams until she could recite the material back word for word. She admitted that she told no one at school how much time she spent study-ing (six to seven hours a night) and acknowledged that by anyone's standards but her own and her father's, it was excessive.

Tina was still extremely preoccupied with her weight and shape after her hospitalization, as evidenced by her continuing restricted eating, exercising, and constant self-criticism. She often said to her mother, "I hate how I look. Do I look fat to you? Would you tell me if I did?" Her mother did not know how to respond to this "barrage of questions," and Tina remained unconvinced by her attempts at reassurance. Tina denied bingeing or purging, and her mother confirmed this report.

The above behaviors and ideas were not bothersome to Tina; in fact she didn't understand why her parents and psychiatrist were making such a fuss over them, as she had always been this way. "My father is a perfectionist, too," she said. Her parents were stymied by her behaviors and especially angered by her monopolization of the bathroom in the morning. Yelling at her, punish-ing her, reprimanding her—all came to naught. Tina was "stuck" in her behav-iors despite her stated desire to change them. She worried constantly that she was fat and had a great deal of difficulty accepting the recommendation of continued weight gain.

Tina is the younger of two children and reports being close to her brother, three years her senior. Her parents are of mixed ethnicity; her father is a second-generation Korean and her mother is American. Both parents are intelligent and accomplished; her father is an academic scientist and her mother a pianist who limits herself to teaching students privately, having given up her career when the children were born. Tina's relatives lived across the United States, and she typically only saw them once a year. She said she doesn't feel particularly close to anyone in her extended family. Tina has never drunk or used drugs, and her parents report being social drinkers, which they defined as an occasional glass of wine.

Tina's father is obsessed with being thin and in shape and gives her mixed messages about food. He wants her to eat, but is not unhappy that she eliminated "fatty, junk food" and is critical of "the American diet." His wife is of healthy weight, although she gained weight after having children. The household environment is conflicted, angry, and tense due to their marital problems, mostly about parenting differences. Tina's father is often critical of her mother for being too "permissive" with the children and for letting herself go. He feels that children are raised too loosely in this country, whereas Tina's mother feels that he is too hard on them, often putting them down and calling them "lazy failures," among other pejorative terms. She also reported feeling very controlled by her husband's criticisms and demands. "Nothing I do is right." She reported having thought about leaving him many times, and he, too, often feels hopeless and resigned to a disappointing marriage. Tina's mother has a history of depression, which has been treated with medication in the past; her father has refused to consider the possibility of any emotional difficulties in himself.

In the initial session Tina spoke flatly, showing little expression and eye contact as she talked about what she had been through for the last six months. She gave minimal answers to questions and displayed little response to empathic statements made by the therapist. She said that art was an outlet for her and showed some energy when the therapist suggested she draw a picture in the session to indicate how she felt. When she talked about her drawing, she described feeling "trapped" and "frightened." When questioned further about these feelings, she said that she hated her family and felt no future for herself. Despite this statement, she said she had never felt suicidal or depressed. She also denied having been sexually abused.

Tina described having only one friend, a second-generation Korean girl her age, and said she wasn't interested in having a boyfriend. She said, "What's the point of a relationship? Look at my parents and how their marriage turned out." Tina liked participating in track and cross-country at school for the exercise it provided; she said that she liked long-distance running, although she never placed in races. She admitted that this made her feel a "failure."

Please go to the Appendix for directions to this case. The following questions will help to guide your thinking about a possible multi-axial diagnosis.

Questions to consider when formulating a diagnosis for Tina

1. What symptoms does Tina display in regard to eating and shape? What type of eating disorder characterizes these symptoms?

2. What do you make of Tina's preoccupation with her physical appearance in the mornings?

3. What do you make of the amount of time Tina spends on schoolwork and studying?

4. How can you account for the family problems that seem to have contributed to Tina's current functioning?

5. Is there evidence of a major depressive disorder or dysthymia?

14

— ▼▲▼ —

Borderline Personality Disorders

Kenda Starnes is a 19-year-old single Caucasian female referred to the mental health center by a housemate, a 42-year-old man named John. When John called the agency, he was told that he could not make an appointment on behalf of a nonrelative. "But she's threatening to kill herself," he pleaded. He added that Kenda had recently spent one week in a psychiatric hospital and was refusing to take the antidepressant medications the doctor had prescribed. "She won't listen to the doctor. She won't listen to me. She jerks everyone around, trying to get her way." John was about to arrange to have the discharge summary sent to this agency, but he apparently persuaded Kenda to call on her own behalf, because she contacted the social worker the next day.

Kenda came to her first appointment dressed casually, and appeared her stated age. During the meeting she seemed uncomfortable and suspicious. Her affect was grim, and she rarely made eye contact. Kenda admitted to the social worker that she was in a lot of emotional pain. "I feel so lonely sometimes. I don't know if it will ever go away. I used to wish someone would rescue me, but really I don't think anyone understands me." Kenda added that she tried to stay active, to "keep my mind off myself," spending most of her time with John, his six-year-old daughter, and the two other young adult women who lived at the house. "All of us work as volunteer emergency medical technicians (EMTs) for the Fire Department. That's where we met. John had just gotten divorced and was looking for housemates."

Asked about her current relationships, Kenda said that she liked the other women in the house "OK" but didn't feel that she knew them very well. She was quick to say, "They're not trustworthy." She added, "John is divorced. He's just a friend to all of us." About that relationship, she said "I don't know what he wants from me, but it's a place to stay. Actually, I think he wants sex from me, but I don't like him that way. He's kind of creepy. But it's nice to have people around, even though they don't care much about me. In fact, it's terrible when I'm by myself." When asked to elaborate on that point, Kenda said,

"I feel lonely all the time. I need people to be with me. Sometimes I feel I'm disintegrating when I'm alone, as though I'm just fading into nothingness. It's scary. It's why I hate to go to bed at night. I have to lie there alone in the dark and think. I get more and more afraid, because I'm so empty." Kenda admitted that she feels tired almost all the time, partly because of poor sleep but also because of "feeling frustrated so often."

When asked about other friends, she said, "People don't like me. You can't trust them anyway. In fact, people are always letting me down. I don't do anything to hurt them, but they're always abandoning me when I need them the most. I call them and they can't talk, or I stop by their apartments and they're not home, even when they've said they would be. I don't know why people don't treat me better. I'm a good person."

Alarmingly, the hospital records, which arrived after the first visit, indicated that Kenda had been hospitalized ten times in the year since her high school graduation. These inpatient stays were all precipitated by the onset of depression, fears of losing self-control, and the alarming anxiety she experienced when alone. The episodes often occurred during her chronically sleepless nights. The hospital report also indicated that Kenda was prone when upset to strike her fist into concrete walls. She had broken bones in her hand on at least five occasions by doing this. When the social worker asked about this, Kenda responded, "When I get upset, I have to do something. I'm afraid I'll lose control or fall apart. Sometimes when I hit the wall it brings me back down to earth." There was no history of any mental health intervention prior to her leaving her family's home.

Personality is a difficult concept to define. One noted theorist defined it as a stable set of tendencies and characteristics or thoughts, beliefs, and actions that have continuity over time (Maddi, 1996). The DSM-IV category of personality disorders represents an attempt to identify persons whose chronic problems in social functioning are related to ingrained patterns of thinking, behaving, and feeling. The idea of a personality as *disordered* is controversial, however (Mattaini, 1994). Social workers should be concerned about using these diagnoses because they appear to describe the *total person*, rather than a particular aspect of the person or the result of person-in-environment processes. In this chapter we consider the concept of personality disorder and, more specifically, one personality disorder that is often encountered by clinical practitioners: the borderline type.

Characteristics of Personality Disorders

According to the APA (2000) all of the personality disorders are characterized by enduring cognitions and behaviors that deviate from cultural standards, are pervasive and rigid, are stable over time, have an onset in adolescence or early adulthood, and lead to unhappiness and impairment. They must include maladaptive behavior in at least two of the following areas: *affect* (range and intensity of emotions), *cognition* (how the self and others are perceived), *impulse control*, and *interpersonal functioning*. The DSM classifies the personality disorders into three *clusters*, based on shared core characteristics (Woods, 1999). Cluster A includes the paranoid, schizoid, and schizotypal disorders. These disorders are believed to have a genetic base and are more common in the biological relatives of people with schizophrenia. People with these disorders are considered by others to be odd and eccentric. The cluster B disorders (antisocial, borderline, histrionic, and narcissistic) are characterized by dramatic, emotional, and erratic presentations. These disorders may have a partial genetic base in that they have associations with other DSM Axis I disorders (such as substance abuse, mood, and somatic disorders). The cluster C disorders (avoidant, dependent, and obsessive-compulsive) feature anxious or fearful presentations and are associated with the anxiety disorders. It is estimated that about 9.1 percent of the U.S. population have a personality disorder (Lenzenweger et al., 2007).

All personality disorder diagnoses are recorded on Axis II. The practitioner must be cautious about diagnosing a specific personality disorder, because there is much overlap among the symptoms of the different personality disorders (Skodol, Gunderson, Shea, McGlashan, Morey, et al., 2002). If the social worker plans to focus intervention on the personality disorder, the term *principal diagnosis* should be included. The Cluster A disorders may be specified as premorbid if they were present before the symptoms of the Axis I diagnosis (if the latter will be the primary focus of intervention).

The diagnosing clinician must make judgments about personality functioning in the context of the client's ethnic, cultural, and social background. Some cultures, for example, value interpersonal dependency more than others do. Disproportionately high rates of borderline personality disorder are found in Hispanic relative to Caucasian and African-American populations (Skodol et al., 2002). Hispanic clients have more symptoms reflecting anger, affective instability, and unstable relationships than Caucasians do. Similarly, African-Americans are more likely than Caucasians or Hispanics to be diagnosed with the paranoid and schizotypal personality disorders (Whaley, 2001).

Personality disorder diagnoses should rarely be applied to children and adolescents. Personality patterns are not considered to reach a state of constancy until late adolescence or young adulthood. Further, the diagnosis lacks validity in young people because many symptoms occur in the course of normal adolescence (Chabrol, Montovany, Duconge, Kallmeyer, Mullet, et al., 2004). To diagnose a personality disorder in a client under age 18, the symptoms must have been present for a full year.

Borderline Personality Disorder

With this introduction we now move into a discussion of borderline personality disorder. Persons with this disorder are frequently encountered in clinical settings and are often difficult to engage in an intervention process. Many of the principles of assessment and intervention described here are also relevant to clients with other personality disorders, however.

Borderline personality disorder is characterized by a pattern of instability in interpersonal relationships and self-image and a capacity for frequent and intense negative emotions. While there is disagreement about the core features of the disorder, most observers agree on the characteristics of *highly variable mood* and *impulsive behavior* (Trull, 2001).

Prevalence and Comorbidity

Borderline personality disorder is a significant mental health problem present in many cultures around the world (Freeman, Stone, & Martin, 2005). It occurs in an estimated 1.6 percent of the general U.S. population (Lenzenweger, Lane, Loranger, & Kessler, 2007). Borderline personality disorder is the most common personality disorder found in clinical settings. Borderline personality disorder (BPD) is diagnosed predominantly in women; the estimated gender ratio is 3:1 (Freeman, Stone, & Martin, 2005). Despite the widespread notion that BPD is more commonly experienced by women, however, a recent national study found that actual rates were comparable in women and men (Lenzenweger et al., 2007). Apparently, clinical samples contain more women with borderline personality disorder.

Many disorders are often comorbid with borderline personality disorder. Indeed, a majority (84.5 percent) of cases meet criteria for at least one Axis I disorder in the past year, and the mean number is 3.2 (Lenzenweger et al., 2007). The most commonly seen Axis I disorders include the anxiety disorders (60.5 percent), impulse control disorders (intermittent explosive disorder, attention-deficit hyperactivity disorder [ADHD]) (49 percent), substance use disorders (38.2 percent), and mood disorders (34.3 percent). There is overlap among the symptoms of the personality disorders as well, and borderline personality disorder most often co-occurs with the antisocial and avoidant types (Grilo, Sanislow, & McGlashan, 2002).

Up to 55 percent of inpatients with BPD have a history of suicide attempts, and the actual suicide rate is between 5 and 10 percent (APA, 2000). Up to 80 percent have committed acts of self-mutilation (such as cutting the forearms or face). Studies have shown that nonsuicidal acts of self-mutilation are intended to express anger, punish oneself, generate normal feelings when experiencing depersonalization, or distract oneself from painful feelings (Brown, Comtois, & Linehan, 2002). The risk of suicide appears to be highest when clients are in their 20s. The presence of substance use has major implications for treatment, since clients with borderline personality disorder who abuse substances generally have a poor outcome and are at higher risk for suicide and death or injury from accidents (van den Bosch, Verheul, & van den Brink, 2001).

Assessment

While general assessment guidelines for borderline personality disorder are offered in Figure 14.1, a particular challenge for assessment is to determine whether Axis I symptoms are distinctive enough to justify a diagnosis of the disorder. The social worker

FIGURE 14.1 Assessment of Borderline Personality Disorder.

- Do the client's presenting problems result from patterns of interaction with others?
- Are there recent stressors that may account for the client's symptom presentation? If so, is this an isolated situation or part of a general pattern?
- Is the client under the influence of any substances (alcohol, drugs, or medicine) that may account for the symptoms of anxiety and depression?
- Has the client's personality changed as a result of the presence of a medical condition (in which case the appropriate diagnosis would be a personality change due to a general medical condition)?
- Is there evidence of a history of hypomanic or manic episodes (which may suggest a diagnosis of bipolar disorder)?
- Assess the possibility of a major depressive episode. (Note that features of depression particularly characteristic of BPD are emptiness, self-condemnation, fears of abandonment, sense of hopelessness, self-destructiveness, and repeated suicidal gestures; these would not be diagnosed as a separate major depressive disorder but as indicative of BPD.)
- If the client is an older adolescent/young adult, are the identity concerns related to a developmental phase?
- If there are manipulative behaviors displayed by the client, are they related to a desire for nurturance or to a desire for power, profit, or personal gain?

Source: Yen, Shea, Sanislow, Grilo, et al., 2004.

should remain patient during this phase. When the practitioner combines an Axis I disorder with BPD, intervention should focus on both disorders, since the presence of BPD is a risk influence for recovery from an Axis I disorder (Livesley, 2004).

Depressive disorders are strongly associated with borderline personality disorder. Features of depression that are particularly characteristic of borderline personality disorder are emptiness, self-condemnation, abandonment fears, hopelessness, self-destructiveness, and repeated suicidal gestures (Yen, Shea, Pagano, Sanislow, Grilo, et al., 2003). In this type of presentation, one would diagnose only borderline personality disorder and not a separate major depressive disorder.

Kenda volunteered that she was the fourth of eight children (five girls and three boys) born to a Catholic couple, and the fourth girl. The family was lower middle class. Her father is a struggling furniture salesman. Her parents had a rural background and moved to their present suburban area when Kenda was a few years old. "My dad never felt accepted in the city, because we were country people. He seemed to take his frustrations out on me." Kenda added, "I was always the black sheep. I didn't do anything bad, but that's what my folks always told me. I was always getting yelled at for no reason. They used to get mad, saying I was a dangerous driver. I liked to drive my car fast, but I only did that late at night, and I never had a serious accident. It was fun, and I knew what I was doing. But no one in my family would ride with me. I used to like when people rode with me, because I liked to scare them." Kenda added that she was at best cordial with her family and had little contact with her parents and siblings. She described her parents as "mean." When pressed about this, Kenda shared that, "My parents were together all the time and didn't pay much attention to us. We all had to raise ourselves." Kenda said that she moved out of the house the day after her high school graduation. "I stayed away from home as much as I could all through high school, and I couldn't wait to get away." Kenda stated again that she was frequently singled out as the family scapegoat. Her father in particular always criticized her and told the others that she was worthless. "He's like a lot of people, who don't want to give credit to me when it's due."

During the second interview Kenda was more verbal and the social worker learned more about her background. In high school Kenda showed remarkable athletic ability, starring on her high school's state championship softball team two years in a row. Another impressive accomplishment was her work on the town's volunteer rescue squad. Kenda developed an early interest in nursing and intentionally sought out the EMT position. She hoped to become a registered nurse one day. She admitted to being a bit of a daredevil as well, jumping off high cliffs into reservoirs and sometimes starting fights with other young women she didn't know "just for the excitement of seeing what happens."

Kenda smiled when she talked about her fights but downplayed her accomplishments, saying that "I'm not really good at anything. I don't have any skills. I'm kind of a nobody." Yet, beginning at the age of 18, Kenda had been making emergency squad runs, going to the sites of heart attacks and car accidents and participating in dramatic rescues. Further, she seemed to be very effective in that capacity. "I like to keep busy," she said. "I don't feel so good when I just sit around." Indeed, Kenda and her housemates worked long hours at the Fire Department, attended parties, played sports, and took week-end trips together. When asked if she took pride or pleasure in these activities, she replied, "No. I'm just filling time. If I stop doing things I feel so empty." Kenda did say that she missed a lot of work due to her inability to concentrate on external events and function interpersonally when she felt sad, frightened, or irritable. She usually missed several days of work each week and thus had an unsteady income, which was a concern to her.

Kenda suggested that her parents could provide the social worker with more accurate background information and invited the social worker to meet with them, as long as she didn't have to be present. The social worker had one meeting with her parents and was struck by their defensiveness. Her father said, "Whatever Kenda tells you, don't believe it. I always provided very well for her. We always had food on the table and clothes in the closet. I never cared that Kenda never appreciated anything. She was an ungrateful girl."

Kenda's mother agreed that she was not one to nurture or be soft with her kids. She said, "Children cannot learn too early to stand on their own two feet, and I ran my household accordingly. They had to learn early to take care of themselves." The social worker gained the impression that Kenda's description of an emotionally cold household was accurate.

During the third assessment meeting, Kenda said again that she sometimes felt she deserved to be lonely, because "I'm a bad person," even though she was not able to elaborate on this point. At other times, however, she felt she was "an OK person." Kenda talked about a series of short-term relationships with boys during her last two years of high school, but she insisted that they were superficial. She never let her boyfriends get to know her well and was never physically intimate with them. She said, "They were always smothering me, wanting to be with me all the time, but who wants that? They all seemed nice at first, but then I realized I couldn't count on them for anything, and they eventually wanted sex. That's probably all they ever wanted. So we wound up having lots of arguments and I had to push them away." Still, Kenda said that she always had a new boyfriend within a few weeks of a breakup. She said, somewhat sarcastically, "It was a way for me to pass the time."

After this third visit, the social worker received a letter from Kenda detailing her history of sexual abuse by her father that spanned the ages of 5 through 17. She had never discussed these incidents with anyone. Kenda added that the incest was her own fault, proof that she was a bad person. The social worker asked Kenda why she had finally decided to tell her about the incest. Kenda said she had never trusted anyone and assumed that anyone who knew her secret would reject her. She perceived that the social worker was genuinely interested in her, although she admitted to feeling confused by the social worker's concern. "You're the best therapist I've ever known, and I'm really trusting you with something here. You'd better not let me down."

During the fourth meeting Kenda was again experiencing thoughts of death and fears of losing control. They began the process of writing up a treatment contract and plan, and the social worker arranged for Kenda to be seen by the agency physician for a medication evaluation. "I'll see him," Kenda said, but I've taken meds before and they never do anything for me."

Directions Part I, Multi-Axial Diagnosis: Given the case information and your responses to the questions below, prepare the following: a multi-axial diagnosis, the rationale for the diagnosis and GAF score, and additional information you would have wanted to know in order to make a more accurate diagnosis.

Questions to consider when formulating a diagnosis for Kenda

1. Do Kenda's presenting problems result from patterns of interaction with others?

2. Are there recent stressors that may account for Kenda's symptoms? If so, is this an isolated situation or part of a general pattern?

3. Is Kenda under the influence of any substances or medical conditions that may account for her anxiety and depression?

4. Might Kenda have a mood disorder? Can her self-mutilation behaviors be considered suicidal in nature?

5. Are there any manipulative behaviors displayed by the client? If so, are they related to a desire for nurturance or personal gain?

6. How would you characterize Kenda's sense of identity?

Multi-Axial Diagnosis

Axis I:

Axis II:

Axis III:

Axis IV:

Axis V:

Rationale and Differential Diagnosis

Additional Information Needed

Biopsychosocial Risk and Resilience Influences

Onset

Borderline personality disorder most likely results from a combination of biological and environmental processes. It is approximately five times more common among first-degree biological relatives of those with the disorder than in the general population (APA, 2000). Borderline personality disorder also increases familial risk for substance abuse disorders, antisocial personality disorder, and mood disorders. Still, these risks may be related to environmental conditions as well as personal constitution. One theorist writes that the person seems to have a predisposition to affective instability and a childhood history of neglect, abuse, loss, or lack of validation (Linehan, 1993). Additional risks for people from oppressed and vulnerable populations are listed in Figure 14.2.

BIOLOGICAL INFLUENCES

The biological causes of BPD are speculative (Johnson, 1999). Some of its symptoms (impulsivity, irritability, hypersensitivity, emotional lability, and intensity) are associated with a biological foundation. Researchers have studied the link between BPD and two neurotransmitters: serotonin (which is diminished) and norepinephrine (which is overactive) (Gurvits, Koenigsberg, & Siever, 2000). Serotonin has been linked to both external and self-directed aggression. As noted earlier, a relationship between the personality and affective disorders has long been argued. Persons with BPD are said to have mood swings that resemble bipolar disorder (the interpersonal conflicts are a differentiating factor). Biological contributors to this process may include elevations of the person's catecholamines (neurotransmitters that mediate mood states and aggression) and dysfunctions in the locus coeruleus (used for information processing and memory), the amygdala in the limbic system (that manages fear and anxiety), and the hippocampus (a center of emotional experience) (Skodol, Siever, Livesley, Gunderson, Pfohl, et al., 2002).

FIGURE 14.2 **Borderline Personality Disorder in Vulnerable and Oppressed Populations.**

Youth
- Childhood history of neglect, abuse, loss, or lack of validation places youth at risk for development of BPD.[1]
- Ongoing sexual abuse in childhood is a major predictor of the severity of borderline syndromes.[2]

Females
- BPD is diagnosed more often in women,[3] although in a national study, rates were comparable for men and women living in the community.[4]
- Men with BPD are more likely to present with comorbid substance abuse disorders, whereas women are more likely to present with PTSD and eating disorders.[5]

Racial Minorities
- Hispanic persons have a disproportionately higher rate of BPD when compared with Caucasian and African-American groups.[6]

Low Socioeconomic Status (SES)
- A background of poverty places a person with BPD at risk of lower success rates in the realms of intimacy and work because of additional stresses associated with low SES.[7]
- Out of all the personality disorders, BPD puts people at greatest risk for unemployment, which is associated with low SES.[8]

PSYCHOLOGICAL INFLUENCES

Although there is limited evidence to support their validity, psychodynamic theorists have produced a rich literature on persons with borderline personality disorder (St. Clair, 1999). These clients are said to have failed to negotiate successfully the delicate task of separating from primary caregivers while maintaining an internalized sense of being cared for. During infancy they either were or felt themselves to be abandoned. They feel that when a parent or other close attachment figure is not physically present or immediately available, he or she may be gone forever. The person often experiences intense separation anxiety as a result. For these reasons, the person carries into new relationships the sense that abandonment by significant others is always a real threat.

[1]Yen et al., 2004.
[2]Zanarini, Yong, Frankenburg, Hennen, Reich, et al., 2002.
[3]APA, 2000.
[4]Lenzenweger et al., 2007.
[5]Skodol et al., 2005.
[6]Skodol et al., 2005.
[7]Skodol et al., 2005.
[8]Lenzenweger et al., 2007.

SOCIAL INFLUENCES

Most empirical research shows a positive relationship between childhood trauma and borderline symptoms (Yen et al., 2002). Such trauma includes loss, sexual and physical violence, neglect, abuse, firsthand observation of domestic violence, and parental substance abuse or criminality. In general, clients with borderline personality disorder report significantly more negative life events than do persons with other personality disorders or depression (Skodol et al., 2005). Ongoing sexual abuse in childhood is a major predictor of the severity of borderline syndromes (Zanarini, Yong, Frankenburg, Hennen, Reich, et al., 2002). Dissociative symptoms are positively associated with inconsistent treatment by a caregiver, sexual abuse by a caregiver, firsthand observation of sexual violence as a child, and an adult rape history (Zanarini, Ruser, Frankenburg, Hennen, & Gunderson, 2000).

The role of childhood trauma as a risk mechanism also appears to be related to the person's biological sensitivity to environmental stimuli. This mechanism is thought to act through the neurotransmitters described above during the person's physical development. In studies of predictor variables for the borderline personality disorder diagnosis, *interpersonal sensitivity* emerged as most significant (Blais, Hilsenroth, & Fowler, 1999). Sensitivity to intense experiences of negative emotions may be a stronger predictor of the disorder than childhood sexual abuse. When experiencing intense emotions, persons with this disorder tend to lose their sensitivity to the feelings of others (Bland, Williams, Scharer, & Manning, 2004). This may produce a situation in which the person uses impulsive and self-destructive behavior to manage the stress related to his or her hypersensitive reactions to negative stimuli.

Course and Outcome

Long-term studies of clients with borderline personality disorder indicate that its course is variable (Fonagy & Bateman, 2006). The person's early adulthood is often characterized by instability, episodes of affective and impulse control problems, and high usage of general health and mental health resources. One study of young adults found that borderline personality disorder predicted negative outcomes in the areas of academic achievement and social maladjustment over the subsequent two years, regardless of the presence of any other diagnoses (Bagge, Nickell, Stepp, Durrett, Jackson, et al., 2004).

There is some evidence, however, that the course of borderline personality disorder is more benign than formerly believed, in part because of the availability of effective interventions (Fonagy & Bateman, 2006). Later in life a majority of individuals with the disorder attain greater stability in social and occupational functioning, even in the absence of intervention, in part because their acting-out symptoms tend to decrease (Himelick & Walsh, 2002). It has also been found that the symptoms of this disorder may wax and wane throughout its course. In a longitudinal study of clients with a variety of personality disorders, affective instability and inappropriate anger were the most stable characteristics over a two-year span for persons with borderline personality disorder, while self-injury and efforts to avoid abandonment were the least stable (Skodol et al., 2005).

TABLE 14.1 Risk and Resilience Influences for Course of the Disorder

RISK INFLUENCES	RESILIENCE INFLUENCES
Biological None	None
Psychological Attachment deficits Presence of a comorbid disorder Substance use Major symptoms: higher levels of affective instability, identity disturbance, and impulsivity	Resolution of attachment issues, childhood trauma, and neglect Absence of substance use Major symptoms: self-injury, efforts to avoid abandonment
Social Lack of structure in daily life Failure to establish relationships with others Absence of enduring relationships Poor academic achievement Poor occupational functioning Living in poverty	Structured lifestyle Some stable relationships High academic achievement Stable occupational functioning Absence of poverty conditions

Sources: Fonagy & Bateman, 2006; Livesley, 2004; Skodol et al., 2005; Paris, 2003; Bagge et al., 2004; Zanarini et al., 2002; Gurvits, Koenigsberg, & Siever, 2000.

Longitudinal studies also indicate that about one-third of clients with BPD appear to recover from the disorder within ten years after initial diagnosis, solidifying their identities and replacing self-damaging acts with modulated behavior patterns (Paris, 2003). After ten years of intervention, 50 percent of clients no longer meet the full criteria for the disorder. Studies of hospitalized clients with borderline personality disorder indicate that even though they may gradually attain functional roles 10 to 15 years after admission to psychiatric facilities, only about 50 percent of the women and 25 percent of the men will have attained enduring success in intimacy (as indicated by marriage or long-term partnership) (Paris, 2003). From 50 to 75 percent of clients will have achieved stable, full-time employment by that time. Clients with the disorder from backgrounds of poverty may have substantially lower success rates in the spheres of intimacy and work because of the additional stresses associated with that condition. Clients with comorbid drug use disorders have a higher risk of suicide attempts, as do those with affective instability, identity disturbance, and impulsivity (Skodol et al., 2005).

Directions Part II, Biopsychosocial Risk and Resilience Assessment: Formulate a risk and resilience assessment, both for the onset of the disorder and the course of the disorder, including the strengths that you see for this individual.

TABLE 14.2 Biopsychosocial Risk and Resilience Assessment for the Onset of the Disorder

RISK INFLUENCES	PROTECTIVE INFLUENCES
Biological	
Psychological	
Social	

TABLE 14.3 Biopsychosocial Risk and Resilience Assessment for the Course of the Disorder

RISK INFLUENCES	PROTECTIVE INFLUENCES
Biological	
Psychological	
Social	

What techniques could you use to elicit additional strengths in this client?

Intervention

Clients with borderline personality disorder show a greater lifetime use of most categories of medication, and most types of psychotherapy, than clients with other personality disorders or major depressive disorder (Zanarini, Frankenburg, Hennen, et al., 2004). According to the National Comorbidity Replication Survey, 42.4 percent of those with borderline personality disorder were in treatment during the past year (Lenzenweger et al., 2007). Still, it is challenging for practitioners to engage them in a sustained process of intervention. It is estimated that 40 to 60 percent of these clients drop out of intervention prematurely (Marziali, 2002). Further, there is a dearth of empirically validated methods of intervention, although psychodynamic writers have theorized extensively about clinical intervention (Goldstein, 2000; St. Clair, 1999). Much of this literature is case studies and small samples.

Between 1974 and 1998, 15 clinical studies that included pre- and post-treatment effects were conducted (Perry, Banon, & Ianni, 1999). All of the studies were based on psychodynamic, interpersonal, cognitive-behavioral, and supportive therapies and reported positive outcomes. Four studies focused specifically on BPD, and while all of these had limitations, their pooled results indicate a 25 percent recovery rate per year for clients receiving intervention.

In standard interventions the practitioner establishes and maintains a therapeutic alliance, responds to crises, monitors the client's safety, provides education about the disorder, offers consistent supportive or insight-oriented therapy, and coordinates interventions by other providers (Livesley, 2004). In one research study clients and practitioners alike emphasized the theme of trust as crucial for the establishment and maintenance of a therapeutic relationship (Langley & Klopper, 2005). In his review of outcome studies, Livesley (2004) concluded that comprehensive intervention in BPD requires an array of interventions from different therapeutic models, delivered in a coordinated way. The practitioner must be able to build an effective alliance with the client and then treat both the core interpersonal pathology and the various behavioral manifestations of the disorder. Group interventions are often productive for persons with borderline personality disorder (Marziali, 2002). They can provide opportunities for identification with other members, more opportunities for learning and experimenting with new patterns of behaviors, and opportunities to provide and receive empathic feedback in a supportive environment.

Because of clients' labile moods, changing motivation, and self-harm tendencies, many practitioners establish an explicit "contract" agreement with the client about how the relationship will proceed (Yeomans, Gutfreund, Selzer, & Clarkin, 1993). The contract should address the timing and frequency of sessions; plans for crisis management; the practitioner's after-hours availability (if any); and expectations about scheduling, attendance, and payment. Because of the client's potential for impulsive behavior, practitioners must be comfortable with setting limits on self-destructive behaviors.

Psychosocial Interventions

While validating clients' suffering, practitioners must also help them to take appropriate responsibility for their actions. Effective intervention helps clients realize that although they are not responsible for their past traumas, they are responsible for controlling self-destructive patterns in the present and future (Ryle, 2004). Interpretations of here and now behavior as it links to events in the past are useful for helping clients learn about their repetitive and maladaptive behavior patterns. As previously noted, splitting is a major defense mechanism of clients with borderline personality disorder. Intervention must be geared toward helping the client begin to experience the shades of gray between these extremes and integrate the positive and negative aspects of the self and others.

Some clients with borderline personality disorder may need to be seen in protective environments, usually for short periods of time until their mood symptoms stabilize. Indications for partial or brief hospitalization include dangerous, impulsive behavior that cannot be managed in an outpatient setting; nonadherence to outpatient intervention and a deteriorating clinical picture; complex comorbidity that requires intensive assessment of response to intervention; symptoms that significantly interfere with functioning and are unresponsive to outpatient intervention; and transient psychotic episodes associated with a loss of impulse control or impaired judgment (Van Kesssel, Lambie, & Stewart, 2002).

PSYCHODYNAMIC INTERVENTION

Psychodynamic interventions involve careful attention to the therapist-client relationship with thoughtfully timed interpretations of the client's transference. They draw from the theoretical perspectives of ego psychology, object relations, and self-psychology. Psychodynamic intervention is usually conceptualized as operating on an exploratory-supportive continuum of interventions (Berzoff, 1996). On the supportive end of the continuum, goals involve the strengthening of defenses and self-esteem, validation of feelings, internalization of the therapeutic relationship, and development of a greater capacity to cope with disturbing feelings. At the exploratory end of the continuum the goals are to make unconscious patterns more consciously available, increase affect tolerance, build a capacity to delay impulsive action, provide insight into relationship problems, and develop reflective functioning toward a greater appreciation of internal motivation in the self and others (Goldstein, 1995). A meta-analysis of psychological therapies for borderline personality disorder showed that psychodynamic interventions lower levels of anxiety and depression and reduce use of medications (Binks, Fenton, McCarthy, Lee, & Adams, et al., 2006a).

DIALECTICAL BEHAVIOR THERAPY

This intervention approach assumes that the client's core difficulty is one of affective instability (Robins, 2002). Dialectical behavior therapy (DBT) is based on cognitive-behavioral and learning theories and is an intensive, one-year outpatient intervention that combines weekly individual sessions with skills-training groups. The purposes of the groups are to teach adaptive coping skills in the areas of emotional regulation, distress tolerance, interpersonal effectiveness, and identity confusion, and to correct maladaptive cognitions. The individual interventions, provided by the same practitioner, address maladaptive behaviors while strengthening and generalizing coping skills. Some client-practitioner phone contact is permitted between sessions for support and crisis intervention. An important component of DBT is the consultation team, which can help the practitioner maintain objectivity during the often intensive intervention process.

DBT can be considered a well-established intervention for a client with borderline personality disorder as evidenced by seven randomized clinical trials across four different research teams (Lynch, Chapman, & Rosenthal, 2006). Another summary of studies that compared DBT with other treatments indicated that DBT is more effective than less structured interventions in reducing client suicidality, although overall outcome differences were modest (Binks, Fenton, McCarthy, Lee, Adams, et al., 2006a). A 12-week psychoeducational family intervention program based on the DBT model has been developed for parents and spouses, family member burden and grief, as well as increased coping skills for family members (Fruzzetti, Buteau, Neiditch, Panny, Bruce, et al., 2005).

MEDICATIONS

Many clients with borderline personality disorder receive medications to help manage their symptoms of depression, suicidal ideation, anger, and impulsive behavior. In fact, because of their problematic behaviors and frequency of comorbid symptoms, clients with borderline personality disorder are prescribed more psychotropic medications than are other psychiatric outpatients (Sansone, Rytwinski, & Gaither, 2003). Medications generally target cognitive symptoms, mood lability, and impulsivity. Prescribing effective medications is difficult, however, because of the disorder's symptom heterogeneity, diagnostic unreliability, presence of comorbid disorders, and potential for self-destructiveness.

Only 40 to 50 studies have been done on the drug treatment of borderline personality disorder, and drug effects are modest (Soloff, 2005). Looking at double-blind, placebo-controlled studies of antidepressant, anti-anxiety, antipsychotic, anticonvulsant, and lithium medications, this researcher found either modest or no relief of symptoms from medications from each class. Thus, medication should be used only as an adjunct to psychotherapy, as there is little evidence that it yields significant positive symptom outcomes for clients.

Several other recent meta-analyses of comparison group studies support the above points. One such study found that selective serotonin reuptake inhibitors (SSRIs) (particularly fluoxetine) appear to be helpful in reducing anger and hostility, but that haloperidol may be a better choice for controlling hostility and psychotic symptoms (Binks, Fenton, McCarthy, Lee, Adams, et al., 2006b). Another meta-analysis of 22 randomized, placebo-controlled clinical trials concluded that antidepressant and mood-stabilizing drugs were mildly effective against affective instability and anger but did not produce significant benefits in relation to impulsivity, aggression, unstable relationships, suicidal ideation, and global functioning (Nose, Cipriani, Biancosino, Grassi, & Barbui, 2006). Antipsychotic drugs as a class had a positive effect in terms of impulsivity, aggression, interpersonal relationships, and global functioning.

Directions Part III, Goal Setting and Treatment Planning: Given your risk and resilience assessment of the individual, your knowledge of the disorder, and evidence-based practice guidelines, formulate goals and a possible treatment plan for this individual.

Critical Perspective

Borderline personality disorder, like all of the personality disorders, is a highly problematic diagnostic category. First, it is based on a concept (personality) that is itself difficult to capture. Second, a personality disorder is supposed to represent an enduring pattern of experience and behavior. However, the DSM does not specify how long the pattern needs to persist. Without stating a time frame, clinicians may make a diagnosis without a history of interactions with the client. Specifically, the borderline personality disorder diagnosis lacks strong validity and reliability in research studies (Skodol, Gunderson, Shea, McGlashan, Morey, et al., 2005). Different clients with this diagnosis may have quite different symptom clusters and as a result present very differently to practitioners. Indeed, considering the different symptoms, people can meet the criteria in 126 different ways (Truti & Burrett, 2004). Further, because one's *personality* is synonymous with the *person*, the diagnosis seems to present practitioners with an ethical dilemma in reinforcing a deficits perspective on human functioning.

Third, some researchers and theorists believe that personality disorders would be more legitimately conceptualized as *dimensional* rather than categorical (Skodol et al., 2005). That is, clients should be assessed with regard to the functionality of each one of a stable set of common personality traits, rather than as having a disorder relating to all of them. In other words, personality disorders could be redefined as sets of generally stable personality traits with intermittent symptomatic behaviors tied to some of these traits. Such a conceptual shift would also create a diagnostic practice that was less stigmatizing to clients.

Finally, and related to the previous criticism, the division in the DSM between Axis I disorders and Axis II personality disorders seems somewhat arbitrary. Originally, this division was based on psychodynamic notions, although now the DSM promotes itself as an atheoretical manual. More recently, the National Comorbidity Replication Survey results showed that impairment displayed by people with personality disorders was due largely to a high number of Axis I disorders in such persons rather than the effect of the personality disorder itself (Lenzenweger et al., 2007). This evidence of frequent Axis I comorbidity further raises questions about the separation of personality disorders from Axis I disorders in the DSM nomenclature.

In spite of these concerns, clients with symptoms of borderline personality disorder have very real, ongoing problems, and practitioners should remain committed to working with them so that they can achieve their goals of improved relationships and social integration.

Directions Part IV, Critical Perspective: Formulate a critique of the diagnosis as it relates to this case example. Questions to consider include: Does this diagnosis represent a valid mental disorder from the social work perspective? Is this diagnosis significantly different from other possible diagnoses? Your critique should be based on the values of the social work profession (which are incongruent in some ways with the medical model) and the validity of the specific diagnostic criteria applied to this case.

CASE 2

Marcy is a 36-year-old Caucasian woman who came to the women's counseling center several weeks ago reporting feelings of anger and "wanting an outlet to vent" about several of her relationships. She has never seen a psychiatrist or counselor before coming to the counseling center.

Marcy's childhood years were riddled with stresses. Her mother, Gloria, was "beautiful," "high-spirited," "highly dramatic," and an alcoholic. Her father, Michael, was (and remains, accordingly to Marcy) emotionally imma- ture and ineffectual in his career, parenting, and many of his relationships. He was emotionally bereft over the marriage's dissolution, which came about because of Gloria's drinking. The couple divorced when Marcy was two years old.

Marcy was an only child, and when her parents divorced she remained in her mother's custody. Gloria's addiction caused a rapid deterioration in her physical and emotional state, to the extent that when Michael's mother (Marcy's paternal grandmother) came to visit several years later, after not having seen her granddaughter in several months, she found Marcy emaci- ated with sores over much of her body. Marcy's paternal grandparents took temporary custody of her but made it clear to Gloria that they wanted her "to get herself together" so that Marcy could eventually return to her mother. Her grandparents described Marcy as a "difficult child," in that she cried easily and was hard to soothe. Gloria's former in-laws ended up paying for two lengthy stays in a drug and alcohol rehabilitation center for Gloria; however, she was unable to stop drinking.

Within several years of Marcy's arrival in their lives, her grandparents sought permanent legal custody through the judicial system to facilitate certain decisions for Marcy, such as schooling and medical care. But they still hoped Gloria would "dry out" and "get herself together" so that she and Marcy could be together again. These hopes were dashed when Gloria died in a Las Vegas hotel room, "unintentionally drinking herself to death," when Marcy was ten.

It is clear that from the time Marcy's grandparents took custody of her, they were her primary caregivers. She refers to them as Mom and Dad and refers to her biological father (Michael) as "the big kid." Michael, who also lived with his parents through much of the rest of Marcy's childhood, was always in the background of her life. He took no visible parenting role, for which Marcy continues to hold him in contempt.

Three years ago Marcy married a man named Zach, six years her junior. Marcy has no female friends and professes to dislike most women strongly. She rarely drinks alcohol and no longer uses illicit substances, as she fears she may have inherited a propensity toward addiction from her mother. She admitted to drinking "a great deal," and doing her "fair share of drugs" in college, but she now avoids drugs and (mostly) alcohol. She admits to impulsivity in "binge shopping," but the behavior does not appear to cause marital strife, presumably because her grandmother continues to allow Marcy to use her credit cards at several fine department stores.

Marcy admits to a lengthy history of instability in her interpersonal relationships, dating back to when she was in high school, until she married. Whenever she became convinced that a boyfriend was going to leave her, she would "beg and humiliate herself." If that didn't work, she said, she would "dump him before he could do it to me." Her romantic relationships prior to her marriage lasted for six months at the most.

At some point in college, she reported "getting really skinny. It was great! I would run a few miles a day, eat next to nothing, and drink my dinner at bars every night." She was not diagnosed or treated for an eating disorder, and the behavior seemed to resolve itself after graduation.

Marcy acknowledges that she goes through periods of feeling profoundly depressed, empty, and abandoned, no matter how her husband Zach tries to console her. She fears that "something," by which she means death, will "happen to my husband." In the session she emphasized loudly, "I would kill myself if anything happened to my Zach. He's my world. He fills me up. Every day, I live for the moment he gets home from work. I get so lonely and depressed whenever I am apart from him." She then quickly asserted, "He knows better than to have an affair. I would throw him out, scratch his eyes out, and literally cut the crotches of every pair of pants he owns. He knows better than to fuck with me. I'd make him wish he'd never been born!"

Marcy claims she and her husband are very happy and do everything together. They have no outside friends but feel that their family (of two dogs and a cat) is their world. When Marcy mentioned that she had thrown a party for her husband recently on his birthday, the social worker asked who was invited. Marcy retorted that it was only she and Zach and their animals. "Why the hell would I want to invite anyone else? Zach is my world."

Early in Marcy's counseling, she confided that until very recently, she was quite close to her husband's sister, Jessica, but that she had flown into a rage when Jessica apparently set personal boundaries related to Marcy's unsolicited and disparaging advice about Jessica's new boyfriend, whom Marcy had never met. Marcy felt disrespected, that Jessica was "treating me like a neighbor, not like a sister. I hate her. I hate all of my husband's family. Zach and I decided it's just us against the world, and I am fine with that. We don't need anyone else." Since then the two women have "made up," and Marcy has changed her perception of Jessica to one of adoration and admiration. "I can't live without my sister." She also has fluctuated between adoration and devaluation of her mother-in-law during her short tenure at the counseling center.

Marcy says that she made clear to her husband's family when she and Zach became engaged that once her grandparents were gone, she was completely alone and she expected them to be her family. She forbade them to refer to her as an "in-law," stated that she was their daughter or sister, and declared that she wanted a family with whom she could be "naked and vulnerable."

Marcy readily acknowledges that her feelings about people are very "all or nothing," that she "is pretty honest," that she "either loves you or hates you," a quality she highly values in herself.

Marcy has been fired from two jobs in the past two years. Marcy's version of events is, "They're all a bunch of assholes anyway, who set me up to fail from the beginning." She is not receptive to seeing any other possible interpretation and denies the possibility that she may have had any culpability in the outcomes.

Three months ago Marcy secured a software training position that allows her to work from home, which minimizes her interpersonal actions with supervisors and coworkers. This arrangement has apparently worked out quite well for her. Some strife and friction occurred recently, however, in her relationships with her employers and coworkers, with whom she deals primarily via e-mail, telephone, and biweekly meetings. Concurrently, Marcy was under significantly increased stress with a heavy travel and training schedule.

Marcy exhibits remarkably little insight into her behavior, and her husband appears to align with Marcy's interpretations in all instances, whether regarding her troubled career path or her relationships with coworkers, former friends, or even his sister. Marcy acknowledges that early in their relationship, she demanded that of him (as she did of her grandmother): "You are either with me or you are against me. I mean, if I can't count on him to side with me no matter what, who can I count on?"

Please go to the Appendix for directions to this case. The following questions will help to guide your thinking about a possible multi-axial diagnosis.

Questions to consider when formulating a diagnosis for Marcy

1. From information gathered in the social history, is the client's presenting problem resulting from a pattern of interaction with others?

2. Are there any recent stressors that may account for the client's symptoms presentation? Is an adjustment disorder warranted?

3. Is the client under the influence of any substances that may account for the symptoms?

4. Are any changes in personality or mood related to the presence of a medical condition?

5. Is there evidence of current or past history of manic episodes?

6. Is there evidence of a major depressive episode?

7. If there are manipulative behaviors, are they related to a desire for nurturance rather than a desire for power, profit, or personal gain?

8. Does the client seem at risk for suicide?

CASE 3

Erica is a 23-year-old single Jewish Caucasian woman who says she's "devastated" over her recent breakup with her boyfriend and her sudden relocation to Virginia from Florida two months ago. She is currently staying with her sister and her sister's fiancé in a suburb of Washington, D.C., while she assesses her future. Their relationship is contentious; Erica feels "controlled by her sister," who she says "nags" her to "clean" around the house and "judges" her when she spends money going clubbing with her new friends instead of on groceries for the household. Erica admits that her sister feels she abuses her hospitality.

Erica graduated from college a year ago with a degree in criminal justice, which is a field she claims to feel "passionate" about. After graduation, Erica spent June in Europe with her father. Upon returning to the United States she began an intimate relationship with a man who had recently been released from prison and needed a place to stay. She allowed him to move into her apartment and paid for his room and board over the summer, using her father's credit card to pay for their expenses. In early September, upon realizing that the man was cheating on her, she abruptly moved out and came to Virginia because she wanted "to show him that I didn't care" and because "I wanted to escape." At the same time, her father cut off her access to his credit card. Currently, her mother is helping her with basic expenses but is threatening to stop supporting her as well. Her sister has given her a deadline of two months to move out on her own.

Erica details a history of unstable relationships and making "unhealthy" choices in her relationships, with men in particular. She had a boyfriend throughout high school, by whom she became pregnant twice (she aborted in each case) and comments that he was similar in character to her most recent boyfriend. She remained emotionally involved in that relationship throughout college. She is puzzled by the men she dates, stating, "I don't know why I always like the guys that I know my father won't approve of." Erica remained sexually active in college, "You know, getting drunk and sleeping with guys I didn't even know," but did not have a monogamous relationship with anyone. She has been in "almost daily" phone contact with a young African-American man who lives in New Jersey whom she met two years ago over spring break. Despite admitting that this man "has some problems"—he still lives at home, is in debt, is a heavy drinker, dropped out of college, and never comes to see her (she always drives to see him)—she has strong feelings for him and is considering moving to New Jersey to be near him.

She now holds a part-time job waiting tables at an area bar, for which she receives no health insurance. After one week at her new job, she began dating one of the waiters, a 27-year-old African-American male who has a four-year-old daughter. Erica states that she wants to "take it slow," yet she is already intensely emotional about the course of the relationship and had sex with him within their first week of dating. She says "she just knows" they are supposed to be together. She worries about what her family will think of these relationships, because they want her to marry a white Jewish man.

Erica grew up in Miami, Florida, the younger of two sisters. Her parents divorced when she was six years old and shared custody of her. She denies any history of sexual or physical abuse. Her father fought her mother over child support for many years, and money is a controlling force in Erica's relationship with her father. Erica has "many issues" with her father, and her feelings about him tend to shift. When he is financing her lifestyle, he is a "good guy." When she does something he does not approve of, he cuts off contact with her and she views him as "Castro." She repeatedly asked the social worker if her father is to blame for her problems.

Erica chose to live with her father and his new wife and stepchildren through most of her high school years, because his rules and supervision were much more lax than those of her mother. She used marijuana heavily throughout high school and began using other drugs (alcohol, Ecstasy, cocaine, acid) extensively in college. In her junior year in college Erica started experiencing panic attacks and was unable to attend classes. She was given paroxetine, which she took for six months, and her symptoms alleviated. She said her doctor told her the panic attacks could have been caused by her recreational drug use. She denies current drug use at this time and continues to drink socially. She is no longer taking any psychoactive medications and stated a strong aversion to taking any at this time. She declined to see the staff psychiatrist for a consultation.

Erica describes a close and supportive relationship with her mother. She says she has a similar personality to her mother and that they are both "passive," although she wasn't able to provide any details about what this meant. She believes her father resents her because she is so much like her mother. Erica reports that her mother suffered from major depression for over two years after breaking up with a long-term boyfriend and was finally helped through therapy. Her mother is currently remarried and has stepchildren much younger than Erica.

Erica's mother sent her to therapy numerous times when she was growing up, blaming Erica's problems on the divorce. Erica has little recollection of the therapy and usually stopped attending after only a few visits. She reports several traumatic events in her life thus far: having a driver on her street pull out a gun at her and her mother while at a stop sign when she was in the fifth grade; allowing gang members to come to a party held at her mother's house (while her mother was away), which resulted in the house being robbed; and undergoing two abortions while in high school.

Erica says she doesn't think about these past events in more than fleeting ways, and she doesn't have bad dreams about them. She recounted the events in detail and did not, in session, seem to be avoiding memories of them. Erica states that while she has thought about "what it would be like if I was no longer here," she has never had suicidal ideation with a plan or intent to carry it out.

Erica is an intelligent young woman with an engaging and outgoing personality and a good sense of humor. When asked how these traits were "passive," as she had described herself earlier, Erica wasn't able to reconcile these aspects of herself. Erica admits to having very low self-esteem and no sense of "who I am" beyond what others identify for her. Her values and goals change from day to day depending on whom she is talking to. She describes herself as "too generous and kind," but has strong expectations about what she must get in return for her nurturance of others.

She states that she has a group of close friends in Florida with whom she maintains contact, but she is reluctant to move back to Florida because of their negative influence on her life (excessive partying). Still, she is bored in Virginia and "just wants to go out and have some fun." She says she goes clubbing with her coworkers most nights after work and likes the restaurant trade for that reason; there is typically an instant social life attached to it. She says she feels bored and empty when she stays home at night and then usually spends her time talking on the phone to the young man in New Jersey or her friends in Florida. She says she feels restless, tense, and "empty" when there is no one in the house and she is alone. Because she doesn't like feeling this way, she says that she avoids the feelings by being with other people as much as possible and talks on the phone almost constantly when she is by herself. She states that one of the reasons she moved to Virginia is that she didn't want to live by herself in the apartment after she broke up with her boyfriend.

Erica believes that money would answer all of her problems and yearns for life in college when she could do whatever she wanted and her father paid her expenses. She has little insight into her pattern of behaviors in relationships and seeks therapy hoping that the social worker can advise her "what to do." Erica identifies "figuring out what I want to do with my life" as her major goal and is also interested in having a "healthy relationship." Erica has committed to only eight therapy sessions because of her financial situation, and since beginning therapy two months ago she has either missed or rescheduled half her appointments, allegedly due to work conflicts.

Erica completed a Beck's Assessment for depression and scored a 19 out of 60, putting her in the low depression range. She denied insomnia, decreased or increased appetite, lack of energy, an inability to concentrate, or recurrent thoughts of death. When asked about episodes of major depression in the past, she said she has sometimes "felt depressed" but can "snap out of it" if she talks to a boyfriend or meets someone new.

Please go to the Appendix for directions to this case. The following questions will help to guide your thinking about a possible multi-axial diagnosis.

Questions to consider when formulating a diagnosis for Erica

1. From information gathered in the social history, is Erica's presenting problem the result of a pattern of interaction with others?

2. Are there any recent stressors that may account for Erica's symptoms presentation? Is an adjustment disorder warranted?

3. Is Erica using any substances that may account for the symptoms?

4. Is there evidence of current or past history of manic episodes?

5. Is there evidence of a major depressive episode?

6. If there is manipulative behavior, is it related to a desire for nurturance rather than a desire for power, profit, or personal gain?

7. Are Erica's identity concerns related to a developmental phase?

8. Does Erica seem at risk for suicide?

Rationale and Differential Diagnosis

Additional Information Needed

Directions Part II, Biopsychosocial Risk and Resilience Assessment: Formulate a risk and resilience assessment, both for the onset of the d isorder and the course of the disorder.

TABLE 1 Biopsychosocial Risk and Resilience Assessment for the Onset of the Disorder

RISK INFLUENCES	PROTECTIVE INFLUENCES
Biological	
Psychological	
Social	

TABLE 2 Biopsychosocial Risk and Resilience Assessment for the Course of the Disorder

RISK INFLUENCES	PROTECTIVE INFLUENCES
Biological	
Psychological	
Social	

What techniques could you use to elicit additional strengths in this client?

Directions Part III, Goal Setting and Treatment Planning: Given your risk and resilience assessments of the individual, your knowledge of the disorder, and evidence-based practice guidelines, formulate goals and a possible treatment plan for this individual.

Directions Part IV, Critical Perspective: Formulate a critique of the diagnosis as it relates to this case example. Questions to consider include: Does this diagnosis represent a valid mental disorder from the social work perspective? Is this diagnosis significantly different from other possible diagnoses? Your critique should be based on the values of the social work profession (which are incongruent in some way with the medical model) and the validity of the specific diagnostic criteria applied to this case.

Arean, P., & Cook, B. (2002). Psychotherapy and combined psychotherapy/pharmacotherapy for late life depression. *Biological Psychiatry, 52*, 293–303.

Armstrong, T., & Costello, J. (2002). Community studies on adolescent substance use, abuse, or dependence and psychiatric comorbidity. *Journal of Consulting & Clinical Psychology, 70*, 1224–1239.

Arnold, L. (1996). Sex differences in ADHD. *Journal of Abnormal Child Psychology, 24*, 555–569.

Asarnow, J. R., Jaycox, L. H., & Tompson, M. C. (2001). Depression in youth: Psychosocial interventions. *Journal of Clinical Child Psychology, 30*(1) 33–47.

Ascher-Svanum, H., Faries, D., Zhu, B., Ernst, F., Swartz, M., & Swanson, J. (2006). Medication adherence and long-term functional outcomes in the treatment of schizophrenia in usual care. *Journal of Clinical Psychiatry, 67*(3), 453–460.

Ashley, O., Marsden, M. E., & Brady, T. (2003). Effectiveness of substance abuse treatment programming for women: A review. *American Journal of Drug and Alcohol Abuse, 29*, 19–54.

Atchley, R. (2000). *Social forces and aging: An introduction to social gerontology.* Belmont, CA: Wadsworth.

Bacaltchuk, J., & Hay, P. (2003). Antidepressants versus placebo for people with bulimia nervosa (Cochrane Review). In *The Cochrane Library*, Issue 4. Chichester, UK: John Wiley.

Bacaltchuk, J., Hay, P., & Trefiglio, R. (2001). *Antidepressants versus psychological treatments and their combination for bulimia nervosa* (Cochrane Review). In: *The Cochrane Library*, Issue 4. Chichester, UK: John Wiley & Sons, Ltd.

Bagge, C., Nickell, A., Stepp, S., Durrett, C., Jackson, K., & Trull, T. J. (2004). Borderline personality disorder features predict negative outcomes 2 years later. *Journal of Abnormal Psychology, 113*(2), 279–288.

Bailey, R. K., & Owens, D. L. (2005). Overcoming challenges in the diagnosis and treatment of attention-deficit/hyperactivity disorder in African Americans. *Supplement to the Journal of the National Medical Association, 97*, 5–16.

Bains, J., Birks, J. S., & Dening, T. T. (2005). Antidepressants for treating depression in dementia (Review). *Cochrane Database of Systematic Reviews, 2002*, 4, Art. No. CD003944.

Baker, J. A. (1999). Teacher-student interaction in urban at-risk classrooms: Differential behavior, relationship quality, and student satisfaction with school. *Elementary School Journal, 100*(1), 57–70.

Bakker, A., van Balkom, A., & Spinhoven, P. (2002). SSRIs vs. TCAs in the treatment of panic disorder: A meta-analysis. *Acta Psychiatrica Scandinavica, 106*(3), 163–167.

Baldessarini, R. J., Tondo, L., Davis, P., Pompili, M., Goodwin, F. K., & Henne, J. (2006). Decreased risk of suicides and attempts during long-term lithium treatment: A meta-analytic review. *Bipolar Disorders, 2006, 8*[5, pt 2], 625–639.

Ballard, C., & Howard, R. (2006). Neuroleptic drugs in dementia: Benefits and harm. *Nature Reviews Neuroscience, 7*(6), 492–500.

Ballard, C., & Waite, J. (2006). The effectiveness of atypical antipsychotics for the treatment of aggression and psychosis in Alzheimer's disease. *Cochrane Database of Systematic Reviews, 1*, Art. No. CD003476.

Bandelow, B., Spath, C., Tichauer, A., Broocks, A., Hajak, G., & Ruther, E. (2002). Early traumatic life events, parental attitudes, family history, and birth risk factors in patients with panic disorder. *Comprehensive Psychiatry, 43*, 269–278.

Barber, J. G., & Gilbertson, R. (1996). An experimental study of brief unilateral intervention for the partners of heavy drinkers. *Research on Social Work Practice, 6*, 325–336.

Barkley, R. A. (2000). *Taking charge of ADHD (revised edition).* New York: Guilford Press.

Barkley, R. A. (2004). Adolescents with attention-deficit/hyperactivity disorder: An overview of empirically based treatments. *Journal of Psychiatric Practice, 10*, 39–56.

Barkley, R. A. (2006). Attention-Deficit/Hyperactivity Disorder. In D. A. Wolfe & E. J. Mash (Eds.), *Behavioral and emotional disorders in adolescents: Nature, assessment, and treatment* (pp. 91–152). New York: Guilford Press.

Barkley, R. A., & Murphy, K. R. (2006). *Attention-deficit hyperactivity disorder: A clinical workbook (3rd ed.).* New York: Guilford Press.

Barkley, R. A., Fischer, M., & Smallish, L. (2006). Young adult outcome of hyperactive children: Adaptive functioning in major life activities. *Journal of the American Academy of Child and Adolescent Psychiatry, 45*(2), 192–202.

Barnes, C., & Mitchell, P. (2005). Considerations in the management of bipolar disorder in women. *Australian and New Zealand Journal of Psychiatry, 39*(8), 662–673.

Barnett S. M., Sirey, J. A., Bruce, M., Hamilton, M., Raue, P., Friedman, S. J., Rickey, C., Kakuma, T., Carroll M. K., Kiosses, D., & Alexopoulos, G. (2002). Predictors of early recovery from major depression among persons admitted to community-based clinics. *Archives of General Psychiatry, 59*, 729–735.

Baron-Cohen, S., Ring, H. A., & Bullmore, E. T. (2000). The amygdala theory of autism. *Neuroscience & Biobehavioral Reviews, 24*(3), 355–364.

Basco, M. R., & Rush, A. J. (2005). *Cognitive-behavioural therapy for bipolar disorder (2nd ed.).* New York: Guilford Press.

Beach, S., & Jones, D. (2002). Marital and family therapy for depression in adults. In I. Gotlib & C. Hammen (Eds.), *Handbook of depression* (pp. 422–440). New York: Guilford Press.

Beattie, E. R. A., Algase, D. L., & Song, J. (2004). Keeping wandering nursing home residents at the table: Improving food intake using a behavioral communication intervention. *Aging and Mental Health, 8*(2), 109–116.

Beatty, R., Geckle, M., Huggins, J., Kapner, C., Lewis, K., & Sandstrom, D. (1999). Gay men, lesbians, and bisexuals. In B. McCrady & E. Epstein (Eds.), *Addictions: A comprehensive guidebook* (pp. 542–551). New York: Oxford University Press.

Beck, A., Rush, A., Shaw, B., & Emery, G. (1979). *Cognitive therapy of depression.* New York: Guilford Press.

Behan, J., & Carr, A. (2000). Oppositional defiant disorder. In A. Carr (Ed.), *What works with children and adolescents? A critical review of psychological interventions with children, adolescents and their families* (pp. 102–130). Florence, KY, US: Taylor & Frances/Routledge.

Bell, L. (2003). What can we learn from consumer studies and qualitative research in the treatment of eating disorders? *Eating and Weight Disorders, 8*, 181–187.

Bennett, D., & Gibbons, T. (2000). Efficacy of child cognitive-behavioral interventions for antisocial behavior: A meta-analysis. *Child and Family Behavior Therapy, 22*, 1–15.

Bentley, K., & Walsh, J. (2006). *The social worker and psychotropic medication (3rd ed.).* Pacific Grove, CA: Brooks/Cole.

Berger, P. L., & Luckmann, T. (1966). *The social construction of reality.* New York: Doubleday.

Berkman, N. D., Lohr, K. N., & Bulik, C. M. (2007). Outcomes of eating disorders: A systematic review of the literature. *International Journal of Eating Disorders, 40*(4), 293–309.

Bernard, L., Young, A. H., Pearson, J., Geddes, J., & O'Brien, G. (2002). Systematic review of the use of atypical antipsychotics in autism. *Journal of Psychopharmacology, 16*(1), 93–101.

Bernstein, G., & Shaw, K. (1997). Practice parameters for the assessment and treatment of children and adolescents with anxiety disorders. *Journal of the American Academy of Child and Adolescent Psychiatry, 36*(10S) Supplement, 69S–S.

Bertolino, B., & O'Hanlon, B. (2002). *Collaborative, competency-based counseling and therapy.* Boston: Allyn & Bacon.

Berument, S., Rutter, M., Lord, C., Pickles, A., & Bailey, A. (1999). Autism Screening Questionnaire: Diagnostic validity. *British Journal of Psychiatry, 175,* 444–451.

Berzoff, J. (Ed.) (1996). *Inside out and outside in: Psychodynamic clinical theory and practice in contemporary multicultural contexts.* Northvale, NJ: Jason Aronson.

Bharani, N., & Snowden, M. (2005). Evidence-based interventions for nursing home residents with dementia-related behavioral symptoms. *Psychiatric Clinics of North America, 28,* 985–1005.

Bhutta, A., Cleves, M., Casey, P., Cradock, M., & Anand, K. (2002). Cognitive and behavioral outcomes of school-aged children who were born preterm: A meta-analysis. *Journal of the American Medical Association, 288,* 728–737.

Biederman, J., Farone, S., Milberger, S., Jetton, J., Chen, L., Mick, E., Greene, R., & Russell, R. (1996). Is childhood oppositional defiant disorder a precursor to adolescent conduct disorder? Findings from a four year follow-up study of children with ADHD. *Journal of the American Academy of Child and Adolescent Psychiatry, 35,* 1193–1204.

Billstedt, E., Gillberg, C., & Gillberg, C. (2005). Autism after adolescence: Population-based 13- to 22-year follow-up study of 120 individuals with autism diagnosed in childhood. *Journal of Autism and Developmental Disorders, 35*(3), 351–360.

Binks, C., Fenton, M., McCarthy, L., Lee, T., Adams, C., & Duggan, C. (2006a). Psychological therapies for people with borderline personality disorder. *The Cochrane Database System Review, 1,* Art No. CD005652.

Binks, C., Fenton, M., McCarthy, L., Lee, T., Adams, C., & Duggan, C. (2006b). Pharmacological interventions for people with borderline personality disorder. *Cochrane Database of Systematic Reviews,* Art. No. CD005653.

Bird, M., & Parslow, R. (2002). Potential for community programs to prevent depression in older people. *The Medical Journal of Australia, 7,* 107–110.

Birks, J., Grimley-Evans, J., Iakovidou, V., & Tsolaki, M. (2007). Rivastigmine for Alzheimer's disease. *The Cochrane Database of Systematic Reviews.* Issue 1, DOI: 10.1002/14651858. CD001191.

Birmaher, B., Axelson, D., Strober, M., Gill, M. K., Valeri, S., Chiapetta, L., Ryan, N., Leonard, H., Hunt, J., Iyengar, S., & Keller, M. (2006). Clinical course of children and adolescents with bipolar spectrum disorders. *Archives of General Psychiatry, 63*(2), 175–183.

Birmaher, B., Ryan, N., Williamson, D., Brent, D., Kaufman, J., & Dahl, R. (1996). Childhood and adolescent depression: A review of the past 10 years, Part I. *Journal of the American Academy of Child and Adolescent Psychiatry, 35,* 1427–1439.

Bishop, D. V. M. (1998). Development of the Children's Communication Checklist (CCC): A method for assessing qualitative aspects of communicative impairment in children. *Journal of Child Psychology and Psychiatry, 39,* 879–891.

Bisson, J., & Andrew, M. (2005). Psychological treatment of post-traumatic stress disorder (PTSD). *Cochrane Database of Systematic Reviews, 3,* 1–2.

Blais, M. A., Hilsenroth, M. J., & Fowler, J. C. (1999). Diagnostic efficiency and hierarchical functioning of the DSM-IV borderline personality disorder criteria. *Journal of Nervous and Mental Diseases, 187*(3), 167–173.

Bland, A. R., Williams, C. A., Scharer, K., & Manning, S. (2004). Emotion processing in borderline personality disorder. *Issues in Mental Health Nursing, 25,* 655–672.

Blehar, M. C. (2006). Women's mental health research: The emergence of a biomedical field. *Annual Review of Clinical Psychology, 2,* 135–160.

Bloom, B., & Dey, A. N. (2006). Summary health statistics for U.S. children: National Health Interview Survey, 2004, (227):1–85.

Bockting, C. L., Spinhoven, P., & Koeter, M. W. (2006). Prediction of recurrence in recurrent depression and the influence of consecutive episodes on vulnerablity for depression: A 2-year prospective study. *Depression Evaluation Longitudinal Therapy Assessment (DELTA) Study Group; Journal of Clinical Psychiatry, 67*(5), 747–755.

Bogenschneider, K. (1996). An ecological risk/protective theory for building prevention programs, policies, and community capacity to support youth. *Family Relations: Journal of Applied Family & Child Studies, 45,* 127–138.

Bohlmeijer, E., Smit, F., & Cuijpers, P. (2003). Effects of reminiscence and life review on late-life depression: A meta-analysis. *International Journal of Geriatric Psychiatry, 18,* 1088–1094.

Boise, L., Neal, M. B., & Kaye, J. (2004). Dementia assessment in primary care: Results from a study in three managed care systems. *The Journals of Gerontology Series A: Biological Sciences and Medical Sciences, 59,* M621.

Bolen, R., & Scannapieco, M. (1999). Prevalence of child sexual abuse: A corrective meta-analysis. *Social Service Review, 73,* 281–301.

Bonavita, V., Iavarone, A., & Sorrentino, G. (2001). Depression in neurological diseases: A review. *Archives of General Psychiatry* (Suppl. 7), 49–66.

Bond, G. R. (2004). Supported employment: Evidence for and against evidence-based practice. *Psychiatric Rehabilitation Journal, 27*(4), 345–359.

Bond, J., Kaskutas, L., & Weisner, C. (2003). The persistent influence of social networks and Alcoholics Anonymous on abstinence. *Quarterly Journal of Studies on Alcohol, 64,* 579–588.

Borges, G., Angst, J., Nock, M., Ruscio, A. M., Walters, E., & Kessler, R. (2006). A risk index for 12-month suicide attempts in the National Comorbidity Survey Replication (NCR-S). *Psychological Medicine,* 1–11.

Bosquet, M., & Egeland, B. (2006). The development and maintenance of anxiety symptoms from infancy through adolescence in a longitudinal sample. *Development and Psychopathology, 18,* 517–550.

Bourgeois, M. S., Dijkstra, K., & Hickey, E. M. (2005). Impact of communication interaction on measuring self- and proxy-related depression in dementia (Electronic Version). *Journal of Medical Speech-Language Pathology, 13,* 37–51.

Bowden, C. L., Ketter, T. A., Sachs, G. S., & Thase, M. E. (2005). Focus on bipolar disorder treatment. *Journal of Clinical Psychiatry, 66*(12), 1598–1609.

Bowden, C. L. (2000). Efficacy of lithium in mania and maintenance therapy of bipolar disorder. *Journal of Clinical Psychiatry, 61*(Suppl. 9), 35–40.

Bowen, G., Richman, J., Brewster, A., & Bowen, N. (1998). Sense of school coherence, perceptions of danger at school, and teacher support among youth at risk of summary, and critique. *American Journal of Geriatric Psychiatry, 9*(4), 361–381.

Cole, M. G. (2005). Evidence-based review of risk factors for geriatric depression and brief preventive interventions. *Psychiatric Clinics of North America, 28,* 785–803.

Conklin, H. M., & Iacono, W. G. (2003). At issue: Assessment of schizophrenia: Getting closer to the cause. *Schizophrenia Bulletin, 29*(3), 409–412.

Conner, K. R., Sorensen, S., & Leonard , K. E. (2005). Initial depression and subsequent drinking during alcoholism treatment. *Journal of Studies on Alcohol,* 401–406.

Conners, C. K., Epstein, J. N., March, J. S., Angold, A., Wells, K. C., Klaric, J. M., Swanson, J. M., Arnold, L. E., Abikoff, H. B., Elliott, G. R., Greenhill, L. L., Hechtman, L., Hinshaw, S. P., Hoza, B., Jensen, P. S., Kraemer, H. C., Newcorn, J. H., Pelham, W. E., Severe, J. B., Vitiello, B., & Wigal, T. (2001). Multimodal treatment of ADHD (MTA): An alternative outcome analysis. *Journal of the American Academy of Child and Adolescent Psychiatry, 40,* 159–167.

Connor, D., Glatt, S., Lopez, I., Jackson, D., & Melloni, R. (2002). Psychopharmacology and aggression; I. A meta-analysis of stimulant effects on overt/covert aggression-related behaviors in ADHD. *Journal of the American Academy of Child and Adolescent Psychiatry, 41,* 253–262.

Constantino, J. N., & Todd, R. D. (2003). Autistic traits in the general population: A twin study. *Archives of General Psychiatry, 60*(5), 524–530.

Cooper, C., Katone, C., Orrell, M., & Livingston, G. (2004). Coping strategies and anxiety in caregivers of people with Alzheimer's disease: The LASER-AD study. *Journal of Affective Disorders, 90*(1), 15–20.

Cooper, R. (2004). What is wrong with the DSM? *History of Psychiatry, 15*(57, Pt1), 5–25.

Cooper, Z. (1995). The development and maintenance of eating disorders. In K. D. Brownell & C. G. Fairburn (Eds.), *Eating disorders and obesity: A comprehensive handbook* (pp. 199–206). New York: Guilford Press.

Corcoran, J., & Dattalo, P. (2006). Parent involvement in treatment for ADHD: A meta-analysis of the published studies. *Research in Social Work Practice.*

Corcoran, J., & Walsh, J. (2006). *Clinical assessment and diagnosis in social work practice.* New York: Oxford University Press.

Corrao, G., Bagnardi, V., Zambon, A., & Arico, S. (1999). Exploring the dose-response relationship between alcohol consumption and the risk of several alcohol-related conditions: A meta-analysis. *Addiction, 94,* 1551–1573.

Cottrell, D., Fonagy, P., Kurtz, Z., Phillips, J., & Target, M. (2002). What works for whom? A critical review of treatments for children and adolescents. *Depressive Disorders* (pp. 89–105). New York, London: Guilford Press.

Council on Social Work Education. (2004). *Education Policy and Accreditation Standards.* Retrieved June 1, 2007, from http://www.cswe.org/NR/rdonlyres/111833A0 -C4F5-475C-8FEB-EA740FF4D9F1/0/EPAS.pdf.

Counts, C. A., Nigg, J. T., Stawicki, J. A., Rappley, M., & Eye, A. V. (2005). Family adversity in DSM-IV ADHD combined and inattentive subtypes and associated disruptive behavior problems. *Journal of the American Academy of Child & Adolescent Psychiatry, 44*(7), 690–698.

Cozolino, L. (2002). *The neuroscience of psychotherapy: Building and rebuilding the human brain.* New York: W. W. Norton.

Creamer, M., McFarlane, A. C., & Burgess, P. (2005). Psychopathology following trauma: The role of subjective experience. *Journal of Affective Disorders, 86*(2–3), 175–182.

Crisp, A. H., Norton, K., Gowers, S., Halek, C., Bowyer, C., Yeldham, D., Levett, G., & Bhat, A. (1991). A controlled study of the effect of therapies aimed at adolescent and family psychopathology in anorexia nervosa. *British Journal of Psychiatry, 159,* 325–333.

Cronk, N., Slutske, W., Madden, P., Bucholz, K., & Heath, A. (2004). Risk for separation anxiety disorder among girls: Paternal absence, socioeconomic disadvantage, and genetic vulnerability. *Journal of Abnormal Psychology, 113,* 237–247.

Crow, T. J., Honea, R., Passingham, D., & Mackay, C. E. (2005). Regional deficits in brain volume in schizophrenia: A meta-analysis of voxel-based morphometry studies. *American Journal of Psychiatry, 162,* 2233–2245.

Cuffe, S. P, McKeown, R. E., Jackson, K. L., Addy, C. L., Abramson, R., & Garrison, C. Z. (2001). Prevalence of attention-deficit/hyperactivity disorder in a community sample of older adolescents. *Journal of the American Academy of Child and Adolescent Psychiatry, 40*(9), 1037–1044.

Cuijpers, P. (1997). Bibliotherapy in unipolar depression: A meta-analysis. *Journal of Behavior Therapy and Experimental Psychiatry, 28,* 139–147.

Cuijpers, P. (1998). A psychoeducational approach to the treatment of depression: A meta-analysis of Lewinsohn's "Coping with Depression" course. *Behavior Therapy, 29,* 521–533.

Cummings, L. J., & Cole, G. (2002). Alzheimer's disease. *Journal of the American Medical Association, 287,* 2335–2339.

Currie, J., & Thomas, D. (1995). Does Head Start make a difference? *American Economic Review, 85*(3), 341–365.

Davidson, P., & Parker, K. (2001). Eye movement desensitization and reprocessing (EMDR): A meta-analysis. *Journal of Consulting and Clinical Psychology, 69,* 305–316.

Davila, J., Ramsay, M., Stroud, C. B., & Steinberg, S. J. (2005). Attachment as vulnerability to the development of psychopathology. In B. L. Hankin & J. R. Z. Abela (Eds.), *Development of psychopathology: A vulnerability-stress perspective* (pp. 215–242). Thousand Oaks, CA: Sage Publications.

De Beurs, E., Beekman, A., Geerlings, S., Deeg, D., Van Dyck, R., & Van Tilburg, W. (2001). On becoming depressed or anxious in late life: Similar vulnerability factors but different effects of stressful life events. *British Journal of Psychiatry, 179*(5), 426–431.

de Jong, P., & Berg, I. K. (2002). *Interviewing for solutions (2nd ed.).* Pacific Grove, CA: Brooks/Cole.

Deater-Deckard, K., Dodge, K. A., & Sorbring, E. (2005). Cultural differences in the effects of physical punishment. In M. Rutter, & M. Tienda (Eds.), *Ethnicity and causal mechanisms* (pp. 204–226). New York, NY: Cambridge University Press.

Deater-Deckard, K., Ivy, L., & Smith, J. (2005). Resilience in gene-environment transactions. In S. Goldstein, & R. B. Brooks (Eds.), *Handbook of resilience in children* (pp. 49–63). New York, NY, US: Kluwer Academic/Plenum Publishers.

DeGrandpre, R. (1999). *Ritalin nation: Rapid fire culture and the transformation of human consciousness.* New York: W. W. Norton.

Dekovic, M. (1999). Risk and protective factors in the development of problem behavior during adolescence. *Journal of Youth and Adolescence, 28*(6), 667–685.

DeRose, L., Wright, A., & Brooks-Gunn, J. (2006). Does puberty account for the gender differential in depression? In C. L. M. Keyes & S. H. Goodman (Eds.), *Women and depression: Handbook for the social, behavioral, and biomedical sciences* (pp. 89–128). New York: Cambridge University Press.

DeRubeis, R., Gelfand, L., Tang, T., & Simons, A. (1999). Medications versus cognitive behavior therapy for severely depressed outpatients: Mega-analysis of four randomized comparisons. *American Journal of Psychiatry, 156*, 1007–1013.

Desai, H., & Jann, M. (2000). Major depression in women: A review of the literature. *Journal of the American Pharmaceutical Association, 40*, 525–537.

Detera-Wadleigh, S. D., & McMahon, F. J. (2006). G72/G30 in schizophrenia and bipolar disorder: Review and meta-analysis. *Biological Psychiatry, 60*(2), 106–114.

DeVane, C. L., Chiao, E., Franklin, M., & Kru, E. J. (2005). Anxiety disorders in the 21st century: Status, challenges, opportunities, and comorbidity with depression. *American Journal of Managed Care*, 344–353.

Diamond, G. S., Reis, B. F., Diamond, G. M., Siqueland, L., & Isaacs, L. (2002). Attachment-based family therapy for depressed adolescents: A treatment development study. *Journal of the American Academy of Child and Adolescent Psychiatry, 41*(10), 1190–1197.

Dodge, K. (2003). Do social information-processing patterns mediate aggressive behavior? In B. Lahey, T. E. Moffitt, & A. Caspi (Eds.), *Causes of conduct disorder and juvenile delinquency* (pp. 254–276). New York: Guilford Press.

Donovan, C., & Spence, S. (2000). Prevention of childhood anxiety disorders. *Clinical Psychology Review, 20*, 509–531.

Duffy, M., Gillig, S. E., & Tureen, R. M. (2002). A critical look at the DSM-IV. *Journal of Individual Psychology, 58*(4), 363–373.

DuPaul, G. J., & Eckert, T. (1997). The effects of school-based interventions for attention deficit hyperactivity disorder: A meta-analysis. *School Psychology Review, 26*, 5–27.

DuPaul, G. J., & Power, T. J. (2000). Educational interventions for students with attention-deficit disorders. In T. Brown (Ed.), *Attention-deficit disorders and comorbidities in children, adolescents, and adults* (pp. 607–634). Washington, DC: American Psychiatric Publishing.

Durlak, J. A. (1998). Common risk and protective factors in successful prevention programs. *American Journal of Orthopsychiatry, 68*(4), 512–520.

Ebmeier, K. P., Donaghey, C., & Steele, J. D. (2006). Recent developments and current controversies in depression. *Lancet, 367*, 153–167.

Eddy, K. T., Dutra, L., Bradley, R., & Westen, D. (2004). A multidimensional meta-analysis of psychotherapy and pharmacotherapy for obsessive-compulsive disorder. *Clinical Psychology Review, 24*(8), 1011–1030.

Edwards, M. E., & Steinglass, P. (1995). Family therapy treatment outcomes for alcoholism. *Journal of Marital and Family Therapy, 21*, 475–509.

Egger, H., & Angold, A. (2006). Common emotional and behavioral disorders in preschool children: Presentation, nosology, and epidemiology. *Journal of Child Psychology and Psychiatry, 47*(3–4).

Ehrensaft, M. K. (2005). Interpersonal relationships and sex differences in the development of conduct problems. *Clinical Child and Family Psychology Review, 8*(1), 39–63.

Eikeseth, S., Smith, T., Jahr, E., & Eldevik, S. (2002). Intensive behavioral treatment at school for 4- to 7-year-old children with autism: A 1-year comparison controlled study. *Behaviour Modification: Special Issue: Autism*, Part 2, 26, 49–68.

Ellen, I. G. (2000). *Sharing America's neighborhoods: The prospects for stable racial integration*. Cambridge, MA: Harvard University Press.

Epps, S., & Jackson, B. (2000). *Empowered families, successful children*. Washington, DC: American Psychiatric Publishing.

Essock, S. M. (2002). Editor's introduction: Antipsychotic prescribing practices. *Schizophrenia Bulletin, 28*(1), 1–4.

Evans, D. L. (2000). Bipolar disorder: Diagnostic challenges and treatment considerations. *Journal of Clinical Psychiatry, 61*(Suppl. 13), 26–31.

Evans, J. G., Wilcock, G., & Birks, J. (2004). Evidence-based pharmacotherapy of Alzheimer's disease. *International Journal of Neuropsychopharmacology, 7*(3), 351–369.

Fairburn, C. G., Agras, W. S., Walsh, B. T., Wilson, G. T., & Stice, E. (2004). Prediction of outcome in bulimia nervosa by early change in treatment. *American Journal of Psychiatry, 161*, 2322–2324.

Fairburn, C. G., Cooper, Z., Doll, H. A., & Davies, B. A. (2005). Identifying dieters who will develop an eating disorder: A prospective, population-based study. *American Journal of Psychiatry, 162*, 2249–2255.

Fairburn, C. G., Cooper, Z., Doll, H. A., & Welch, S. L. (1999). Risk factors for anorexia nervosa: Three integrated case-control comparisons. *Archives of General Psychiatry, 56*(5), 468–476.

Fairburn, C. G., Jones, R., Peveler, R. C., Carr, S. J., et al. (1991). Three psychological treatments for bulimia nervosa: A comparative trial. *Archives of General Psychiatry, 48*(5), 463–469.

Fairburn, C. G., Marcus, M. D., & Wilson, G. T. (1993). Cognitive-behavioral therapy for binge eating and bulimia nervosa: A comprehensive treatment manual. In C. G. Fairburn & G. T. Wilson (Eds.), *Binge eating: Nature, assessment, and treatment* (pp. 361–404). New York: Guilford Press.

Fairburn, C. G., Norman, P. L., Welch, S. L., O'Connor, M. E., Doll, H. A., & Peveler, R. C. (1995). A prospective study of outcome in bulimia nervosa and the long-term effects of three psychological treatments. *Archives of General Psychiatry, 52*(4), 304–312.

Fals-Stewart, W., O'Farrell, T. J., & Birchler, G. R. (2005). Behavioral couples therapy for alcoholism and drug abuse: Where we've been, where we are, and where we're going. *Journal of Cognitive Psychotherapy, 19*(3), 229–246.

Faraone, S. V., Biederman, J., Spencer, T., Mick, E., Murray, K., Petty, C., Adamson, J. J., & Monuteaux, M. C. (2006). Diagnosing adult attention deficit hyperactivity disorder: Are late onset and subthreshold diagnoses valid? *American Journal of Psychiatry, 163*(10), 1720–1729.

Faraone, S. V., & Khan, S. A. (2006). Candidate gene studies of attention-deficit/hyperactivity disorders. *Journal of Clinical Psychiatry, 67*(8), 13–20.

Faraone, S., Spencer, T., Aleardi, M., Pagano, C., & Biederman, J. (2004). Meta-analysis of the efficacy of methylphenidate for treating adult attention-deficit/hyperactivity disorder. *Journal of Clinical Psychopharmacology, 24*, 24–29.

Faravelli, C., Rosi, S., & Scarpato, M. A. (2006). Threshold and subthreshold bipolar disorders in the Sesto Fiorentino Study. *Journal of Affective Disorders, 94*(1–3), 111–119.

Farrer, L. A., Cupples, L. A., & Haines, J. L. (1997). Effects of age, sex, and ethnicity on the association between apolipoprotein E genotype and Alzheimer disease: A meta-analysis. *JAMA: Journal of the American Medical Association, 278*(16), 1349–1356.

Fava, G. A., Ruini, C., & Rafanelli, C. (2005). Sequential treatment of mood and anxiety disorder. *Journal of Clinical Psychiatry, 66*(11), 1392–1400.

Fava, G. A., Ruini, C., Rafanelli, C., Kupka, R. W., Luckenbaugh, D. A., & Post, R. M, Comparison of rapid-cycling and non-rapid-cycling bipolar disorder based on prospective mood ratings in 539 outpatients. *American Journal of Psychiatry, 162*(7), 1273–1280.

Favaro, A., Tenconi, E., & Santonastaso, P. (2006). Prenatal factors and the risk of developing anorexia nervosa and bulimia nervosa. *Archives of General Psychiatry, 63,* 82–88.

Fawcett, J. (2006). Depressive disorders. In R. L. Simon & R. E. Hales (Eds.), *The American Psychiatric Publishing textbook of suicide assessment and management (1st ed.)* (pp. 255–275). Washington, DC: American Psychiatric Publishing.

Ferdinandi, A. D., Yoottanasumpun, V., Pollack, S., & Bermanzohn, P. C (1998). Rehab rounds: Predicting rehabilitation outcome among patients with schizophrenia. *Psychiatric Services, 49,* 907–909.

Fergusson, D. M., Beautrais, A. L., & Horwood, L. J. (2003). Vulnerabilty and resiliency to suicidal behaviours in young people. *Psychological Medicine, 33*(1), 61–73.

Fergusson, D., Horwood, L., & Lynskey, M. (1996). Childhood sexual abuse and psychiatric disorder in young adulthood: II. Psychiatric outcomes of childhood sexual abuse. *Journal of the American Academy of Child and Adolescent Psychiatry, 35,* 1365–1374.

Fichter, M. M., Quadflieg, N., & Hedlund, S. (2006). Twelve-year course and outcome predictors of anorexia nervosa. *International Journal of Eating Disorders, 39,* 87–100.

Fink, M. (2006). ECT in therapy-resistant mania: Does it have a place? *Bipolar Disorders, 8*(3), 307–309.

Finlay, J. M. (2001). Mesoprefontal dopamine neurons and schizophrenia: Roles of developmental abnormalities. *Schizophrenia Bulletin, 27*(3), 431–442.

First, M. B., Frances, A., & Pincus, H. A. (2002). *DSM-IV-TR handbook of differential diagnosis.* Washington, DC: American Psychiatric Publishing.

Fischer, J., & Corcoran, K. (2007). *Measures for clinical practice and research: A sourcebook: Volume 1 and Volume 2: Couples, families, and children (4th ed.).* NY: Oxford University Press.

Fitzsimmons, S., & Buettner, L. L. (2003). Therapeutic recreation intervention for need-driven dementia-compromised behaviors in community dwellers. *American Journal of Alzheimer's Disease and Other Dementias, 17*(6), 367–381.

Fletcher, K. (1996). Childhood post-traumatic stress disorder. In E. J. Mash & R. Barkley (Eds.), *Child psychopathology* (pp. 248–276). New York: Guilford Press.

Floyd, M. (2003). Bibliotherapy as an adjunct to psychotherapy for depression in older adults. *Journal of Clinical Psychology, 59*(2), 187–195.

Floersch, J. (2003). The subjective experience of youth psychotropic treatment. *Social Work in Mental Health, 1*(4), 51–69.

Foa, E. B., Keane, T. M., & Friedman, M. J. (Eds.). (2000). *Effective treatments for PTSD: Practice guidelines from the International Society for Traumatic Stress Studies.* New York: Guilford Press.

Folstein M. F., Folstein, S. E., & McHugh, P. R. (1975): Mini-mental state: A practical method for grading the state of patients for the clinician. *Journal of Psychiatric Research, 12,* 189–198.

Fonagy, P., & Bateman, A. W. (2006). Progress in the treatment of borderline personality disorder. *British Journal of Psychology, 188*(1), 1–3.

Fonagy, P., & Kurtz, Z. (2002). Disturbance of conduct. In P. Fonagy, M. Target, D. Cottrell, J. Phillips, & Z. Kurtz (Eds.), *What works for whom? A critical review of treatments for children and adolescents.* New York: Guilford Press.

Fonagy, P., Target, M., Cottrell, D., Phillips, J., & Kurtz, Z. (2002). *What works for whom? A critical review of treatments for children and adolescents.* New York: Guilford Press.

Fonseca, A. C., & Perrin, S. (2001). Clinical phenomenology, classification and assessment of anxiety disorders in children and adolescents. In W. K. Silverman & P. D. A. Treffers (Eds), *Anxiety disorders in children and adolescents: Research, assessment and intervention* (pp. 126–158). New York: Cambridge University Press.

Ford, J. D., Stockton, P., & Kaltman, S. (2006). Disorders of extreme stress (DESNOS) symptoms are associated with type and severity of interpersonal trauma exposure in a sample of healthy young women. *Journal of Interpersonal Violence, 21*(11), 1399–1416.

Ford, T., Goodman, R., & Meltzer, H. (2004). The relative importance of child, family, school and neighborhood correlates of childhood psychiatric disorder. *Social Psychiatry and Psychiatric Epidemiology, 39*(6), 487–496.

Forehand, R. L., & McMahon, R. J. (1981). *Helping the non-compliant child: A clinician's guide to parent training.* New York: Guilford Press.

Foreyt, J., Poston, W., Winebarger, A., & McGavin, J. (1998). Anorexia nervosa and bulimia nervosa. In E. Mash & R. Barkley (Eds.), *Treatment of childhood disorders (2nd ed.)* (pp. 647–691). New York: Guilford Press.

Franco, K. N., & Messinger-Rapport, B. (2005). Pharmacological treatment of neuropsychiatric symptoms of dementia: A review of the evidence. *JAMA: Journal of the American Medical Association, 293*(5), 596–608.

Frank, E., & Novick, D. (2002). Progress in the psychotherapy of mood disorders: Studies from the Western Psychiatric Institute and Clinic. *Epidemiologia e Psichiatria Sociale, 10*(4), 245–252.

Frank, E., Kupfer, D. J., Ehlers, C. L., Monk, T. H., Cornes, C., Carter, S., & Frankel, D. (1994). Interpersonal and social rhythm therapy for bipolar disorder: Integrating interpersonal and behavioral approaches. *Behavior Therapy, 17,* 143–149.

Franko, D. L., & Keel, P. K. (2006). Suicidality in eating disorders: Occurrence, correlates, and clinical implications. *Clinical Psychology Review, 26,* 769–782.

Franko, D. L., Dorer, D. J., Keel, P. K., Jackson, S., Manzo, M. P., & Herzog, D. B. (2005). How do eating disorders and alcohol use disorder influence each other? *International Journal of Eating Disorders, 38,* 200–207.

Franko, D., Wonderlich, S., Little, D., & Herzog, D. (2004). Diagnosis and classification of eating disorders. In J. K. Thompson (Ed.), *Handbook of eating disorders and obesity* (pp. 58–80). Hoboken, NJ: John Wiley.

Freeman, A., Stone, M., & Martin, D. (2005). Introduction: A review of borderline personality disorder. In A. Freeman, M. H. Stone, & D. Martin (Eds.), *Comparative treatments for borderline personality disorder* (pp. 1–20). New York: Springer.

French, K., Finkbiner, R., & Duhamel, L. (2002). Patterns of substance use among minority youth and adults in the United States: An overview and synthesis of national survey findings. Prepared by the Center for Substance Abuse Treatment, Department of Health and Human Services under the NEDS contract No. 270-97-7016. Fairfax, VA: Caliber Associates.

Frick, P. J. (2006). Developmental Pathways to Conduct Disorder. *Child and Adolescent Psychiatric Clinics of North America, 15,* 311–331.

Fuller, R., & Hiller-Sturmhofel, S. (1999). Alocholism treatment in the United States: An overview. *Alcohol Research and Health, 23,* 69–77.

Gallagher-Thompson, D., Lovett, S., & Rose, J. (2000). Impact of psychoeducational interventions on distressed family caregivers. *Journal of Clinical Geropsychology, 6*(2), 91–110.

Gambrill, E. (2002). Encouraging transparency. *Journal of Social Work Education, 38*(2), 211–214.

Garfinkel, I., Heintze T., & Huang, C. (2001). The effects of child support enforcement on women's incomes. *Poverty Research News, 5*(3), 5–7.

Garmezy, N. (1993). Children in poverty: Resilience despite risk. *Psychiatry, 56*, 127–136.

Gatz, J. L., Tyas, S. L., St. John, P., & Montgomery, P. (2005). Do depressive symptoms predict Alzheimer's disease and dementia? *Journal of Gerontology: Medical Sciences, 60A*(6), 744–747.

Gatz, M., Reynolds, C. A., Fratiglioni, L., Johansson, B., Mortimer, J. A., Berg, S., Fishe, A., & Pedersen, N. L. (2006). Role of genetics and environments for explaining Alzheimer's disease. *Archives of General Psychiatry, 63*, 168–174.

Gavin, N., Gaynes, B., Lohr, K., Meltzer-Brody, S., Gartlehner, G., & Swinson, T. (2005). Perinatal depression: A systematic review of prevalence and incidence. *Obstetrician Gynecology, 106*, 1071–1083.

Geanellos, R. (2005). Adversity as opportunity: Living with schizophrenia and developing a resilient self. *International Journal of Mental Health Nursing, 14*(1), 7–15.

Geddes, J. R., Burgess, S., Hawton, K., Jamison, K., & Goodwin, G. M. (2004). Long-term lithium therapy for bipolar disorder: Systematic review and meta-analysis of randomized controlled trials. *American Journal of Psychiatry, 161*(2), 217–222.

Gijsman, H. J., Geddes, J. R., & Rendell, J. M. (2004) Antidepressants for bipolar depression: A systematic review of randomized, controlled trials. *American Journal of Psychiatry, 161*(9), 1537–1547.

Gillies, D., Beck, A., McCloud, A., & Rathbone, J. (2005). Benzodiazepines alone or in combination with antipsychotic drugs for acute psychosis. *Cochrane Database of Systematic Reviews, 4*, Art. No. CD003079.

Ginsberg, L. D. (2006). Carbamazepine extended-release capsules: A retrospective review of its use in children and adolescents. *Annals of Clinical Psychiatry, 18*(Suppl. 1), 9–14.

Girgus, J. S., & Nolen-Hoeksema, S. (2006). Cognition and Depression. In C. L. Keyes, & S. H. Goodman (Eds.), *Women and depression: A handbook for the social, behavioral, and biomedical sciences* (pp. 147–175). New York, NY, US: Cambridge University Press.

Glueckauf, R. L., Stine, C., Bourgeois, M., Pomedor, A., Rom, P., Young, M. E., Massey, A., & Ashley, P. (2005). Alzheimer's rural care healthline: Linking rural care givers to cognitive-behavioral intervention for depression. *Rehabilitation Psychology, 50*(4), 346–354.

Godart, N. T., Perdereau, F., Rein, Z., Berthoz, S., Wallier, J., Jeammet, P. H., & Flament, M. F. (2007). Comorbidity studies of eating disorders and mood disorders. Critical review of the literature. *Journal of Affective Disorders, 97*, 37–49.

Goff, D. C., Sullivan, L. M., McEvoy, J. P., Meyer, J. M., Nasrallah, H. A., Dumit, G. I., Lamberti, S., D'Agostino, R. B., Stroup, T. S., Davis, S., & Lieberman, J. A. (2005). A comparison of ten-year cardiac risk estimates in schizophrenia patients from the CATIE study and matched controls. *Schizophrenia Bulletin, 80*(1), 45–53.

Golden, N., Katzman, D., Kreipe, R., Stevens, S., Sawyer, S., Rees, J., Nicholls, D., & Rome, E. (2003). Eating disorders in adolescents: Position paper of the Society for Adolescent Medicine. *Journal of Adolescent Health, 33*, 496–503.

Golding, J. M. (1999). Intimate partner violence as a risk factor for mental disorders: A meta-analysis. *Journal of Family Violence, 14*(2), 99–132.

Goldstein, E. G. (1995). *Ego psychology and social work practice* (2nd ed.). New York: Free Press.

Goldstein, E. G. (2000). *Object relations theory and self psychology in social work practice.* New York: Free Press.

Gonzalez-Tejara, G., Canino, G., Ramirez, R., Chavez, L., Shrout, P., Bird, H., Bravo, M., Martinez-Taboas, A., Ribery, J., & Bauermeister, J. (2005). Examining minor and major depression in adolescents. *Journal of Child Psychology and Psychiatry, 46*, 888–899.

Goodman, S. H., & Gotlib, I. H. (1999). Risk for psychopathology in the children of depressed mothers: A developmental model for understanding mechanisms of transmission. *Psychological Review, 106*, 458–461.

Goodwin, R., Fergusson, D., & Horwood, L. J. (2004). Association between anxiety disorders and substance use disorders among young persons: Results of a 21-year longitudinal study. *Journal of Psychiatric Research, 38*, 295–304.

Gordon, D. A., Arbuthnot, J., Gustafson, K. E., & McGreen, P. (1988). Home-based behavioral-systems family therapy with disadvantaged juvenile delinquents. *American Journal of Family Therapy, 16*, 243–255.

Gorman, J., Shear, K., Cowley, D., Cross, C. D., March, J., Roth, W., Shehi, M., & Wang, P. (2002). Practice guidelines for the treatment of patients with panic disorder. In *American Psychiatric Association practice guidelines for the treatment of psychiatric disorders. Compendium 2002* (pp. 635–696). Washington, DC: American Psychiatric Publishing.

Gowers, S., & Bryant-Waugh, R. (2004). Management of child and adolescent eating disorders: The current evidence base and future directions. *Journal of Child Psychology and Psychiatry, 45*, 63–83.

Graber, J. A., Brooks-Gunn, J., & Warren, M. F. (2006). Pubertal effects on adjustment in girls: Moving from demonstrating effects to identifying pathways. *Journal of Youth and Adolescence, 35*(3), 413–423.

Grant, B. F., Hasin, D. S., Blanco, C., Stinson, F. S., Chou, S. P., Goldstein, R. B., Dawson, D. A., Smith, S., Saha, T. D., & Huang, B. (2005). The epidemiology of social anxiety disorder in the United States: Results from the National Epidemiologic Survey on Alcohol and Related Conditions. *Journal of Clinical Psychiatry, 66*, 1351–1361.

Grant, B. F., Stinson, F. S., Hasin, D. S., Dawson, D. A., Chou, S. P., Ruan, W. J., & Huang, B. (2005). Prevalence, correlates, and comorbidity of bipolar I disorder and axis I and II disorder: Results from the national epidemiological survey on alcohol and related conditions. *Journal of Clinical Psychiatry, 66*, 1205–1215.

Grant, B. F., Hasin, D. S., Stinson, F. S., Dawson, D. A. S., Chou, P. W., Ruan, J., & Huang, B. (2005). Co-occurrence of 12-month mood and anxiety disorders and personality disorders in the US: Results from the national epidemiologic survey on alcohol and related conditions. *Journal of Psychiatric Research, 39*(1), 1–9.

Grassel, E., Wiltfang, J., & Kornhuber, J. (2003). Non-drug therapies for dementia: An overview of the current situation with regard to proof of effectiveness. *Dementia and Geriatric Cognitive Disorders, 15*(3), 115–125.

Graybeal, C. (2001). Strengths-based social work assessment: Transforming the dominant paradigm. *Families in Society, 82*, 233–242.

Greenberg, M., Speltz, M., DeKlyen, M., & Jones, K. (2001). Correlates of clinic referral for early conduct problems: Variable- and person-oriented approaches. *Development and Psychopathology, 13*, 255–276.

Grilo, C. M., Sanislow, C. A., & McGlashan, T. H. (2002). Co-occurrence of DSM-IV personality disorders with borderline personality disorder. *Journal of Nervous and Mental Disease, 190*(8), 552–553.

Groesz, L. M., Levine, M. P., & Murnen, S. K. (2002). The effect of experimental presentation of thin media images on body satisfaction: A meta-analytic review. *International Journal of Eating Disorders, 31*, 1–16.

Gurvits, I. G., Koenigsberg, H. W., & Siever, L. J. (2000). Neurotransmitter dysfunction in patients with border-line personality disorder. *Psychiatric Clinics of North America, 23*(1), 27–40.

Gutman, L. M., & Sameroff, A. J. (2004). Continuities in depression from adolescence to young adulthood: Contrasting ecological influences. *Development and Psychopathology, 16*, 967–984.

Hagopian, L., & Ollendick, T. (1997). Anxiety disorders. In R. Ammerman & M. Hersen, (Eds.), *Handbook of prevention and treatment with children and adolescents: Intervention in the real world context* (pp. 431–454). New York: John Wiley.

Halfon, N., Regaldo, M., McLearn, K. T., Kuo, A. A., & Wright, K. (2003). *Building a bridge from birth to school: Improving developmental and behavioral health services for young children.* New York: Commonwealth Fund.

Hamre, B. K., & Pianta, R. C. (2001). Early teacher-child relationships and the trajectory of children's school outcomes through eighth grade. *Child Development, 72*(2), 625–638.

Hanes, R. B., Yao, X., Degani, A., Kripalani, S. Garb, A., & McDonald, H. P. (2005). Interventions to enhance medication adherence. *Cochrane Database of Systematic Reviews, 4*, Art. No. CD000011.

Hankin, B. L., Abela, J. R. Z., Auerbach, R. P., McWhinnie, C. M., & Skitch, S. A. (2005). Development of behavioral problems over the life course: A vulnerability and stress perspective. In B. L. Hankin & J. R. Z. Abela (Eds.), *Development of psychopathology: A vulnerability-stress perspective* (pp. 385–416). Thousand Oaks, CA: Sage Publications.

Hankin, B. L., & Abela, J. R. Z. (2005). Depression from childhood through adolescences and adulthood: A developmental vulnerability and stress perspective. In B. L. Hankin & J. R. Z. Abela (Eds.), *Development of psychopathology: A vulnerability-stress perspective* (pp. 245–288). Thousand Oaks, CA: Sage Publications, Inc.

Hanklin, B., Kassel, J. D., & Abela, J. R. (2005). Adult attachment dimensions and specificity of emotional distress symptoms: Prospective investigations of cognitive risk and interpersonal stress generation as mediating mechanisms. *Personality and Psychology Bulletin, 31*, 136–151.

Harlap, S. (2001). Schizophrenia: Older fathers substantially raise the risk of having children with disease. *Genomics and Genetics Weekly*, 17–18.

Haupt, M., Karger, A., & Jänner, M. (2000). Improvement of agitation and anxiety in demented patients after psychoeducative group intervention with their caregivers. *International Journal of Geriatric Psychiatry, 15*(12), 1125–1129.

Hawton, K., Sutton, L., Haw, C., Sinclair, J., & Harriss, L. (2005). Suicide and attempted suicide in bipolar disorder: A systematic review of risk factors. *Journal of Clinical Psychiatry, 66*(6), 693–704.

Hay, P. J., & Bacaltchuk, J. (2003). Psychotherapy for bulimia nervosa and binging (Cochrane Review). In *The Cochrane Library*, Issue 1. Oxford: Update Software.

Hay, P., Bacaltchuk, J., Claudino, A., Ben-Tovim, D., & Yong, P. (2003). *Individual psychotherapy in the outpatient treatment of adults with anorexia nervosa* (Cochrane Review). In *The Cochrane Library*, Issue 4. Chichester, UK: John Wiley.

Hayes, R. L., & McGrath, J. J. (2000). Cognitive rehabilitation for people with schizophrenia and related conditions. *Cochrane Database of Systematic Reviews, 3*, Art. No. CD000968.

Hayward, C., Wilson, K. A., Lagle, K., Killen, J. D., & Taylor, C. B. (2004). Parent-reported predictors of adolescent panic attacks. *Journal of the American Academy of Child and Adolescent Psychiatry, 43*, 613–620.

Hazan, C., Campa, M., & Gur-Yaish, N. (2006). Attachment across the lifespan. In P. Noller & J. Feeney (Eds.), *Close relationships: Functions, form and processes* (pp. 189–209). Hove, England: Psychology Press/Taylor & Francis.

Hazell, P., O'Connell, D., Heathcote, D., & Henry, D. (2003). Tricyclic drugs for depression in children and adolescents (Cochrane Review). In *The Cochrane Library*, Issue 1 2003. Oxford: Update Software.

Healy, D. (2002). *The creation of psychopharmacology.* Cambridge, MA: Harvard University Press.

Heering, P. W., & Wilder, D. A. (2006). The use of dependent group contingencies to increase on-task behavior in two general education classrooms. *Education and Treatment of Children, 29*(3), 459–468.

Helgeson, V., Reynolds, K., & Tomich, P. (2006). A meta-analytic review of benefit finding and growth. *Journal of Consulting and Clinical Psychology, Special issue: Benefit-Finding, 74*, 797–816.

Henggeler, S. W., Schoenwald, S. K., Borduin, C., Rowland, M., & Cunningham, P. B. (1998). *Multisystemic treatment of antisocial behavior in children and adolescents.* New York: Guilford Press.

Herbert, L. A., Beckett, L. A., Schurr, P. A., & Evans, D. A. (2001). *Annual incidence of Alzheimer's disease in the United States projected to the years 2000 through 2050.* Philadelphia: Lippincott Williams & Wilkins, Inc., 15*(4), 169–173.

Hersen, M. (2006). *Clinician's handbook of child behavioral assessment.* San Diego, CA: Elsevier.

Hettema, J. M., Neale, M. C., & Kendler, K. S. (2001). A review and meta-analysis of the genetic epidemiology of anxiety disorders. *American Journal of Psychiatry, 1574*, 1568–1578.

Heyn, P. (2003). The effect of a multisensory exercise program on engagement, behavior, and selected physiological indexes in persons with dementia. *American Journal of Alzheimer's Disease and Other Dementias, 18*(4), 247–251.

Hill, D., Rozanski, C., Carfagnini, J., & Willoughby, B. (2005). Gender identity disorders in childhood and adolescence: A critical inquiry. *Journal of Psychology and Human Sexuality, 17*(3/4), 7–33.

Hill, J. (2002). Biological, psychological and social processes in conduct disorders. *Journal of Child Psychology and Psychiatry, 43*(1), 133–164.

Hilty, D., Brady, K., & Hales, R. (1999). A review of bipolar disorder among adults. *Psychiatric Services, 50*, 201–213.

Himelick, A. J., & Walsh, J. (2002). Nursing home residents with borderline personality traits: Clinical social work interventions. *Journal of Gerontological Social Work, 37*(1), 49–63.

Hingson, R. W., Hereen, T., & Winter, M. R. (2006). Age at drinking onset and alcohol dependence. *Archives of Pediatrics and Adolescent Medicine, 160*, 739–746.

Hino, T., Takeuchi, T., & Yamanouchi, N. (2002). A 1-year follow-up study of coping in patients with panic disorder. *Comprehensive Psychiatry, 43*, 279–284.

Hinshaw, S. P., Owens, E. B., Sami, N., & Fargeon, S. (2006). Prospective follow-up of girls with attention-deficit/hyperactivity disorder into adolescence: Evidence for continuing cross-domain impairment. *Journal of Consulting and Clinical Psychology, 74*(3), 489–499.

Hinshaw, S., & Anderson, C. (1996). Conduct and oppositional defiant disorders. In E. Mash & R. Barkley (Eds.),

Child psychopathology (pp. 113–149). New York: Guilford Press.

Hirschfeld, R. M. A., Lewis, L., & Vornik, L. A. (2003). Perceptions and impact of bipolar disorder: How far have we come? Results of the National Depressive and Manic Depressive Association's 2000 survey of individuals with bipolar disorder. *Journal of Clinical Psychiatry, 64*(2), 161–174.

Hogarty, G. E. (2002). *Personal therapy for schizophrenia and related disorders.* New York: Guilford Press.

Hogarty, G. E., Greenwald, D., & Ulrich, R. F. (1997). Three-year trials of personal therapy among schizophrenic patients living with or independently of family, II: Effects on adjustment of patients. *American Journal of Psychiatry 154*, 1514–1523.

Hogarty, G. E., Kornblith, S. J., & Greenwald, D. (1997). Three-year trials of personal therapy among schizophrenic patients living with or independently of family, I: Description of study and effects on relapse rates. *American Journal of Psychiatry, 154*, 1504–1513.

Holahan, C. J., Moos, R. H., Holahan, C. K., Brennan, P. L., & Schutte, K. K. (2005). Stress generations, avoidance coping, and depressive symptoms: 10-year model. *Journal of Consulting and Clinical Psychology, 73*(4), 658–666.

Holter, M. (2004). Autistic spectrum disorders: Assessment and intervention. In P. Allen-Meares & M. Fraser (Eds.), *Intervention with children and adolescents: An interdisciplinary perspective* (pp. 205–228). Washington, DC: NASW Press.

Hopfer, C . J., Stallings, M. C., Hewitt, J. K., & Crowley, T. J. (2003). Family transmission of marijuana use, abuse, and dependence. *Journal of the American Academy of Child Adolescent. Psychiatry, 42*, 834–841.

Horowitz, K., McKay, M., & Marshall, R. (2005). Community violence and urban families: Experiences, effects, and directions for intervention. *American Journal of Orthopsychiatry, 75*(3), 356–368.

Howlin, P. (2005). Outcomes in autism spectrum disorders. In F. R. Volkmar, R. Paul, A. Klin, & D. Cohen (Eds.), *Handbook of autism and pervasive developmental disorders Vol. 1: Diagnosis, development, neurobiology, and behavior* (3rd ed.) (pp. 201–220). Hoboken, NJ: John Wiley.

Huang, B., Grant, B. F., Dawson, D. A., Frederick, F. S., Chou, S. P., Saha, T. D., Goldstein, R. B., Smith, S. M., Ruan, W. J., & Pickering, R. P. (2006). Race-ethnicity and the prevalence and co occurrence of *Diagnostic and Statistical Manual of Mental Disorders,* alcohol and drug use disorders and Axis I and II disorders.

Hudson, J., Hiripi, E., Pope, H., & Kessler, R. (2006). The prevalence and correlates of eating disorders in the National Comorbidity Survey Replication. *Biological Psychiatry, 61*, 348–358.

Humphreys, K., Wing, S., McCarty, D., Chappel, J., Gallant, L., Haberle, B., Horvath, T., Kaskutas, L. A., Kirk, T., Kivlahan, D., Laudet, A., McCrady, B. S., McLellan, T., Morgenstern, J., Townsend, M., & Weiss, R. (2004). Self-help organizations for alcohol and drug problems: Towards evidence-based practice. *Journal of Substance Abuse Treatment, 26*, 151–158.

Huxley, N. A., Rendell, M., & Sederer, L. (2000). Psychosocial treatments in schizophrenia: A review of the past 20 years. *Journal of Nervous and Mental Disease, 188*(4), 187–201.

Hypothyroidism. (2006). Retrieved on October 20, 2006, at http://www.mayoclinic.com/health/hypothyroidism/DS00353/DSECTION=7.

Iliffe, S., & Manthorpe, J. (2004). The hazards of early recognition of dementia: A risk assessment. *Aging & Mental Health, 8*(2), 99–105.

Jackson, A., Cavanaugh, J., & Scott, J. (2003). A systematic review of manic and depressive prodromes. *Journal of Affective Disorders, 74*(3), 209–217.

Jacobvitz, D., Hazen, N., Curran, M., & Hitchens, K. (2004). Observations of early triadic family interactions: Boundary disturbances in the family predict symptoms of depression, anxiety, and attention-deficit/hyperactivity disorder in middle childhood. *Development and Psychopathology, 16*, 577–592.

Jaffee, S. R., Caspi, A., & Moffitt, T. E. (2005). Nature x nurture: Genetic vulnerabilities interact with physical maltreatment to promote conduct problems. *Development and Psychopathology, 17*(1), 67–84.

Jatzko, A., Rothenhofer, S., & Schmitt, A. (2006). Hippocampal volume in chronic posttraumatic stress disorder (PTSD): MRI study using two different evaluation methods. *Journal of Affective Disorders, 94*(1–3), 121–126.

Jedziewski, M. K., Lee, V. M., & Trojanowski, J. Q. (2005). Lowering the risk of Alzheimer's disease: Evidence-based practices emerging from new research.

Jessor, R., Van Den Bos, J., Vanderryn, J., Costa, F. M., & Turbin, M. S. (1997). Protective factors in adolescent problem behavior: Moderator effects and developmental change. In G. A. Marlatt & G. R. Van Den Bos (Eds.), *Addictive behaviors: Readings on etiology, prevention, and treatment* (pp. 239–264). Washington, DC: American Psychological Association.

Jewell, J. D., & Stark, K. D. (2003). Comparing the family environments of adolescents with conduct disorder or depression. *Journal of Child and Family Studies, 12*, 77–89.

Jobe, T., & Harrow, M. (2005). Long-term outcome of patients with schizophrenia: A review. *Canadian Journal of Psychiatry, 50*(14), 892–900.

Johnson, B. R., Jang, S. J., Li, S. D., & Larson, D. (2000). The "invisible institution" and black youth crime: The church as an agency of local social control. *Journal of Youth and Adolescence, 29*(4), 479–498.

Johnson, D. R., & Lubin, H. (2006). The counting method: Applying the rule of parsimony to the treatment of posttraumatic stress disorder. *Traumatology, 12*(1), 83–99.

Johnson, H. C. (1999). Borderline personality disorder. In F. J. Turner (Ed.), *Adult psychopathology: A social work perspective* (pp. 430–456). New York: Free Press.

Johnson, J. G., McGeoch, P. G., Caskey, V. P., Abhary, S. G., Sneed, J. R., & Bornstein, R. F. (2005). The developmental psycho-pathology of personality disorders. In B. L. Hankin & J. R. Z. Abela (Eds.), *Development of psychopathology: A vulnerability-stress perspective* (pp. 417–464). Thousand Oaks, CA: Sage Publications.

Johnston, L. (2000). *Users and abusers of psychiatry: A critical look at psychiatric practice* (2nd ed.). Philadelphia: Routledge.

Johnstone, P., & Zolese, G. (2005). Length of hospitalization for people with severe mental illness. *The Cochrane Database of Systematic Reviews, 2*, Art. No. CD000384.

Joiner, T. E., Walker, R. L., Pettit, J. W., Perez, M., & Cukrowicz, K. (2005). Evidence-based assessment of depression in adults. *Psychological Assessment, 17*(3), 267–277.

Jones, C., Cormac, I., Silvera da Monta Neto, J. I., & Campbell, C. (2004). Cognitive behavior therapy for schizophrenia. *Cochrane Database of Systematic Reviews, 4*, Art. No. CD000524.

Jones, R. S., Chow, T. W., & Gelz, M. (2005). Asian Americans and Alzheimer's disease: Assimilation, culture, and beliefs. *Journal of Aging Studies, 20*(1), 11–25.

Jordan, R. (2001). Multidisciplinary work for children with autism. *Educational and Child Psychology, 18*(2), 5–14.

Jorm, A. F., & Griffiths, K. M. (2006). Population promotion of informal self help strategies for early intervention against depression and anxiety. *Psychological Medicine, 36*(1), 3–6.

Julien, R. M. (2001). *A primer of drug action: A concise, non-technical guide to the actions, uses, and side effects of psychoactive drugs (9th ed.).* New York: W. H. Freeman.

Kahn, R. S., Khoury, J., Nichols, W. C., & Lanphear, B. P. (2003). Role of dopamine transporter genotype and maternal prenatal smoking in childhood hyperactive-impulsive, inattentive, and oppositional behaviors. *Journal of Pediatrics, 143*(1), 104–110.

Kalb, C., & Rosenberg, D. (2004). Nancy's next campaign. *Newsweek, 143*(25), 39–44.

Kalil, A., & Kuntz, J. (1999). First births among unmarried adolescent girls: Risk and protective factors. *Social Work Research, 23,* 197–208.

Kaminski, K. M., & Garber, J. (2002). Depressive spectrum disorders in high-risk adolescents: Episode duration and predictors of time to recovery. *Journal of the American Academy of Child and Adolescent Psychiatry, 41*(4), 410–418.

Kanas, N. (2000). Group therapy and schizophrenia: An integrative model. In B. Martindale & A. Bateman (Eds.), *Psychosis: Psychological approaches and their effectiveness* (pp. 120–133). London: Gaskell/Royal College of Pharmacists.

Kaplow, J., Curran, P., & Dodge, K. (2002). Conduct problems prevention research group. Child, parent, and peer predictors of early-onset substance use: A multisite longitudinal study. *Journal of Abnormal Child Psychology, 30,* 199–216.

Karageorge, K., & Wisdom, G. (2001). *Physically and sexually abused women in substance abuse treatment: Treatment services and outcomes.* Report to the Center for Substance Abuse Treatment. Fairfax, VA: Caliber Associates.

Karasu, T. B., Gelenberg, A., Merriam, A., & Wang, P. (2002). Practice guidelines for the treatment of patients with major depressive disorder. In *American Psychiatric Association practice guidelines for the treatment of psychiatric disorder: Compendium 2002 (2nd ed.)* (pp. 463–545). Washington, DC: American Psychiatric Publishing.

Kasari, C., & Rotheram-Fuller, E. (2005). Current trends in psychological research on children with high-functioning autism and Asperger disorder. *Current Opinion in Psychiatry, 18*(5), 497–501.

Kaslow, N., & Thompson, M. (1998). Applying the criteria for empirically supported treatment to studies of psychosocial interventions for child and adolescent depression. *Journal of Clinical Child Psychology, 27,* 146–155.

Kazdin, A. (2001). Treatment of conduct disorders. In J. Hill & B. Maughan (Eds.), *Conduct disorders in childhood and adolescence* (pp. 408–448). New York: Cambridge University Press.

Keel, P. K., & Klump, K. L. (2003). Are eating disorders culture-bound syndromes? Implications for conceptualizing their etiology. *Psychological Bulletin, 129,* 747–769.

Keel, P., & Mitchell, J. (1997). Outcome in bulimia nervosa. *American Journal of Psychiatry, 154,* 313–321.

Keel, P., Dorer, D., Franko, D., Jackson, S., & Herzog, D. (2005). Postremission predictors of relapse in women with eating disorders. *American Journal of Psychiatry, 162,* 2263–2268.

Kelly, J., Myers, M., & Brown, S. (2002). Do adolescents affiliate with 12-step groups? A mulivariate process model of effects. *Journal of Studies on Alcohol, 63,* 293–305.

Kendall, P. C., Kane, M., Howard, B., & Siqueland, L. (1990). *Cognitive-behavioral treatment of anxious children: Treatment manual.* (Available from P. C. Kendall, Department of Psychology, Temple University, Philadelphia, PA 19122.)

Kendall, P., Safford, S., Flannery-Schroeder, E., & Webb, A. (2004). Child anxiety treatment: Outcomes in adolescence and impact on substance use and depression at 7.4 year follow-up. *Journal of Consulting and Clinical Psychology, 72,* 276–287.

Kessler, R. (2004). The epidemiology of dual diagnosis. *Biological Psychiatry, 56,* 730–737.

Kessler, R., Adler, L., Barkley, R., Biederman, J., Conners, K., Demler, O., Faraone, S., Greenhill, L., Howes, M., Secnik, K., Spencer, T., Ustun, B., Walters, E., & Zaslavsky, A. (2006). The prevalence and correlates of adult ADHD in the United States: Results from the National Comorbidity Survey Replication. *American Journal of Psychiatry, 163,* 716–723.

Kessler, R. C., Adler, L. A., Barkely, R., Biederman, J., Conners, C. K., Faraone, S. V., Greenhill, L. L., Jaeger, S., Secnik, K., Spencer, J., Ustun, T. B., & Zaslavsky, A. M. (2005). Patterns and predictors of attention deficit/hyperactivity disorder persistence into adulthood: Results from the National Comorbidity Survey Replication. *Biological Psychiatry, 57,* 1442–1451.

Kessler, R. C., Berglund, P., Demler, O., Jin, R., Merikangas, K. R., & Walters, E. E. (2005). Lifetime prevalence and age-of-onset distributions of DSM-IV disorders on the National Comorbidity Survey Replication. *Archives of General Psychiatry, 62*(6), 593–602.

Kessler, R. C., Adler, L., Ames, M., Barkley, R., Bimbaum, H., Greenberg, P., Johnston, J., Spencer, T., & Ustun, T. B. (2005). The prevalence and effects of adult attention deficit/hyperactivity disorder on work performance in a nationally representative sample of workers. *Journal of Occupational and Environmental Medicine, 47*(6), 565–572.

Kessler, R. C., Birnbaun, H., Demler, O., Falloon, I. R., Gagnon, E., Guyer, M., Howes, J., Kendler, K. S., Shi, L., Walters, E., & Wu, E. Q. (2005). The prevalence and correlates of nonaffective psychosis in the National Comorbidity Survey Replication. *Biological Psychiatry, 58*(8), 668–676.

Kessler, R. C., Chiu, W. T., Demler, O., & Walters, E. E. (2005). Prevalence, severity, and comorbidity of 12-month *DSM-IV* disorders in the National Comorbidity Survey Replication. *Archives of General Psychiatry, 62*(6), 617–627.

Kessler, R. C., Chiu, W. T., Jin, R., Ruscio, A. M., Shear, K., & Walters, E. E. (2006). The epidemiology of panic attacks, panic disorder, and agoraphobia in the National Comorbidity Survey Replication. *Archives of General Psychiatry, 63*(4), 415–424.

Kessler, R. C., Mickelson, K. D., & Williams, D. R. (1999). The prevalence, distribution, and mental health correlates of perceived discrimination in the United States. *Journal of Health and Social Behavior, 40*(3), 208–231.

Kessler, R.C. (2003). Epidemiology of women and depression. *Journal of Affective Disorders, 74*(1), 5–13.

Killick, S., & Allen, C. (1997). "Shifting the balance": Motivational interviewing to help behaviour change in people with bulimia nervosa. *European Eating Disorders Review, 5,* 33–41.

King, R., Leonard, H., & March, J. (1998). Practice parameters for the assessment and treatment of children and adolescents with obsessive-compulsive disorder. *Journal of the American Academy of Child and Adolescent Psychiatry, 37* (Suppl. 10), 27S–45S.

Kinney, D. K., Yurgelun-Todd, D. A., Tohen, M., & Tramer, S. (1998). Pre- and perinatal complications and risk for bipolar disorder: A retrospective study. *Journal of Affective Disorders, 50*(2–3), 117–124.

Kinney, J. M., & Rentz, C. A. (2005). Observed well-being among individuals with dementia: Memories in the making, an art program, versus other structured activity. *American Journal of Alzheimer's Disease and Other Dementias, 20*(4), 220–227.

Kirkpatrick, B., Herrera Catanedo, S., & Vazquez-Barquero, J. (2002). Summer birth and deficit schizophrenia: Cantabria, Spain. *Journal of Nervous and Mental Disease, 190*(8), 526–532.

Klein, D. N., Dougherty, L. R., & Olino, T. M. (2005). Towards guidelines for evidence-based assessment of depression in children and adolescents. *Journal of Clinical Child and Adolescent Psychology, 34*(3), 412–432.

Klein, D. N., Shankman, S. A., & Rose, S. (2006). Ten-year prospective follow-up study of the naturalistic course of dysthymic disorder and double depression. *American Journal of Psychiatry, 163*(5), 872–880.

Klerman, L. (2004). *Another chance: Preventing additional births to teen mothers.* Washington, DC: National Organization on Adolescent Pregnancy, Parenting, and Prevention.

Knapp, P. (2006). Evolutionary biology of stress disorders. In P. S. Jensen, P. Knapp, & D. A. Mrazek (Eds.), *Toward a new diagnostic system for child psychopathology: Moving beyond the DSM* (pp. 131–149). New York: Guilford Press.

Knouse, L. E., Bagwell, C. L., Barkley, R. A, & Murphy, ADHD evidence from a driving study. *Journal of Attention Disorders, 8*(4), 221–234.

Kobak, K. A., Greist, J. H., Jefferson, J. W., Katzelnick, D. J., & Henk, H. J. (1998). Behavioral versus pharmacological treatments of obsessive compulsive disorder: A meta-analysis. *Psychopharmacology,* 211–214.

Kolevzon, A., Mathewson, K. A., & Hollander, E. (2006). Selective serotonin reuptake inhibitors in autism: A review of efficacy and tolerability. *Journal of Clinical Psychiatry, 67*(3), 407–415.

Kolodziej, M. E., Griffin, M. L., & Najavits, L. M. (2005). Anxiety disorders among patients with co-occurring bipolar and substance use disorders. *Drug and Alcohol Dependence, 80*(2), 251–257.

Kotler, L. A., Cohen, P., Davies, M., Pine, D. S., & Walsh, B. D. (2001). Longitudinal relationships between childhood, adolescent, and adult eating disorders. *Journal of the American Academy of Child and Adolescent Psychiatry, 40,* 1434–1441.

Kotlyar, M., Dysken, M., & Adson, D. E. (2005). Update on drug-induced depression in the elderly. *American Journal of Geriatric Pharmacotherapy, 3,* 288–300.

Kovacs, M. (2001). Gender and the course of major depressive disorder through adolescence in clinically referred youngsters. *Journal of the American Academy of Child and Adolescent Psychiatry, 40,* 1079–1085.

Kovacs, M., Obrosky, S., Gatsonis, C., & Richards, C. (1997). First-episode major depressive and dysthymic disorder in childhood: Clinical and sociodemographic factors in recovery. *Journal of the American Academy of Child and Adolescent Psychiatry, 36*(6), 777–784.

Kownacki, R., & Shadish, W. (1999). Does Alcoholics Anonymous work? The results from a meta-analysis of controlled experiments. *Substance Use and Misuse, 34,* 1897–1916.

Koyama, T., Tachimor, H., & Osada, H. (2006). Cognitive and symptom profiles in high-functioning pervasive developmental disorder not otherwise specified and attention-deficit/hyperactivity disorder. *Journal of Autism and Developmental Disorders, 36*(3), 373–380.

Kraaij, V., Arensman, E., & Spinhoven, P. (2002). Negative life events and depression in elderly persons: A meta analysis. *Journals of Gerontology Series B-Psychological Sciences & Social Sciences, 57B*(1), 87–94.

Kranzler, H., & Van Kirk, J. (2001). Efficacy of nalrexone and acamprosate for alcoholism treatment: A meta-analysis. *Alcoholism, 25,* 1335–1341.

Kreppner, J., O'Connor, T., & Rutter, M. (2001). Can inattention/overactivity be an institutional deprivation syndrome? *Journal of Abnormal Child Psychology, 29,* 513–529.

Krishnakumar, A., & Buehler, C. (2000). Interparental conflict and parenting behaviors: A meta-analytic review. *Family Relations, 49,* 25–44.

Krishnan, K. R. (2005). Psychiatric and medical comorbidities of bipolar disorder. *Psychosomatic Medicine, 67,* 1–8.

Kronenberger, W. S., & Meyer, R. G. (2001). *The child clinician's handbook (2nd ed.).* Needham Heights, MA: Allyn & Bacon.

Kuhn, D., & Fulton, B. R. (2004). Efficacy of an educational program for relatives of persons in the early stages of Alzheimer's disease. *Journal of Gerontological Social Work, 42*(3–4), 109–130.

Kuipers, E., Garety, P., & Fowler, D. (2006). Cognitive, emotional, and social processes in psychosis: Refining cognitive behavioral therapy for persistent positive symptoms.

Kunz, J. A. (2002). Targeted reminiscence interventions for older adults with dementia. *Journal of Geriatric Psychiatry, 35*(1), 25–49.

Kupka, R. W., Luckenbaugh, D. A., & Post, R . M. (2005). Comparison of rapid-cycling and non-rapid-cycling bipolar disorder based on prospective mood ratings in 539 outpatients. *American Journal of Psychiatry, 162*(7), 1273–1280.

Kushner, M., Sher, K., & Erickson, D. (1999). Prospective analysis of the relation between DSM-III anxiety disorders and alcohol use disorders. *American Journal of Psychiatry, 156,* 723–732.

Kutchins, H., & Kirk, S. A. (1997). *Making us crazy; DSM: The psychiatric bible and the creation of mental disorders.* New York: The Free Press.

Lahey, B. B., Loeber, R., Burke, J., & Rathouz, P. J. (2002). Adolescent outcomes of childhood conduct disorder among clinic-referred boys: Predictors of improvement. *Journal of Abnormal Child Psychology, 30*(4), 333–349.

Lahey, B., & Waldman, I. (2003). A developmental propensity model of the origins of conduct problems during childhood and adolescence. In B. Lahey, T. E. Moffitt, & A. Caspi (Eds.), *Causes of conduct disorder and juvenile delinquency* (pp. 76–117). New York: Guilford Press.

Laidlow, K., Thompson, L., Gallagher-Thompson, Dick-Siskin, L. (2003). *Cognitive behaviour therapy with older people.* Hoboken, NJ.: John Wiley & Sons.

Lainhart, J. (1999). Psychiatric problems in individuals with autism, their parents and siblings. *International Review of Psychiatry, 11,* 278–298.

Lam, K. S. L., Aman, M. G., & Arnold, L. E. (2005). Neurochemical correlates of autistic disorder: A review of the literature. *Research in Developmental Disabilities, 27*(3).

Langley, G. C., & Klopper, H. (2005). Trust as a foundation for the therapeutic intervention for patients with borderline personality disorder. *Journal of Psychiatric and Mental Health Nursing, 12*(1), 23–32.

Larimer, M., Palmer, R., & Marlatt, A. (1999). Relapse prevention: An overview of Marlatt's cognitive-behavioral model. *Alcohol Research and Health, 23,* 151–160.

Latimer, J. (2001). A meta-analytic examination of youth delinquency, family treatment, and recidivism. *Canadian Journal of Criminology, 43,* 237–252.

Lauque, S., Arnaud-Battandier, F., Gillette, S., Plaze, J. M., Andrieu, S., Cantet, C., & Vellas, B. (2004). Improvement of weight and fat-free mass with oral nutritional supplementation in patients with Alzheimer's disease at risk of malnutrition: A prospective randomized study. *Journal of the American Geriatrics Society, 52*(10), 1702–1707.

Lavretsky, H., Nguyen, L. H., & Goldstein, M. Z. (2006). Diagnosis and treatment of neuropsychiatric symptoms in Alzheimer's disease. *Psychiatric Services, 57*(5), 617–619.

Le, H. N., Munoz, R., Ippen, C. G., & Stoddard, J. (2003). Treatment is not enough: We must prevent major depression in women. *Prevention and Treatment.* Retrieved on December 31, 2003, at http://80gateway1.ovid.com .proxy.library.vcu.edu/ovidweb.cgi.

Ledingham, J. (1999). Children and adolescents with oppositional defiant disorder and conduct disorder in the community: Experiences at school and with peers. In H. Quay & A. Hogan (Eds.), *Handbook of disruptive behavior disorders* (pp. 353–370). New York: Kluwer Academic/Plenum Publishers.

Leiberman, J., Stroup, S., McEvoy, J., Swartz, M., Rosenheck, R., Perkins, D., Keefe, R., Davis, S., Davis, C., Lebowitz, B., Severe, J., & Hsiao, J. (2005). Effectiveness of antipsychotic drugs in patients with chronic schizophrenia. *New England Journal of Medicine, 353,* 1209–1223.

Lemery, K. S., & Doelger, L. (2005). Genetic vulnerabilities to the development of psychopathology. In B. L. Hankin & J. R. Z. Abela (Eds.), *Development of psychopathology: A vulnerability-stress perspective* (pp. 161–198). Thousand Oaks, CA: Sage Publications.

Lenoir, M. E., Dingemans, P., Schene, A. H., Hart, A. A., & Linszen, D. H. (2002). The course of parental expressed emotion and psychotic episodes after family intervention in recent-onset schizophrenia: A longitudinal study. *Social Psychiatry and Psychiatric Epidemiology, 39*(2), 69–75.

Lenzenweger, M. F., Lane, M. C., Loranger, A. W., & Kessler, R. C. (2007). DSM-IV personality disorders in the National Comorbidity Survey Replication. *Biological Psychiatry,* in press, corrected proof.

Leonard, B. E. (2003). *Fundamentals of psychopharmacology.* New York: Martin Duwitz.

Leucht, S., McGrath, J., White, P., & Kissling, W. (2002). Carbamazepine for schizophrenia and schizoaffective psychosis. *Cochrane Database of Systematic Reviews, 3,* Art. No. CD001258.

Leventhal, T., & Brooks-Gunn, J. (2003). Children and youth in neighborhood contexts. *Current Directions in Psychological Sciences, 12*(1), 27–31.

Levy, F., Hay, D. A., & Bennett, K. S. (2006). Genetics of attention-deficit/hyperactivity disorder: A current review and future prospects. *International Journal of Disability, Development and Education, 53*(1), 5–20.

Lewinsohn, P. M., Streigel-Moore, R. H., & Seeley, J. R. (2000). Epidemiology and natural course of eating disorders in young women from adolescence to young adulthood. *Journal of the American Academy of Child and Adolescent Psychiatry, 39,* 1284–1292.

Lewinsohn, P., & Essau, C. (2002). Depression in adolescents. In I. H. Gotlib & C. Hammen (Eds.), *Handbook of depression* (pp. 541–559). New York: Guilford Press.

Lewinsohn, P., Clarke, G., Hops, H., & Andrews, J. (1990). Cognitive-behavioral treatment for depressed adolescents. *Behavior Therapy, 21,* 385–401.

Lewinsohn, P., Clarke, G., Rhode, P., Hops, H., & Seeley, J. (1996). A course in coping: A cognitive-behavioral approach to the treatment of adolescent depression. In E. D. Hibbs & P. S. Jensen (Eds.), *Psychosocial treatments for child and adolescent disorders: Empirically based strategies for clinical practice* (pp. 109–135). Washington, DC: American Psychological Association.

Lichtenberg, P. A., Kemp-Havican, J., MacNeill, S. E., & Johnson, A. S. (2005). Pilot study of behavioral treatment in dementia care units. *Gerontologist, 45,* 406–410.

Liddle, H. A., Dakof, G. A., & Parker, K. (2001). Multidimensional family therapy for adolescent drug abuse:

Results of a randomized clinical trial. *American Journal of Drug and Alcohol Abuse, 27*(4), 651–688.

Lieberman, J., Stroup, S., McEvoy, J., Swartz, M., Rosenheck, R., Perkins, D., Keefe, R., Davis, S., Davis, C., Lebowitz, B., Severe, J., & Hsiao, J. (2005). Effectiveness of antipsychotic drugs in patients with chronic schizophrenia. *New England Journal of Medicine, 353,* 1209–1223.

Linehan, M. M. (1993). *Cognitive behavioral treatment of borderline clients.* New York: Guilford Press.

Linnet, K. M., Dalsgaard, S., Obel, C., Wisborg, K., Henriksen, T. B., Rodriguez, A., Kotimaa, A., Moilanen, I., Thomsen, P. H., Olsen, J., & Jarvelin, M. R. (2003). Maternal lifestyle factors in pregnancy risk of attention deficit hyperactivity disorder and associated behaviors: Review of the current evidence. *American Journal of Psychiatry, 160*(6), 1028–1040.

Littell, J. H., Popa, M., & Forsythe, B. (2005). Multisystemic therapy for social, emotional, and behavioral problems in youth aged 10–17 (Cochrane Review). In (Ed.), *The Cochrane Library, Issue 3.* Chichester, UK: John Wiley & Sons, Ltd.

Livesley, W. J. (2004). Changing ideas about the treatment of borderline personality disorder. *Journal of Contemporary Psychotherapy, 34*(3), 185–192.

Loeber, R., & Coie, J. (2001). Continuities and discontinuities of development, with particular emphasis on emotional and cognitive components of disruptive behaviour. In J. Hill & B. Maughan (Eds.), *Conduct disorders in childhood and adolescence* (pp. 379–407). NY: Cambridge University Press.

Loeber, R., Burke, J. D., Lagey, B. B., Winters, A., & Zera, M. (2000). Oppositional defiant and conduct disorder: A review of the past 10 years, part I. *Journal of the American Academy of Child and Adolescent Psychiatry, 39*(12), 1468–1484.

Loeber, R., Farrington, D., Stouthamer-Loeber, M., & Van Kammen, W. (1998). *Antisocial behavior and mental health problems: Explanatory factors in childhood and adolescence.* Mahwah, NJ: Lawrence Erlbaum.

Loeber, R., Green, S. M., Lahey, B. B., Frick, P. J., & McBurnett, K. (2002). Findings on disruptive behavior disorders from the first decade of the Developmental Trends Study. *Clinical Child and Family Psychology Review, 3,* 37–60.

Lonergan, E., Luxenberg, J., Colford, J., & Birks, J. (2007). Haloperidol for agitation in dementia. *The Cochrane Database of Systematic Reviews.* Issue 1 DOI: 10.1002/14651858.CD002852.

Longabaugh, R., Wirtz, P., Zweben, A., & Stout, R. (1998). Network support for drinking: Alcoholics Anonymous and long term matching effects. *Addiction, 93,* 1313–1333.

López, A., & Birks, J. (2007). Nimodipine for primary degenerative, mixed and vascular dementia. *The Cochrane Database of Systematic Reviews.* Issue 1 DOI: 10.1002/14651858.CD000147.

Lord, C., Risi, S., & Lambrecht, L. (2000). The Autism Diagnostic Observation Schedule—Generic: A standard measure of social and communication deficits associated with the spectrum of autism. *Journal of Autism and Developmental Disorders, 30*(3), 205–223.

Lord, C., Rutter, M., & LeCouteur, A. (1994). Autism Diagnostic Interview—Revised: A revised version of a diagnostic interview for caregivers of individuals with possible pervasive developmental disorders. *Journal of Autism and Developmental Disorders, 24*(5), 659–685.

Lott, L., & Klein, D.T. (2003). Psychotherapeutic interventions. In D. P. Hay, D. T. Klein, L. K. Hay, G. T. Grossberg, & J. S. Kennedy (Eds.), *Agitation in patients with dementia: A practical guide to diagnosis and management* (pp. 103–118). Washington, DC: American Psychiatric Publishing.

Lowe, M. R. (2002). Dietary restraint and overeating. In K. D. Brownell (Ed.), *Eating disorders and obesity* (pp. 88–92). New York: Guilford.

Lowe, M. R., & Timko, C. A., (2004). What a difference a diet makes: Towards an understanding of differences between restrained dieters and restrained nondieters. *Eating Behaviors, 5*(3), 199–208.

Lu, P. H., Masterlund, D. A., Mulnard, R., Cotman, C., Miller. B., Yaffe, K., Reback, E., Porter, V., & Swerdloff, R. (2006). Effects of testosterone on cognition and mood in male patients with mild Alzheimer's disease and healthy elder men. *Archives of Neurology, 63*(2), 177–185.

Lu, Y. Y., & Austrom, M. G. (2005). Distress responses and self-care behaviors in dementia family caregivers with high and low depressed mood. *Journal of the American Psychiatric Nurses Association, 11*(4), 231–240.

Lundahl, B., Risser, H. J., & Lovejoy, M. C. (2006). A meta-analysis of parent training: Moderators and follow-up effects. *Clinical Psychology Review, 26*, 86–104.

Lyketsos, C. G., Steinberg, M., Tschanz, J. T., Norton, M. C., Steffens, D. C., & Breitner, J. C. S. (2000). Mental and behavioral disturbances in dementia: Findings from the Cache County study on memory in aging. *American Journal of Psychiatry, 157*, 708–714.

Lynch, T. R., Chapman, A. L., & Rosenthal, M. Z. (2006). Mechanisms of change in dialectical behavior therapy: Theoretical and empirical observations. *Journal of Clinical Psychology, 62*(4), 459–480.

Lynch, W. J., Roth, M. E., & Carrol, M. E. (2002). Biological basis of sex differences in drug abuse: Preclinical and clinical studies. *Psychopharmacology, 164*, 121–137.

Mackinnon, D., Potash, J., McMahon, F., & Simpson, S. (2005). Rapid mood switching and suicidality in familial bipolar disorder. *Bipolar Disorders: An International Journal of Psychiatry and Neurosciences, 7*(5), 441.

Mackin, R. S., & Arean, P. (2005). Evidence-based psychotherapeutic interventions for geriatric depression. *Psychiatric Clinics of North America, 28*, 805–820.

Maddi, S. R. (1996). *Personality theories: A comparative analysis (6th ed.)*. Pacific Grove, CA: Brooks/Cole.

Magda, C., Schopler, E., Cueva, J. E., & Hallin, A. (1996). Treatment of autistic disorder. *Journal of the American Academy of Child and Adolescent Psychiatry, 35*(2), 134–143.

Mahoney, D. F., Tarlow, B. J., & Jones, R. B. (2003). Effects of an automated telephone support system on caregiver burden and anxiety: Findings from the REACH for TLC intervention study. *Gerontologist, 43*(4), 556–567.

Malaspina, D., Goetz, R. R., Friedman, J. H., Kaufmann, C. A., Faraone, S. V., Tsuang, M., C.lininger, C. R., Nurnberger, J. I., & Blehar, M. C. (2001). Traumatic brain injury and schizophrenia in members of schizophrenia and bipolar disorder pedigrees. *American Journal of Psychiatry, 158*(3), 440–446.

Malmberg, L., & Fenton, M. (2005). Individual psychodynamic psychotherapy and psychoanalysis for schizophrenia and severe mental illness. *The Cochrance Database of Systematic Reviews, 4*, Art. No. CD001360.

Mandell, D. S., & Palmer, R. (2005). Differences among states in the identification of autistic spectrum disorders. *Archives of Pediatric and Adolescent Medicine, 159*, 266–269.

Mandell, D. S., Listerud, J., Levy, S. E., & Pinto-Martin, J. A. (2002). Race differences in the age at diagnosis among Medicaid-eligible children with autism. *Journal of the American Academy of Child and Adolescent Psychiatry, 41*(12), 1447–1454.

Mandell, D. S., Novak, M. & Zubritsky, L. (2005). The role of culture in families' treatment decisions for children with autism spectrum disorders. *Mental Retardation and Developmental Disabilities Research Reviews, 11*(2), 110–115.

Mann, K., Lehert, P., & Morgan, M. Y. (2004). The efficacy of Acamprosate in the maintenance of abstinence in alcohol-dependent individuals: Results of a meta-analysis. *Alcoholism: Clinical and Experimental Research, 28*(1), 51–63.

Mannuzza, S., & Klein, R. (1999). Adolescent and adult outcomes in attention-deficit/hyperactivity disorder. In H. Quay & A. Hogan (Eds.), *Handbook of disruptive behavior disorders* (pp. 279–294). New York: Plenum Publishers.

Mannuzza, S., Klein, R., & Moulton, J. (2002). Young adult outcome of children with "situational" hyperactivity: A prospective, controlled, follow-up study. *Journal of Abnormal Child Psychology, 30*, 191–198.

Mantere, O., Melartin, T. K., Suominen, K., Rytsala, H. J., Valtonen, H. M., Arvilommi, P., Leppamaki, S., & Isometsa, E. T. (2006). Differences in axis I and axis II comorbidity between bipolar I and II disorders and major depressive disorder. *Journal of Clinical Psychiatry, 67*(4), 584–593.

Marangell, L. B., Kupfer, D. J., Sachs, G. S., & Swann, A. C. (2006). Emerging therapies for bipolar depression. *Journal of Clinical Psychiatry, 67*(7), 1140–1151.

Maracek, J. (2006). Social suffering, gender, and women's depression. In C. L. M. Keyes & S. H. Goodman (Eds.), *Women and depression: Handbook for the social, behavioral, and biomedical sciences* (pp. 283–308). New York: Cambridge University Press.

Marriott, R., Neil, W., & Waddingham, S. (2006). Antipsychotic medication for elderly people with schizophrenia. *Cochrane Database of Systematic Reviews, 1*, Art. No. CD005580.

Marshall, M., & Lockwood, A. (2003). Early intervention for psychosis. *Cochrane Database of Systematic Reviews, 2*, Art. No. CD004718.

Marshall, M., Crowther, R., Almaraz-Serrano, A., Creed, F., Sledge, W., Kluiter, W., Perkins, D. O., Miller-Anderson, L., & Lieberman, J. A. (2006). Natural history and predictors of clinical course. In J. A Lieberman, T. S. Stroup, & D. O. Perkins (Eds.), *The American Psychiatric Publishing textbook of schizophrenia* (pp. 289–301). Washington, DC: American Psychiatric Publishing.

Martin, C., Kelly, T., Rayens, M. K., Brogli, B. R., Brenzel, A., Smith, W. J., & Omar, H. (2002). Sensation seeking, puberty and nicotine, alcohol and marijuana use in adolescence. *Journal of the American Academy of Child and Adolescent Psychiatry, 41*, 1495–1502.

Martin, M. M., Orsillo, S. M., & Roemer, L. (2001). Practitioner's guide to empirically based measures of anxiety. In (Ed.), (pp. 159–164). Dordrecht, Netherlands: Kluwer Academic Publishers.

Martin-Cook, K., Remakel-Davis, B., Svetlick, D., Hynan, L. S., & Weiner, M. F. (2003). Caregiver attribution and resentment in dementia care. *American Journal of Alzheimer's Disease and Other Dementias, 18*(6), 366–374.

Martino, S., Carroll, K., Kostas, D., Perkins, J., & Rounsaville, B. (2002). Dual diagnosis motivational interviewing: A modification of motivational interviewing for substance-abusing patients with psychotic disorders. *Journal of Substance Abuse Treatment, 23*, 297–308.

Marziali, E. (2002). Borderline personality disorders. In A. R. Roberts & G. J. Greene (Eds.), *Social workers' desk reference* (pp. 360–364). New York: Oxford University Press.

Mason, D., & Frick, P. (1994). The heritability of antisocial behavior: A meta-analysis of twin and adoption studies. *Journal of Psychopathology and Behavioral Assessment, 16,* 301–323.

Matson, J. L., & Minshawi, N. F. (2006). *Early intervention for autism spectrum disorders: A critical analysis.* New York: Elsevier Science

Matson, J. L., & Minshawi, N. F. (2006). *Early intervention for autism spectrum disorders: A critical analysis.* New York: Elsevier Science.

Mattaini, M. (1994). Can personalities be disordered? No. In S. A. Kirk & S. D. Einbinder (Eds.), *Controversial issues in mental health* (pp. 48–54). Boston: Allyn and Bacon.

Matza, L. S., Rajagopalan, K. S., Thompson, C. L., & Lissovoy, G. (2005). Misdiagnosed patients with bipolar disorder: Comorbidities, treatment patterns, and direct treatment costs. *Journal of Clinical Psychiatry, 66*(11), 1432–1440.

Maughan, B., & Rutter, M. (2001). Antisocial children grown up. In J. Hill & B. Maughan (Eds.), *Conduct disorders in childhood and adolescence* (pp. 507–552). New York: Cambridge University Press.

McClellan, J., & Werry, J. (2000). Summary of the practice parameters for the assessment and treatment of children and adolescents with schizophrenia. *Journal of the American Academy of Child and Adolescent Psychiatry, 39*(12), 1580–1582.

McClellan, J., & Werry, J. S. (2003). Evidence-based treatments in child and adolescent psychiatry: An inventory. *Journal of the American Academy of Child and Adolescent Psychiatry, 42,* 1388–1400.

McClelland, G. M., Elkington, K. S., Teplin, L. A., & Abram, K. M. (2004). Multiple substance use disorders in juvenile detainees. *American Academy of Child and Adolescent Psychiatry, 43,* 1215–1224.

McClendon, M. J., Smyth, K. A., & Neundorfer, M. M. (2004). Survival of persons with Alzheimer's disease: Caregiver coping matters. *Gerontologist, 44*(4), 508–519.

McCrady, B. (2005). Alcohol use disorders and the Division 12 task force of the American Psychological Association. *Psychology of Addictive Behaviors, 14,* 267–276.

McCrady, B. S., Noel, N. E., Abrams, D. B., Stout, R. L., Nelson, H. F., & Hay, W. M. (1986). Comparative effectiveness of three types of spouse involvement in outpatient behavioral alcoholism treatment. *Journal of Studies on Alcohol, 47,* 459–467.

McCullough, M. E., Larson, D. B., Hoyt, W. T., & Koenig, H. G. (2000). Religious involvement and mortality: A meta-analytic review. *Health Psychology, 19*(3), 211–223.

McDermut, W., Miller, I. W., & Brown, R. A. (2001). The efficacy of group psychotherapy for depression: A meta-analysis and review of the empirical research. *Clinical Psychology: Science and Practice, 8*(1), 98–116.

McGee, R., & Williams, S. (1999). Environmental risk factors in oppositional-defiant disorder and conduct disorder. In H. Quay, C. Herbert, & A. Hogan (Eds.), *Handbook of disruptive behavior disorders* (pp. 419–440). Dordrecht, Netherlands: Kluwer Academic Publishers.

McGlashan, T. H., Miller, T. J., & Woods, S. W. (2001). Pre-onset detection and intervention research in schizophrenia psychoses: Current estimates of benefit and risk. *Schizophrenia Bulletin, 27*(4), 563–570.

McGuffin, P., Rijsdijk, F., Andrew, M., Sham, P., Katz, R., & Cardino, A. (2003). The heritability of bipolar affective disorder and the genetic relationship to unipolar depression. *Archives of General Psychiatry, 60,* 497–502.

McHugo, G. J., Mooney, D., Racusin, R., Ford, J. D., & Fleischer, A. (2000). Predicting posttraumatic stress after hospitalization for pediatric injury. *Journal of the American Academy of Child and Adolescent Psychiatry, 39*(5), 576–583.

McIntosh, D. E., & Trotter, J. S. (2006). Early onset bipolar spectrum disorder: Psychopharmacological, psychological, and educational management. *Psychology in the Schools, 43*(4), 451–460.

McIntosh, V. V., Jordan, J., Carter, F. A., Luty, S. E., McKenzie, J. M., Bulik, C. M., Frampton, C. M., & Joyce, P. R. (2005). Three psychotherapies for anorexia nervosa: A randomized, controlled trial. *American Journal of Psychiatry, 162,* 741–747.

McKay, J. (1999). Studies of factors in relapse to alcohol, drug and nicotine use: A critical review of methodologies and findings. *Journal of Studies on Alcohol, 60,* 566–576.

McKerchar, P. M., & Thompson, R. H. (2004). A descriptive analysis of potential reinforcement contingencies in the preschool classroom. *Journal of Applied Behavior Analysis, 37*(4), Win 2004., pp. 431–444.

McMahon, R. J. (1994). Diagnosis, assessment, and treatment of externalizing problems in children: The role of longitudinal data. *Journal of Consulting and Clinical Psychology, 62,* 901–917.

McMahon, R. J., & Frick, P. J. (2005). Evidence-based assessment of conduct problems in children and adolescents. *Journal of Clinical Child and Adolescent Psychology, 34*(3), 477–505.

McMurtray, A. M., Ringman, J., & Chao, S. Z. (2006). Family history of dementia in early-onset versus very late-onset Alzheimer's disease. *International Journal of Geriatric Psychiatry, 21*(6), 597–598.

McShane, R., Areosa-Sastre, M., & Minakaran, N. (2007). Memantine for dementia. *The Cochrane Database of Systematic Reviews.* Issue 1 DOI: 10.1002/14651858. CD003154 .pub5

Meeks, T. W., Ropacki, S. A., & Jeste, D. V. (2006). The neurobiology of neuropsychiatric syndromes in dementia. *Current Opinion in Psychiatry, 19*(6), 581–586.

Meinecke, D. L. (2001). Editor's introduction: The developmental etiology of schizophrenia hypothesis: What is the evidence? *Schizophrenia Bulletin, 27*(3), 335–336.

Merikangas, K. R., Akiskal, H. S., Angst, J., Greenberg, P. E., Hirschfeld, R. M. A., Petukhova, M., & Kessler, R. C. (2007). Lifetime and 12-month prevalence of bipolar spectrum disorder in the national comorbidity survey replication. *Archives of General Psychiatry, 64,* 543–552.

Metiteri, T., Zanetti, O., Geroldi, C., Frisoni, G. B., DeLeo, D., Dello Buono, M., Bianchetti, A., & Trabucchi, M. (2001). Reality orientation therapy to delay outcomes of progression in patients with dementia: A retrospective study. *Clinical Rehabilitation, 15*(5), 471–478.

Miklowitz, D. J., & Otto, M. W. (2006). New psychosocial interventions for bipolar disorder: A review of literature and introduction of the systematic treatment enhancement program. *Journal of Cognitive Psychotherapy, 20*(2).

Miklowitz, D. J., Otto, M. W., & Frank, E. (2007). Psychosocial treatments for bipolar depression: A 1-year randomized trial from the Systematic Treatment Enhancement Program. *Archives of General Psychiatry, 64*(4), 419–427.

Miklowitz, D. J., Wisniewski, S. M., Otto, M. W., & Sachs, G. S. (2005). Perceived criticism from family members as a predictor of the one-year course of bipolar disorder. *Psychiatry Research, 136*(2–3), 101–111.

Miller, I. W., Keitner, G. I., Ryan, C. E., Solomon, D. A., Beevers, C. G., & Cardemil, E. V. (2005). Treatment matching in the posthospital care of depressed patients. *American Journal of Psychiatry, 162,* 2131–2138.

Miller, L., Davies, M., & Greenwald, S. (2000). Religiosity and substance use and abuse among adolescents in the National Comorbidity Survey. *Journal of the*

American Academy of Child and Adolescent Psychiatry, 39(9), 1190–1197.

Miller, W., & Rollnick, S. (2002). *Motivational interviewing: Preparing people to change addictive behavior (2nd ed.).* New York: Guilford Press.

Miller-Johnson, S., Coie, J. D., Maumary-Gremaud, A., & Bierman, K. (2002). Peer rejection and aggression and early starter models of conduct disorder. *Journal of Abnormal Child Psychology, 30*(3), 217–231.

Mineka, S., & Zinbarg, R. (2006). A contemporary learning theory perspective on the etiology of anxiety disorders: It's not what you thought it was. *American Psychologist, 61*, 1–25.

Mirin, S., Batki, S., Bukstein, O., Isbell, P., Kleber, H., Schottenfeld, R., Weiss, R., & Yandow, V. (2002). Practice guideline for the treatment of patients with substance use disorders: Alcohol, cocaine, opioids. *American Psychiatric Association practice guidelines for the treatment of psychiatric disorders: Compendium 2002* (pp. 249–348). Washington, DC: American Psychiatric Association.

Mittelman, M. S., Roth, D. L., Haley, W. E., & Zarit, S. H., (2004). Effects of a caregiver intervention on negative caregiver appraisals of behavior problems in patients with Alzheimer's disease: Results of a randomized trial. *Journals of Gerontology: Series B: Psychological Sciences and Social Sciences, 59B*(1), 27–P34.

Mizes, J. S., & Palermo, T. M. (1997). Eating disorders. In R. T. Ammerman & M. Hersen (Eds.), *Handbook of prevention and treatment with children and adolescents: Intervention in the real world context* (pp. 238–258). New York: John Wiley.

Moffitt, T. (2003). Life-course persistent and adolescence-limited antisocial behavior: A 10-year research review and research agenda. In B. Lahey, T. Moffitt, & A. Caspi (Eds.), *Causes of conduct disorder and juvenile delinquency* (pp. 49–75). New York: Guilford Press.

Moffitt, T., Caspi, A., Harrington, H., & Milne, B. (2002). Males on the life-course-persistent and adolescence-limited antisocial pathways: Follow-up at age 26 years. *Development and Psychopathology, 14*, 179–207.

Moffitt, T., Caspi, A., Rutter, M., & Silva, P. (2001). *Sex differences in antisocial behavior: Conduct disorder, delinquency, and violence in the Dunedin longitudinal study.* New York: Cambridge University Press.

Mohr, D. C., Hart, S. L., & Julian, L. (2005). Telephone-administered psychotherapy for depression. *Archives of General Psychiatry, 62*, 1007–1014.

Moncrieff, J., Hopker, S., & Thomas, P. (2005). Psychiatry and the pharmaceutical industry: Who pays the piper? *Psychiatric Bulletin* (2005) 29: 84–85.

Moncrieff, J., Wessely, S., & Hardy, R. (2004). Active placebos versus antidepressants for depression. *Cochrane Database of Systematic Reviews, 1*, 1–2.

Mond, J. M., Hay, P. J., Rodgers, B., & Owen, C. (2006). An update on the definition of "excessive exercise" in eating disorders research. *International Journal of Eating Disorders, 39*, 147–153.

Morano, C. L. (2003). Appraisal and coping: Moderators or mediators of stress in Alzheimer's disease caregivers. *Social Work Research, 27*(2), 116–128.

Morano, C. L., & Saunders, S. (2006). Exploring differences in depression, role captivity, and self-acceptance in Hispanic and non-Hispanic adult children caregivers. *Journal of Ethnic and Cultural Diversity in Social Work, 14*(1–2), 27–46.

Moreau, D., Mufson, L., Weissman, M., & Klerman, G. (1991). Interpersonal psychotherapy for adolescent depression: Description of modification and preliminary application. *Journal of the American Academy of Child and Adolescent Psychiatry, 30*, 642–651.

Mueller, T. I., Leon, A. C., Keller, M. B., Solomon, D. A., Endicott, J., Coryell, W., Warshaw, M., & Maser, J. D. (1999). Recurrence after recovery from major depressive disorder during 15 years of observational follow-up. *American Journal of Psychiatry, 156*, 1000–1006.

Mueser, K. T., Bond, G. R., Drake, R. E., & Resnick, S. G. (1998). Models of community care for severe mental illness: A review of research on case management. *Schizophrenia Bulletin, 24*, 37–74.

Muise, A., Stein, D., & Arbess, G. (2003). Eating disorders in adolescent boys: A review of the adolescent and young adult literature. *Journal of Adolescent Health, 33*, 427–435.

Multimodal Treatment Study of Children with Attention-Deficit/Hyperactivity Disorder Cooperative Group. (1999). A 14-month randomized clinical trial of treatment strategies for attention-deficit/hyperactivity disorder. *Archives of General Psychiatry, 56*, 1073–1086.

Mulvany, F., O'Callaghan, E., Takei, N., Byrne, M., & Fearon, P. (2001). Effects of social class at birth on risk and presentation of schizophrenia: Case-control study. *British Medical Journal, 323*(7326), 1398–1401.

Murray, R. M., Jones, P. B., & Susser, E. (2003). *The epidemiology of schizophrenia.* New York: Cambridge University Press.

Murphy, K. R., & Adler, L. A. (2004). Assessing attention-deficit/hyperactivity disorder in adults: Focus on rating scales. *Journal of Clinical Psychiatry, 65*(3), 12–17.

Nakash-Eisikovitz, O., Dierberger, A., & Westen, D. (2002). A multidimensional meta-analysis of pharmacotherapy for bulimia nervosa: Summarizing the range of outcomes in controlled clinical trials. *Harvard Review of Psychiatry, 10*, 193–211.

Nelson-Zlupko, L., Kauffman, E., & Dore, M. M. (1995). Gender differences in drug addiction and treatment: Implications for social work intervention with substance-abusing women. *Social Work, 40*, 45–54.

Nemeroff, C. B. (2000). An ever-increasing pharmacopoeia for the management of patients with bipolar disorder. *Journal of Clinical Psychiatry, 61*(Suppl. 13), 19–25.

Newcomer, S., & Udry, J. (1985). Parent-child communication and adolescent sexual behavior. *Family Planning Perspectives, 17*, 169–174.

Newman, C. F. (2006). Bipolar disorder. In F. Andrasik (Ed.), *Comprehensive handbook of personality and psychopathology: Vol. 2: Adult psychopathology* (pp. 244–261). Hoboken, NJ: John Wiley.

Nguyen, N., Fakra, E., & Pradel, V. (2006). Efficacy of etifoxine compared to lorazepam monotherapy in the treatment of patients with adjustment disorders with anxiety: A double-blind controlled study in general practice. *Human Psychopharmacology: Clinical and Experimental, 21*(3), 139–149.

Ni, X., Chan, K., & Bulgin, N. (2006). Association between serotonin transporter gene and borderline personality disorder. *Journal of Psychiatric Research, 40*(5), 448–453.

Nigg, J., & Huang-Pollock, C. (2003). An early-onset model of the role of executive functions and intelligence in conduct disorder/delinquency. In B. Lahey, T. E. Moffitt, & A. Caspi (Eds.), *Causes of conduct disorder and juvenile delinquency* (pp. 227–253). New York: Guilford Press.

Nock, M. K., Kazdin, A. E., Hiripi, E., & Kessler, R. C. (2006). Prevalence, subtypes, and correlates of DSM-IV conduct disorder in the National Comorbidity Survey Replication. *Psychological Medicine, 1*–12.

Nolen-Hoeksema, S. (2002). Gender differences in depression. In I. H. Gotlib & C. Hammen (Eds.), *Handbook of depression* (pp. 492–509). New York: Guilford Press.

Norcross, J., Beutler, L., & Levant, R. (Eds.) (2006). *Evidence-based practices in mental health.* Washington, DC: American Psychological Association.

Nose, M., Cipriani, A., Biancosino, B., Grassi, L., & Barbui, C. (2006). Efficacy of pharmacotherapy against core traits of borderline personality disorder: Meta-analysis of randomized controlled trials. *International Clinical Psychopharmacology, 21*(6), 345–353.

Nowotny, P., Smemo, S., & Goate, A. M. (2005). Genetic risk factors for late-onset Alzheimer's disease. In C. F. Zorumski & E. H. Rubin (Eds.), *Psychopathology in the genome and neuroscience era* (pp. 51–62). Washington, DC: American Psychiatric Publishing.

O'Hara, M. W., & Swain, A. M. (1996). Rates and risk of postpartum depression-A meta-analysis. *International Review of Psychiatry, 8,* 37–54.

Ohan, J., & Johnston, C. (2005). Gender appropriateness of symptom criteria for attention-deficit/hyperactivity disorder, oppositional-defiant disorder, and conduct disorder. *Child Psychiatry and Human Development, 35,* 359–381.

Olfson, M., Blanco, C., Liu, L., Moreno, C., & Laje, G. (2006). National trends in the outpatients treatment of children and adolescents with antipsychotic drugs. *Archives of General Psychiatry, 63,* 679–685.

Olfson, M., Marcus, S. C., Druss, B., Elinson, L., Tanielian, T., & Pincus, H. A. (2002). National trends in the outpatient treatment of depression. *Journal of the American Medical Association, 287,* 203–209.

Olfson, M., Marcus, S. C., Tedeschi, M., & Wan, G. J. (2006). Continuity of antidepressant treatment for adults with depression in the United States. *American Journal of Psychiatry, 163,* 101–108.

Olsen, C. E., Poulsen, H. D., & Lubline, H. K. F. (2005). Drug therapy of dementia in elderly patients: A review. *Nordic Journal of Psychiatry, 59*(2), 71–77.

Onder, G., Orazio, Z., & Ezio, G. (2005). Reality orientation therapy combined with cholinesterase inhibitors in Alzheimer's disease: Randomized controlled trial. *British Journal of Psychiatry, 187*(5), 450–455.

O'Neill, S. (2003). African American women and eating disturbances: A meta-analysis. *Journal of Black Psychology, 29,* 3–16.

Orwin, R., Maranda, M., & Brady, T. (2001). *Impact of prior physical and sexual victimization on substance abuse treatment outcomes.* Report prepared under Contract No. 270-97-7016 for the Center for Substance Abuse Treatment. Fairfax, VA: Caliber Associates.

Ownby, R. L., Crocco, E., Acevedo, A., John, V., & Loewenstein, D. (2006). Depression and risk for Alzheimer's disease. *Archives of General Psychiatry, 63,* 530–538.

Ozer, E., Best, S., Lipsey, T., & Weiss, D. (2003). Predictors of posttraumatic stress disorder and symptoms in adults: A meta-analysis. *Psychological Bulletin, 129,* 52–73.

Ozonoff, S., Rogers, S. J., & Hendren, R. L. (Eds.) (2005). *Autism spectrum disorders: A research review for practitioners.* Washington, DC: American Psychiatric Publishing.

Papassotiropoulos, A., Fountoulakis, M., Dunckley, T., Stephan, D. A., & Reiman, E. M. (2006). Genetics, transcriptomics, and proteomics of Alzheimer's disease. *Journal of Clinical Psychiatry, 67*(4), 652–670.

Pappadopulos, E., Woolston, S., Chait, A., Perkins, M., Connor, D. F., & Jensen, P. S. (2006). Pharmacotherapy of aggression in children and adolescents: Efficacy and effect size. *Journal of the Canadian Academy of Child and Adolescent Psychiatry, 15*(1), 27–39.

Paris, J. (2003). *Personality disorders over time: Precursors, course, and outcome.* Washington, DC: American Psychiatric Publishing.

Patrick, L., Perugini, M., & Leclerc, C. (2002). Neuropsychological assessment and competency for independent living among geriatric patients. *Topics in Geriatric Rehabilitation, 17*(4), 65–78.

Patterson, G., & Guillon, M. (1968). *Living with children: New methods for parents and teachers.* Champaign, IL: Research Press.

Patton, G. C., Selzer, R., Coffey, C., Carlin, J. B., & Wolfe, R. (1999). Onset of adolescent eating disorders: Population based cohort study over 3 years. *British Medical Journal, 318,* 765–768.

Pelham, W. E., Fabiano, G. A., & Massetti, G. M. (2005). Evidence-based assessment of attention deficit hyperactivity disorder in children and adolescents. *Journal of Clinical Child and Adolescent Psychology, 34*(3), 449–476.

Peliosa, L., & Lund, S. (2001). A selective overview of issues on classification, causation, and early intensive behavioral intervention for autism. *Behavior Modification, 25*(5), 678–697.

Penza, K., Heim, C., & Nemeroff, C. (2006). Trauma and depression. In C. L. M. Keyes & S. H. Goodman (Eds.), *Women and depression: Handbook for the social, behavioral, and biomedical sciences* (pp. 360–381). New York: Cambridge University Press.

Perkins, D. O., Miller-Anderson, L., & Lieberman, J. A. (2006). Natural history and predictors of clinical course. In J. A. Lieberman, J. A. Stroup, & D. O. Perkins (Eds.), *The american psychiatric publishing textbook of schizophrenia* (pp. 289–301). Washington, DC: American Psychiatric Publishing.

Perlis, R. H., Welge, J. A., Vornik, M. S., Herschfeld, R. M. A., & Keck, P. E. (2006). Atypical antipsychotics in the treatment of mania: A meta-analysis of randomized, placebo-controlled trials. *Journal of Clinical Psychiatry, 67*(4), 509–516.

Perrin, S., Smith, P., & Yule, W. (2000). Practitioner review: The assessment and treatment of post-traumatic stress disorder in children and adolescents. *Journal of Child Psychology and Psychiatry and Allied Disciplines, 41*(3), 277–289.

Perry, J. C., Banon, E., & Ianni, F. (1999). Effectiveness of psychotherapy for personality disorders. *American Journal of Psychiatry, 156,* 1312–1321.

Petrakis, I., Gonzalez, G., Rosenheck, R., & Krystal, J. (2002). Comorbidity of alcoholism and psychiatric disorders: An overview. *Alcohol Research and Health, 26,* 81–90.

Petticrew, M., & Roberts, H. (2006). *Systematic reviews in the social sciences: A practical guide.* Malden, MA: Blackwell Publishing.

Pfammatter, M., Junghan, U. N., & Brenner, H. D. (2006). Efficacy of psychological therapy in schizophrenia: Conclusions from meta-analyses. *Schizophrenia Bulletin, 32*(S1), S64.

Pharoah, F. M., Rathbone, J., Mari, J. J., & Streiner, D. (2003). Family intervention for schizophrenia. *Cochrane Database of Systematic Reviews, 3,* Art. No. CD000088.

Phillipe, T., Lalloue, F., & Preux, P. (2006). Dementia patients' caregivers' quality of life: The PIXEL study. *International Journal of Geriatric Psychiatry, 21*(1), 50–56.

Phillips, N. K., Hammen, C. L., Brennan, P. A., Najman, J. M., & Bor, W. (2005). Early adversity and the prospective prediction of depressive and anxiety disorders in adolescents. *Journal of Abnormal Child Psychology, 33,* 13–24.

Pike, K. M., Walsh, B. T., Vitousek, K., Wilson, T., & Bauer, J. (2003). Cognitive behavior therapy in the posthospitalization treatment of anorexia nervosa. *American Journal of Psychiatry, 160,* 2046–2049.

Pilling, S., Bebbington, P., Kuipers, E., Garety, P., Geddes, J., Martindale, B., Orbach, G., & Morgan, C. (2002). Psychological treatments in schizophrenia: II. Meta-analysis of randomized controlled trials of social skills training and cognitive remediation. *Psychological Medicine, 32*(5), 783–791.

Pilowsky, D. J., Wickramaratne, P. J., Rush, A. J., Hughes, C. W., Garber, J., Malloy, E., King, C. A., Cerda, G., Sood, A. B., Alpert, J. E., Wisniewski, S. R., Trivedi, M. H., Talati, A., Carlson, M. M., Lui, H. H., Fava, M., & Weissman, M. M. (2006). Children of currently depressed mothers: A STAR*D ancillary study. *Journal of Clinical Psychiatry, 67*(1), 126–136.

Pinikahana, J., Happell, B., & Keks, N. A. (2003). Suicide and schizophrenia: A review of literature (1990–1999) and implications for mental health nursing. *Issues in Mental Health Nursing, 24*, 24–27.

Pinquant, M., & Sorensen, S. (2006). Ethnic differences in stressors, resources, and psychological outcomes of family caregiving: A meta-analysis. *Gerontologist, 45*, 90–106.

Pliszka, S. (2000). Patterns of psychiatric comorbidity with attention-deficit/hyperactivity disorder. *Child and Adolescent Psychiatric Clinics of North America, 9*, 525–540.

Pliszka, S. R., Crismon, M. L., Hughes, C. W., Conners, C. K., Emslie, G. J., Jensen, P. S., McCracken, J. T., Swanson, J. M., & Lopez, M. (2006). The Texas Children's Medication Algorithm Project: Revision of the algorithm for pharmacotherapy of attention-deficit/hyperactivity disorder. *Journal of the American Academy of Child and Adolescent Psychiatry 45*(6), 642(16).

Pollard, J., Hawkins, D., & Arthur, M. (1999). Risk and protection: Are both necessary to understand diverse behavioral outcomes in adolescence? *Social Work Research, 23*, 145–158.

Polleux, F., & Lauder, J. M. (2004). Toward a developmental neurobiology of autism. *Mental Retardation and Developmental Disabilities Research Reviews, 10*(4), 303–317.

Pompili, M., Mancinelli, I., Girardi, P., Ruberto, A., & Tatarelli, R. (2004). Suicide in anorexia nervosa: A meta-analysis. *International Journal of Eating Disorders, 36*, 99–103.

Popkin, J., & Skinner, C. H. (2003). Enhancing academic performance in a classroom serving students with serious emotional disturbance: Interdependent group contingencies with randomly selected components. *School Psychology Review, 32*, 282–295.

Portzky, G., Audenaert, K., & van Heeringen, K. (2005). Suicide among adolescents: A psychological autopsy study of psychiatric psychosocial and personality-related risk factors. *Social Psychiatry and Psychiatric Epidemiology, 40*(11), 922–930.

Posey, D. J., Erickson, C. A., Stigler, K. A., & McDougle, C. J. (2006). The use of selective serotonin reuptake inhibitors in autism and related disorders. *Journal of Child and Adolescent Psychopharmacology, 16*(1–2), 181–186.

Post, R. M., & Kowatch, R. A. (2006). The health care crisis of childhood-onset bipolar illness: Some recommendation for its amelioration. *Journal of Clinical Psychiatry, 67*(1), 115–125.

Post, R.M., & Kowatch, R.A. (2006). The health care crisis of childhood-onset bipolar illness: Some recommendation for its amelioration. *Journal of Clinical Psychiatry, 67*(1), 115–125.

Post, R. M., Leverich, G. B., King, Q., & Weiss, S. R. (2001). Developmental vulnerabilities to the onset and course of bipolar disorder. *Development and psychopathology, 13*(1), 581–598.

Potvin, S., Sepehry, A. A., & Strip, E. (2006). A meta-analysis of negative symptoms in dual diagnosis schizophrenia. *Psychological Medicine, 36*(4), 431–440.

Pratt, B. M., & Woolfenden, S. R. (2003). Interventions for preventing eating disorders in children and adolescents (Cochrane Review). In *The Cochrane Library,* Issue 1. Oxford: Update Software.

Prendergast, M., Podus, D., & Change, E. (2000) Program factors and treatment outcomes in drug dependence treatment: An examination using meta-analysis. *Substance Use and Misuse, 35*, 1931–1965.

Prinz, R. J., & Miller, G. E. (1991). Issues in understanding and treating childhood conduct problems in disadvantaged populations. *Journal of Clinical Child Psychology, 20*, 379–385.

Project MATCH Research group. (1997). Matching alcoholism treatments to client heterogeneity: Project MATCH posttreatment drinking outcomes. *Journal of Studies on Alcohol, 58*, 7–29.

Punnoose, S., & Belgamwar, M. (2006). Nicotine for schizophrenia. *Cochrane Database of Systematic Reviews, 1*, Art. No. CD004838.

Purdie, N., Hattie, J., & Carroll, A. (2002). A review of the research on interventions for attention deficit hyperactivity disorder: What works best? *Review of Educational Research, 72*(1), 61–99.

Quraishi, S., & Frangou, S. (2002). Neuropsychology of bipolar disorder: A review. *Journal of Affective Disorders, 72*(3), 209–226.

Raicu, R. G., & Workman, R. H. (2000). Management of psychotic and depressive features in patients with vascular dementia. *Topics in Stroke Rehabilitation, 7*(3), 11–19.

Reichenberg, A., Gross, R., Weiser, M., Bresnahan, & Silverman, et al. (2006). Advancing paternal age and autism. *Archives of General Psychiatry, 63*(9), 1026–1032.

Reinecke, M., Ryan, N., & Dubois, D. (1998). Cognitive-behavioral therapy of depression and depressive symptoms during adolescence: A review and meta-analysis. *Journal of the American Academy of Child and Adolescent Psychiatry, 37*, 26–34.

Resnick, M. D., Bearman, P. S., Blum, R. W., Bauman, K. E., Harris, K. M., Jones, J., Tabor, J., Beuhring, T., Sieving, R. E., Shew, M., Ireland, M., Bearinger, L. H., & Udry, J. R. (1997). Protecting adolescents from harm: Findings from the National Longitudinal Study on Adolescent Health. *Journal of the American Medical Association, 278*(10), 823–893.

Rhee, S. H., & Waldman, I. D. (2002). Genetic and environmental influences on antisocial behavior: A meta-analysis of twin and adoption studies. *Psychological Bulletin, 128*(3), 490–529.

Rice, C. (2007). *Prevalence of autism spectrum disorders— Autism and developmental disabilities monitoring network, 14 sites, United States, 2002.* Retrieved 2007, from CDC MMWR surveillance summaries, 56(SS01), 12–28.

Richdale, A. (1999). Sleep problems in autism: Prevalence, cause, and intervention. *Developmental Medicine and Child Neurology, 41*(1), 60–66.

Riggs, D., & Foa, E. (1993). Obsessive compulsive disorder. In D. Barlow (Ed.), *Clinical handbook of psychological disorders: A step-by-step treatment manual* (pp. 189–239). New York: Guilford Press.

Riggs, P., & Whitmore, E. (1999). Substance use disorders and disruptive behavior disorders. In R. Hendren (Ed.), *Disruptive behavior disorders in children and adolescents, Vol. 18, No. 2. Review of psychiatry series* (pp. 133–173). Washington, DC: American Psychiatric Publishing.

Rivera, P. A. (2000) Effectiveness of a psychoeducational intervention for the reduction of distress in Mexican American caregivers of dementia patients. *Dissertation Abstracts International: Section B: The Sciences and Engineering, 60*(8-B), 4248.

Roberson, E. D., & Mucke, L. (2004). 100 years and counting: Prospects for defeating Alzheimer's disease. *Science, 314*(5800), 781–784.

Robin, A. L., Seigel, P. T., Moye, A. W., Gilroy, M., Barker Dennis, A., & Sikand, A. (1999). A controlled comparison of family versus individual therapy for adolescents with anorexia nervosa. *Journal of the American Academy of Child and Adolescent Psychiatry, 38,* 1482–1489.

Robin, A. L., Siegel, P. T., & Moye, A. (1995). Family versus individual therapy for anorexia: Impact on family conflict. *International Journal of Eating Disorders, 17*(4), 313–322.

Robins, C. J. (2002). Dialectical behavior therapy for borderline personality disorder. *Psychiatric Annals, 32*(10), 608–616.

Romano, C. J. (2004). Posttraumatic stress disorder—A continuing controversy in neuropsychiatry. *Neuropsychiatry Reviews, 5,* 9–12.

Rome, E., & Ammerman, S. (2003). Medical complications of eating disorders: An update. *Journal of Adolescent Health, 33,* 418–426.

Root, R. W. II., & Resnick, R. (2003). An update on the diagnosis and treatment of attention-deficit/hyperactivity disorder in children. *Professional Psychology: Research and Practice, 24,* 34–41.

Rosen, A. (2000). Ethics of early prevention in schizophrenia. *Australian and New Zealand Journal of Psychiatry, 34*(Suppl.), S208.

Rosenfarb, I. S., Miklowitz, D. J., Goldstein, M. J., Harmon, L., Nuechterlein, K. H., & Rea, M. M. (2001). Family transactions and relapse in bipolar disorder. *Family Process, 40*(1), 5–14.

Rosenthal, R., & Westreich, L. (1999). Treatment of persons with dual diagnoses of substance use disorder and other psychological problems. In B. McCrady & E. Epstein (Eds.), *Addictions: A comprehensive guidebook* (pp. 439–476). New York: Oxford University Press.

Rothe, E. (2005). Considering cultural diversity in the management of ADHD in Hispanic patients. *Journal of the National Medicine Association, 97,* S17.

Rovner, B. W., Steel, C. D., Shmuely, Y., & Folstein, M. F. (1996). A randomized trial of dementia care in nursing homes. *Journal of the American Gerontological Society, 44,* 7–13.

Rubin, A. (1992). Case management. In S. M. Rose (Ed.), *Case management and social work practice* (pp. 5–24). New York: Longman.

Rucklidge, J. J., & Tannock, R. (2001). Psychiatric, psychosocial, and cognitive functioning of female adolescents with ADHD. *Journal of the American Academy of Child and Adolescent Psychiatry, 40*(5), 530–540.

Rudolph, K. (2002). Gender differences in emotional responses to interpersonal stress during adolescence. *Journal of Adolescent Health, 30,* 3–13.

Rugulies, R. (2002). Depression as a predictor for coronary heart disease: A review and meta- analysis. *American Journal of Preventive Medicine, 23,* 51–61.

Runyan, D. K., Hunter, W. M., Socolar, R. R., Amaya-Jackson, L., English, D., Landsverk, J., Dubowitz, H., Browne, D. H., Bangdiwala, S. I., & Mathew, R. M. (1998). Children who prosper in unfavorable environments: The relationship to social capital. *Pediatrics, 10,* 12–20.

Rush, A. J., Sackeim, H. A., & Marangell, L. B. (2005). Effects of 12 months of vagus nerve stimulation in treatment-resistant depression: A naturalistic study. *Biological Psychiatry, 58*(5), 355–363.

Rush, A. J., Trivedi, M. H., Wisniewski, S. R., Stewart, J. W., Nierenberg, A. A., Thase, M. E., Ritz, L., Biggs, M. M., Warden, D., Luther, J. F., Shores-Wilson, K., Niederehe, G., & Fava, M. (2006). Bupropion-ST, sertraline, or venlafaxine-XR after failure of SSRIs for depression. *Archives of General Psychiatry, 354,* 1231–1242.

Rushton, J., Forcier, M., & Schectman, R. (2002). Epidemiology of depressive symptoms in the national longitudinal study of adolescent health. *Journal of American Academy of Child and Adolescent Psychiatry, 41,* 199–205.

Ruitenberg, A., Ott, A., van Swieten, J. C., Hofman, A., & Breteler, M. M. B. (2001). Incidence of dementia: Does gender make a difference? *Neurobiology of Aging, 22,* 575–580.

Rutter, M., Bailey, A., & Lord, C. (2003). *Social Communication Questionnaire (SCQ) manual.* Los Angeles: Western Psychological Services.

Ryan, M. M., Lockstone, H. E., & Huffaker, S. J. (2006). Gene expression analysis of bipolar disorder reveals downregulation of the ubiquitin cycle and alterations in synaptic genes. *Molecular Psychiatry, 11*(10), 965–978.

Rychtarik, R. G., & McGillicuddy, N. B. (2005). Coping skills training and 12-steps facilitation for women whose partner has alcoholism: Effects on depression, the partner's drinking, and partner physical violence. *Journal of Consulting and Clinical Psychology, 73,* 249–261.

Ryle, A. (2004). The contribution of cognitive analytic therapy to the treatment of borderline personality disorder. *Journal of Personality Disorders, 18*(1), 3–35.

Sachs, G. S., Printz, D. J., Kahn, D. A., Carpenter, D., & Docherty, J. P. (2000). *Medication treatment of bipolar disorder. Expert consensus guideline series.* New York: McGraw-Hill.

Sackett, D., Straus, S., Richardson, W., Rosenberg, W., & Haynes, R. (2000). *Evidence-based medicine: How to practice and teach EMB (2nd ed.).* London: Churchill Livingstone.

Saigh, P., Yasik, A., Sack, W., & Koplewicz, H. (1999). Child-adolescent posttraumatic stress disorder: Prevalence, risk factors, and comorbidity. In P. Saigh & J. Bremner (Eds.), *Posttraumatic stress disorder: A comprehensive text* (pp. 18–43). Boston: Allyn & Bacon.

Saleeby, D. (2001) *Human behavior and social environments: A biopsychosocial approach.* New York: Columbia University Press.

Samudra, K., & Cantwell, D. (1999). Risk factors for attention-deficit/hyperactivity disorder. In H. Quay & A. Hogan (Eds.), *Handbook of disruptive behavior disorders* (pp. 199–230). New York: Plenum Publishers.

Sanderson, W., & McGinn, L. (2001). Cognitive-behavioral therapy of depression. In M. M. Weissman (Ed.), *Treatment of depression: Bridging the 21st century* (pp. 249–279). Washington, DC: American Psychiatric Publishing.

Sansone, R. A., Rytwinski, D., & Gaither, G. A. (2003). Borderline personality and psychotropic medication prescription in an outpatient psychiatry clinic. *Comprehensive Psychiatry, 44*(6), 454–458.

Sareen, J., Cox, B. J., Clara, I., & Asmundson, G. J. (2005). The relationship between anxiety disorders and physical disorders in the U.S. National Comorbidity Survey. *Depression and Anxiety, 21,* 193–202.

Sareen, J., Cox, B. J., Goodwin, R. D., & Asmundson, G. (2005). Co-occurrence of posttraumatic stress disorder with positive psychotic symptoms in a nationally representative sample. *Journal of Trauma and Stress, 18,* 313–322.

Sareen, J., Houlahan, T., Cox, B. J., & Asmundson, G. J. (2005). Anxiety disorders associated with suicidal ideation and suicide attempts in the National Comorbidity Survey. *Journal of Nervous and Mental Disease, 193*(7), 450–454.

Sax, L., & Kautz, K. J. (2003). Who first suggests the diagnosis of attention-deficit/hyperactivity disorder? *Annals of Family Medicine, 1*(3), 171–174.

Schatzberg, A. F., & Nemeroff, C. B. (Eds.) (2001). *The American Psychiatric Publishing Press textbook of psychiatry (2nd ed.).* Washington, DC: American Psychiatric Publishing.

Scheeringa, M. S., Peebles, C. D., Cook, C. A., & Zeanah, C. H. (2001). Toward establishing procedural, criterion, and discriminant validity for PTSD in early childhood. *Journal of the American Academy of Child and Adolescent Psychiatry, 40*(1), 52–60.

Scheeringa, M. S., Zeanah, C. H., Drell, M. J., & Larrieu, J. A. (1995). Two approaches to the diagnosis of post-traumatic stress disorder in infancy and early childhood. *Journal of the American Academy of Child and Adolescent Psychiatry, 34*(2), 191–200.

Schnurr, P. P., Friedman, M. J., & Bernardy, N. C. (2002). Research on posttraumatic stress disorder: Epidemiology, pathophysiology, and assessment. *JCLP/In Session: Psychotherapy in Practice, 58*, 877–889.

Scholz, J. K., & Levine, K. (2000). The evolution of income support policy in recent decades. *Focus, 21*(2), 9–15. Madison, WI: University of Wisconsin-Madison, Institute for Research on Poverty.

Schreibman, L., Stahmer, A. C., & Akshoomoff, N. (2006). Pervasive developmental disorders. In *Clinical handbook of child behavioral assessment* (pp. 503–524). San Diego: Elsevier Academic Press.

Scogin, F. R., Hanson, A., & Welsh, D. (2003). Self-administered treatment in stepped-care models of depression treatment. *Journal of Clinical Psychology, 59*(3), Mar 2003, 341–349.

Scott, J., McNeil, Y., & Cavanaugh, J. (2006). Exposure to obstetric complications and subsequent development of bipolar disorder: Systematic review. *British Journal of Psychiatry, 189*, 3–11.

Searle, J. (1995). *The Construction of Social Reality.* New York: Free Press.

Seeman, M. V. (2003). Gender differences in schizophrenia across the life span. In C. I. Cohen (Ed.), *Schizophrenia into later life: Treatment, research, and policy* (pp. 141–154). Washington, DC: American Psychiatric Publishing.

Serretti, A., & Olgiati, P. (2005). Profiles of "manic" symptoms in bipolar I, bipolar II and major depressive disorders. *Journal of Affective Disorders, 84*(2–3), Special issue: Bipolar Depression: Focus on Phenomenology, 159–166.

Shanmugham, B., Karp, J., Drayer, R., Reynolds, C. F., & Alexopoulos, G. (2005). Evidence-based pharmacologic interventions for geriatric depression. *Psychiatric Clinics of North America, 28*(4), 821–835.

Shapiro, F. (1995). *Eye movement desensitization and reprocessing: Basic principles, protocols and procedures.* New York: Guilford Press.

Shear, K., Jin, R., & Ruscio, A. M. (2006). Prevalence and correlates of estimated DSM-IV child and adult separation anxiety disorder in the National Comorbidity Survey Replication. *American Journal of Psychiatry, 163*(6), 1074–1083.

Sheehan, T., & Owen, P. (1999). The disease model. In B. McCrady & E. Epstein (Eds.), *Addictions: A comprehensive guidebook* (pp. 268–286). New York: Oxford University Press.

Shepard, B., Carter, A., & Cohen, J. (2000). Attention-deficit/hyperactivity disorder and the preschool child. In T. E. Brown (Ed.), *Attention-deficit disorders and comorbidities in children, adolescents, and adults* (pp. 231–295). Washington, DC: American Psychiatric Publishing.

Sher, L. (2003). Daily hassles, cortisol, and the pathogenesis of depression. *Medical Hypotheses, 62*(2), 198–202.

Shirk, S., Talmi, A., & Olds, D. (2000). A developmental psychopathology perspective on child and adolescent

treatment policy. *Development and Psychopathology, 12*, 835–855.

Siebenbruner, J., Englund, M. M., Egeland, B., & Hudson, K. (2006). Developmental antecedents of late adolescence substances use patterns. *Development and Psychopathology, 18*, 551–571.

Siegel, B., & Hayer, C. (1999). *Detection of autism in the 2nd and 3rd year: The Pervasive Developmental Disorders Screening Test (PDDST).* Presented at the Society for Residential Child Development, Albuquerque, NM.

Siller, M., & Sigman, M. (2002). The behaviors of parents with children with autism predict the subsequent development of their children's communication. *Journal of Autism & Developmental Disorders, 32*(2), 77–89.

Silva, R. R., Gabbay, V., & Minami, H. (2005). When to use antidepressant medication in youths. *Primary Psychiatry, 12*(9), 42–50.

Simon, N., Otto, M. W., Wisniewski, S. R., Fossey, M., Sagduyu, K., Frank, E., Sachs, G. S., Nierenberg, A. A., Thase, M. E., & Pollack, M. H. (2004). Anxiety disorder comorbidity in bipolar disorder patients: Data from the first 500 participants in the systematic treatment enhancement program for bipolar disorder. *American Journal of Psychiatry, 161*, 2222–2229.

Sisson, R. W., & Azrin, N. H. (1986). Family-member involvement to initiate and promote treatment of problem drinkers. *Journal of Behavioral Therapy and Experiential Psychiatry, 17*, 15–21.

Skodol, A. E., Gunderson, J. G., Shea, M. T., McGlashan, T. H., Morey, L. C., Sanislow, C. A., Bender, D. S., Grilo, C. M., Zanarini, M. C., Yen, S., Pagano, M. E., Skodol, A. E., Siever, L. J., Livesley, W. J., Gunderson, J. G., Pfohl, B., & Widiger, T. A. (2002). The borderline diagnosis II: Biology, genetics, and clinical course. *Biological Psychiatry, 51*(12), 951–963.

Skodol, A. E., Gunderson, J. G., Shea, M. T., McGlashan, T. H., Morey, L. C., Sanislow, C. A., Bender, D. S., Grilo, C. M., Zanarini, M. C., Yen, S., Pagano, M. E., & Stout, R. L. (2005). The Collaborative Longitudinal Personality Disorders Study (CLPS): Overview and implications. *Journal of Personality Disorders, 19*(5), 487–504.

Skodol, A. E., Siever, L. J., Livesley, W. J., Gunderson, J. G., Pfohl, B., & Widiger, T. A. (2002). The borderline diagnosis II: Biology, genetics, and clinical course. *Biological Psychiatry, 51*(12), 951–963.

Smith, N., Floyd, M., Jamison, C., & Scogin, F. (1997). Three-year follow-up of bibliotherapy for depression. *Journal of Consulting and Clinical Psychology, 65*, 324–327.

Smith, T., Magyar, C., & Arnold-Saritepe, A. (2002). *Autism spectrum disorder.* New York: John Wiley.

Smolak, L., & Murnen, S. K. (2002). A meta-analytic examination of the relationship between child sexual abuse and eating disorders. *International Journal of Eating Disorders, 31*, 136–150.

Solar, J., & Weatherall, R. (2005). *Cognitive behavioral therapy for anxiety disorders in children and adolescents* (Cochrane Review). In: *The Cochrane Library*, Issue 1. Chichester, UK: John Wiley and Sons, Ltd.

Soloff, P. H. (2005). Somatic treatments. In J. M. Oldham, A. E. Sokil, & D. S. Bender (Eds.), *The American Psychiatric Publishing textbook of personality disorders* (pp. 387–403). Washington, DC: American Psychiatric Publishing, Inc.

Spector, A., Davies, S., Woods, B., & Orrell, M. (2000). Reality orientation for dementia: A systematic review on the evidence of effectiveness from randomized controlled trials. *The Gerontologist, 40*, 206–212.

St. Clair, M. (1999). *Object relations and self-psychology: An introduction* (3rd ed.). Pacific Grove, CA: Brooks/Cole.

Stahl, S. M. (2000). *Essential psychopharmacology: Neuroscientific basis and practical applications (2nd ed.)*. New York: Cambridge University Press.

Stanton, M. D., & Shadish, W. R. (1997). Outcome, attrition, and family-couples treatment for drug abuse: A meta-analysis and review of the controlled, comparative studies. *Psychological Bulletin, 122,* 170–191.

Stark, K., Reynolds, W., & Kaslow, N. (1987). A comparison of the relative efficacy of self-control therapy and a behavioral problem-solving therapy for depression in children. *Journal of Abnormal Child Psychology, 15,* 91–113.

Stark, K., Rouse, L., & Livingston, R. (1991). Treatment of depression during childhood and adolescence: Cognitive-behavioral procedures for the individual and family. In P. Kendall (Ed.), *Child and adolescent therapy* (pp. 165–206). New York: Guilford Press.

Steen, R. G., Mull, C., McClure, R., Hamer, R. H., & Lieberman, J. A. (2006). Brian volume in first-episode schizophrenia: Systematic review and meta-analysis of magnetic resonance imaging studies. *British Journal of Psychiatry, 188,* 510–518.

Stein, D. J., Zungu-Dirwayi, N., Van der Linden, G. J. H., & Seedat, S. (2003). Pharmacotherapy for posttraumatic stress disorder (Cochrane Review). In *The Cochrane Library*, Issue 1. Oxford: Update Software.

Stein, L. I., & Test, M. A. (1980). Alternative mental hospital treatment: I. Conceptual model, treatment program, and clinical evaluation. *Archives of General Psychiatry, 37,* 392–397.

Stein, M. B., Sherbourne, C. D., Craske, M. G., Means-Christensen, A., Bystritsky, A., Katon, W., Sullivan, G., & Roy-Byrne, P. P. (2004). Quality of care for primary care patients with anxiety disorders. *American Journal of Psychiatry, 161,* 2230–2237.

Steinberg, L. (April 1, 2000). We know some things: Parent-adolescent relations in retrospect and prospect. Presidential address, The Society for Research on Adolescence, Chicago, IL. Retrieved on March 25, 2004, at http://astro.temple.edu/~lds/sra.htm.

Steiner, M., Dunn, E., & Born, L. (2003). Hormones and mood: From menarche to menopause and beyond. *Journal Affect Disorders, 74*(1), 67–83.

Stice, E. (2002). Risk and maintenance factors for eating pathology: A meta-analytic review. *Psychological Bulletin, 128*(5), 825–848.

Stinson, F. S., Grant, B. F., Dawson, D. A., Ruan, W. I., Huang, B., & Saha, T. (2005). Comorbidity between DSM-IV alcohol and specific drug use disorders in the United States: Results from the National Epidemiologic Survey on Alcohol and Related Conditions. *Drug and Alcohol Dependence, 80*(1), 105–116.

Stone, M. H. (2006). Relationship of borderline personality disorder and bipolar disorder. *American Journal of Psychiatry, 163*(7), 1126–1128.

Stone, W. L., Coonrod, E. E., & Ousley, O. Y. (2000). Screening Tool for Autism Two-Year-Olds (STAT): Development and preliminary data. *Journal of Autism and Developmental Disorders, 30*(6), 607–612.

Streeton, C., & Whelan, G. (2001). Nalrexone, a relapse prevention maintenance treatment of alcohol dependence: A meta-analysis of randomized controlled trials. *Alcohol and Alcoholism, 36,* 544–552.

Striegel-Moore, R. H. (1993). Etiology of binge eating: A developmental perspective. *International Journal of Social Psychiatry, 32,* 383–387.

Striegel-Moore, R. H., & Cachelin, F. M. (1999). Body image concerns and disordered eating in adolescent girls: Risk and protective factors. In N. G.Johnson, M. C. Roberts, & J. Worell (Eds.), *Beyond appearance: A new look at adolescent girls* (pp. 85–108). Washington, DC: American Psychological Association.

Striegel-Moore, R. H., Franko, D. L., Thompson, D., Barton, B., Schreiber, G. B., & Daniels, S. R. (2005). An empirical study of the typology of bulimia nervosa and its spectrum variants. *Psychological Medicine, 35,* 1563–1572.

Substance Abuse and Mental Health Services Administration (2006). *Results from the 2005 National Survey on Drug Use and Health: National Findings* (Office of Applied Studies, NSDUH Series H-30, DHHS Publications No. SMA 06-4194). Rockville, MD.

Suh, G. H., & Shah, A. (2001). A review of the epidemiological transition in dementia—Cross-national comparisons of the indices related to Alzheimer's disease and vascular dementia. *Acta Psychiatrica Scandinavia, 104*(4–11).

Sukhodolsky, D. G., Kassinove, H., & Gorman, B. S. (2004). Cognitive-behavioral therapy for anger in children and adolescents: A meta-analysis. *Aggression and Violent Behavior, 9*(3), 247–269.

Sullivan, P. F., Neale, M. C., & Kendler, K. S. (2000). Genetic epidemiology of major depression: Review and meta-analysis. *American Journal of Psychiatry, 157*(10), 1552–1562.

Sund, A. M., & Wichstrom, L. (2002). Insecure attachment as a risk factor for future depressive symptoms in early adolescence. *Journal of the American Academy of Child and Adolescent Psychiatry, 41*(12), 1478–1486.

Swann, A. C. (2006). Neurobiology of bipolar depression. In R. S. El-Mallakh & N. S. Ghaemi (Eds.), *Bipolar depression: A comprehensive guide* (pp. 37–68). Washington, DC: American Psychiatric Publishing.

Swann, A. C., & Ginsberg, D. L. (2004). Special needs of women with bipolar disorder. *CNS Spectrums, 9*(8), 1–11.

Swanson, J. (1992). *School Based Assessments and Interventions for ADD Students*. Irvine, CA: KC.

Swanson, J., Schuck, S., Mann, M., Carlson, C., Hartman, K., Sergeant, J., Clevenger, W., Wasdell, M., & McCleary, R. (2001). Categorical and dimensional definitions and evaluations of symptoms of ADHD: The SNAP and SWAN ratings scales. Retrieved 2007, from http://www.adhd.net.

Swartz, H. A., & Markowitz, J. C. (1995). Interpersonal psychotherapy. In I. D. Glick (Ed.), *Treating depression* (pp. 71–84). San Francisco: Jossey-Bass.

Szapocznik, J., & Williams, R. A. (2000). Brief strategic family therapy: Twenty-five years of interplay among theory, research and practice in adolescent behavior problems and drug abuse. *Clinical Child and Family Psychology Review, 3,* 117–135.

Tannock, R., & Brown, T. E. (2000). Attention-deficit disorders with learning disorders in children and adolescents. In T. E. Brown (Ed.), *Attention-deficit disorders and comorbidities in children, adolescents, and adults* (pp. 231–295). Washington, DC: American Psychiatric Publishing.

Tantillo, M., Bitter, C. N., & Adams, B. (2001). Enhancing readiness for eating disorder treatment: A relational/motivational group model for change. *Eating Disorders, 9,* 203–216.

Taylor, R. J., Ellison, C. G., Chatters, L. M., Levin, J. S., & Lincoln, K. D. (2000). Mental health services in faith communities: The role of clergy in black churches. *Social Work, 45,* 73–87.

Taylor, V., & MacQueen, G. (2006). Associations between bipolar disorder and metabolic syndrome: A review. *Journal of Clinical Psychiatry, 67,* 1034–1041.

Taylor, W., & Doraiswamy, P. M. (2004). A systematic review of antidepressant placebo-controlled trials for geriatric depression: Limitations of current data and directions for the future. *Neuropsychopharmacology, 29,* 2285–2299.

Teri, L., McCurrry, S. M., Logsdon, R., & Gibbons, L. E. (2005). Training community consultants to help families improve dementia care: A randomized controlled trial. *Gerontologist, 54*(6), 802–811.

Tharyan, P., & Adams, C. E. (2005). Electroconvulsive therapy for schizophrenia. *Cochrane Database of Systematic Reviews, 2,* Art. No. CD000076.

Thienemann, M., Moore, P., & Tompkins, K. (2006). A parent-only group intervention for children with anxiety disorders: Pilot study. *Journal of the American Academy of Child & Adolescent Psychiatry, 45*(1), 37–46.

Thomas, E. J., Santa, C., Bronson, D., & Oyserman, D. (1987). Unilateral family therapy with the spouses of alcoholics. *Progress in Behavioral Social Work,* 145–162.

Thompson, L. A., & Kelly-Vance, L. (2001). The impact of mentoring on academic achievement of at-risk youth. *Children and Youth Services Review, 23*(3), 227–243.

Thompson-Brenner, H., Glass, S., & Westen, D. (2003). A multidimensional meta-analysis of psychotherapy for bulimia nervosa. *Clinical Psychological Science Practice, 10,* 269–287.

Thorgrimsen, L., Schweitzer, P., & Orrell, M. (2002). Evaluating reminiscence for people with dementia: A pilot study. *Arts in Psychotherapy, 29*(2), 93–97.

Tondo, L., Albert, M. J., & Baldessarini, R. J. (2006). Suicide rates in relation to health care access in the United States: An ecological study. *Journal of Clinical Psychiatry, 67,* 517–523.

Tozzi, F., Thornton, L. M., Klump., K. L., Fichter, M. M., Halmi, K. A., Kaplan, A. S., Strober, M., Woodside, D. B., Crow, S., Mitchell, J., Rotondo, A., Mauri, M., Cassano, G., Keel, P., Plotnicov, K. H., Pollice, C., Lilenfeld, L. R., Berrettini, W. H., Bulik, C. M., & Kaye. W. H. (2005). Symptom fluctuation in eating disorders: Correlates of diagnostic crossover. *The American Journal of Psychiatry, 162,* 732–740.

Treasure, J., & Ward, A. (1997). A practical guide to the use of motivational interviewing in anorexia nervosa. *European Eating Disorders Review, 5,* 102–114.

Treasure, J., Katzman, M., Schmidt, U., Troop, N., Todd, G., & de Silva, P. (1999). Engagement and outcome in the treatment of bulimia nervosa: First phase of a sequential design comparing motivation enhancement therapy and cognitive behavioural therapy. *Behaviour Research and Therapy, 37,* 405–418.

Treatment for Adolescents with Depression Study Team. (2004). Fluoxetine, cognitive-behavioral therapy, and their combination for adolescents with depression: Treatment for Adolescents with Depression Study (TADS) randomized controlled trial. *Journal of the American Medical Association, 292,* 807–820.

Trierweiler, S. J., Neighbors, H. W., Munday, C., Thompson, E. E., Binion, V. J., & Gomez, J. P. (2000). Clinician attributions associated with the diagnosis of schizophrenia in African-American and non African-American patients. *Journal of Consulting and Clinical Psychology, 68*(1), 171–175.

Trivedi, M. H., Rush, A. J., Wisniewski, S. R., Nierenberg, A. A., Warden, D., Ritz, L., Norquist, G., Howland, R. H., Lebowitz, B., McGrath, P. J., Shores-Wilson, K., Biggs, M. M., Balasubramani, G. K., & Fava, M. (2006). Evaluation of outcomes with citalopram for depression using measurement-based care in STAR*D: Implications for clinical practice. *The American Journal of Psychiatry, 163,* 28–40.

Trivedi, M. H., Fava, M., Wisniewski, S. R., Thase, M. E., Quitkin, F., Warden, D., Ritz, L., Nierenberg, A. A.,

Lebowitz, B. D., Biggs, M. M., Luther, J. F., Shores-Wilson, K., & Rush, A. J. (2006). Medication augmentation after the failure of SSRIs for depression. *The New England Journal of Medicine, 354,* 1243–1252.

Trull, T. J. (2001). Structural relations between borderline personality disorder features and putative etiological correlates. *Journal of Abnormal Psychology, 110*(3), 471–481.

Twamley, E. W., Jeste, D. V., & Lehman, A. F. (2003). Vocational rehabilitation in schizophrenia and other psychotic disorders: A literature review and meta-analysis of randomized controlled trials. *Journal of Nervous and Mental Disease, 191*(8), 515–523.

Tyrer, S. (2006). What does history teach us about factors associated with relapse in bipolar affective disorder? *Journal of Psychopharmacology, 20* (Suppl. 2), 4–11.

U.S. Department of Health and Human Services. (1999). *Mental Health: A report of the surgeon general.* Retrieved 2007, from http://www.surgeon general.gov/library/mentalhealth/home.html.

U.S. Department of Health and Human Services. (2001). *Culture, race, and ethnicity: A supplement to mental health: A report of the surgeon general.* Retrieved 2007, from http://www.surgeongeneral.gov/library/mentalhealth/cre/.

Uebelacker, L. A., & Whisman, M. A. (2006). Moderators of the association between relationship discord and major depression in a national population-based sample. *Journal of Family Psychology, 20,* 40–46.

Valenstein, E. (1998). *Blaming the brain: The truth about drugs and mental health.* New York: The Free Press.

Van Boeijen, C. A., Van Balkom, A. J., Van Oppen, P., Nettie Blankenstein, N., Cherpanath, A., & van Dyck, R. (2005). Efficacy of self-help manuals for anxiety disorders in primary care: A systematic review. *Family Practice, 22*(2), 192–196.

van den Bosch, L. M., Verheul, R., & van den Brink, W. (2001). Substance abuse in borderline personality disorder: Clinical and etiological correlates. *Journal of Personality Disorders, 15*(5), 416–424.

Van Kessel, K., Lambie, I., & Stewart, M. W. (2002). The impact of brief planned admissions on inpatient mental health unit utilization for people with a diagnosis of borderline personality disorder. *New Zealand Journal of Psychology, 31*(2), 93–97.

Veenstra-Vanderweele, J., & Cook, E. H. (2003). Genetics of childhood disorders: XLVI. Autism, part 5: Genetics of autism. *Journal of the Academy of Child and Adolescent Psychiatry, 42*(1), 116–119.

Velting, O., Setzer, N., & Albano, A. M. (2004). Update on and advances in assessment and cognitive-behavioral treatment of anxiety disorders in children and adolescents. *Professional Psychology: Research and Practice, 35,* 42–54.

Verdoux, H., Geddes, J. R., Takei, N., Lawrie, S. M., Bovet, P., Eagles, J. M., Heun, R., McCreadie, R. G., McNeil, T. F., O'Callaghan, E., Stober, G., Willinger, M. U., Wright, P., & Murray, R. M. (1997). Obstetric complications and age at onset in schizophrenia: An international collaborative meta-analysis of individual patient data. *American Journal of Psychiatry, 154*(9), 1220–1227.

Vink, A. C., Birks, J. S., Bruinsma, M. S., & Scholten, R. J. (2007). Music therapy for people with dementia. *The Cochrane database of Systematic Reviews, 1,* New York: Wiley.

Vinton, L., & Wambach, K. (2005). Alcohol and drug use among elderly people. In C. A. McNeese & D. DiNitto (Eds.), *Chemical dependency: A systems approach* (pp. 484–502). Boston: Pearson.

Virginia Commission on Youth. (2005). *Collection of evidence-based treatment modalities for children and adolescents with mental health treatment needs, (2nd ed.).* Retrieved 2007, from http://coy.state.va.us/Modali-ties2005/contents05.htm.

Vita, A., Silenzi, C., & Dieci, M. (2006). Brian morphology in first episode schizophrenia: A meta-analysis of quantitative magnetic resonance imaging studies. *Schizophrenic Research, 82*(1), 75–88.

Volkmar, F. R., Lord, C., Bailey, A., Schultz, R. T., & Klin, A. (2004). Autism and pervasive developmental disorders. *Journal of Child Psychology and Psychiatry, 45*(1), 135–170.

Volkmar, F., Charwanda, K., & Klin, A. (2004). Autism in infancy and early childhood. *Annual Review of Psychology 56*, 315–336.

Von Ranson, K. M., & Robinson, K. E. (2006). Who is providing what type of psychotherapy to eating disorder clients? A survey. *International Journal of Eating Disorders, 39*(1), 27–34.

Wachs, T. (2000). *Necessary but not sufficient.* Washington, DC: American Psychological Association.

Wade, T. J., Cairney, J., & Pevalin, D. J. (2002). Emergence of gender differences in depression during adolescence: National panel results from three countries. *Journal of the American Academy of Child and Adolescent Psychiatry, 41*, 190–199.

Wadsworth, M. E., & Achenbach, T. M. (2005). Explaining the link between low socioeconomic status and psychopathology: Testing two mechanisms of the social causation hypothesis. *Journal of Consulting and Clinical Psychology, 73*(6), 1146–1153.

Waldman, I. D., & Gizer, I. R. (2006).The genetics of attention deficit hyperactivity disorder. *Clinical Psychology Review, 26*(4), 396–432.

Walitzer, K. S., & Dearing, R. L. (2006). Gender differences in alcohol and substance use relapse. *Clinical Psychology Review, 26*, 128–148.

Walitzer, K., Dermen, K., & Conners, G. (1999). Strategies for preparing clients for treatment: A review. *Behavior Modification, 23*, 129–151.

Walters, G. (2002). The heritability of alcohol abuse and dependence: A meta-analysis of behavior genetic research. *American Journal of Drug and Alcohol Abuse, 28*, 557–584.

Wampold, B., Minami, T., Baskin, T., & Tierney, S. (2002). A meta-(re) analysis of the effects of cognitive therapy versus "other therapies" for depression. *Journal of Affective Disorders, 69*, 159–165.

Wang, P. S., Berglund, P., Olfson, M., Pincus, H. A., Wells, K. B., & Kessler, R. C. (2005). Failure and delay in initial treatment contact after first onset of mental disorders in the National Comorbidity Survey Replication. *Archives of General Psychiatry, 62*, 603–613.

Wang, P. S., Lane, M., Olfson, M., Pincus, H. A., Wells, K., & Kessler, R. C. (2005). Twelve-month use of mental health services in the United States. *Archives of General Psychiatry, 62*, 629–640.

Warren, S., Huston, L., Egeland, B., & Sroufe, L. A. (1997). Child and adolescent anxiety disorders and early attachment. *Journal of the American Academy of Child and Adolescent Psychiatry, 36*, 637–644.

Warshaw, M., Massion, A., Shea, T., Allsworth, J., & Keller, M. (1997). Predictors of remission in patients with panic with and without agoraphobia: Prospective 5-year follow-up data. *Journal of Nervous and Mental Disease, 185*, 517–519.

Waschbusch, D. (2002). A meta-analytic examination of comorbid hyperactive-impulsive-attention problems and conduct problems. *Psychological Bulletin, 128*, 118–150.

Waslick, B. D., Kandel, B. A., & Kakouros, B. S. (2002). Depression in children and adolescents: An overview. In D. Shaffer & B. D. Waslick (Eds.), *The many faces of depression in children and adolescents* (pp. 1–36). Washington, DC: American Psychiatric Publishing.

Webster-Stratton, C. (1981, revised 2001). *Incredible years parents and children training series.* Retrieved on November 7, 2003, at www.incredibleyears.com.

Wei, E. H., Loeber, R., & White, H. R. (2004). Teasing apart the developmental associations between alcohol and marijuana use and violence. *Journal of Contemporary Criminal Justice, 20*(2), 166–183.

Wei, W., Sambamoorthi, U., Olfson, M., Walkup, J. T., & Crystal, S. (2005). Use of psychotherapy for depression in older adults. *American Journal of Psychiatry, 162*, 711–717.

Weinberg, N., Rahdert, E., Colliver, J., & Meyer, G. (1998). Adolescent substance abuse: A review of the past 10 years. *Journal of the American Academy of Child and Adolescent Psychiatry, 37*, 252–262.

Weinstein, D., Staffelbach, D., & Biaggio, M. (2000). Attention-deficit hyperactivity disorder and post-traumatic stress disorder: Differential diagnosis in childhood sexual abuse. *Clinical Psychology Review, 20*(3), 359–378.

Weiss, G., & Hechtman, L. T. (1993). *Hyperactive children grown up: ADHD in children, adolescents, and adults (2nd ed.).* New York: Guilford Press.

Weiss, G., & Trokenberg-Hechtman, L. (1993). *Hyperactive children grown up: ADHD in children, adolescents, and adults.* New York: Guilford Press.

Weiss, M., & Weiss, J. (2004). A guide to the treatment of adults with ADHD. *Journal of Clinical Psychiatry, 65* (Suppl. 3), 27–37.

Weissman, M. M., Wickramaratne, P., Nomura, Y., Warner, V., Pilowsky, D., & Verdeli, H. (2006). Offspring of depressed parents: 20 years later. *American Journal of Psychiatry, 163*, 1001–1008.

Wells, K., Klap, R., Koike, A., & Sherbourne, C. (2001). Ethnic disparities in unmet need for alcoholism, drug abuse, and mental health care. *American Journal of Psychiatry, 158*, 2027–2032.

Werner, E. (2000). Protective factors and individual resilience. In J. Shonoff & S. Meisels (Eds.), *Handbook of early childhood intervention (2nd ed.)* (pp. 115–133). Cambridge: Cambridge University Press.

Werner, E. E., & Smith, R. S. (2001). *Journeys from childhood to midlife: Risk, resilience, and recovery.* Ithaca, NY: Cornell University Press.

Westen, D. (2005). Patients and treatments in clinical trials are not adequately representative of clinical practice. In J. C. Norcross, L. E. Beutler, & R. F. Levant (Eds.), *Evidence-based practices in mental health: Debate and dialogue on the fundamental questions* (pp. 161–171). Washington, DC: American Psychological Association.

Wetherell, J. L., Lenze, E. J., & Stanley, M. A. (2005). Evidence-based treatment of geriatric anxiety disorders. *Psychiatric Clinics of North America, 28*(4).

Whaley, A. L. (2001). Cultural mistrust: An important psychological construct for diagnosis and treatment of African Americans. *Professional Psychology: Theory and Practice, 32*(6), 555–562.

White, J. (2000). The prevention of eating disorders: A review of the research on risk factors with implications for practice. *Journal of Child and Adolescent Psychiatric Nursing, 13*, 76–78.

White, M., & Epston, D. (1990). *Narrative means to therapeutic ends.* New York: W.W. Norton.

Whitehead, C., Moss, S., Cardno, A., & Lewis, G. (2002). Antidepressants for people with both schizophrenia and depression. *Cochrane Database of Systematic Reviews, 2*, Art. No. CD002305.

Whittal, M., Agras, W. S., & Gould, R. (1999). Bulimia nervosa: A meta-analysis of psychosocial and pharmacological treatments. *Behavior Therapy, 30*, 117–135.

Whittington, C. J., Kendall, T., Fonagy, P., Cottrell, D., Cotgrove, A., & Boddington, E. (2004). Selective serotonin reuptake inhibitors in childhood depression: Systematic review of published versus unpublished data. *Lancet, 363*, 1341–1345.

Wiggins L. D., Baio, J., & Rice, C. (2006). Examination of the time between first evaluation and first autism spectrum diagnosis in a population-based sample. *Journal of Developmental & Behavioral Pediatrics, 27*(Suppl. 2), S79–S87.

Wildes, J. E., & Emery, R. E. (2001). The roles of ethnicity and culture in the development of eating disturbance and body dissatisfaction: A meta-analytic review. *Clinical Psychology Review, 21*(4), 521–551.

Wiley, A. (2004) Abnormal psychology textbooks exclude feminist criticism of the DSM. In P. J. Caplan & L. Cosgrove (Eds.), *Bias in psychiatric diagnosis* (pp. 41–46). Lanham, MD: Jason Aronson.

Willer, M. G., Thuras, P., & Crow, S. J. (2005). Implications on the changing use of hospitalization to treat anorexia nervosa. *American Journal of Psychiatry, 162*, 2374–2376.

Williams, J., & Brayne, C. (2006). Screening for autism spectrum disorders: What is the evidence? *Autism, 10*(1), 11–35.

Williams, N. L., Reardon, J. M., Murray, K. T., & Cole, T. M. (2005). Anxiety disorders: A developmental vulnerability-stress perspective. In B. L. Hankin & J. R. Z. Abela (Eds.), *Development of psychopathology: A vulnerability-stress perspective* (pp. 289–327). Thousand Oaks, CA: Sage Publications.

Willoughby, M. T., Curran, P. T., Costello, E. J., & Angold, A. (2000). Implications of early versus late onset of attention-deficit/hyperactivity disorder symptoms. *Journal of the American Academy of Child and Adolescent Psychiatry, 39*(12), 1512–1514.

Wilson, G., Heffernan, K., & Black, C. (1996). Eating disorders. In E. Mash & R. Barkley (Eds.), *Child psychopathology* (pp. 541–571). New York: Guilford Press.

Wilson, G.T. (1999). Eating disorders and addictive disorders. In C. Fairburn & K. D. Brownell (Eds.), *Eating disorders and obesity: A comprehensive handbook* (pp. 199–203). New York: Guilford Press.

Wilson, S., Lipsey, M., & Soydan, H. (2003). Are mainstream programs for juvenile delinquency less effective with minority youth than majority youth? A meta-analysis of outcomes research. *Research on Social Work Practice, 13*, 3–26.

Wilson, T. G., Loeb, K., Walsh, T. B., Labouvie, E., Petkova, E., Xinhua, L., & Waternaux, C. (1999). Psychological versus pharmacological treatments of bulimia nervosa: Predictors and processes of change. *Journal of Consulting and Clinical Psychology, 67*(4), 451–459.

Wolraich, M. L., Wibbelsman, C. J., Brown, T. E., Evans, S. W., Gotlieb, E. M., Knight, J. R., Ross, E. C., Shubiner, H. H., Wender, E. H., & Wilens, T. (2005). Attention-deficit/hyperactivity disorder among adolescents: A review of the diagnosis, treatment, and clinical implications. *Pediatrics, 115*, 1734–1747.

Woods, B., Spector, A., Jones, C., Orrell, M., & Davies, S. (2007). Reminiscence therapy for dementia. *The Cochrane Database of Systematic Reviews, 1*, New York: Wiley.

Woods, M. E. (1999). Personality disorders. In F. J. Turner (Ed.), *Adult psychopathology: A social work perspective* (pp. 374–429). New York: Free Press.

Wright, J. H., Wright, A. S., Albano, A. M., Basco, M. R., Goldsmith, L. J., Raffield, T., & Otto, M. W. (2005).

Computer-assisted cognitive therapy for depression: Maintaining efficacy while reducing therapist time. *American Journal of Psychiatry, 162*, 1158–1164.

Xue, Y., Leventhal, T., & Brooks-Gunn, J. (2005). Neighborhood residence and mental health problems of 5- to 11-Year-olds. *Archives of General Psychiatry, 62*(5), 554–563.

Yager, J., Anderson, A., Devlin, M., Egger, H., Herzog, D., Mitchell, J., Powers, P., Yates, A., & Zerbe, K. (2002). Practice guideline for the treatment of patients with eating disorders (*2nd ed.*) In *American Psychiatric Association practice guidelines for the treatment of psychiatric disorders: Compendium 2002* (pp. 697–766). Washington, DC: American Psychiatric Publishing.

Yehuda, R. (2006). *Psychobiology of posttraumatic stress disorders: A decade of progress (Vol. 1071).* Malden, MA: Blackwell Publishing.

Yen, S., Shea, M. T., Sanislow, C. A., Grilo, C. M., Skodol, A. E., Gunderson, J. G., McGlashan, T. H., Zanarini, M. C., & Morey, L. C. (2004). Borderline personality disorder criteria associated with prospectively observed suicidal behavior. *American Journal of Psychiatry, 161*, 1296–1298.

Yen, S., Shea, T., Pagano, M., Sanislow, C. A., Grilo, C. M., McGlashan, T. H., Skodol, A. E., Bender, D. S., Zanarini, M. C., Gunderson, J. G., & Morey, L. C. (2003). Axis I and axis II disorders as predictors of prospective suicide attempts: Findings from the Collaborative Longitudinal Personality Disorders Study. *Journal of Abnormal Psychology, 112*(3), 375–381.

Yeomans, F. E., Gutfreund, J., Selzer, M. A., & Clarkin, J. F. (1993). Factors related to drop-outs by borderline patients: Treatment contract and therapeutic alliance. *Journal of Psychotherapy Practice and Research, 3*(1), 16–24.

Young, A. S., Klap, R., Sherbourne, C. D., & Wells, K. B. (2001). The quality of care for depressive and anxiety disorders in the United States. *Archives of General Psychiatry, 58*, 55–61.

Young, E. W., Jensen, L. C., Olsen, J. A., & Cundick, B. P. (1991). The effects of family structure on the sexual behavior of adolescents. *Adolescence, 26*, 977–986.

Young, K., Greenwood, C. E., Van Reekum, R., & Binns, M. A. (2004). A randomized, crossover trial of high-carbohydrate foods in nursing home residents with Alzheimer's disease: Associations among intervention response, body mass index, and behavioral and cognitive function. *Journal of Gerontology: Series A: Biological Sciences and Medical Sciences, 60A*(8), 1039–1045.

Young, R. C. (2005). Evidence-based pharmacological treatment of geriatric bipolar disorder. *Psychiatric Clinics of North America, 28*, 837–869.

Young, S. E., Rhee, S. H., Stallings, M. C., Corley, R. P., & Hewitt, J. K. (2006). Genetic and environmental vulnerabilities underlying adolescent substance use and problem use: General or specific?. *Behavior Genetics, 36*(4), 603–615.

Youngstrom, E. A., Findling, R. L., Youngstrom, J. K., & Calabrese, J. R. (2005). Toward an evidence-based assessment of pediatric bipolar disorder. *Journal of Clinical Child and Adolescent Psychology, 34*(3), 433–448.

Zanarini, M. C., Frankenburg, F. R., Hennen, J., Reich, B., & Silk, K. R. (2004). Axis I comorbidity in patients with borderline personality disorder: 6-year follow-up and prediction of time to remission. *American Journal of Psychiatry, 161*(11), 2108–2114.

Zanarini, M. C., Ruser, T. F., Frankenburg, F. R., Hennen, J., & Gunderson, J. G. (2000). Risk factors associated with the dissociative experiences of borderline patients. *Journal of Nervous and Mental Disease, 188*(1), 26–30.

Zanarini, M. C., Yong, L., Frankenburg, F. R., Hennen, J., Reich, D. B., Marino, M. F., & Vujanovic, A. A. (2002). Severity of reported childhood sexual abuse and its relationship to severity of borderline psychopathology and psychosocial impairment among borderline inpatients. *Journal of Nervous and Mental Disease, 190*(6), 381–387.

Zeltzer, B. B. (2003). Guest Editorial: To lie or not to lie: That is the question. *American Journal of Alzheimer's Disease and Other Dementias, 18*(6), 325–326.

Ziabreva, I., Perry, E., & Perry, R. (2006). Altered neurogenesis in Alzheimer's disease. *Journal of Psychosomatic Research, 61*(3), 311–316.

Zimmerman, M., McGlinchey, J. B., Young, D., & Chelminski, I. (2006). Diagnosing major depressive disorder IV: Relationship between number of symptoms and the diagnosis of disorder. *Journal of Nervous and Mental Disease, 194*(6), 450–453.

Zimmermann, P., Wittchen, H.-U., Hofler, M., Pfister, H., Kessler, R. C., & Lieb, R. (2003). Primary anxiety disorders and the development of subsequent alcohol use disorders: A 4-year community study of adolescents and young adults. *Psychological Medicine, 33*, 1211–1222.

Zientz, J., Rackley, A., & Chapman, S. B. (2007); Evidence-based practice recommendations for dementia: Educating caregivers on Alzheimer's disease and training communication strategies. *Journal of Medical Speech-Language Pathology, 15*(1), 3–14.